GRACE IN CHINA

A bridge to China:
no engineer could dream
such arches, drape them over
monstrous pylons, ask armies
of ironworkers to hurl
enough highway across
a planet already curved,
tense with spilled rivers,
heavy with salt.

Yet one woman sailed
across more than an ocean
to join a man who dreamed
his country out of the dark.
Their lives spun silk
over distances, wove
legends of Sian's warriors
and tales of Tennessee
women, tempered like steel.

Now their families face
each other across deep
water, pull tight
between two continents
the invisible threads.

—ELINOR DIVINE BENEDICT

GRACE IN CHINA

AN AMERICAN WOMAN
BEYOND THE GREAT WALL, 1934-1974

ELEANOR McCALLIE COOPER

WILLIAM LIU

To Susan,
for your journey to China
Eleanor McCallie Cooper

Black Belt Press

Montgomery

Black Belt Press
P.O. Box 551
Montgomery, AL 36101

www.black-belt.com

Library of Congress Cataloging-in-Publication Data
Cooper, Eleanor, 1946-
Grace in China : an American woman beyond the Great Wall, 1934-1974 / Eleanor Cooper,
William Lu
p. cm.
Includes bibliographical references and index
ISBN 1-57966-024-X (alk. paper)
1. Divine, Grace McCallie, 1901-1979—journeys—China. 2. China—Description and
travel. 3. China—Social life and customs. I. Title: American woman beyond the Great Wall,
1934-1974. II. Liu, William, 1941-III. Title
DS710 .C715 1999
951.05'092—dc21
99-052288

Edited and Designed by Randall Williams

Printed in the United States of America
by the Maple-Vail Book Manufacturing Group.

*The Black Belt, defined by its dark, rich soil, stretches across central Alabama. It was the heart
of the cotton belt. It was and is a place of great beauty, of extreme wealth and grinding poverty,
of pain and joy. Here we take our stand, listening to the past, looking to the future.*

This book is dedicated
to those who build bridges between peoples.

This book is dedicated
to those who build bridges between peoples.

CONTENTS

WILLIAM'S FOREWORD

I N MID-August 1979 I watched my sisters Nini and Ellen take off from the Tampa Airport, returning to our home in China. After our mother, Grace, had died that April in Berkeley, California, my sisters and I, with our cousin Eleanor, drove cross country to visit our American roots in Chattanooga, Tennessee. Nini had been there forty-five years earlier, as an eighteen-month-old baby, when Grace was bidding farewell to her family on her way to China to reunite with her Chinese husband. Now, after visiting my uncle and aunt in Naples, Florida, my sisters were taking our mother's ashes back to China to rejoin her husband for the final time.

After their plane took off, I began driving toward Massachusetts and a new teaching job at Wellesley College. I drove right into a fierce thunderstorm. It was early evening, and the rain and wind were so strong that I had to pull onto the shoulder of the highway. The wind rocked the car and the rain pounded the windshield. When lightning flashed, I could only see a waterfall in every direction, while an impenetrable darkness enveloped the car.

Sitting there in the dark, I felt for the first time in my life completely alone, and, for the first time, I tried to look at my parents not through the eyes of their child, but to see them as a couple who had lived their lives with love and respect; an American woman and a Chinese man who had maintained a deep respect for each other's values, beliefs, and commitments. They came from vastly different backgrounds, from cultures that to others often generated seemingly irreconcilable values. Yet each was able to absorb the excellent qualities of the other into a union that defied the then-prevalent deep-seated prejudice against mixed marriages, the devastation of wars, the turbulence of revolutions, and, ultimately, even death.

The most important legacy my parents gave their children was the loving family they created under the most difficult conditions which demonstrated to us the power of our combined cultural heritage. On that stormy night, as the intermittent lightning flashes gave me glimpses of the box on the car seat beside me, a box filled with my mother's writings, I reaffirmed my determination to tell their story.

My mother had been writing her memoirs for a couple of years before she died. My cousin Eleanor McCallie, who had lived with us in Berkeley and helped take care of Mother when she became sick, and I encouraged her to write the story of her life. Encouragement also came from the Oral History Project at the Bancroft Literary of the University of California, Berkeley, with a proposal for Mother to do an oral history about her life. Unfortunately, she became too ill to start the oral history project or to complete her written memoir.

Over the years Eleanor and I had made many efforts to continue what Grace had started, but we were never able to find the time to carry it out. Now, thanks mainly to Eleanor's perseverance, we finally got the story told.

We both strongly believe that we must let Grace tell her own story, and any other voices we use are intended to represent her attitude and point of view or reflect aspects of her character. We were fortunate to have taped recollections of my sisters Nini and Ellen that tell parts of the story. I take great comfort in the fact that represented in the book are the voices of both Nini, who at the age of nine was reading English classics and entertaining our bedridden neighbor, Mrs. Holmberg, with Dickens and George Elliot, and whose brilliant intellect set a tough path for me to follow, and Ellen, whose beauty, honesty, and goodness awed many.

With courage and intellectual inquisitiveness, Grace witnessed and took part in gigantic social upheavals. Her strong mental power helped her through many difficult periods that would have been daunting even to someone physically much stronger than she was. People were always surprised that such courage came from a woman scarcely over five feet tall and who often weighed less than a hundred pounds.

Grace was born in 1901 and died in 1979. As the twentieth century comes to a close, the story of her life will soon be in the hands of the reader. In the new century, the new millennium, we face a fast-shrinking world with swiftly changing boundaries, with races, cultures, social systems, religious beliefs, and economic interests colliding in rapid succession.

If one slight and fragile woman, under horrendous circumstances, could have the courage to follow her heart, the conviction to stare down prejudices, and the self-sacrificing determination to give all her effort to educate and to foster understanding, is there any reason to doubt that the rest of us can try, in our own ways, to do the same?

ELEANOR'S FOREWORD

I FIRST heard of Grace Divine in 1968 when I was heading West to go East. At the time, I didn't know that Grace had set out on a similar journey thirty-four years before. Like me, she left from Chattanooga, Tennessee. We had grown up in the same home town in the same family—a large extended, conservative, Southern family. Coincidentally, we were both the only girl and the middle child with five brothers. Being independent of spirit, we both determined to find our own way out from under the shadow of our male-dominated families.

But there the similarities ended. The times in which we set out on our journeys were very different. She departed during the Great Depression, when the nation was suffering economically and when interracial marriages like hers were shocking news. I left in the sixties just after the assassinations of Martin Luther King, Jr., and Robert Kennedy. Students like myself were torn by the nation's racial strife, anti-war demonstrations, and urban conflicts.

Grace's break was much more dramatic than mine. I had just finished college and was to teach English in Japan. She was starting a new life in China, taking her eighteen-month-old daughter and joining her husband, a Chinese man she had met and married in New York. She followed her heart; I went for a job. My stint lasted two years; she did not come back for forty. During those intervening years she survived floods and famine, wars and revolution.

I try to imagine her feelings as she boarded that train in Chattanooga on a hot summer day in 1934. Was she excited as I was to be setting out on her own adventure? By 1968, train service to Chattanooga had been discontinued. I had to fly to Chicago to catch an Amtrak train to San Francisco. In August 1968, Chicago was preparing for the Democratic National Convention which became a nationally televised confrontation between armed police and angry students protesting the war in Vietnam.

In California, I watched the disturbing events on TV with my aunt, Mary McCallie Ware.

"You know that you are not the first member of the family to go to the Orient, don't you?" she said in a way characteristic of the older generation, putting me in my place. I hadn't thought about it. I really hadn't thought much about anyone doing anything before me.

"No," I answered. "Who else?"

"Well, let's start with your great-grandmother. She went around the world in 1914 at age seventy-four, visiting missions in Japan and Korea, then took the Siberian railway across Russia and was in Moscow when the First World War broke out."

I was impressed. But Aunt Mary went on. "Then there was your Great Uncle Ed, who went to China in the twenties on the throes of a divorce and married an English woman at the Astor Hotel, then crossed the Gobi desert with her in a jeep while he beat off wild dogs and tried to sell electric generators to nomads."

Hard to top, I thought.

"Then my husband Bob and I were in China when the Japanese invaded in 1937."

All right. She'd made her point. But she then showed me a framed photograph from her desk. It was an engaging shot of three happy children on a beach, wearing nothing but underpants and coolie hats, all three toddlers beaming with joy and holding hands as they walked toward the camera. She pointed to the one in the middle, her son. The other two looked "mixed."

"That one," she said, pointing to the Chinese-looking girl in the lead, slightly older than the two little boys, "is Grace Divine's daughter."

"Grace Divine?" I mused. "Is that a real name?"

"Haven't you heard of Grace Divine!" she exclaimed, again emphasizing my ignorance. "She married a Chinaman!"

MY AUNT MARY didn't know, at that time, if Grace was still alive. No one in the family had heard from her in years. Because she had always been "frail" (as the family said), they assumed she was dead. I imagined that she had met some cruel and violent death under the Communist Chinese regime. But I couldn't have imagined that she was very much alive, had been teaching at a university and was, at that very moment, facing her own angry students.

Nevertheless, as I flew off to Japan, I had a strong feeling that someday I would go to China and find Grace—or at least the remains of her—and that someday I would tell her story.

Ironically, Grace found me.

In 1974, out of the blue, a letter arrived in Chattanooga from Grace herself. Subsequently, she returned to America with her son William and was reunited with her family in Tennessee. In an unexpected turn of events, I lived with her and William the last year of her life in Berkeley, California. Those days in Berkeley were set apart from any other period in my life. I would relive them if I could. Her daughters, Nini and Ellen, joined us there when Grace became ill with cancer. Before they came, she began writing her life story. Unfortunately, she died before she finished.

Not knowing what to do with the unfinished work, William and I collected her papers, photos, and tapes of recent interviews and put them in a medium-sized cardboard box. William took the box with him to Wellesley College where he had accepted a teaching position. Nini and Ellen took Grace's ashes to China. And I moved back home, back to the South.

Not long before she died, sensing that I was at a turning point in my own life, Grace advised me to go home. Her death spurred me to make the move. It was here in the hometown where Grace and I both were born, with the family to which we both belong, that I got back in touch with the remarkable story that she had told me.

For years William and I talked about finishing the book she had started, but we were too caught up in living our own lives to write about hers. For seventeen years I kept hearing Grace's voice muffled in that box, feeling her push against the cardboard and try to peek through the cracks. Finally, when William and I re-opened that box, Grace's presence poured out. Her voice on the tapes was clear and strong, the memoirs were fresh and full of details, the letters were brimming with life, all communicating a world not witnessed by many other Westerners. We knew that her voice wanted to be heard. We realized that no one else was left to tell this story. It was up to us.

Filling in her life within China's tumultuous history was like constructing a giant jigsaw puzzle whose pieces were scattered all over the world, hidden in attics, and lost in memories. So many people who once held those pieces were gone, but sometimes they had left old papers or photographs in the hands of unsuspecting descendants or friends whose whereabouts we had to find.

The very nature of Grace's story, as well as the survival of her papers, is a testament to the power of relationships. The strong ties with her American family made it possible for Grace to write them such impassioned letters and to be reunited with them even after twenty years of silence and forty years of separation. Grace's foremost relationship was with her husband, a relationship composed of a deep emotional and intellectual attraction that lasted a lifetime. Grace and her children shared a love for history and literature that allowed them to transcend their time and place and to see the universal elements of human nature during the revolutionary times in which they lived.

In 1998, thirty years after I first heard about Grace and determined that someday I would go to China and find her story, I finally made that journey. As I walked from the terminal into the bustling city of Beijing, tears filled my eyes—I was there at last, but so much had changed. I was met at once by Grace's youngest granddaughter and I stayed with my Chinese cousins. They took me to places where Grace had lived. I met and talked with her former students and colleagues at Nankai University, where she taught from 1957 through 1974. There were a few Westerners in China during the Cultural Revolution, but we know of no other foreigner who was publicly condemned on stage before jeering crowds.

AS MUCH AS possible, the story you are about to read is told in Grace's words. We had four basic sources in her own voice—memoirs, letters, articles, and interviews. Unfortunately, her memoirs ended too soon and left many important years uncovered. Because Grace died before she could finish her book or even edit her memoirs, in respect for what we believe were her intentions, we have taken the liberty to edit as needed. When her materials (letter, memoir, article or interview) provided two or more renditions of the same event, we chose the most appropriate one or combined the most appropriate elements of each, always honoring the spirit of Grace's voice.

Her letters, though incomplete, supplement the first twenty of her China years. All of Grace's papers in China had been destroyed on two occasions, once when the Japanese occupied China during the Second World War and later when her house was ransacked during the Cultural Revolution. The only letters preserved were those that had been sent home to the U.S., many of which ended up with her closest brother, Tom Divine, and his wife Mary Hills. When we began writing this book, Tom had already died. I called Mary Hills and asked her about Grace's letters. She said she remembered putting the letters in a box but she didn't know where it was. My heart sank. Then one day, just before Christmas 1997, Mary Hills's daughter, Elinor Divine Benedict, called and said she had found the box while going through her mother's things. Did we still want it?

Then the box arrived, indeed full of old letters in Grace's handwriting. Some were addressed to Tom and Mary Hills, others to Cousin Eula, or Aunt Ellen or brother Sam. And then I found one beginning, "Dear Mama and Everybody, Well, I'm here at last . . ."

The first letter from China! Tears came to my eyes. There was another dated a week later . . . and the next.

The letters ended in the 1950s. The intensity of the Cold War made it impossible for Grace and her family to continue corresponding. This was not because mail from either side was restricted or forbidden; rather, the intense silence ensued because Grace's letters from "Red China" became threatening to her brother whose livelihood during the Second World War was in top-security defense work. During and after the Korean War, America's hyper-sensitivity to Communism made it problematic for him to correspond with a relative in a Communist country. It is a tribute to him and his wife that they kept her letters intact despite that threat.

During the twenty-year gap of the so-called "bamboo curtain" era, Grace began writing articles for English-language publications. We tracked down copies of these articles in the archives of the Center for Chinese Studies in Berkeley. These articles give us a rarely seen view during the years 1949-59, describing life in revolutionary China as an American wife and mother would experience it.

Where there are gaps in Grace's written materials, interviews fill in. I taped a conversation with Grace and William in 1976, which provided additional stories to those covered in written accounts. However, most of the interview material in the text comes from individual sessions with William and his two sisters, Nini and Ellen, conducted by our friend Paul Kivel in Berkeley in 1979. We are most grateful for these interviews because both Nini and Ellen died before the writing of this book.

Grace was witness to a social transformation that few foreigners and no media saw from the inside. Her perspective is unique—not just for the duration of her stay—other Westerners lived there as long; and not just for the years that she covered—from the semi-colonial period through the Cultural Revolution. She was neither missionary, journalist, diplomat, or political activist. She was not politically or religiously allied. Grace lived as both outside observer and inside participant—a foreigner married to a native, at first raising her children and tending to her household and later trying to support herself and contribute to the society she had chosen. She came from the heart of traditional American culture, but because of her husband and children, she identified with the Chinese. After the flood and the war, she began to understand China's plight. Her personal transformation is gradual, yet dramatic, witnessed in her own writings.

Ultimately, it was Grace's love for the truth that drove her to write. She had a keen intellect, a fine curiosity, and an indomitable spirit. She speaks with passion through letters, with immediacy in published articles and, finally, at the end of her life, with reflection through her memoirs. As we journey through China's history with her, she takes us not only "inside" a world rarely glimpsed by foreigners but "beyond" our usual assumptions, stereotypes, ideologies, and knowledge.

WILLIAM LIU is Grace's only surviving child. He was born in 1941, just before the Japanese occupation. He lived with his mother throughout her life and, in those years, grew from child to colleague to companion. Their sharing of family history and values, their love of Western literature and music, and their delight in verbal wit and humor bonded them and enabled them to survive extreme difficulties. From this crucible of experience, William has emerged with a unique view of both East and West. He has been a researcher at the Chinese Studies Center at the University of California at Berkeley and a professor of Chinese and Comparative Literature at Wellesley College in Massachusetts. He is currently director of the Advanced Interpreter Program and other cross-cultural educational programs at Simon Fraser University in Vancouver, Canada.

Writing Grace's story is the fulfillment of a dream William and I have shared for a quarter century. Why tell this story now? To honor Grace is our first motivation—to honor a life lived in integrity against sweeping forces beyond one's control. Our second goal is to present some of the most dramatic changes of the twentieth century from a perspective rarely seen. As the twentieth century draws to a close, we will see retrospective reviews and critical analyses of all kinds. The most powerful will be the stories that take us on a journey with the many remarkable lives of this century.

Grace's life (1901–1979) spanned more than three quarters of the century. She lived a life that contemporary women find engaging—she followed her heart, educated herself, challenged wrongs, spoke her mind, and changed over time. It was the love for one man that made Grace willing to defy cultural norms, leave her family and her nation, and face insurmountable odds. Hers is a moving love story, deeper than romance, larger even than one marriage. In a real sense, this is not a book about China, or for that matter about Grace, but about "grace in life"—about ordinary people, living through history in all its complexities, tending to families, passing on values, and carrying forward a renewed commitment to each generation.

Twenty years after Grace's death, I have completed what I felt one day I would do—tell her story. She gave me a gift; now, with her son, I give it back, to you.

A NOTE ON THE FORMATTING

In the text of the book, beginning on page 21, passages set in plain roman type, like this, indicate that the words are written by the authors or are quoted from a third party. Extended quotations are indented.

Letters written by Grace have been set in italics like this.

And Grace's words, from the portion of her memoir that she completed before her death, occasionally from articles that she wrote for publication while still in China, and occasionally from interviews, are set in bold like this.

All historical books on China face the problem of spelling Chinese words in English. Because Grace used the traditional *Wade-Giles* system throughout her writings, we have followed that usage for consistency. The currently accepted spelling in *pinyin* is indicated in brackets the first time a word is used or when needed for clarification. By the end of the book we use pinyin exclusively, indicating its accepted use by that time.

ACKNOWLEDGMENTS

WE ARE grateful to many people for their support, encouragement, and contributions without which this book would be less, if at all.

Special thanks must be given to Mary Hills Divine, who saved her sister-in-law's letters for more than fifty years. We regret she did not get to see them in print—she died on Grace's birthday, the year the book was published. Elinor Divine Benedict, Mary Hills's daughter and Grace's niece, who has written her own version of the story in poems, helped us in many ways, donated letters and papers and read early drafts. Paul Kivel interviewed Ellen and Nini in 1979, after Grace's death, which made their contributions possible. Randall Williams, our editor and publisher, saw a good story and gave us the support we needed to make it happen. For photographs we thank Desmond Powers, Giles Brooks, Jimmy Lail, Franklin Ruas, Bertha Wen, Joyce Blessinger, Luby Bubeshko, Alex Liu, Rolfie Gartner, and Mark Leef.

The archives of the following institutions contributed: Nankai University, Qing Hua University, Tianjin Water Works, University of California at Berkeley Center for Chinese Studies, Cornell University, New York City Library, Chattanooga Hamilton County Bicentennial Library, Girls' Preparatory School, and the McCallie School.

Our many friends and family kept us going and provided needed resources: Zachary Adelson, Beverly Bayette, John Bennett, Penny Campbell, Robert Clarke, Mel, Mae and Katie Cooper, Ray Feenstra, Kay and Ford Hart, Iris Hill, Jennifer Hsu, Zhang Kelin, Jo Kleiboer, Jenny Lea, Margaret Leach, Kaimin Liu, Mary Liu, John Louton, Louise Mann, Ellen McCallie, Franklin and Tresa McCallie, Mrs. and Mrs. T. Hooke McCallie, Gretchen McCausland, Dorothy Mingle, Bill and Sylvia Powell, Charles Ruas, Nancy Smith, Dr. Jan Walls, both Mary Wares, and Grace's family, both in China and in the U.S.: her sons-in-law, Liu Enhua and Li Rei-sheng, and her granddaughters, Yun Liu, and Julia Yanhui, Tracy Yancui, and Ellen Yanyu Li.

GRACE IN CHINA

Sat 'Aug. 4, 1934

Dear Mama and Everybody,
                                    Well, I'm here
at last. I got to Tientsin Tuesday afternoon
at two o'clock. I thought I would write
back right away but I have been completely
exhausted ever since I got here. I had
absolutely reached the end of my endurance
and I just collapsed. The last part of
my journey was quite interesting and
very beautiful but with no chance at all
to rest a second. I guess I'd better go
back to where I left off in my last letter

1

TO THE ORIENT

THE BOX was full of old letters, many yellowed. Most were still in their
envelopes but some had been taken out, typed and copied, others refolded
and stuffed back in, a few pages missing, stamps torn off. Some were bundled
and held together with an old rubber band that had practically melted. The dates
were fory, fifty, sixty years ago. There were old newspaper clippings and a few photographs scattered among them. One began, "Dear Mama and Everybody, . . ." It was
Grace's first letter from China.

Saturday, August 4, 1934

Dear Mama and Everybody,

*Well, I'm here at last. I got to Tientsin Tuesday afternoon at two o'clock. I thought I
would write back right away but I have been completely exhausted. I had absolutely
reached the end of my endurance and I just collapsed. The last part of my journey was
quite interesting and very beautiful but with no chance at all to rest a second. I guess I'd
better go back to where I left off in my last letter.*

*When the train reached Vancouver, some of my fellow passengers, a kind man carry-
ing Fuchina for me and another one taking my bags, got us safely on to* The Empress of
Asia. *It was just an hour to sailing time. When Uncle Park took me to the train station in
Chattanooga, he had scolded me for leaving so little leeway between the train's arrival and
the sailing of the boat: Only diplomats and important people travel like that. Any unfore-
seen accident could make a train several hours late, he said. I was thankful that the cow on*

the tracks hadn't held us up any longer than it did and happy to be unpacking in my cabin when I felt the ship's impatient throbbing and thumping to be off.

Life on the boat was pretty much what it had been on the train except there was a lot more room for Fuchina to run around and more places for her to explore. When the weather was fine and the sea was calm, I spent most of the day walking her around the deck and swinging her in one of the swings. We made friends with cabin boys and fellow passengers. On cloudy or stormy days we investigated everything below we could get into. No wonder I lost ten pounds by the time I reached Tientsin.

One night there was a big storm. The ship seemed to roll almost over on its side and back again. The waves dashed and banged against the porthole. I heard the cabin boy going around knocking on doors. I sat up quickly, fearing the worst, but when he got to my door, he just asked to come in and lock the porthole securely. He explained that the porthole might come open during such strenuous rolling and banging and the sea would rush in.

I had planned to get off the Empress in Kobe and take a Japanese boat through the Yellow Sea to Tangu. But as we neared Japan, I began having a sore throat and the thought of being ill in Japan where I knew no one was alarming. Better stay on the Empress for the next four days to Shanghai, I decided. That would give me time to recover. Mr. Liu had friends in Shanghai who would put me on the train to Tientsin. I promptly cabled Mr. Liu to have me met in Shanghai instead of Tangu.

But by the time we reached Kobe I felt fine. Now I was anxious to follow my original schedule, and when Mr. Buckberough, the Canadian Pacific agent, came on board I told him what I'd done and that I had changed my mind again. I feel perfectly well, I said, so I want to get off here and take a Japanese boat to Tangu.

Fine, he agreed, there's a boat leaving tomorrow at noon. Get your things together and we'll get right off. I'll send your husband a cable, get you settled in a hotel and put you on the Chuan Maru tomorrow.

Just as easy as that. And I had been so worried about how troublesome this change of plans might be. We were soon off the boat, in my hurry leaving behind a stack of music with some of my favorite songs which has caused me much regret. I also forgot Fuchina's beloved woolly monkey and little chair made on Lookout Mountain.

Mr. Buckberough said his assistant would take care of my cable to Mr. Liu. He took us to dinner and bought Fuchina some powdered milk and other things to use on the Japanese boat. He was wonderful to me and carried Fuchina everywhere for me. The next morning he checked us out of the hotel and gave me a cable that had come to the Empress of Asia

in the night from Mr. Liu in answer to my first cable, saying that Mr. Tung would meet me in Shanghai. At eleven o'clock he sent me to the boat in his car with his assistant Mr. Shimada to see that I got on all right.

The Chuan Maru was a much smaller ship than the Empress, of course, but it was a pretty good-sized boat, bigger than a river boat and it was very clean and nice. As it was a last minute cancellation, my accommodations were not the most choice. The cabins were quite small with four berths and a very narrow hard sofa. There were two other women in the cabin with me and three grown women and a baby in such little space is anything but comfortable. The berths were so narrow that I couldn't possibly sleep with the baby, so I put a chair and two pillows down at the lower part where there was a railing and let her sleep by herself and I slept on the narrow little sofa. I was so tired at night that I slept in spite of its hardness.

We sailed from Kobe at twelve o'clock Friday. Sailing thru the little Japanese islands was perfectly beautiful. The weather was marvelous and the water as smooth as glass. Saturday morning we stopped at Moji and Japanese officials came on board. Most of the passengers seemed to be nervous about the inspection and that made me nervous. It was my first encounter with Japanese officialdom. However they showed me only the most kindly and friendly interest and paid much more attention to Fuchina than to me.

The weather was so beautiful that we stayed out on deck all day long and I really had a good time in spite of the wild little Fuchina. Everybody was simply crazy about the baby. There was an awfully attractive French couple from Paris, the Count and Countess de Chevegnac, on board. Madame de Chevegnac wanted to take care of Fuchina an hour or two everyday for me. They all thought I had accomplished a remarkable feat in keeping the baby so well all through such a long trip. She really looked grand. We sat at the captain's table, and Col. and Mrs. Drysdale of the American Legation in Peking sat next to me. Anybody who thought that I would be cut off and ostracized by people was certainly mistaken. I was treated marvelously by everybody. Mrs. Drysdale begged me to come visit her at the Legation in Peking.

The nights were like something out of a picture, with a full moon shining on the smooth water and the graceful little Japanese sailboats with their little lanterns. Those nights on the Yellow Sea, I watched the fishing boats drifting across the moon's path in the water and thought happily that the long trip would soon be over and the long separation ended. We would be two more days reaching Tangu which is only an hour's train ride away from Tientsin.

Monday afternoon the day before we landed was the most beautiful of all. We were out of Japanese waters and were nearly to China. The water looked just like green jade and we saw the Chinese junks floating around. It didn't even look real. We docked at Tangu the next morning at five o'clock; I was up long before that watching the sunrise. I put on the new outfit I'd bought in New York specially for my first appearance. I woke up Fuchina at 5:30 and put on her new dress and bonnet. We went out on deck to see if Mr. Liu had come to meet us. It was raining, a nice soft shower that looked awfully pretty coming down on the green fields. The boat was surrounded by little Chinese boats with coolies in blue suits and funny pointed hats. There were lots of people on the dock. Men in long gowns, coolies, soldiers, and all sorts of people. But I didn't see a soul I knew.

We walked up and down the deck for a long time and I looked carefully at each new arrival on the wharf. Suddenly I noticed a man facing away from the boat. There was something familiar about his back view—the height, the build—but to my horror, I felt an instant dislike for this person whose back I was staring at! It was a shocking moment. Had I followed across the world a man I didn't like? Fortunately the man turned around before I could work myself into a panic and I saw beyond doubt that he resembled no one I'd ever seen before.

I need food, I thought, faint with relief, and hurried off with Fuchina to join the Colonel and his wife at breakfast, but I was so excited I couldn't swallow a bite. I thought that Mr. Liu would be down later, but seven, eight, nine o'clock and still he hadn't come.

The docks at Tangu.

Most of the people on board were going up to Peking on the 12:45 train, so everybody stayed on board as it was still raining. At nine I went and asked the purser if any message had come for me. He said no. Col. Drysdale said perhaps Mr. Liu would come down on the 10:00 train. When he didn't come on that train, the Colonel asked me if I didn't want him to take me ashore to telephone or telegraph. So we went to the telegraph office and sent Mr. Liu a telegram saying I would arrive in Tientsin at 1:45. The Colonel said that they would take me with them. He said he was sure Mr. Liu had misunderstood my second cable or it was possible that he never got it at all. On the way back to the boat it started pouring down rain and I got soaked. The rain didn't hurt my dress but it ruined my big white hat.

At lunch time I couldn't eat a thing again. Mrs. Drysdale begged me to eat just a little soup. She said I mustn't worry that they would take care of me. After lunch, we left the boat and walked slowly to the train. I expected Mr. Liu to appear at any minute, but he didn't. The minutes went by and the train was ready to leave. We had to get on.

Col. Drysdale bought my ticket and I went in their compartment with them. Mrs. Drysdale said she is crazy about the Chinese and has lots of Chinese friends. She said I mustn't feel strange at all, that there were at least a hundred American girls in Peking married to Chinese. Col. D. was evidently putting the worst construction on Mr. Liu's non-appearance. He finally said, If anything has gone wrong, you must come to us in Peking. You have our address and phone number. Promise you will. I promised, but I was not at all worried. I was sure that changing my mind and sending two cables had caused some confusion.

During the one hour's ride to Tientsin, the glimpses I had of the countryside from the train window did not fit my idea of Chinese scenery. This flat, flat land with nothing higher than grave mounds and no trees at all jolted my preconceived notions of graceful willow trees and fantastic misty mountains. The Colonel explained that most of this land was "filled in" land, that the seashore used to be much further inland.

When we reached Tientsin the Colonel got off the train with me. We stepped down into the midst of a great crowd milling noisily around with the bewildering sound of Chinese shouted in chorus—passengers calling to friends or for transportation, rickshaw men and taxi drivers shouting for customers—adding to the confusion. We looked anxiously in every direction. The Colonel had to raise his voice to ask me if I saw my husband. I shook my head and stood as tall as possible so I could be readily seen, but there was nobody looking for me.

25

In Tientsin, street scenes depicting the contrast in Western and Chinese styles, 1930s.

We had only a few minutes before the train went on to Peking, so according to the arrangement we'd made on the train, the Colonel put me and Fuchina in a taxi with all my baggage and told the driver to take me to the Water Works Co.

We rode through streets that looked neither American nor Chinese. Along the main street high brick buildings with white porticoed fronts intimidated the neighboring stores and shops. Rickshaw men, running in the hot summer sun, pulling complacent-looking passengers, didn't seem to fit in with the late-Victorian Western style of the buildings. A short ride brought us to the front of a large building beside a walled compound with a sign on the gatepost—the Tientsin Native City Water Works.

Here I was at the end of my long journey. What a way we'd come, Fuchina and I! From New York to Tennessee—then across the United States to Vancouver, across the Pacific to Japan and across the China Sea to Tientsin.

I was so excited I just handed Fuchina to the taxi driver and hurried through the big gate of the compound, past stacks of pipes and groups of workmen and up some steps into a side entrance. I stepped immediately into a big room. I had the impression of heads being raised and of many eyes staring at me in amazement.

I asked the room at large where I could find Mr. Fu-chi Liu. Most continued to stare. There were actually only five or six men writing at desks and one of them got up and came

26

over to me. He said very politely and in good English that Mr. Liu had gone out on some business that morning and hadn't come back yet. But he said I could go into his office and wait.

As we stepped out into the hall, I heard Mr. Liu's voice and saw him coming down the hall with a tall European-looking man.

"Well, there you are!" he said, heavy accent on "there" with both relief and reproof in his voice.

"Yes, here I am and I got here all by myself. Why didn't you meet the boat at Tangu or the train in Tientsin?" I felt as if we were speaking lines in a play. We sounded as if we had parted only last week instead of a year and eight months before.

"I didn't know you were on that boat or on the train. I just this minute found your second cable." He had it in his hand.

The whole thing was a terrible mix up due to the stupidity of Mr. Buckberough's assistant. All he put in the cable was, "Sailing instead Chuan Maru. " It didn't say where I was landing or when, so Mr. Liu naturally thought I was still going to Shanghai. Mr. Tung had cabled him that I was not among the passengers leaving the Empress of Asia. *He said he had the China Travelers Association looking for me. He was just about to take an airplane to Shanghai himself to try to find out something about me.*

Mr. Liu then introduced me to the gentleman with him, Monsieur Ruas, the Water Works' French engineer, and I felt sure the sentimental Frenchman was shocked and disappointed at not witnessing a more touching scene of reunion. But I knew better than to commit such a faux pas—*a public display of that sort would not be considered proper behavior. However, Mr. Ruas did what he could at least to add some ceremony to the welcome. He bowed elegantly and kissed my hand and assured me that monsieur, my husband, had been so longing for my coming.*

Suddenly Mr. Liu realized that something was missing. "The baby!" he exclaimed, "Where is the baby?"

We rushed out and found the taxi man standing on the sidewalk holding her and a lot of Chinese workers standing around looking at her. She wasn't a bit afraid of all the strange people. She knew her daddy right away and went right to him. She was used to seeing his picture and calling it "Daddy," so he probably looked familiar to her.

As we drove off in a big car, waiting with its chauffeur in the compound, to the apartment Mr. Liu had been preparing for several weeks, he turned to me and said very seriously, "I'm sure when Ruas heard you speak, he had never heard such a beautiful voice

The Grand Canal in Tientsin as Grace would have seen it on her arrival.

before in his whole life." And into that blunt statement I could read a whole declaration of love and welcome.

Mr. Liu had rented an apartment, but the furniture hadn't come, so Tuesday night we stayed in a hotel. Fuchina had to sleep with us of course and she had either eaten too much or was too excited, for she rolled around all night long and cried and jumped from one side to the other and from the head to the foot, so we didn't get much rest. Mr. Liu was a wreck from worry and loss of sleep and I was exhausted so we are both just now recovering somewhat.

We went to the apartment Wednesday afternoon. It is in the French concession and is a darling place. The apartment house doesn't open on the street as ours do but onto a courtyard. We have three rooms and bath, a bedroom, living and dining room combined and kitchen. It's awfully pretty. I'm crazy about it. The bedroom opens out on to a little balcony and it has three big windows with shutters. The living room furniture doesn't come till Monday, but we have all the bedroom furniture. Fuchina has a nice little white iron bed with a mosquito net over it. The first night here the mosquitoes almost ate her up. With mosquito net all over her bed, she looks like a little bear in a cage.

I certainly am a lady of ease and luxury now. We have a boy who cooks, cleans, shops and does everything. His name is Sun Pao-san and he certainly is a marvel compared to American servants. He is a grand cook. He cooks American food marvelously. I don't have

28

to think of what to eat, buy it or go get it. All I do is to eat it when it is ready. Yesterday for lunch we had omelettes and tomatoes stuffed with shrimp and mayonnaise. Sun makes grand mayonnaise. Ordinarily I hate shrimp but these were delicious. Last night for dinner we had a half small chicken apiece with deliciously cooked potatoes and lettuce salad and ice cold watermelon. I have two qts. of milk every morning from a Chinese dairy. It's not nearly so rich of course as your all's milk but it is very good. Sun cleans the house, fixes Fuchina's food too, and does all the shopping, and you should see how spotless he leaves the kitchen when he is through cooking. I don't need a nurse. I would have nothing to do for all our dirty clothes are sent to the laundry. We are going to rent a piano soon so I can continue my music.

I haven't seen much of Tientsin yet as I have been too tired to go out. We did go to the French Park the other night about six. It was very interesting to see the Chinese men in their long white, blue, or lavender silk gowns and the pretty Chinese girls and cute children. Fuchina had a grand time. She ran her daddy all over the park. I had a hard time keeping up with them. They look so cute together—the big one and the little one.

Mr. Liu was very shy with her at first. But now they are very crazy about each other and the first thing she says in the morning is "Dada." He is going to spoil her rotten. He can't stand for me to spank her and he cries if she cries. Needless to say he thinks she is the cutest, prettiest, and smartest baby in the world. He plays grand with her, so much better than I ever could.

It is time for lunch now. I have written such a long letter and still I haven't told nearly all I wanted to. Give my love to everybody. I am very, very happy. Mr. Liu is all I thought he was and more.

Lots of love,
Grace

2

GRACE AND FU-CHI

G RACE had been in New York for two years when she met Liu Fu-chi in 1928. Mr. Liu had come to America as a student at Cornell University, and when he graduated with a degree in hydraulic engineering, he went to New York City to gain some practical experience before returning to China. He had a job with a civil engineering firm and found a room in an apartment house on West 112th Street.

The New York that Mr. Liu entered in 1928 was the ideal place for a young engineer. Following the First World War, New York rose above the ashes of Europe as the emerging commercial and artistic center of the world. American technological innovation was symbolized by skyscrapers rising higher than any civilization had dared to erect. The Empire State Building was under construction, as were many other of the elegant "art deco" buildings of this era—the Chrysler Building, with its graceful spire, the Waldorf Astoria Hotel bringing elegance to Park Avenue, and the Irving Trust Company building on Wall Street. The construction that would have interested a young engineer the most was the George Washington Bridge crossing the Hudson River. This dramatic expanse of steel over water was the largest suspension bridge ever built and was touted as the most beautiful bridge in the world. The continually expanding underground subways were another showcase of American engineering. Over water, in the air, and even underground New York was breaking the limits of the past.

Grace had come to New York to pursue a singing career. From childhood she had been known for a voice like "the sound of silver bells." In 1920, she had trained in

Chicago with Franz Proschowsky, a noted teacher from Berlin who specialized in coloratura soprano and had trained many well-known opera singers such as Amalita Galli-Curci and Tito Schipa. When Mr. Proschowsky moved to New York, Grace's mother urged her to return home to help nurse her younger brother Edward who was ill.

When Grace returned to Chattanooga, Tennessee, she discovered that Edward had already recovered and her mother merely wanted her home. Lacking the funds to set off for New York, she continued voice lessons at Cadek Conservatory and directed the glee club at a girls' school that had been started by her aunt and two other teachers. That is where Grace probably would have stayed and been destined, like her aunt, to the life of an unmarried teacher, if it had not been for her voice . . . and a coincidence.

One day someone in the audience at a recital heard Grace sing and took notice. A short time later, Grace was offered a scholarship to continue her studies in New York. The anonymous sponsor had recommended her to Mr. Adolph Ochs, who was then the owner and publisher of the New York *Times*. But Mr. Ochs had his beginnings in publishing in Chattanooga and had not forgotten his hometown. No matter how successful he had become in New York, Mr. Ochs was known in Chattanooga for his patronage of the arts. Grace was not the only young artist to win his benevolence.

In her memoirs, Grace writes of her early experiences in the big city:

My first weeks in New York were delightfully hectic. Everything came fully up to my expectations, especially the subway rush hour—hordes of people shoved, squashed and squeezed into a tiny space and hurled at terrific speed from place to place. Once I had a shoe literally squeezed off my foot when I made a precipitate entrance. It finally reached me, traveling overhead from hand to hand, at the other end of the car.

I tried to see as many Broadway shows as possible while I settled down in a girls' club for music students to do some serious work with my singing. Thus my life in New York began, and it continued, with the usual music student's activities—lessons, hours of practicing exercises and learning new songs, auditions, singing engagements, and attending concerts and opera.

Grace Divine in New York in the 1920s.

This time, instead of urging her daughter to return home, Grace's mother, Julia McCallie Divine, joined her in New York. The move suited Mrs. Divine because her husband had died and her five sons had all married and left home. She brought along her sixteen-year-old grand-daughter Julianne. Mrs. Divine rented an apartment on West 112th Street, in the flourishing Morningside Heights area, nearby to Grace's conservatory and many institutions of learning, worship, and the arts— Columbia University, Barnard College, Union Theological Seminary, the Jewish Theological Seminary, and Juilliard Institute of Musical Art.

Their apartment house was a simple eight-story, yellow brick build-ing with geometric patterns in the brickwork and a wrought iron front gate. If Grace walked out of the front door and turned left down the tree-lined street to Amsterdam Avenue, she would walk almost straight into the "Portals of Paradise" of the magnificent Cathedral of St. John the Divine, a newly built, medieval-style anomaly in the burgeoning metropolis. Looking down Amsterdam Avenue beside the cathedral, she could see in the distance the towers of New York's emerging skyline, silhouetted against the sky. Grace often mused that her mother had picked this location because being called "Mrs. Divine" in the proximity of the Cathedral of St. John the Divine made her feel like a relative of the saint.

But on her way to her music lessons, she would go the other way—out her apart-ment building and to the right, across Broadway to Riverside Drive, where a statue of Samuel Tilden, former Governor of New York and 1876 nominee for President, bore the inscription "I trust the people." The double promenade along Riverside Park afforded wide walkways with two rows of trees atop a rocky ledge overlooking the Hudson River and a parkway below. Residents from the magnificent apartment build-ings along Riverside Park walked their dogs or fed pigeons on the sidewalks. Nannies played with children on the swings or pushed them in perambulators. At the top of the park at 123rd Street, just past Riverside Church, a religious edifice built by John D. Rockefeller, was the tomb of President Ulysses S. Grant—a person Grace knew through her grandfather's accounts of the Civil War, when the then-general of the Union forces came to break the siege on Chattanooga in 1863.

IT WAS her mother who first struck up a conversation with the rather short, bespec-tacled, somewhat serious Chinese student she met in the elevator of their apartment building. When Mrs. Divine discovered that the young foreign student was staying alone in a room without a kitchen, she invited him to dinner. He soon became a frequent visitor. Grace, her mother, and Grace's niece Julianne found Liu Fu-chi appealing and his broken English quite charming. Over time, with her mother's constant questioning, she came to know a good deal about the young man, as she recounted in her memoirs:

At first I was merely interested and intrigued by his talk, his speech full of original and amusing imperfections, his opinions and his stories of his home province, bedeviled with rival warlords and bandits, and his participation in the big anti-Japanese student movement of 1919. But gradually as his English became more fluent, his unusual intellect and character impressed me and his calm self-confidence without conceit won my respect and admiration.

Mama, Julianne, and I listened, fascinated, to Mr. Liu talk about China and his home province of Shensi [Shaanxi], called the "Cradle of Chinese Civilization." A part of Shensi, we learned, was the ancient feudal state of Chin, which eventually conquered the other feudal states in 221 B.C. The city of Sian [Xian], once called Changan, was the capital of the first Emperor of China more than 2,000 years ago.

He told us that when he was a boy, he lived in West Liu Village which was made up of about one hundred families, most of them named Liu. West Liu Village was located in the heart of China, in Shensi province, and had a written history of over eight hundred years. His family were considered a well-to-do peasant family, doing their own farm work and having many different roles in the village—teachers, doctors, and even merchants.

His father died before he was born and Fu-chi was brought up under the strict supervision of his three uncles. At an early age he set to memorizing Confucian classics in parrot-fashion recitation as was the custom of the day. He said it was the teaching and training from his uncles that molded his character and shaped his life. This training emphasized the traditional moral concepts and high principles of the Chinese people: honesty, discipline, hard work, education, and respect for family and authority. This interested Mama tremendously and she enjoyed discussing Confucian principles with Fu-chi. They differed little, she thought, from the strict Calvinist upbringing of her own youth and her father's Scotch Presbyterian code of behavior.

33

Fu-chi's uncle, a schoolmaster in Fuping county, taught him the importance of study, but his methods were purely Confucian and his outlook was narrow and fearful of change at a time of intense political ferment. In 1911 large numbers of Manchus were murdered in Sian, near where Fu-chi lived. It was the beginning of the overthrow of the emperor. Warlords vied for power and bandits roamed the countryside while foreign powers dismembered China. Natural disasters caused massive social upheaval. Catastrophic flooding in 1910 and 1911 destroyed crops in the usually fertile valleys around Fu-chi's homeland and caused death, starvation, and displacement of millions of people. The dikes built to control the Yellow River were managed by political appointees. The systems were unattended and silt had built up. The young Fu-chi saw that it was the human system that failed, leaving people helpless in the wake of natural forces. The natural crisis, perhaps, could not be avoided, but the human disaster could be lessened, he thought.

Fu-chi's observations led him to believe in the importance of studying Western science. He knew that China must change and that he must study to find solutions to the nation's problems. He was influenced by the thinking of other young people of that time, by the desire to study everything Western—religion, philosophy, history, literature, political and organizational ways, social values and customs—but most of all to bring what they learned back to China, to make China a better nation.

The dilemma was that China needed foreign expertise, technology, and finance, yet the Western nations who could provide these were unraveling the very fabric of Chinese culture. For more than two thousand years China had enjoyed a relatively stable civilization managed by a Confucian code of order and a systematic bureaucracy that survived even when dynasties collapsed and emperors died. But by the nineteenth century, the system had become cumbersomely bureaucratic and the population had grown faster than the the ability of the system to respond. Pressure to change was building from within at the same time that foreign powers were applying pressure from without.

Initially China resisted foreign demands. The government limited foreigners' access to only a few coastal ports and refused to import foreign goods. Instead China became an exporter, known in the West for its fine teas, silks, furs, porcelain, timber, and other products. To reverse this imbalance of trade, Britain secretly smuggled opium into China, a product cheaply produced in the British colony of India. The

British Opium Wars of 1839–42 were fought to assure Britain's dominance over China, and the Treaty of Nanking which ended the fighting granted Britain just that. The British were granted the island of Hong Kong to do with as they "shall see fit" and five ports where British subjects were allowed "extraterritoriality," or the right to govern under their own jurisdiction, immune from Chinese law. Other nations soon joined the frenzy until parts of China were divided into territories where foreign nations were granted greater control, through a series of unequal treaties. Furthermore, the Sino-Japanese War of 1895 resulted in the loss of Formosa [Taiwan], an island off the coast of China, to Japanese control.

Although the West was considered barbaric to China's ruling elite, it was becoming increasingly clear to many Chinese that the Emperor system and the Manchu government were unable to manage this crisis.

The Boxer Rebellion in 1900 was a turning point in Chinese history. The Boxers were a late nineteenth century secret society that fueled the flames of anti-foreign resentment. The killing of hundreds of foreigners, mostly missionaries, enraged Western nations. Troops from the eight "predator" nations (England, France, Germany, Austria, Russia, Japan, Italy, and the United States) marched into Peking [Beijing] in a dramatic show of force, squelched the rebellion, and then exacted an indemnity, or payment for damages, from the imperial government of $330 million.

The United States later returned its portion of the indemnity funds back to China in the form of scholarships for Chinese students to study in the United States.

When Fu-chi was around twelve, his uncles decided that without a father, his future depended on having a good education. Tsing Hua [Qinghua], near Peking, was a high school with two years of college and Western-trained teachers. Through a careful selection process, each province in China sent two students a year there. With the advice of his uncles and the help of a cousin who had become an official in the province, Fu-chi won a scholarship to Tsing Hua. The scholarship had been established with the United States' Boxer Rebellion Indemnity Funds. He left for Peking at age thirteen.

Fu-chi told us how he started out on the long and dangerous trip from West Liu Village to Peking in 1917. The railroad came only part of the way and a traveler from beyond that point must reach it on foot or by whatever conveyance he was lucky enough to find. Rivaling warlords and bandits roamed the countryside,

reminding Fu-chi of a terrifying childhood memory. **One day when he had been going home from school in a nearby village, taking his time along an old familiar road, he saw human heads hanging like some monstrous fruit on the tree branches just ahead of him. After one frozen moment, he fled home on wings of terror. He later heard that the severed heads of marauding bandits had been hung there to discourage other roving bandits.**

At the end of the Boxer Rebellion, it was evident to many that dynastic rule in China was at an end and a new order was needed. When the Empress Dowager died and the child emperor Pu Yi assumed the throne, political pressures began to mount. Many educated Chinese wanted a democratic government and hoped to attain the political reform, industrial development, and military build-up that Japan had accomplished after opening to the West. The idea of a constitutional monarchy, as Japan had chosen, was rejected in favor of a democratic republic. A National Assembly of representatives from each province convened in Nanking on December 29, 1911. The Assembly declared the establishment of the Republic of China and elected Dr. Sun Yat-sen its first president. A few weeks later, on February 12, 1912, the emperor abdicated.

President Sun Yat-sen.

The presidency of Sun Yat-sen was short-lived, but the life of the republic continued under the leadership of his Nationalist party or Kuomintang (KMT). His slogan "China for the Chinese" inspired Fu-chi and many of his classmates. Convinced that China could overcome its backwardness, these young students set out to learn all they could from the West and bring it back to build China's future. However, their disillusionment with the West lay just ahead, at the end of the First World War.

At first things proceeded normally at Tsing Hua. Fu-chi played on the basketball and track teams and even learned American baseball. He was short and squarely built but tough and fast enough to make a name for himself in sports. I learned this from his classmates who came to visit in New York. He began learning English from a young American woman who taught him to read. He apologized for his spoken English, but

he said that his ability to read English had given him much joy, especially in the long summers when he was not able to return home. He stayed at the school in Peking and read under the trees of the campus. I was surprised to find that he had read James Fenimore Cooper, Robert Louis Stevenson, Sir Walter Scott, Charles Dickens, Victor Hugo, Mark Twain—many of the same books I had enjoyed as a youth.

I was fascinated by Fu-chi's descriptions of the anti-Japanese movement and the student demonstrations in 1919. On May 4, 1919, the world outside became a greater teacher to him than the world inside books. On that morning, the students of Peking marched in protest against the signing of the Treaty of Versailles in Paris. The Western nations had transferred the former German-held territories in China to Japan. When news reached China, thousands of students in Peking gathered at Tiananmen Square in front of the Forbidden City and marched toward the foreign Legation Quarter. Fu-chi marched with the Tsing Hua students through the streets of Peking carrying placards, handing out leaflets and shouting protest slogans. Barred from the legation by Chinese police and foreign guards, violent outbreaks occurred. Many students were jailed and one killed. A terrific blow from the butt of a police rifle sent Fu-chi limping back to school, unable to sit down for several days.

LIU FU CH'I
劉弗禔
陝西富平

Liu has been for years a member of the varsity, basket ball and base ball teams and a wearer of the college sweater. He has held the first place in 800 meters and mile run for two successive seasons without counting his sure success in the coming spring.

小胖子運動精熟，肌肉發達，將來擬當工程師。平居常以苦力自命。近來大樓上常聞他跟[加油]隆隆對笑，其樂不可言也。此君開來無事，便高唱[自幼兒……]遇見好東西，必大呼 [marvelous;] 你若惹他 張口便道 [秋!]

A photocopy of Fu-chi's Tsinghua class photo, 1925. The description notes his prowess in basketball, baseball, and track.

The years following the 1919 protests witnessed an outpouring of intellectual exuberance known as the "May Fourth Movement." It engaged all levels of Chinese society in a quest to determine the country's direction. Study groups, socialist clubs, and new periodicals and magazines attempted to redefine China's culture and its role in the world. China plunged into an exploration of every form of political and social organization that promised transformation. Many different approaches were advocated. Some opposed Western ways, others adulated the West. Many of China's rising generation of young reformers traveled to other countries in the 1920s. There were pragmatists and radicals, but the spirit of nationalism galvanized the whole nation.

After participating in the march at age fifteen, Fu-chi began to consider how he

Fu-chi's Cornell
class photo,
1928.

could help build a new China. Fu-chi was attracted neither to the communist radicals nor to the militarist isolationists. His pragmatism led him to a practical path of reconstruction. Through education, engineering, and structural reform, he thought, China could change the devastating problems and social disorder he had witnessed in his youth. Grace wrote in her memoirs how his decision was made:

The scholarship stipulated that the recipients should go to an American university of their choice to complete their college degree. Since his commitment was to China's future, Fu-chi debated whether he would be more useful as a doctor or as an engineer. Finally engineering won out over medicine as the skill that he needed to help build modern China. He chose Cornell University in Ithaca, New York, as the best school for his purpose.

After graduation, Fu-chi came to work for Allen Hazen in New York, a specialist in flood control and large city water systems. Hazen was the author of many of the texts Fu-chi had studied at Cornell. In the winters Fu-chi drew plans and did design work, and in the summers he worked as a surveyor on construction sites in New Jersey and the Catskills. Fu-chi learned a great deal from the construction workers, including a large vocabulary of choice American invectives.

When he was not working outside the city, Julianne and I often went with him to movies, plays, and sometimes an opera, going afterwards to have a Chinese dinner. It was a delightful and rewarding friendship for the three of us. His background of ancient civilization and culture, his modern education, both Chinese and Western, his pleasant courtesy, poise, and quiet assurance made him a fascinating and stimulating person to know.

The Tennessee girl was sensitive about her first date with a Chinese native, Grace recalled later. Fu-chi must have noticed her hesitancy for he remained respectful and at a distance. He acted more at ease with Julianne. Grace noticed his attentiveness to Julianne, the younger and prettier of the two. She thought that because of her age, F. C. must be interested in Julianne. Grace did not yet know that he watched her every movement and listened attentively when she sang.

Grace did not say in her memoirs when they actually fell in love. She described their budding relationship with a decorum characteristic of women of her generation. She insisted it was not a sudden infatuation but a gradual growing of respect and admiration for each other. They both valiantly resisted the idea before she found herself "desperately" in love. She first noticed the change the night they went to hear Rosa Ponselle.

There were many reasons why this evening was magical. It was one of the rare times that Grace was alone with Mr. Liu. Neither her mother nor Julianne accompanied them. Grace wanted to show her foreign friend the very best that New York offered—the Metropolitan Opera. The "old Met" on Broadway, with its curving horse-shoe auditorium in ivory and gold, radiated glamor and elegance in the 1930s. It was a time of long gloves and top hats, jewels and flowers.

Rosa Ponselle emerged on the stage of the Met that night with haunting beauty and a sumptuous voice. She played the leading role in Bellini's *Norma*, a role acknowledged to be a cruel test of a singer. It required full range of three octaves, as well as agility in the fast-paced coloratura passages, all the while expressing the powerful emotion required by the drama.

I wanted to show Fu-chi the very best singer in the type of role for which I had been training. I was anxious that he might not like it or that the performance would not be satisfactory. In my nervousness I had forgotten that the story of *Norma* is one of illicit love between two people of different cultures. In this case, a noble Druidess, who is living in a country conquered by the Romans, is caught in a love affair with a Roman soldier. She contemplates murdering her two children and is finally heroically burned at the stake.

The story and the music had such a mesmerizing effect on us both that we left the theatre in a daze. The music had made Fu-chi so absent-minded that he forgot his hat and when we went back to find it, he said, "I think music like that could make people a little crazy." He loved to use contemporary slang. "Crazy" was a popular phrase at the time with lots of meanings, but in this case, I knew he was enchanted. All of New York declared *Norma* an unadulterated success, but for me it was much more than that.

Grace did not have the rounded face of a Rosa Ponselle, with her natural built-in resonators, nor the wide girth characteristic of many opera singers. In fact, she was slim and had a thin face. With brunette hair and clear gray eyes, she was not particularly known for her beauty. But when she sang, her whole appearance took on a radiance that made her seem larger and fuller in the eyes of the listener. Grace thought she saw that transformation begin to happen in Mr. Liu's eyes one evening after the opera.

In the evenings at our apartment, I often sang, sometimes practicing old songs or enjoying new ones. But on this night, I noticed something different about Fu-chi's gaze. It started out as an evening like many before—first a dinner that Mama had prepared, then I went to the piano after we all helped clear the table. Mama called to me from the kitchen, "Sister, sing my favorite, 'All Those Endearing Young Charms.' I am sure Mr. Liu would love to hear it."

When I sang, he had the habit of standing beside me and leaning his elbow on the piano. Although he was usually very circumspect in speech and manner, I caught an unguarded look that put me in a turmoil of conflicting thought and feelings. I began to realize that my feelings were getting beyond the safe "respect and admiration" stage. Was I ready to challenge all the prejudices of race, religion, culture, and customs?

Interracial marriage was illegal in her home state of Tennessee. Although the law did not specify Chinese, it would have been considered shocking for a white woman to marry across any race lines. Even in New York with its polyglot of languages and cultures such a marriage was not common. Her family would have been against it as much for religious reasons as racial ones.

Her short acquaintance with Mr. Liu had grown in her own cultural context. Western music, literature and art were her life and livelihood. Seldom did they venture outside the milieu in which she existed except for an occasional excursion into Chinatown or to a Chinese restaurant. Consequently her cultural habits, customs and ways of thinking and doing were not yet challenged. And she had no reason to think they would be.

I knew it was Fu-chi's plan to go to Germany in the fall to study hydraulics at Karlruhe University. His plan was to go back to China through Russia and Siberia, and not return to New York. That should settle the matter, I thought. As the sailing

date neared, I thought, "Yes, this is the wisest way." But being wise did not console me. Fu-chi was going through the same struggle.

He could not let anything, no matter what it meant to him personally, jeopardize his longtime purpose to devote his life and work to the Chinese people. So we were both silently and unhappily determined to let wisdom prevail.

And so it did, until our farewell on the night that the Queen Mary sailed revealed what we really felt. Thinking we would never see each other again, what did it matter if we dropped the mask this one time?

It would have been hard to resist an emotional farewell at the scene of Fu-chi's departure. The dock was full of people hugging and kissing, waving farewell, crying and trying to get in one last goodbye before separating. Besides the bands and fanfare and the horns in the port on the Hudson River were so loud the noise would have drowned out a normal conversation. An embrace was the only way to say goodbye. If it was their first embrace, it was one of farewell, not one of beginnings. Or so Grace thought.

Days followed when I felt my heart was utterly broken and my life desolate. Mama was sympathetic. She was fond of Fu-chi and thought he was quite a wonderful person, but I could tell she was glad he was gone.

For three months he wrote impersonal letters, addressed to the three of us, about his life in Germany—the kind people in his boarding house, the landlady who was an artist and doing a portrait of him, the nice old professor who liked to talk to him, the beauty of the country, his walks along the Rhine, and how the German students applauded with their feet, stamping on the floor—very interesting letters.

Then at last came a letter addressed only for me, saying he had made up his mind—he was coming back. He'd already written to the Chinese Education Ministry in Washington, the organization that had charge of the Chinese scholarship students in the U.S., telling them he was disappointed in the course and wanted to come back to New York and continue working. The Ministry, knowing well his real reason, refused to give him permission to return to New York but told him to do as he had planned and go back to China via Russia and Siberia.

"I told them," Fu-chi wrote, "that I was coming back no matter what they said and I asked them to transfer my allowance to someone else. It's no use my staying here. I'm just wasting time. I can't study. I see your face on every page. On the bank of the Rhine, I hear you singing."

I came to life again. Julianne was delighted. And in spite of her doubts and fears, Mama was pleased, too. She was a romantic soul and I knew she liked Fu-chi's daring.

Not long afterwards, he was back in New York, and I heard his voice on the telephone say, "Can you meet me on the corner of 113th Street and Morningside Drive tomorrow morning at nine?" I walked the two and a half blocks the next morning on clouds. The first words he said were, "I'd forgotten how beautiful you are!" What love can do to the eyesight, I thought. Aside from being in good health at the time, young and happy, I hadn't the slightest claim to beauty.

We walked down to 110th Street and got on the upper deck of a Fifth Avenue bus and rode to Washington Square and back again. Maybe we did it twice; we had a great deal to discuss and decide. All doubt and hesitation were gone now, for both of us. I knew that this was the one man I wanted now and forever to live with and be with, to face life with whatever the years might bring.

I asked Fu-chi what made him decide to defy all warnings and advice against a foreign marriage. All his friends—but one—and the education ministry had warned him about the relationship. While in Germany, Fu-chi told me, he had written his uncle to break the engagement that his uncle had negotiated for him when he was twelve years old with a Chinese girl from his home village, whom he had never met. When his uncle refused, he wrote the girl himself telling her that she was educated in the old school and he in the new, and they would never be congenial. The girl wrote back that she would try to adapt herself to his life. But he did not believe in the old traditional customs of his country and he made his own choice. I asked him what gave him the courage to make such a decision.

He said that what gave him the final confidence to go against all of the warnings of others was the fact that I was the daughter of my remarkable mother. He thought her daughter would have the character and understanding to cope with life in a strange land and culture and perhaps unaccustomed circumstances.

3

A MARRIAGE OF CULTURES

W<small>E DON'T</small> know what thoughts Julia Divine really had about the marriage. Although Grace was twenty-seven when she met Fu-chi, Mrs. Divine considered herself responsible for her unmarried daughter's welfare. Her family—especially the men in her family, her brothers and her sons—would hold her accountable "if anything went wrong."

It was not unusual in that age for a girl's family to protest her choice of a beau. Mrs. Divine's brothers had prevented their youngest sister from marrying a man they thought inadequate. She could guess where they stood on the matter. Perhaps she also thought of her own marriage at age nineteen to a man nearly twice her age. He died in 1915, leaving her with six children and a little rental property for income. Her father had tried to talk her out of marrying Mr. Divine. Or perhaps she thought about her two sisters who remained unmarried despite the fact that they were good, intelligent, and kind women. Undoubtedly, she wanted more for her daughter.

Grace thought it would take only a little time to gain her mother's approval. After giving Mrs. Divine some time to get used to the idea, they would get married and wait for the proper time to leave for China. This plan was not so easily carried out.

Mr. Liu arranged to get back his old job. But when he was unable to get his room in the same building again, Mrs. Divine offered to sublet him a room in their apartment. This gesture came naturally to her and stemmed from her religious convictions. She had grown up in a household that considered giving a room to someone in need as "entertaining angels unawares."

43

After Fu-chi moved into our apartment, Mama couldn't give up the idea of converting him. Along with her unconventional belief in faith healing, Mama was also a rebel against what she considered the cold formality of the established churches. She wanted her religion to be more alive, to have more of the feeling of being in touch with God, qualities she thought lacking in conventional churchgoing. When I was a child, she often went to a church in an underprivileged section of Chattanooga where the people were mostly factory workers. Its members spoke in tongues, fell to the floor in trances, shouted and saw visions.

Papa was not at all religiously inclined, but he never criticized Mama's religious beliefs and activities. But storms of criticisms came from her brothers, shocked and dismayed by what they called her irrational and fanatical behavior and her association with the poor and uneducated.

Mama and Fu-chi had long philosophical discussions, going back to Confucius, Mencius, and the Greek philosophers, on up to John Dewey—whom Mama didn't like.

A conversation between Mrs. Divine and Mr. Liu would have touched on religious and social thinking in both East and West. Confucian values, Mrs. Divine agreed, like education, family, and respect for authority, had been the basis for a stable social order with moral and ethical standards for centuries in China but, she argued, they were not Christian. Precisely, Fu-chi explained. In China, a religious basis for government was not necessary. Besides, he said, the youth of China were opposed to Confucianism, believing that it ran counter to all that they wanted for a new society in China. They also discussed John Dewey, whom Mrs. Divine disliked because he debunked religion. Mr. Liu was familiar with the ideas of Dewey, then a professor at nearby Columbia University. Dewey's works had been translated into Chinese by Hu Shi, another Boxer Indemnity Fund scholar at Columbia in 1910. Fu-chi liked Dewey's emphasis on pragmatism, on social reform, and education for change rather than "isms." Young people in China, like himself, were torn between wanting to free China of feudalism and imperialism and to replace it with something more than nationalism. He wanted to find a way to replace the old Confucian bureaucratic system with a practical, scientific, and progressive social order that was continuous with his own culture and with civilization worldwide, not just Chinese.

Grace wrote in her memoirs that her mother took Fu-chi to hear a Christian evangelist, Father Divine. There were many popular evangelists at the time, such as "Brother Brown" of the Pentecostal Church, and Aimee Semple McPherson, who wore white and stressed divine healing. But Julia Divine had been introduced by her son John to Father Divine, an African-American evangelist whose controversial Peace Mission Movement became a haven for the downtrodden during the Depression. Although his primary followers were lower-class blacks, mostly older women, Father Divine welcomed people of every social background, economic level, and racial group. White women participated in the movement, as secretaries or servers at the communal meals, thereby reversing the usual roles at this time where blacks would have served whites at the tables. Mrs. Divine's experiences of black churches in the South made her comfortable in the highly charged religious and interracial setting, a shocking contrast to segregated society at that time which allowed few opportunities of social mixing between race and class.

It was not far from their apartment to Father Divine's headquarters, but in a very real sense, it was a world away. From Morningside Drive, you literally descended from a high plateau, down zig-zagging steps along a sheer rock cliff to a flat plain below, from where you could not see the Hudson River or even know that you were on Manhattan. Through the heart of Harlem ran a wide, bustling boulevard, 125th Street, lined with stores, churches, and various commercial and cultural activities. The Apollo Theatre was the center of activity, and many famous blues and jazz musicians and singers, such as W. C. Handy and Bessie Smith, made their appearances here. Writers like Langston Hughes, James Weldon Johnson, Richard Wright, and Countee Cullen, and musicians Roland Hayes and Paul Robeson were names that Julia Divine became familiar with while she was in New York. A block behind the Apollo Theatre was a long row of three-story walk-ups, low-rent and run-down dwellings. Over a door on a storefront on West 126th Street was a sign, "The Kingdom of Father Divine."

This was one place where the name "Mrs. Divine" would have fit right in, but so as not to confuse herself with Father Divine's wife, Julia took the name "Faithful Joy," similar to the adopted names of other disciples, "June Peace," or "Faithful Mary." Every day hundreds gathered at the center for "The Feast," a massive feeding of disciples and the hungry. Long banquet tables were set with linens and flowers, a splendor unusual for feedings of the poor, especially during the Depression. As one of the servers, Mrs. Divine wore a white dress and a white apron. She and the other servers would convey from the kitchen huge platters of green beans, fried okra, stewed tomatoes, lima beans, steamed rice, pork chops, roast beef, fried chicken, baked ham, and all kinds of breads, hot rolls, corn bread, fried bread, brown bread, and rye bread, along with quantities of coffee, milk, and butter. Like Jesus feeding the multitudes, the abundance bespoke of God's outpouring to all people, especially to the faithful in time of need.

The meals were accompanied by singing that seemed to spontaneously grow from the crowd's joy. Hand clapping, foot patting, swaying of the body, and occasional "shouts of the spirit" grew sometimes into a rhythm of a repeated phrase set by one of the guests. After the food quit coming and the singing stopped, Father Divine began to talk. His sermons spoke of hope for mankind in this world and most of all for the discouraged and downtrodden. He believed that men and women had an unlimited capacity to do good and could lead upstanding and prosperous lives without waiting to go to heaven. With religious fervor, Father Divine advocated self-respect, hard work, celibacy, and economic cooperation to end poverty.

Father Divine and his wife at the daily feast, New York, 1930s.

There was an economic side of the Peace Mission that would have interested Fu-chi. Followers of Father Divine did not believe in welfare; instead they formed many small and cooperative businesses—restaurants, groceries, barber shops, fresh food vendors, and cleaning stores—which in the Depression created an economy of the poor. It is unlikely that Fu-chi observed the economic side of the mission or saw past the religious overtones. Grace wrote in her memoirs that he listened docilely to the long sermon, but when they returned home, he said to her mother, "It's of no use. I'm just a born heathen, Juie." (This was the name that Julianne and all her other grandchildren called her.)

Fu-chi claimed that he had no religion. Growing up in the countryside, he had heard stories of ghosts and other spirits, but these were more like folk tales and superstitions to him. They had nothing to do with God. He always resented it when someone tried to manipulate these tales to control people's behavior. His religion, he tried to explain to her, was of a more practical nature. What he believed was manifested in what he did. He didn't have to have a religious reason, it was just important to him to be a good man, to use his reason and to follow his inner direction.

Fu-chi's letter to Mrs. Divine's brother, the Reverend Thomas S. McCallie, was not intended to be a statement of his beliefs. Apparently Fu-chi had loaned Mrs. Divine some money which her brother, "Dr. Tom," then pastor of Central Presbyterian Church in Chattanooga, had returned to him with a letter. Fu-chi was aware that her brothers considered her practice of Christianity circumspect. He responded to the letter by praising Mrs. Divine and by speaking his own view of "Truth." This is the only existing letter from Fu-chi.

New York City
August 10, 1931

My dear Dr. McCallie:

I thank you so much for your kind letter and the check. What I did for Mrs. Divine is so little should never be mentioned.

Now I have the honor and opportunity to write you, a dear brother of Mrs. Divine who, I am absolutely sure, loves her dearly and always has full sympathy with her, no matter, what course she follows.

Sometimes in our life, things good, or bad, happen to us beyond our expectation. I do know—anybody is helpless in such a case. I do not know how some people can better it, which they think is unwise, or foolish.

I am heathen. I do not want to judge other people with my own yardstick which may be ridiculous and sometimes full of ignorance. There is one thing, which I think is true all peoples. May I say "Truth"?

I never saw anyone who lives up so true to the teachings of Christianity as Mrs. Divine. As I know the main teaching of Christianity is to please God. It does look very simple, but it is impossible to all peoples. In the present day, with the results of the bad practices of the old churches, the unbelievable development of industry and science, and the backwardness in the social, political, and economical practices and reforms, all religions are in a dark period. In the States, people generally live with a philosophy of "do as I please, nobody's business." In Europe people ask God's help with hatred, jealousy, and

47

national pride. I think, the western world can only be saved by the true practice of the teachings of Christianity. But it is still a test.

May I at the same time quote what Confucius said once, "I do not murmur against Heaven. I do not grumble against men. My studies lie low, and my penetration rises high. But there is Heaven;—that knows me!"

I traveled in Asia, America, and Europe. I saw, bad people are bad ones; good ones are good ones; fact is fact; and truth is truth. I do not want to bother you any more by my useless writing. May I thank you again for your kind letter.

Respectfully yours,

Fu-chi Liu

Grace had not counted on her brothers' interference with her plans to marry Fu-chi. First came Edward, the baby of the family, three years younger than Grace. He was supremely good looking, with an athletic build and a luminous face. In his youth he had jumped off the high Walnut Street Bridge over the Tennessee River just to prove he could do it. He came to New York after his own marriage had failed and he was down on his luck. His mother took him in. Eventually he got a job at the YMCA, but not before he had taken advantage of his mother's generosity with his sister's limited resources. Mrs. Divine wrote a letter on May 16, 1932 to her son Tom in Chattanooga. Tom was only a year younger than Grace and the one on whom his mother depended. After thanking him for some money he had loaned her, she admitted in the letter that Grace "had much that was given her by others taken from her by me."

Next came Robert, the number two son and Julianne's father. Robert himself had married against the family wishes at age nineteen to a girl only sixteen and had had four children in succession. Unable to support them, he had sent Julianne to live with his mother. However, Robert was outraged at what his daughter was witnessing. He spoke crudely to his mother and threatened to have Fu-chi deported.

One day at work, Mr. Liu was summoned brusquely to the front office. Two dark-suited men demanded to see his papers. After examining the papers and asking some questions, they left suddenly. Mr. Liu was given no explanation.

Despite these intrusions, Grace thrived. She had been asked to sing opera on radio. She lacked the appearance for stage, but the new and exciting medium of radio was perfect for her. Still, it was recommended that she gain weight by drinking more milk. In her letter to Tom, Mrs. Divine wrote that "Grace looks wonderfully well. She weighs almost 125 pounds, due to the persistent milk diet." She added a poignant note: "I do not know what is before us."

Mrs. Divine's uncertainty and Grace's weight gain had to do with more than a milk-enhanced diet.

Mama knew that if I married, I would go to China. She held it off as long as she could so that she would not lose me. When she found out that I was expecting, she cried and cried. She knew then that our love would not go away.

Soon after the incident with the plainclothesmen, we went down to City Hall and were married, with Julianne and a clerk as witnesses. Julianne was delighted with her important part in the procedure and was in high spirits. A walk over to nearby Chinatown and lunch in a Cantonese restaurant was a suitable and lively celebration.

The marriage of Grace McCallie Divine and Liu Fu-chi was announced in the *Chattanooga Times* on June 29, 1932. The article listed her uncles and her brothers.

Grace in New York, Winter 1931.

THE DEPRESSION was in full swing by this time. The homeless and unemployed filled the streets of New York. The Empire State Building, which opened in 1931, was unable to find tenants. By 1932 bread lines were prevalent and shantytowns had sprung up in Central Park. Political unrest began to ferment. A riot broke out in Union Square at the close of a meeting of thousands of Communists and sympathizers. The elections in the fall brought Fiorello La Guardia to the mayoralty of New York and Franklin D. Roosevelt to the Presidency. These two men, although of opposite political parties, united in their efforts to turn the tide. Following their elections, millions of dollars of federal aid relief began to flow into New York. Changes were in store for Grace, too.

With the end of summer 1932, things had become serious. The Depression had grown deeper with no end in sight. Even men with good educations were

selling apples on the street. Fu-chi knew that his office must soon be letting people go. He felt he must begin preparing immediately to go back to China.

"You can find another job," pleaded Mama.

"Impossible, Juie. And I mustn't waste any time hunting for I must go quickly before my bank account begins to shrink."

There was no question of my going with him. My baby was due in December and Fu-chi's situation was too uncertain. There was no job waiting for him in China. His search to find one would take time. It was his plan to leave me his money in the bank and travel to China very cheaply—to Seattle by Greyhound bus and third class passage to Shanghai. He would get a job and save every penny, and when the baby was big enough to travel, he would send for me.

In the last week in September the inevitable happened.

"We are terribly sorry, Liu—but, you see how it is . . ."

There was very little in the way of preparation left to do, and on October 4, 1932, he left New York on the five-day bus trip to Seattle. I remember the afternoon I said good-bye to Fu-chi at the door and watched him as he walked down the hall with his two old schoolmates who were seeing him off. At the elevator he turned, raised his hand and smiled at me. I did not cry. I was very brave until I went in and closed the door.

Grace said she may have been the only one who had absolute faith that this plan would be carried out successfully. She waited, hoping, while others waited, fearing. Grace recalled the first letter after Fu-chi left.

I answered the door bell one afternoon to find our landlord standing there with a letter in his hand. He bowed and made me a little speech. "I am very glad," he said, "to be the one to bring you this first news," and he handed me the letter with the Seattle postmark. I tried to thank him.

"Ah," he smiled with sympathy and understanding. "I knew it would make you happy."

As I turned back inside and shut the door, Julianne came running, snatched the letter and ran back to the kitchen where Mama was ironing.

"Juie, Juie, the letter has come!"

"Julianne," I pleaded, "Give me my letter! It's for me!"

"No, no, it's not just for you. Juie and I must hear it too. I'll read it aloud." She began to tear it open begging Mama to be on her side. "Juie, can't I read it to all of us? She would leave something out, I know."

Mama smiled. "Let her read it, Sister," she said to me.

So I sat and listened to my letter read aloud. Julianne read with emotion, interrupting herself several times to exclaim, "Oh, Juie, isn't that wonderful?"

Toward the end when there was a sentence about the "baby angel for whom we've had this separation," Mama's tears fell sizzling on the hot iron.

There were other letters, one every week. He had landed in Shanghai with five dollars in his pocket, he wrote, and was staying with an old school friend while he looked around for a job. I knew he had no wealthy or influential family or friends, none of that "pull" so important in China of that day. But his confidence and self-assurance were high that he could make his way solely on his ability. Another letter said there was nothing suitable in Shanghai—he was going on to Nanking. From Nanking he wrote of success. He was now the deputy chief engineer of sanitation for the Nanking municipal government. The chief engineer was an American whom he liked immediately. He would be paid the highest salary a Chinese in that position could get, but it was only a third of what a foreigner would be paid—evidence of China's semicolonial condition. His letters arrived once a week, usually on Friday afternoon or Saturday mornings. I was so excited to get them that I hesitated to open them. Even the longest ones were too brief and no matter how slowly I read them they were gone too fast and I had another long week to wait.

Liu Fu-chi (center front), Deputy Chief Engineer of Sanitation, Nanking, 1933.

A mail boat to the Far East sailed from San Francisco once a week and Grace tried to get a letter on every boat. On Christmas Eve, December 24, 1932, a cable to Nanking announced the good tidings, "Mother and daughter doing well."

With Mr. Liu's suggestion, Grace named her daughter Ju-Lan, which in Chinese meant "Pure Lotus" but in English sounded like her mother's name. Her

51

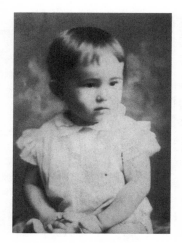

Ju-lan, the
"China Doll,"
New York,
1933.

mother, however, said the baby looked just like Fu-chi and called her "Fuchina," accent on the "chi" pronounced like a long e.

As the Depression progressed, Mrs. Divine's income from the property she owned in the South diminished, so she and Julianne went to work for a Swedish friend who had opened a tearoom in the neighborhood. Resourceful as a cook, Mrs. Divine helped in the kitchen and Julianne, pretty, vivacious, and energetic, served the customers. With Mama and Julianne at work, the housekeeping, as well as taking care of the baby, fell to Grace:

I was exceedingly tired but glad to be so busy, and if I had not had the baby I don't know how I would have made it. Ju-Lan's daily outings in her carriage made us a familiar sight on Broadway and Amsterdam, the Columbia University campus and the grounds of St. John's Cathedral. Dressed in a short, short dress and wearing a little pink bonnet, she looked exactly like an animated doll. The nurses at the New York hospital where she was born had called her "the China doll." When she went with me to the fruit store on Broadway, everybody, men, women, and children stopped to stare and exclaim. I wrote to Fu-chi that his daughter was a sensation on Broadway.

Grace wrote of her conflicting feelings to her sister-in law Mary Hills Divine, on January 10, 1934: "Now I am between the 'devil and the deep blue sea.' As crazy as I am to go I can't stand to think of leaving Mama. She loves the baby to death, and the baby loves Mama better than she does me. I know they will feel terrible when I go. It is very painful to be so torn."

About this time, according to her memoirs, Grace heard from Fu-chi that his situation had changed:

Fu-chi began writing me about the negotiations he was having with the Tientsin Water Works Company. It was then a British-Chinese company registered in Hong Kong and had a Danish chief engineer. Patriotic Chinese directors of the company were trying to oust the British and reorganize as a Chinese company registered in Nanking. According to new Chinese government regulations the chief engineer must be Chinese. The Chinese directors were having difficulty finding a suitable

Chinese to take the chief engineer's position. In the search for one they heard about Fu-chi. He seemed to be just what they needed and the two top Chinese directors came to Nanking to talk to him.

The American chief engineer had gone home on a short leave and Fu-chi was the acting chief in his place. This looked most impressive to the Tientsin men and they were anxious to get Fu-chi to come to Tientsin. "I have a good job here," he told them. "I like it and I'm satisfied with my work here, but there's nothing I'd like better than to help you take your company from British hands." The arrogant colonial British were the most disliked foreigners in China. But when he named the salary he wanted, they were horrified, just as he knew those wealthy North China industrialists would be. For it was considerably more than a Chinese engineer was ever paid. When they said as much, Mr. Liu replied,

Ju-lan on roof of apartment, New York, 1933.

"It's much less than the foreign engineer is paid." They tried to argue, but Fu-chi implied politely that they could take it or leave it. He was perfectly satisfied where he was. They left saying they must discuss it with the other Chinese directors.

A telegram came within a week saying all the Chinese directors agreed to the salary Fu-chi named and asked him to come as soon as he could. But now, the American chief engineer in Nanking had returned from his home leave and protested Fu-chi's leaving. He tried to persuade him to stay, offering more money and the promise of going to the States for further study. But to Fu-chi the prospect of ousting the British was more appealing. He would soon be leaving Nanking, he wrote, and when he settled in Tientsin, he would borrow the money and wire for me and the baby to come.

Now Grace quickly set about getting her passport. This was a troublesome task because she had no birth certificate. She had to ask her Uncle Park McCallie in Tennessee to sign a statement before a notary public attesting to her birth on February 23, 1901. She also had to take Ju-Lan to the Chinese division on Ellis Island where she was fingerprinted and footprinted. Then they took a passport picture together and were all ready for the journey.

Mrs. Divine and Julianne moved south at the end of June. Grace followed a little later with a ticket to Vancouver through Chattanooga for a week. Grace's whirlwind visit home was big news in the Southern town. The front page of the *Chattanooga News* carried her story. Her aunts hosted parties in her honor, signaling acceptance to others.

Her brother Sam invited her to stay with his family. Sam, the third brother, was shorter than Grace's other older brothers and had been permanently crippled by something he drank during Prohibition. He had met Fu-chi early on in New York and liked him. He and Grace's younger brother Tom hosted her. Tom described later how he felt when he first saw his sister and her "mixed" baby: "My sister Grace came in the door of our house with her chubby little black-haired baby toddling along beside her. She [the baby] had never seen me before, yet she stretched out her arms to me and ran to greet me. Grace hugged me and all my resentment of her marriage melted away."

Grace's memoir described her departure from Chattanooga:

On a scorching hot mid-July day in 1934, I stood in the big railway station in Chattanooga, surrounded by my family. I was on my way to China with my eighteen-month-old daughter.

We had spent a week in my brother Sam's home, seeing and greeting relatives and friends again, some for the first time since I'd left Chattanooga eight years before, and at the same time saying good-bye—a sort of "hail and farewell" visit.

While waiting for the train to come in, everyone was giving me last-minute advice, suggestions, and warnings.

"And don't lose your passport," said Uncle Park. "Have you got it in a safe place?"

My passport! It hit me with a blow.

"No, no," I almost shrieked. "I've left it. It's on the dining room table in Sam's house!" I wailed, wringing my hands in despair.

"All right, all right," said Sam, "Don't have a fit. I'll get it."

Mama, Uncle Park, Aunt Hattie, and my brother Tom were quite speechless. Aunt Hattie shook her head in consternation. I knew they were thinking, "If she begins like this, how will such an absent-minded addle pate get herself and baby safely halfway round the world?"

Sam took his car on two wheels around corners and was back with the passport just as the train pulled into the station.

THE CHATTA.

ASSOCIATED PRESS AND UNITED PRESS SERVICE   CHATTANOOGA, TENN., FRI

Chattanooga Girl Who Broke Racial Ties And Married Chinese Engineer Paying Visit Here

East and West Become One for Grace Divine, Now Mrs. Liu Fuchi.

By NELLIE KENYON

All of her life Grace Divine, talented Chattanooga girl, has wanted to travel to foreign lands, live in strange places, fall "frightfully" in love, marry and have a nice baby. Somehow she has always felt that the fairy prince of whom she read in her childhood story books would some day come along and make possible this fantastic dream.

Today Grace Divine, as Mrs. Liu Fuchi, wife of a native Chinese, who is a brilliant scholar, feels that this dream has come true. She is deeply in love, has a beautiful baby and is in Chattanooga to tell her relatives good-by before sailing for the Orient to join her husband.

"I had to pinch myself several times coming down on the train from New York to see if it was really me, and then I wouldn't believe it," said Mrs. Liu Fuchi, as she sat holding in her arms her 15-months-old daughter, Ju Lann (Little Orchid in Chinese).

Little did Grace Divine realize several years ago when she had her first date with Liu Fuchi and went to see "Good News," a musical comedy then playing in New York, that it would mean good news to her and that she was sitting beside her future husband. Little did this Southern girl realize then that she was destined to give up a musical future and go with this man from the Land of the Rising Sun back to his native country as his wife.

Was Sensitive at First.

The Tennessee girl was somewhat skeptical and sensitive over her first date with a native Chinese, and he too, detected this sensitiveness and

(Continued on Page 10.)

China's Far Away, But Now It's Home

"East is East and West is West, and never the twain shall meet." But for Grace Divine, a Chattanooga musician, the twain have met. She is now Mrs. Liu Fuchi, the wife of a young Chinese engineer. With her 15-months-old daughter, she is finding her new home far away China. She will sail soon to join him and make her home there.

Grace's visit to Chattanooga before embarking for China was front-page news, June 22, 1934.

THE CHATTA.

:IATED PRESS AND UNITED PRESS SERVICE   CHATTANOOGA, TENN., FRI

Chattanooga Girl Who Broke Racial Ties And Married Chinese Engineer Paying Visit Here

East and West Become One for Grace Divine, Now Mrs. Liu Fuchi.

China's Far Away, But Now It's Home

By NELLIE KENYON

All of her life Grace Divine, talented Chattanooga girl, has wanted to travel to foreign lands, live in strange places, fall "frightfully" in love, marry and have a nice baby. Somehow she has always felt that the fairy prince of whom she read in her childhood story books would some day come along and make possible this fantastic dream.

Today Grace Divine, as Mrs. Liu Fuchi, wife of a native Chinese, who is a brilliant scholar, feels that this dream has come true. She is deeply in love, has a beautiful baby and is in Chattanooga to tell her relatives good-by before sailing for the Orient to join her husband.

"I had to pinch myself several times coming down on the train from New York to see if it was really me, and then I wouldn't believe it," said Mrs. Liu Fuchi, as she sat holding in her arms her 15-months-old daughter, Ju Lann (Little Orchid in Chinese).

Little did Grace Divine realize several years ago when she had her first date with Liu Fuchi and went to see "Good News," a musical comedy then playing in New York, that it would mean good news to her and that she was sitting beside her future husband. Little did this Southern girl realize then that she was destined to give up a musical future and go with this man from the Land of the Rising Sun back to his native country as his wife.

Was Sensitive at First.

The Tennessee girl was somewhat skeptical and sensitive over her first date with a native Chinese, and he, too, detected this sensitiveness and

(Continued on Page 18.)

"East is East and West is West, and never the twain shall meet." But for Grace Divine, a Chattanooga musician, the twain have met. She is now Mrs. Liu Fuchi, the wife of a young Chinese engineer. With her 15-months-old daughter, she is finding her new home—far away China. She will sail soon to join him and make her home there.

It was hay fever weather in Tennessee and my last words of farewell were lost in fits of sneezing and weeping. A miserable start to my long journey.

My emotions were mixed. It was heartbreaking to leave Mama and all the family and yet there was the deep happiness and excitement of being on my way at last.

First, to the Chicago train station, then three days and three nights to Vancouver, ten days across the Pacific and four days across the China Sea, before I reached my new home—No one, not even myself, dreamed it would be forty years before I saw this country again.

4

STARTING LIFE IN CHINA

G RACE'S first three years in Tientsin were the end time of a disappearing world. Unaware of what was passing and what was coming, life in semicolonial China was for her an extraordinary interlude of untroubled happiness. She saw and heard much that was shocking and troublesome, but none of it adversely affected her life. It was like having a box seat at an opera where she could be shocked, saddened, and even frightened and still feel safely beyond the play going on. She lived in a small, confined world inside a larger, unpredictable one. Grace wrote home after three months that she had "really not seen anything of China"— that was the feeling of one living in the foreign-controlled territories inside China in the 1930s.

Since the end of the British Opium War in 1842, foreign countries had claimed rights to areas of China, called "concessions," exempt from Chinese law. When Grace arrived, Tientsin was divided into the British, French, Japanese, Russian, Italian, and Belgian concessions; the former German and Austrian concessions were called the "Special Areas." Each of these foreign-controlled territories had their own businesses, parks, police, schools, languages, architecture, banks, restaurants, and laws. The combined effect made Tientsin a busy cosmopolitan and commercial city. It served as both the port for Peking and the center of foreign trade, commerce, banking, and military operations in Northern China—smaller but similar to Shanghai in the south.

Life inside the foreign concessions was like a country club. Servants were abundant and cheap. Whatever one's activity during the day, it ceased at five o'clock when the drinking began. The social life was extraordinary. Horse races, costume balls,

57

movie theaters, and private clubs both brought together and kept separate the lines of class, race, and national origin. Most of the Lius' associates were foreign-born or foreign-educated, mixed marriages or mixed blood. Grace did not like most of the foreigners she met, calling them "tacky," meaning they lacked values like her own. And she, in turn, was snubbed by the Westerners who looked down on the Chinese and those who married them. This prejudice permeated all aspects of colonial society, even the church that Grace attended.

The French Park in the French Concession, Tientsin, 1930s.

Fascinated by her newly acquired status and privilege, Grace wrote glorious details of her new life, intending to impress and reassure her family that she had not "married down" and was not suffering with the masses in China, as they may have assumed. Her letters provide intimate, immediate images of her first impressions, untroubled by the significance of events. But in her memoirs, written forty years later, she knows what she did not know at the time, that China and her life were about to change dramatically. The distance of time allows her not only to laugh at herself as a blundering, innocent newcomer but also to see the irony of her innocence within a world unconscious of its own demise. Her early letters demonstrate the characteristics which make her a reliable observer and guide—her honesty, straightforwardness, curiosity—and, ultimately, her willingness to change.

Grace had Ju-lan's portrait shot in both Chinese and Western style.

The relationship between Grace and Fu-chi is central. The roles are reversed now. Grace is no longer in her cultural milieu, but in one that operates in ways unknown and unknowable to her. Her husband, whom she calls Mr. Liu when writing to her mother and Fu-chi in her memoirs, is her support and interpreter—of language, customs, and current events. He, in turn, includes her in all he does. She listens in on his conversations with co-workers in the afternoons at their house; she reads his reports and edits his English; she learns from him what is happening around them and the news of the world beyond. At first her assumptions of Chinese politics are based on media reports, but over time she becomes more keenly aware of the difference between what was in the papers and what was really happening. She is not typical of most foreigners in China who saw events only from the foreign perspective.

Ultimately, because she identifies with her husband, she identifies with China.

August 9, 1934
Dear Mama,

I got your first letter yesterday afternoon. I read it aloud to Mr. Liu and Fuchina. Fuchina hung around my neck and tried to get in the letter. When we said it was Juie's letter she took it and looked all over it and hugged it all up under her chin.

LIFE IN TIENTSIN, 1934–35

Our small flat was on the French side of the road that was the boundary between the French and British concessions. Therefore we did not really live in China,

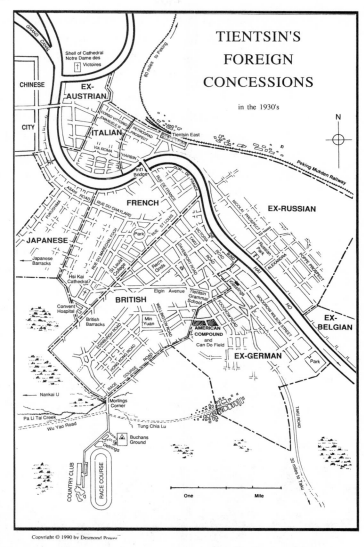

TIENTSIN'S FOREIGN CONCESSIONS

in the 1930's

Copyright © 1990 by Desmond Power

Map of the foreign concessions in Tientsin, as they existed early in the century.

but in French territory in China, under the jurisdiction of the French Municipal Council. It was the same with the British, Japanese, and Italian concessions, all managed by their respective municipal councils under their respective home governments.

These "concessions," as the foreign-controlled territories were called, became the foreigner's paradise that gave even the most insignificant little clerk sent out from home a luxurious lifestyle he could never know in his own country. Ordinary westerners, including missionaries, enjoyed a higher standard of living and had more status than they would have had at home. Here the British were the elite, all other nationalities were inferior to them, either slightly or greatly. Chinese, or "natives," were on the bottom. All the rest of Tientsin was called the Chinese or Native City, and to most foreigners was considered uncivilized territory.

Our snug little flat of three rooms and a tiny balcony overlooking the courtyard was in a racially and internationally conglomerate compound—a Russian Jewess with a German husband, a British newspaper man and his Russian wife, a large Chinese family, a Greek couple, some Italians, and a number of mixed Chinese and western families.

The American barracks in the First Special Area of Tientsin.

October 5, 1934

You asked about the foreign element here. Where I am there's nothing much but foreign element for we live in a foreign concession. Our apartment building is in the French concession but the British concession is across the street. Our street has two names. The French side is called Rue St. Louis and the British side is Bristow Road. Just a block away

is Victoria Road which is the Wall St. of Tientsin with all the big banks and British stores. The same road runs into the French concession on one end and becomes the Rue de France, on the other end. It goes into the Chinese Special Area and becomes Woodrow Wilson Street.

The people around here are mostly French, British, and Rus-

sian. I don't like the foreigners here. They are mostly business people and tacky.

Most of the Americans live in the Special Area which is under Chinese control. It is really the prettiest and nicest part of the city. There are some beautiful houses there. But the trouble is that Mr. Liu can't live out of the district that's furnished water by his company or he will forfeit his house allowance. That means that we have to live in either the French, British, or Italian concessions.

We went to see Wallace Beery in "The Bowery" the other night. The picture was so typically American I don't see how most of the audience understood it. We have been to several picture shows and the audiences are very interesting to me. I never realized how different from each other the various nationalities, much less races, looked.

They always have a ten-minute intermission here in the middle of each picture and I love to watch the audience. There are always quite a lot of Chinese, in foreign dress and Chinese dress, Chinese flappers with permanent waves and long earrings, old fat Chinese gentlemen in long gowns and modern young Chinese men in foreign clothes. But I haven't seen a Chinese girl in foreign clothes. There are some Japanese in kimonos and wooden shoes. There are about an equal number of French, Russian, and British and some Italians and not very many Americans. The British are nearly always dressed in evening clothes.

The other night we were picking out the different nationalities and we couldn't find any Americans. Suddenly I said, "Oh, look, here come the Stones. They are going to sit in front of us." Mr. Liu had to laugh out loud, for here came a family dressed in tailored sport clothes with long sharp faces and slightly dried-up looking and so unmistakably American.

Mr. Liu doesn't like Tientsin nearly as well as he did Nanking. This is just like any city—streets, sidewalks, buildings, and crowds. Nanking was more in the country with fields and farms and water buffalo. He said there were lovely places to walk in the woods and up the mountains. Here there are only the sidewalks and city parks. There's no place to go with a baby. The park is too far to walk to and the streets are so crowded it's not very pleasant walking with a baby. Nanking is much more typically Chinese, not as many foreigners. There he was working in the government and could hear all the political gossip daily that he loves so much. Here you have to depend on just what you read in the papers.

November 23, 1934

I do want to write something about China but I have been here only a little over three months and I really have not seen anything of China. Tientsin is just a big commercial city. Nothing pretty, nothing artistic, and nothing typically Chinese. It is much more for-

A street scene in the Chinese "native city" part of Tientsin.

eign than Chinese. In a foreign concession you would forget you were in China if it weren't for the rickshaws and Chinese people.

One thing that really is Chinese is the little food stand on nearly every street. Some of them look like small hot dog stands and they sell the most delicious smelling concoctions of vegetables, meat, onions, garlic and red peppers in pretty Chinese bowls. There is one right in front of our house. And you can't imagine how tempting the food smells on a cold frosty morning. The rickshaw coolies and people going to work stop there and eat a hot smoking dish or two.

Another kind is just two big trays a man carries around on a bamboo pole across his shoulders. It always looks tempting, too. There are piles of fresh scraped raw carrots, long white turnips, red turnips, long white radishes and other Chinese vegetables that are eaten raw. Then there are big bins of wonderful fat chestnuts roasting in hot charcoal.

You know how the Chinese love tea. On nearly every corner there is a little contriv-

Chinese merchant at curio shop, Tientsin.

ance that looks like a China cupboard. It has pots of boiling water, tea bowls and tea. They are for the outdoor workers, rickshaw men, policemen, watchmen, etc. The other day I saw a policeman during a traffic lull standing in the middle of the street drinking his cup of hot tea as nonchalantly as if he had been sitting at his own table.

In the Chinese native city of course it's very different from the concessions. I have only been thru it once. The streets are very narrow and crowded and swarming with children. I was surprised to see how very fat and healthy most of them look. I suppose the sickly ones simply don't last long. Mr. Liu's office is in the native city and he says it's very interesting. The other day he was walking along the street and a man in front of him was carrying a rather long bundle wrapped in bamboo matting. When he passed the man he saw that the bundle was a little dead baby that the poor man was taking away to bury somewhere. Mr. Liu said it gave him such a shock that he felt bad all the way home.

A CAREFREE EXISTENCE

Charles Ruas, the French engineer at the Water Works, lived in the same compound. He had been divorced for a year and had no wife at that time. His cook found a cook for us, a nineteen-year-old boy named Sun Pao-san who had been a "small cook" (apprentice) at the famous Astor Hotel in the British Concession, and Sun, in his turn, found me an amah. That's the way things were done. If you didn't have a cook, you asked a friend's cook to get you one, and then if you needed an amah or house boy, you asked your own servant to find you one. The cooks, amahs, and house boys of the concessions made up a close community of friends and relatives, a convenient and readily available supply of domestic help.

Ju-lan playing in the park, with amahs in the background.

As young as he was, Sun Pao-san was an excellent cook, but, in my arrogance, I considered him still better after I taught him how to cook vegetables Southern style and how to make American pies.

Wang Nai-nai, the amah, was a middle-aged woman who had been a nurse for British and American families and, therefore, spoke some English. She was experienced and capable and took the baby over without any trouble. A daily routine was soon established that left me time to explore and investigate my new world. Sun Pao-san and Wang Nai-nai were with us altogether for twenty years, until Ju-Lan was a grown woman.

I had never known such a carefree existence before and never knew quite the same again. I had no housework to do, no cooking, no marketing, and no baby tending. I could sit down in the middle of the morning with a new book and not feel guilty, but conscious nevertheless of what Grandma McCallie would think of such sinful idleness.

I was happy and pleased with my new life and so hypnotized and intrigued by the life around me that happenings outside the tight little world of the concessions seemed unreal to me.

October 5, 1934

I have just finished reading yours and Julianne's weekly letters. Mr. Liu hasn't come home yet. I usually read them aloud to him. He is always so interested in everything you all say. He gets quite homesick for N.Y. and you and Julianne.

The weather has turned much colder in the last week. One day it was downright cold. We have no heat on yet. This is not N.Y. There is a fireplace in the living room, but Sun will not build a fire in it unless I insist. He considers it very foolish and extravagant. He is the most "saving" soul I've ever seen. He says oranges and lemons cost too much money and when I insist that he buy oranges every day he shakes his head and looks as if he thought the foreign "missy" were completely crazy. He is an awfully good faithful boy and he is grand to the baby and she likes him fine and calls him "Dun."

Grace and Ju-lan visiting the Water Works Pumping Station.

It is after five o'clock now and Mr. Liu has just come in. He is reading your letter now. Ju Lan is playing out in the court with Amah and the other children. She has been out there since 2:30. She stays out nearly all day long. I can hear the children yelling and screaming and Ju Lan's voice is the loudest of all. She is a little roughneck. You would die if you could hear her imitating amah's Chinese. She wrinkles up her nose and squints her eyes and says "Mei Yo" just exactly like amah. That means "have not."

October 19, 1934

I am studying Chinese at the Y.W. now. We have two lessons a week. Then nearly every

64

night I have another lesson with Mr. Liu. Sometimes he has too many things to study to help me. In the meantime I practice on Sun and amah. They beam with pride on me when I can make them understand something I say in Chinese.

November 11, 1934

Chinese is as hard as the dickens. The writing and reading aren't so hard but speaking!—Each sound has four different tones and each tone means something else. For instance one tone of a certain sound means chair, another tone of the same thing means soap. Yesterday when the rickshaw man took me to the park I told him to come back and get me at 11:30 in Chinese and he understood me. I talked to the amahs in the park, too, and they can understand me. I am always so proud when they know what I say.

Ju Lan talks the funniest language you ever heard now. She tries so hard to talk Chinese. When her father talks to Sun or Amah, she will imitate him. And when she tries to sing Chinese like Sun it's the funniest thing you could imagine.

November 22, 1934

I know it sounds like I would have nothing to do when I have two servants. But I find plenty to occupy my time and I don't read as much as I did in N. Y. When I first came I was so exhausted that I didn't even tell Sun what to get to eat. I just let him do it all. But in two or three weeks I got tired of fancy heavy cooking and it was bad for me, too. So now I plan all the meals and help cook a lot too. I have been teaching Sun real physical culture cooking. I am sure we have the best food in Tientsin. Then I take most of the care of the baby. Amah keeps her clothes clean and mended and plays with her but I do the most important things. My Chinese lessons take up nearly three whole mornings a week and I have to study in the meantime.

OMINOUS CLOUDS GATHERING

But, indeed, my conventional ideas of life and the world were about to be considerably shaken.

I knew that dark and ominous clouds were gathering and spreading, that the Japanese, already in Manchuria, were coming down into Hopei [Hebei], the province we were in, and were establishing a Japanese-controlled demilitarized zone between Peking and Tientsin and were smuggling drugs and Japanese goods into the Chinese cities.

The Japanese concession in Tientsin was full of opium and heroin dens. Dead bodies were nightly picked up around the low-class heroin dives and thrown into the river. I was horrified, of course, when floating bodies were pointed out to me a time or two. But it all seemed to have nothing to do with my life.

At the time of my arrival in Tientsin, the Japanese were encroaching farther and farther into North China, but the Nationalist Kuomintang [Guomindang] Government in Nanking was making no efforts to resist them. Instead, we heard that Chiang Kai-shek, the supreme leader in the Republic of China, was beginning his fifth extermination campaign against the Communists.

But what we didn't hear about was the Red Army's breaking out of Chiang's encirclement in October 1934, two months after I reached Tientsin, and starting on what became known as the "Long March" to Shensi Province. No word of this penetrated the confines of the concessions.

October 5, 1934

The National Government is much stronger than it ever was and fast progress in every line is being made all over China. Chiang Kai-shek is much more popular than he used to be and even those who never liked him say he has changed.

The Chinese government is desperately fighting the opium and drug traffic. There is a death penalty for being caught dealing in drugs and every day the paper tells of some drug dealer being executed. But the Japanese are trying just as hard to force the drugs on the Chinese. Everywhere in N. China where they are in control they protect the drug dealers. Right here in the Japanese concession there are hundreds of shops where drugs are sold openly to Chinese but no Japanese are allowed to buy any. It is the same in Manchuria. Everywhere there are shops selling drugs to Chinese but not to Japanese. Japan is trying to flood China with drugs and make wrecks of as many Chinese as possible.

But China today is stronger and more united than any time since the Revolution [overthrow of emperor in 1911]. The foreigners have been pushed back and are taking a decidedly back seat. The Chinese themselves are in control of the big business, banks, railroads, etc. And the men who are doing the real work and getting things done are the Chinese students who studied in America.

America and Russia are probably the only two countries who would welcome a strong China. England certainly does not want a strong China on account of India, and neither does France. Next to the Japanese, the British are the most disliked people in China.

CULTURAL BLUNDERS

The foreign country club life in that "never never land" of the concessions—
with its horse racing, entertaining and being entertained, the rivalry of hostesses,
the British club where members got respectably drunk at five o'clock, and the constant struggle of the lower ranks to climb into the society of the higher—went on
unconcerned in the path of a coming hurricane that would sweep it away forever.

So ignorant was I of the life and conditions that I had come into that I was apt
to commit stupidities and make blunders. Fu-chi, also a greenhorn about life in the
concessions, couldn't brief me beforehand. He hadn't lived in a Chinese family
since he was thirteen and was more used to Western ways than to Chinese. He
never realized that I knew very little of Chinese social customs. I had only my own
foreign manners and ideas of courtesy to go by.

There were a number of Fu-chi's former Tsing Hua classmates living in or near
Tientsin when I arrived in 1934. Several were teaching at the two nearby universities, two doctors and a businessman. I was soon getting some practice in how to
behave properly in a Chinese social setting.

August 9, 1934

*We have had an awful lot of company since I have been here. All of Mr. Liu's friends
in Tientsin have been to see us and we have had two dinner parties here. The dinners were
absolutely no trouble to me. I didn't even know what we were going to have until it was
put on the table. Our cook, Sun Pao-san, took care of everything.*

Wednesday night we had the Police Commissioner Mr. Yang, his wife, and his secre-

The horse-
racing course
outside the
British
Concession.

67

tary Mr. Chen. Mrs. Yang couldn't stay for dinner as she was going to a party given by Madame Chang, the young Marshal's wife, at the Villa Westlake.

We first had consommé, then baked fish with potato salad, then squash with red cabbage cooked with apple, then stuffed tomatoes, apple pie and coffee, and lastly fruit. Sun makes wonderful coffee. I just tasted a drop but I never drink it. Chinese men are crazy about pie. Sun's pie isn't quite like our pie. It's more like apple short cake. Please tell me how to make pie crust and I can tell Sun. He is very smart and I know he could make it right if I told him what to do.

THE HONORED GUEST

One of the first lessons I got was at a dinner party of these classmates and their wives. It was an elaborate banquet with about fifteen guests seated around a big round table. I did not know that the seating of guests went according to a pre-scribed ritual in which hostess and guests played their accustomed parts. When the hostess told me to sit in a certain seat I did so and was amazed to see every other guest refuse to take the assigned seat with much waving of hands and loud protests of "No, no, let someone else take this seat." After much persuasion and more pro-tests everyone was at last seated and the feast began.

As we walked home I said to Fu-chi, "How terribly rude not to sit where the hostess tells you to."

He burst out laughing. "It was you who were rude. You promptly took the most honorable seat without a word of protest."

"But," I said, "the hostess told me to sit there."

"Of course, she did, but you should have protested loudly your un-worthiness of such an honor until you were practically pushed into the seat."

"That's silly," I said indignantly. "Anyway, why didn't you tell me be-forehand?"

"I never thought of it. Besides, it is just a piece of old Chinese eti-quette that would not suit you at all. Nobody expected it of you. Don't worry, you behaved very properly."

November 11, 1934

I am sending some pictures we took last Sunday at Nankai University right

Fu-chi and Ju-lan, with chickens and rabbits, Nankai campus, 1934.

outside of Tientsin. We were invited to spend the day with Dr. Chang, head of one of the departments. It is a lovely place. So much nicer than inside the city. All the faculty live in cute little bungalows on the grounds. They have tennis courts and a playground for children. Big iron pots were full of beautiful and unusual fish. There are at least a hundred rabbits of all kinds and sizes, including the giant Siberian rabbits with beautiful fluffy white fur, six and seven inches long. Ju Lan had a grand time. She screamed and yelled when it was time to go home.

We invited Dr. and Mrs. Chang here for dinner today. We ate about two o'clock and had a real American dinner. Dr. Chang liked it fine, but I think Mrs. Chang thought it was very flat and tasteless. She tried her best to eat but she couldn't make much of it. We had soup, roast chicken, mashed potatoes with peas and carrots, asparagus with white sauce over it, slaw, and apple pie. I made the pie. It was my second attempt and was not quite as successful as my first. It broke all to pieces when I tried to cut it. My first pie fell to pieces too but not quite as bad as the second.

I had forgotten to buy a pie pan and Sun borrowed one. The system of borrowing that the Chinese servants have is very funny. For instance, if we don't have enough plates or cups or glasses, at the last minute, Sun will go out and borrow some from some other cook, a friend of his, and we will be eating out of somebody's dishes that we don't know at all. Or sometimes I miss a certain bowl or pan and Sun has lent it to somebody's cook.

POT OF RICE

The next lesson I took more seriously and felt very embarrassed when Fu-chi told me what I'd done. This time we were having a family dinner with an old classmate, his wife and two children and another close friend.

At a medium-sized round table there was a bowl of rice at each place and three rather small plates of vegetables stir-fried with slivers of meat. A huge pot of rice stood on a side table. This was the kind of Chinese food I loved. I piled the vegetables and meat on top of my rice, putting more on as I ate it off with a little rice at a time. My one bowl of rice was quite sufficient to last the whole meal, but everyone else got up and refilled their bowls several times. I noticed that by the time my rice was almost gone, so were the vegetable and meat dishes.

Again on the way home I commented. "I loved that food, but there wasn't enough of the vegetable dishes."

"You think that because you eat like an American. Chinese consider rice the main food. They fill up on that with just enough vegetables and meat to help the rice along," he explained. "But you," laughing as if it were a huge joke, "you do just the opposite. You ate up all the vegetables and meat with only a half a bowl of rice."

"Stop laughing. You're mean," I said. "Why didn't you tell me? Why did you let me make such a spectacle of myself?"

"Don't worry. Mrs. Tuan was very pleased that you liked her food so well."

I had to laugh, but I felt terribly embarrassed and determined never to make that blunder again. Naturally in making my way in an alien culture I was bound to get myself laughed at occasionally.

October 27, 1934

We went to a wedding this afternoon of one of Mr. Liu's schoolmates. As they are both Christians they were married in the Chinese Christian church. It was not a Chinese wedding but just like an American one. The bride wore a beautiful white satin wedding gown with a long train and lace veil. The maid of honor was extremely pretty and wore a pink satin foreign style dress. Their hair looked beautiful—they both had permanents.

The church was crowded. There were lots of foreigners, the British Consul General being one of them, and nearly all the prominent Chinese of the city. A famous general sat right in front of us. I can't remember his name. All the Chinese men had on long heavy silk gowns and silk trousers tied around the ankles with bows and velvet slippers. Of course the younger men wore foreign clothes. Most of the women had on Chinese dresses. One of the prettiest women there had on a foreign dress, a black velvet afternoon dress with pearls. She looked stunning. The groom and best man wore tails and high silk hats.

The best man was Mr. Ding, one of the schoolmates that visited us in New York. The groom and Mr. Ding stood beside the pulpit while the maid of honor, the little flower girl and the bride and her father crept down the aisle—and were they painful to see! The groom looked as if he might drop dead any minute and Mr. Ding looked as if he wished he were dead and buried. Mr. Liu just suffered for them. He wouldn't even look at them. And when the procession started down the aisle he said, "Why don't they come faster."

The preacher was an American and he used the ring service. After he got through a Chinese preacher said a long prayer in Chinese and then the audience sang a hymn in Chinese. An American doctor with his wife and daughter sat opposite us and they sang loud and lustily in Chinese.

Sunday October 28

We went to church this morning in the Anglo-Chinese college run by the London Mission. Most of the audience were Chinese students but there were about a dozen English people, at least they looked English. The Superintendent was playing the organ and singing a hymn in Chinese as lustily as Uncle Park. He had a much better voice than Uncle Park. The man who spoke was very good—nothing particularly spiritual, but all right. As we were walking home afterwards, Mr. Liu was picking the preaching to pieces. He said, "Oh, the man was just rambling," when a donkey pulling a big load of coal right beside us on the street suddenly gave a loud "ouk-a-ouk-a-ouk"—or whatever it is they do—right in Mr. Liu's ear. And the poor man almost jumped out of his skin. He laughed and said, "Well, I certainly did get a good horse laugh for saying the preacher was rambling."

THE KITCHEN GOD INCIDENT

One of my favorite pastimes during my first months in Tientsin was wandering around in the curio shops, looking at and often buying fascinating little objects of porcelain, ivory, lacquer, etc.

One morning I bought what I thought was a real find—a scroll picture of a beautiful white-bearded old man in a rose-colored long gown, gesturing with graceful hands to the birds flitting through the flowers and trees. Oh, it was a lovely picture!

I hurried home with it, pleased and excited. I wanted to hang it on our dining-living room wall. It was lunch time and Fu-chi had just come in. I proudly unwrapped my picture and held it up.

"Isn't this lovely? Won't it look wonderful against this wall?"

He stared, shocked, as if he couldn't believe his eyes.

"Oh, no," he said seriously, "not on this wall. You'd better give it to Sun."

I was astonished and hurt. "But, but," I stammered. "What's the matter with it?"

"It's the kitchen god. Here, Sun," he said as the cook came in. "You take this. Tai-tai wants to hang him up on the wall in here."

I knew Sun wanted to laugh out loud, but was too polite to do it.

I later saw my picture in the coal bucket and learned about the kitchen god and the reason for the horrified look when I wanted to hang him up in the living room.

He was a sort of New Year's joke and it was part of the New Year's celebration to put a plate of sticky candy in front of his picture to stick his teeth together so he

71

wouldn't be able to tell tales on people when he made his annual report to heaven at New Year's.

The kitchen god incident didn't cure me of visiting the curio shops, but I was no longer such a gullible greenhorn.

August 9, 1934

It's terribly hard to shop here. Of course I can't go by myself except to one or two English stores and they are so much more expensive. Any time he wants it, Mr. Liu can have a marvelous-looking big car and a chauffeur in uniform. You should see me going shopping in a big car with a chauffeur, having the clerks to take all the packages out to the car instead of carrying anything.

He is quite a "big dog" you know. Every morning the chauffeur comes after him and takes him to work. He usually goes about 8:30. Then he comes home at twelve and goes back to work at two and stays until five.

We have ridden several times in rickshaws too. Fuchina sits in one rickshaw with her daddy and I sit in another. That's lots of fun.

THE WATER WORKS COMPANY

One day I heard a car stop in the courtyard and then another one.

"Sun," I called. "Have you got the beer on ice?"

"Long time on ice, Tai-tai."

Men's voices, loud, coming up the stairs . . . and a minute later, Fu-chi came in with two of his fellow engineers, Charles Ruas, the Frenchman in his thirties, and

Grace and Ju-lan, with a Water Works car, 1934.

Mr. Cudzilo, a middle-aged Pole. I was greeted in three accents and my hand kissed in both French and Polish style.

An after-work discussion of the affairs of the Water Works and of the world, enjoyably helped along with glasses of ice cold Tsing-tao beer, became an almost daily custom. I enjoyed listening in on these discussions. They were both amusing and educational for a rather provincial-minded American.

The fight to wrest control of the Water Works from British to Chinese hands was not finished. It swayed back and forth keeping everything but maintenance work at a standstill. The three engineers were vehement in their criticism of the way the Chinese directors were dilly-dallying—so much needed to be done. The whole company was just wasting time. Charlie Ruas denounced Mr. B——, the Danish chief engineer. "He's no engineer. He was just a ship's mechanic and got that job because he married the daughter of the British manager of Hall and Haltz [a British department store]."

F. C.'s colleague, Charles Ruas, perched on a stylized lion statue.

October 5, 1934

No wonder the Chinese have boiled with fury against the foreigners. Ignorant, incompetent men who probably couldn't get any kind of a job at home have come over here and because they were foreigners have gotten enormous salaries and been put over Chinese who knew ten times as much.

The present chief engineer of the Water Works company is an ignorant Danish mechanic, in no way qualified to be an engineer. He got his job thru pull with the British directors because he married an English girl. Mr. Liu says he is a complete joke. He does nothing at all. They despise him. Mr. Liu does not work under him nor have to take any orders from him.

Mr. Liu is more or less his own boss and is put there by the Chinese directors to gradually take control of everything. When the company becomes Chinese they are going to keep some of the best foreign engineers and mechanics—Mr. Ruas and Mr. Cudzilo and some others. It will be the first time they have had a Chinese boss. But they all like Mr. Liu very much and treat him so respectfully it tickles me.

October 20, 1934

Last night Mr. Liu went to a banquet for the Yellow River Commission. When he came home at 9:30, he read me the report he had written on the condition of the company for the board of directors so I could correct the English. You would be surprised at what good English he can write when he really tries. It was sixteen pages long, though, so it was after twelve when we finished. He is typing it tonight and having an awful time as he is not used to the typewriter. He has already spoiled about a dozen pages and is swearing in both English and Chinese.

November 22, 1934

I had dinner by myself tonight. Mr. Liu was invited to eat with some official of the company. They are going through the red tape of changing the company from a British one to a Chinese one now. It will all be over some time in December. Of course there is an awful lot of feeling, gossip, and crookedness going on. But the Chinese will win out this time, thanks to Mr. Liu. Without him they would be pretty helpless.

November 24, 1934

This is Saturday afternoon and Mr. Liu has just come in. He has been having lunch at Homer Lu's home. Mr. Lu is the richest man here and probably one of the richest in China. He is the chief Chinese director of the Water Co. besides owning the biggest cement company in North China. He is going to Nanking today to arrange with the government about changing the company to a Chinese one. His plan is to get all the private-owned water companies in China in Chinese hands. He has control of a water company in Peking and he is planning to get the water company in the British concession. Mr. Liu will be the chief engineer of them, too. Dr. Li, the head of the Yellow River commission, told Mr. Homer Lu that there was no other engineer in China who knew what Mr. Liu did.

Mr. Liu said Mr. Homer Lu's house was beautiful and his radio must have cost thousands of dollars. He can get any place in the world on it. He gets all the music from America, Paris, Berlin, anywhere—It was especially made for him.

FU-CHI'S COLLEAGUES

. . . Charles Ruas had lived most of his life in Tientsin, as had his father. He had been educated in France, but most of his life had been lived in this port city of old China which was a bad place for young men like Charlie, where the social life centered on drinking. When he was cold sober he was glum and moody, when really drunk he was dreadful, but when he'd had just enough he was a delightful, witty, and charming personality.

Mr. Cudzilo ("sky" had been discarded on the end to make the name easier for Chinese to pronounce) was a relative newcomer to Tientsin, a Polish man of profound education and culture. During the first World War, he was in the Russian army, had been captured by the Germans, escaped, and in the chaos of the Russian Revolution had walked through Siberia down into Manchuria. There, starved and exhausted, he had been jailed as a vagrant. He told me that the Chinese jail seemed to him like heaven—to sleep warm and safe, to eat three delectable meals a day, to be treated with kindness after the horrors and miseries of war, and his long ordeal through Siberia. For this he said he would be eternally grateful to his kind Chinese jailers.

Released when he was able to travel, he came down to Tientsin where there were other Polish refugees. The Danish manager of the Water Works had hired him as an engineer at a salary several times that of a Chinese doing the same work, making him, in the refugee world, a very wealthy man with servants and a big house.

Charlie Ruas declared that on payday, most of the Polish refugees in Tientsin were waiting in the Water Works compound to divide up Cudzilo's salary. Generous-hearted and unselfish, he did, in fact, support many of them. He could not see suffering without trying to relieve it.

In the eight years we knew him, we went many times to Polish gatherings at his house, where we ate Polish food, danced Polish dances, and met all manner of refugees, fled from Poland for diverse reasons. They all flocked around kind, credulous, unsuspicious Cudzilo—once, at least, dealing him a shocking disillusionment.

One night we met at his house a handsome, well-dressed doctor and his strikingly beautiful wife. The tragic look on her face startled me. I thought she must have gone though some unforgettable and terrible experience. Not long afterwards Mr. Cudzilo told us she was dead. Her husband was a blackmailer and had used her to extort money from wealthy men, treating her with the utmost cruelty. She had refused to help her husband blackmail Cudzilo and had shot herself. I don't know what happened to the husband. Of course, we never saw him again.

November 11, 1934

The Armistice was celebrated here in all the concessions and there were French parades, British parades, and American parades. Last night Mr. Cudzilo had another party. There were a Polish doctor and his wife, an English newspaperman and his wife, M. Ruas, another Polish man, and several kinds of wine, beer, whiskey, and vodka. Everybody drank something but me. Mr. Liu drank a little beer but I drank plain water. M. Ruas got drunk

Armistice Day
celebrations
in Tientsin.

and sang at the top of his voice. The Englishman drank vodka until he was terribly drunk. He said I had remarkable self-control not to drink or smoke. I assured him that self-control had nothing to do with it as I had not the slightest temptation in either direction.

THE DAILY CIRCLE EXPANDS

For five or six months, we had been settling down into a pleasant domestic routine, livened by occasional dinner parties and movies, when we unexpectedly acquired an addition to our daily circle.

"Pao-san," Fu-chi said to Sun one morning, "Go down to Ruas' place and tell him I want to see him." Ruas lived three doors away in the same courtyard.

When Sun came back a little later, I heard him talking to Fu-chi in the dining room and they both sounded amused and at one point I could tell that Fu-chi was astonished. When I went in, Sun had gone to the kitchen.

"What's the matter with Ruas?" I asked.

"Sun says he brought a girl home with him last night."

"Oh," I asked. "Is that his custom?"

"Perhaps. He's been divorced about a year. But the funny thing is, this girl brought a child with her, a little boy about Ju Lan's age."

"Well," I exclaimed. "That is something new!"

That afternoon Fu-chi told me that Ruas had talked to him about the girl. She was from Bonn, Germany, and was an actress in German movies. She was part-Chinese and part-German. Ruas said he was very serious about her. He wanted us to meet her and would bring her over that evening.

They arrived promptly after supper.

"This is Erika, Madame Liu. I hope you will be kind to her."

With this simple introduction Charlie ushered in a young woman who, though pleasingly shy and modest, was not at all timid. Fu-chi and I greeted her with matter-of-fact friendliness and she behaved with considerable poise and dignity in a situation that would have been painfully embarrassing to me.

Her voice was clear and well-modulated. She spoke English with a charming accent, undefinable since she spoke German, French, and Chinese fluently. I saw she would be very good-looking made up and dressed properly. She wore no make-up at all and her dress bespoke German, not French influence.

Sun brought in tea and we had a pleasant visit. The conversation was limited and general, of course, I don't remember now what we talked about. But I asked her to come see me the next day and bring the little boy.

And then what a fantastic story I heard! She told me that her father was a Manchu prince who became the ambassador to Germany before the 1911 revolution. He met the daughter of a German manufacturer at a party in Bonn and fell madly in love with her and she with him. When the Dowager Empress called him back to Peking in a time of emergency, he delayed leaving for almost a year. Erika was born at the end of 1910 and when he learned she was a daughter, not a son, he left immediately for China. Erika never saw him. Her mother married her former German boyfriend who adopted her. Erika loved her German stepfather who, she said, always treated her as if she were his own child.

Erika Ruas, who became Grace's closest friend in the early years after Grace's arrival in China.

Erika grew up in Germany under considerable restrictions. She was educated in a Catholic girls' school to protect her. She grew increasingly rebellious and strikingly beautiful. Someone who saw her at age nineteen offered her a role in a German film. After making three films, she was quite well known and loved the attention. A "flashy" character on the staff of a Chinese general traveling around Europe for his "health" enticed her to follow him to Paris, married her and brought her back to China with him.

"It's not an uncommon story," she said, "but when I arrived, I found out that he already had a wife and children. He took me to his parents' home in the Chinese city where his first wife and children lived."

She went on to tell me that the first wife, of course, hated what she considered the foreign interloper. The wife succeeded in turning the husband against her because she was already pregnant and was losing her looks. Her baby turned out to be a boy which increased the first wife's jealousy and fury. The husband, an utter weakling, was completely under the first wife's thumb. She ordered him to turn Erika and her child out of the house and he had done it, first giving her fifty dollars.

"How outrageous!" I exclaimed. "Couldn't you have him arrested?"

Erika laughed, "A woman in China has no protection from a husband."

"What did you do? Where could you go?"

"I tried to find my father, only to discover that he was dead and his family would have nothing to do with me. I knew the German Consulate and he found me a room and a job at the German hotel. Mr. Ruas has been very kind to me. And I appreciate your kindness as well."

They were married soon after, and Erika Ruas became my good friend and almost daily companion through those early years in China. We did not know that in a short time such tragedy would befall her.

Fu-chi, Ju-lan, and the amah, Wang Nai-nai, in Victoria Park in the British Concession.

Jan 15, 1935

We are quite a settled old married couple now, boring everybody with tales of our "extraordinary" child. And I'm even calling Mr. Liu "daddy" myself. You would think we had been married for ten years. But my heart still jumps as it always did when I hear him coming up the steps and he still looks beautiful to me when he comes in.

I think it is so remarkable that two people who are born and brought up at the opposite ends of the earth almost, in different countries, different races, and different civilizations, and yet have customs that could be so very congenial. We like the same books, the same kind of people. We enjoy the same shows, and the same music. We have the same outlook on life, more or less the same philosophy and the same ideals.

Ju Lan speaks a funny mixture of Chinese and English now. She says lots of Chinese words. Mr. Liu says she will beat me in a few more months. Just now she is standing in front of me showing me her hands and saying "Tsang-a, tsang-a" meaning "dirty-dirty." Whenever she doesn't want anything she always says "bu-yow, bu-yow." That means "don't want it." And she calls "Daddy lai, Amah-lai or Gracie-lai when she wants any of us to come—"lai" means come. The amah's name is Wang and Ju Lan calls her "Wang-ma." You always call amahs by putting ma *onto their last names.*

Amah comes a little before seven o'clock and Ju Lan always wakes up a little before she comes. She immediately sits up and begins calling "Wang-ma" at the top of her voice. Amah takes her up, puts her on the "potty," dresses her, and gives her her orange juice and bottle. Then I can sleep till eight.

Mr. Liu and I both get up at eight o'clock and then Ju Lan has some oatmeal with her daddy at nine. Amah takes her to the park at 10:30 and brings her in at 12:30. She eats her lunch, tomato juice, vegetables, and milk, sits on the "potty" again, eats an orange, and then goes to the park again. She comes in at five o'clock, has her supper at 5:30, and goes to bed at 7:30.

She is wild and "woolly" and into everything. She loves to pretend she is Amah or Sun and wash her clothes and scrub the floor and wash and dry the dishes. She says she is amah and holds her dolly out to "pee pee" in a little toy saucer. Right now she is worrying me to death. She says she wants to "write Juie." So I have given her a pencil and piece of paper and I will send you what she wrote. Now Mr. Liu is putting her pajamas on and will put her in bed so I can write a piece. She is talking a blue streak and kissing him and calling him "Daddy Liu." I am "Dacie Liu." And she says her name is "Ann Liu."

All the whole Water Company now is sitting holding its breath waiting for Mr. Homer Lu to come back from Hangchow. Everything is all ready for the final meeting now. I will be glad when it is all settled. Its been an awful strain on Mr. Liu, just sitting . . .

Please send me some sheet music. There is no duty on anything under $10.

Just continue to address me in care of Mr. Liu, Tientsin Native City Water Works Co., Tientsin, China. It certainly takes an awfully long time to get letters back and forth.

I wish you and Julianne were here.

With lots of love,

Grace

5

GRACE'S CIVIL WAR ROOTS

A PACKAGE she received early in 1936 contained a copy of a new best-selling Civil War novel. Grace had grown up on Civil War stories. In fact, she had spent much of her childhood on Civil War battlefields. It is no wonder that she felt as if she had lived this epic novel.

January 31, 1936
Dear Mama,

Your package came early this week—I love the book of songs and I think you know what I did with "Gone with the Wind." I sat down with it and scarcely ate or slept until I finished it. I don't think I have ever read such an enthralling book in my entire life. I started it one evening about six o'clock, skipped my dinner and read steadily until long after midnight. When I saw I couldn't possibly finish it even if I sat up all night, I reluctantly went to bed. I started the next morning at eight o'clock without even dressing and read steadily through the day lost to the world until six when I read the last page. I've never enjoyed a book so much. Sometimes while reading, it felt as if I had lived it . . .

Grace's childhood home was on a hill overlooking the site of the battle of Chickamauga, one of the bloodiest of the war. Chickamauga was the first Civil War battlefield to be memorialized as a national military park in 1890, becoming for her a playground among cannons, pyramid-shaped stacks of cannonballs, and monuments to the Union infantries. Her grandparents' home was on the side of Missionary Ridge, where witnesses described "one of the grandest spectacles ever seen." Union soldiers, without orders, had charged up the steep sides of the ridge and routed the last Confederate defense of Chattanooga. When digging the foundation for their home, the family found the remains of a young Union soldier fallen in this bold advance.

Grace's grandparents had their own Civil War romance, though not in the plantation South with big mansions and slaves in the fields. Instead they came from the mountain South, the hills of East Tennessee, where slavery was rare and sympathies in the war were divided. The young preacher and his new bride tried not to take sides in the conflict but soon found their home to be hotel, hospital, and headquarters to Union and Confederate soldiers alike.

Grace's memoirs open with the fiftieth wedding anniversary dinner of her grandparents, the Reverend and Mrs. Thomas H. McCallie on January 28, 1912:

"Gracie! Gracie!"

I gave a jump, nearly dropping my book on the floor. Untangling my mind from the young martyrs falling on the barricades of Paris in the 1830s, I looked up and again was back in my familiar surroundings. I was sitting in the window alcove wearing only my slip and stockings, my dress still lying beside me. The mid-winter

Chattanooga's Lookout Mountain from Missionary Ridge, Civil War cannon in foreground.

sun, now slanting low to the west, had warmed my journey into Victor Hugo's distant world, lulling my memory of today.

"Stop reading and do what you ought to do! The guests are already arriving," came the command from downstairs.

"I'm coming, Grandma!" I stood up as if to attention, the book under my arm.

I leaned over the alcove to look out the window. The late afternoon sun, just dipping below the top of Lookout Mountain, left the city of Chattanooga shadowed in the valley below.

I looked out at the two magnolia trees, standing one on each side of the brick walk with the sun glistening on their glossy leaves. Beyond the trees, down a long curving drive sloping gently up the ridge, several horse-drawn carriages and one automobile were approaching the house.

Quickly I pulled on my linen dress with the puffy sleeves, which I had not dared to wear earlier for fear of wrinkling it. I reminded myself that I must be especially good tonight. On this night, the whole family would assemble for Grandfather and Grandmother McCallie's fiftieth wedding anniversary celebration. I was supposed to greet the guests at the door, and already I was negligent.

I knew that Grandma considered my mother somewhat lax in the training of her children, so Grandma took on that responsibility herself. She invited me to stay

The Missionary Ridge home of Grace's grandparents, where the 1912 celebration took place. Later, this house was known as the Founder's Home at McCallie School.

at her house for several weeks at a time. I would sit beside her and do hem stitching, work buttonholes, and darn stockings. A gentle tap of the third finger of Grandma's right hand was a reminder to "sit up straight, Gracie." Everyday I must pace up and down the long front hall and go up and down the staircase with a big book on my head, never letting it fall. Grandma's lessons extended beyond how to sit, walk, and stand properly. She wanted me to learn to be responsible, dependable, and to do well whatever I undertook to do. Her best lessons came from our daily life. I remember one in particular:

One night as I was sleeping soundly in my little room next to Grandma's, a firm but gentle hand shook my shoulder.

"Gracie, Gracie."

The far-away familiar voice reached my consciousness, and I struggled up through a well of deep sleep and opened my eyes. Beside the bed stood my grandmother, dressed in her high-neck, black silk dress with the white W.C.T.U. (Women's Christian Temperance Union) ribbon pinned on it—and still wearing her hat. She had just come home from a meeting and had seen the watering can that I left outside.

"You must learn not to forget. Now, put on your slippers and come with me," she said.

"Yes, Ma'am."

Infant Grace with her mother, Julia McCallie Divine, 1901.

I got out of bed and padded after Grandma down the broad polished staircase that curves into the big gloomy hall below. The tall Grandfather clock suddenly chimed. The whole household was asleep except me and Grandma. How frightened I would be alone. But I was not afraid with Grandma. It seemed to me that she was afraid of nothing and never had been.

Down the steps and along the brick walk between the two magnolias—I saw the green can and picked it up. I followed her to the back porch where I hung the can on its particular nail—and back to bed again.

On the night of the anniversary, I descended the same staircase in rapid patter, anxious to do what Grandmother wanted. I was startled to see that the usually dark and rather austere Victorian decor of the hall and dining room was splendid with candlelight and festive with flowers. My mother and two other women were busily arranging the room. The long table was pulled out to its full length to seat as many as possible. The family would sit at the big table while other relatives and friends would sit at tables in the hall and adjoining parlor.

I was the middle child with five brothers. My three elder brothers would be sitting with the adults at the table, and my two younger brothers, as well as my myriad little cousins, would be kept away from the festivities in a separate room. At

Grace (middle row, far left) with her grandparents, parents, uncles, aunts, and brothers, 1908.

eleven years old, I felt vastly superior to the children and longed to be with the adults.

As I stood at the bottom of the stairs, mesmerized by the candlelight, I felt a familiar tap on my shoulder. It was Grandma. "I would like for you to sit at the table tonight, next to your Aunt Grace."

"Yes, Ma'am." I could hardly express my delight before she rushed me on to my duty of greeting the guests.

"Now, see to the door."

Of the sixteen children born to my grandparents, only eight survived to adulthood. And all eight were in attendance this evening—five sons and three daughters, along with their spouses.

At the head of the table, Grandfather stood in benign dignity. He had been a Presbyterian minister for more than fifty years—Scotch Calvinist and thoroughly evangelical in his views. Tall and grave, with stern, deep-set eyes and a full gray beard, he was my childish idea of what God must look like.

My little grandmother stood at the foot of the long table, with back as straight and posture as graceful at seventy as at twenty. She was barely taller than me and equally as small in the waist. The crisp white collar on her black dress made her

Grace (far left) with cousin Mary McCallie (third from left), brother Tom Divine (center), and other cousins, playing on Missionary Ridge.

84

head look like it was floating. Her hair was dark and combed back tightly in a bun. I marveled that such a small woman could produce such large men, the five grand and handsome uncles gathering around the table.

The youngest, Uncle Ed, a dashing all-American football hero in his youth and now twenty-seven, fascinated me the most. His sudden marriage to the beautiful Lillian Griffis of New York had shocked the family. They had married while he was a student at Cornell and she was barely twenty herself. At first Lillian's northern speech and manner were strange to our Southern family. My mother had taught me to call her "ahnt," not "ant," as I called my other aunts. As they came to the table, I spoke in one breath to "Ahnt" Lillian and "Ant" Grace, as if they were different species of aunt.

There was severe Uncle Doug and Aunt Emily, missionaries who had met in Korea and were home on furlough. Uncle Tom, another Presbyterian minister, was short, stout, and jolly, and beside him his stately wife and grown son. Two of my uncles, Spence and Park, were both teachers, now headmasters of their own school for boys, using this very dining room as a study hall during the week. I was in awe of both. Uncle Park was stern and Uncle Spence given to sarcasm, which he mistook as humor. He offended me mightily when he referred to my legs as toothpicks and my arms as pipe stems.

Of the three daughters, only my mother was married. Mama named me, her only daughter, after her sister. Aunt Grace was the eldest and was twenty-three years older than Margaret Ellen, who was the last of Grandmother's sixteen births. Since my mother had married at an early age, she gave birth to her first child the same year that Grandmother gave birth to her last. I had heard that due to Grandma's age at the time, my mother had nursed them both—her son and her sister—at the same time. My mother was like that, always bountiful. Aunt Margaret Ellen had always seemed more like my elder sister. She looked young and lovely to me this night, dressed in the fashion of the day, a bronze silk taffeta, trimmed in brown velvet. Aunt Grace was dressed in an old-fashioned white dress with lace collar broached at her neck. I admired my two aunts terribly, although as a child I dreaded the thought of being a spinster like them.

My father, Sam Divine, seemed a rather incongruous element in this predominantly Scottish and devoutly religious family. He was Irish and was considered worldly. It was said that in his youth he danced, played cards, rode fast horses, and

sowed "wild oats." But whatever that meant made no difference to me—I adored him. Although Papa was Irish, he was Presbyterian, which made matters a little better. His father, John Lowery Divine, was conceived in Tyrone county, Northern Ireland, and born in East Tennessee. He never intended to settle in Chattanooga, but on his way somewhere else, his horse and money were stolen in the night, and he had to get a job the next day in Sam Williams's store. In due time he married Sam Williams's daughter and named his first son, Sam Williams Divine. That was in 1849 when my Papa was born. And like his father, he stayed here and found enormous possibilities for this frontier town on the river.

My father was neither a preacher nor a teacher as my uncles were. He was a real estate dealer, a builder, and a promoter. As the town grew, he developed the streetcar lines and extended them over the top of Missionary Ridge and all the way to the Chickamauga battlefield, where he built a big house near the end of the line. He acquired the Lookout Mountain inclines and was an early promoter of the railroads, but his luck as a business man was not always good. He made a great deal of money, then lost a great deal, and eventually ended up bankrupt.

As I watched him at the anniversary dinner, with his shining bald head and long drooping mustache, Edgar Allen Poe style, I thought how good and kind he looked. All of the McCallies referred to him as "Mr. Divine," even Grandfather, and my mother never called him anything else. I always attributed my singing voice to Papa. I guess you could say it came from the "Divine side," but I always knew it was the Irish in me.

The dinner proceeded with great liveliness, much laughter, and occasional speech making. Just before dessert, Uncle Spence stood up and rapped for attention. He had some papers in his hand and said he was going to read some letters very appropriate to the occasion: "Father's proposal of marriage and Mother's answer."

I had heard the romantic story before from my mother of how Grandfather, when only twenty-two and just starting out as a young preacher in 1859, had fallen in love with a young lady's voice at an afternoon party in nearby Cleveland, Tennessee. She was speaking a few feet behind him, and he was so impressed that he cautiously turned to look and was struck to the heart. "Here she is!" he told himself

Top, Grace's father, Sam Williams Divine (1849–1915) as a young man. Above, Sam Divine toward the end of his life.

86

and promptly prayed to God to give her to him in due time, if it was His Will.

After reading the letters in his great speaking voice, Uncle Spence folded them and put them in his pocket amidst applause and much delighted comment. "All of you know," he said, "the wedding of this young couple took place fifty years ago on January 28, 1862. The Civil War had begun nine months earlier, and if ever two young people got married in a time of great distress, it was these two."

Grandfather had told me that he did not believe in secession. But when several states withdrew, he thought there was no power in the Constitution to bring them back by force. His sympathies were with the South because this was his home. But he felt the Southern leaders had made a woeful mistake: "I felt also," he wrote in his journals, "that our true policy would have been to give up slavery and take away the bone of contention, rather than by holding onto it and seceding, bring the country into a terrible war."

For this reason, he did not take sides in the struggle. He and Grandma tried to serve whomever came to their door. But in the midst of turmoil neutrality was not an easy commitment to keep. Many times they were told to evacuate, but they remained, despite heavy losses. Grandfather wrote in his journals of those days:

Grace's grandmother, Ellen Jarnagin McCallie, at age 20, 1861.

The war was now on and the times were dreadful. Provisions and goods manufactured out of the South were becoming continually more scarce and the price of them continually going up . . . until by the end of the war, scarcity reigned everywhere. Not a pound of meal or flour or rice or potatoes could you buy or beg. Not a loaf of bread or anything to eat. The churches, large warehouses, and old stores were filled with sick and wounded men. One morning at the Baptist church I saw a pile of arms and legs lying on the porch—the very sight was appalling. Going inside I saw a surgeon take off a man's leg so quickly that it sickened me . . .

Our garden and yard fences went for the purpose of making barracks for the men. Our large stable, cow house, and corn crib all went. Away went our turkeys too. Our cows were driven off and disappeared. By and

Grace's extended family on the occasion of the Golden Wedding Anniversary of her McCallie grandparents (center), 1912. Grace (far left, bottom) is sitting next to her "Papa." For more about some of the other persons in this photo, see Appendix, page 394.

by when the last picket was pulled from the fence, the last out house swept away, the last chicken, turkey, and cow gone, and our edifice was left standing alone as in a desert, we felt a sense of relief and rest. A kind Providence was watching over us.

It was near the end of the war, in the spring of 1865, that a child was born to them. They named her Grace because, as Grandfather said, "By the Grace of God, we had been spared through the great ordeal."

Years later my grandparents moved to the side of Missionary Ridge. It was in this big Victorian home that the Golden Wedding Anniversary was celebrated.

The anniversary dinner marked the end of Grace's childhood world. All of the people in that room had shaped her life. Her grandfather died that spring and her grandmother two years after that. In 1915, her beloved Papa died suddenly, leaving his wife with six children and only a little rental property for income.

IF MR. LIU was educated by his uncles, Grace could say that she was educated by her aunts. When Grace was five years old, during one of her extended visits to her grandmother's house, she may have overheard conversations between her Aunt Grace McCallie, their cousin Eula Jarnigan, and a friend of theirs, Miss Tommie Payne Duffy. The three women were discussing the idea of starting a college preparatory school for girls. As teachers at the pubic high school, they knew that girls were not afforded the same courses or opportunities as boys and therefore were not able to attend college. Aunt Grace's two brothers had started the McCallie School earlier that year in the family home, but it was for boys only. As the older of the three, she raised concerns about how they would support themselves with no financial backing. She seemed reluctant to give up her sure salary for an uncertain one, and "Besides," she challenged them, "where are you going to have such a school?"

Eula, the youngest of the three and only twenty-eight at the time, knew she needed her cousin's involvement for the venture to work and had already thought out the answer, "Don't say *you*, say 'where are *we* going to have the school?' We are going to have it at your house!"

Grace McCallie's house was on Oak Street, where her father's original farm had been. Her father had given her this property for rental income because, in an uncommon gesture, he did not think that a married woman should have financial advantage over an unmarried one.

The next fall, the Girls' Preparatory School [G. P. S.] opened with forty-five students in the three-story house on Oak Street, renovated by the three women over the summer from a boarding house to a schoolhouse. The three teachers lived on the third floor over the classrooms, breaking another social custom of the time that single women did not live on their own.

Grace Divine walked up the steps of the Oak Street school when she was twelve and came under the tutelage of these pioneering women. What a refreshing change it must have been from her household of five brothers. Cousin Eula taught her Latin from the texts of Virgil and Cicero and maintained that "a woman is not going to be attractive if she doesn't have something in her head." Miss Duffy taught her that history had "more romance and drama than all your little novels." Her Aunt Grace taught English and mathematics, and kept the accounts of the school. Aunt Grace was an omnivorous reader and often gave an English lesson in her normal conversations. In her memoirs, Grace described her instruction at GPS in this way: "The six year course included five years of Latin and four of French. I was no Latin scholar but I read through Caesar, Cicero, and Virgil without disgrace. I learned French with an American accent, but learned to read well enough to enjoy Victor Hugo and George Sand in the original. The scholastic standards of the school were high and the discipline strict."

Just as in Fu-chi's schooling, memorization of the classics was the accepted style of learning in those days. The students memorized passages from the Aeneid, Shakespeare, and the Bible. But Grace learned more from these three women than recitation. She found in them a model. None had a college degree, but all three continually educated themselves. In the summers they studied at American universitites or traveled to Europe to gain firsthand knowledge of places of literary or historical significance. From them Grace gained her first glimpse of the world beyond the school walls. Through their lives, they taught her that education was not something completed with a degree but grounded in life, always changing, growing deeper with experience and reflection—a lesson she later applied to the fullest.

Grace did not graduate in 1918 with her classmates. She was unable to take chemistry because of her asthmatic condition. But the lack of a credit did not stop her from pursuing a musical career.

When I was sixteen I began singing lessons with a young Chattanooga woman whose operatic career in Germany had been interrupted by the war. In 1920 I went with her to Chicago to study with the teacher she studied under in Germany. I loved Chicago. It was my first look at the world outside the South. Everything was new and tremendously exciting. I made rapid progress in my singing and a successful career was prophesied for me. Chicago was a cultural center and I was encouraged to see and hear the best in the worlds of music, dance, and theater . . . The Chicago climate suited me. I enjoyed being blown along Michigan Blvd. and having to grab lamp posts going around corners. In spite of the fierce cold wind, I had no asthma the entire two seasons I was there. The second year I lived in Evanston to be near my brother Tom who was a student at Northwestern University. This exciting life was interrupted in 1922 when my brother Edward became ill. Mama said she needed me and I went home.

The local newspaper noted her return with the following comments:

LOCAL SINGER HOME FOR XMAS

Miss Grace Divine has been taking vocal for the past two terms under Franz Proschowsky, who was a noted instructor in Berlin up to the time of the World war. Miss Divine has received the highest encomiums from her master tutor who pronounces her voice one of the easiest he has ever undertaken and its qualities most wonderful.

Miss Divine will sing at the coming Shrine minstrel [and] will also sing solo at the opening service of the new Central Presbyterian church on New Year's day. Miss Divine ha[s] made an engagement to sing on Chautauqua program, beginning next spring.

. . . Her talent and success should and certainly will be recognized by her home people . . . She has been much loved as a child and school girl and her beautiful voice promises to win laurels for her in her musical career.

'18

Irregular Jourth Years

GRACE DIVINE

"Music waves eternal wands—
Enchantress of the souls of mortals!"

We are very proud of the fact that we have a "prima donna" in our class. Grace's sweet voice will some day, no doubt, be a welcome addition to the music circles of the city. Her favorite "stunt" is losing her things; but we all hope she won't lose her voice. She is also a good story writer when the spirit moves her, and is a good actress as well. Since starting in the G. P. S. five years ago, she has been a member of the Pansophian Literary Society and has participated in many of their programs as a soloist and as a member of the Pansophian Quartette. She also belongs to the Glee Club.

Page Twenty

Her mother had used the ruse of Edward's illness to get Grace to return home. Grace found that Edward was well, but she no longer had the funds to return to Chicago. Instead she stayed and completed her one missing credit at G.P.S. while she also directed the school's glee club. As a result, her cousin Mary McCallie and Grace graduated from G.P.S. in the same year, 1926, even though Grace was six years older.

By this time, the school had moved to a larger brick building on Palmetto Street. It had spacious, well-lighted rooms and a cafeteria and gymnasium. One hundred and fifty girls were now in attendance. In order to tone down the stylish eccentricities of the day, the school adopted a uniform, which would show up in China years later. Grace described them in her memoirs: "We wore a school uniform—blue serge in

Grace's G.P.S. yearbook, 1918. She was noted for losing things, but her classmates said, "We all hope she won't lose her voice." Her acting and writing were also noted.

G.P.S. uniforms, as seen here on a student in 1926, were made of linen or cotton in any solid color.

winter and fall and a plain linen dress in spring and summer. No high heels or silk stockings and no make-up. The founders of the school thought this was necessary to teach the girls to dress suitably and appropriately for school. Some muttering was heard at first, but the girls soon became proud of the distinction. This plain, severe style of dressing actually created a kind of inverted snobbery."

During these years as a teacher, Grace came to know the co-founders fondly and remained in touch with them through at least her early years in China. They asked Grace not only to teach music but also to live in the top-floor apartment with them. Grace described these years as a teacher at G.P.S. with affection:

The next four years I was kept busy teaching and directing the music at my old school, the G.P.S. My Aunt Grace had died in 1918 and the school had continued under the direction of the remaining two of the original triumvirate, Miss Jarnagin and Miss Duffy. They were large and handsome women and their stiff high-necked collars made their stately posture even more imposing. Studies in the summer at the University of Chicago or at the Sorbonne in Paris kept these remarkable women well-qualified and up-to-date in their work. They controlled and guided their school full of teenage girls with wisdom and kindness—if not indulgence.

While I was teaching at the G.P.S. I lived with Miss Duffy and Cousin Eula in their apartment on the third floor of the school building. Here I was subject to even more than school discipline. Cousin Eula was Grandma's niece and had always loomed large and authoritative in my life. I often felt like a small girl again. Sometimes when I groaned over having to go down two flights of stairs to get some school work I'd forgotten, I got this bit of practical philosophy from Cousin Eula: "If you don't use your head, Grace, you'll have to use your feet."

With no t.v. and radio, we read more and talked more. With teaching, getting up plays and operettas, school picnics and hikes, parties and the friendships of youth, I recall those days with pleasure. They were my last years in Chattanooga.

In 1926, as director of the G.P.S. Glee Club, Grace presented a romantic Chinese operetta, *The Crimson Eyebrows*. She had the starring role as Princess Ting Ling, daugh-

ter of the former emperor. Reviews of the performance, given at the Little Theatre in Chattanooga, were highly favorable: "When the curtain rose for the first act, it seemed as if a beautiful page from a history of ancient China appeared . . . The Princess Ting Ling (Miss Grace Divine) was particularly charming in a rich costume of yellow satin, with which she carried an immense fan . . . Miss Divine's solo, in which she describes herself as the shy, pretty little Ting Ling, with a head full of romance, was particularly appealing."

Her cousin Mary McCallie was in the highly praised chorus. Grace could not have imagined that in a few years she would no longer be acting, but actually living in that ancient land and waiting for her cousin Mary to come visit.

Just before she left for New York, Cousin Eula gave her an envelope with these words: "When we were starting out, your Aunt Grace loaned us the money that made the school possible. She asked that we give to you the money that we owed to her. We know that living in New York will be considerably more expensive than Chattanooga.

We want you to have this now." Grace was deeply touched. These women knew more than anyone what it was for a young girl to want to live her dreams.

She was accompanied on her journey to New York by her Aunt (Margaret) Ellen and her aunt's companion and colleague, Miss Margaret Bright. These two women were also teachers and ran an elementary school. Grace's memoirs recalled her excitement:

I watched out the window as the train pulled out of the station and gathered speed through the outskirts of Chattanooga. "I'm on the way to New York, New York, New York," I chanted to myself. I turned from the window, trying not to look too excited. Miss Bright and Aunt Ellen were smiling at me.

"How I envy you, Grace, going to New York for the first time! Aren't you thrilled?"

Grace (center) had the starring role of Princess Ting Ling in a Chinese operetta, Chattanooga, 1926.

Miss Bright asked. She and Aunt Ellen were making one of their many visits to New York and were bringing me along to continue studying with my Chicago teacher, now established in New York.

Aunt Ellen was the person I most admired. She had always been my ideal of loveliness and elegant charm. Her Southern accent had been disciplined by several years of speaking French and German in universities abroad, and her speaking voice was delightful to listen to. She had never married and I'd sometimes wondered if she regretted allowing her brothers to cut short her romance with a young minister whom they did not consider eligible. I got an answer I think, when I made my own unorthodox marriage against all warning and advice. She wrote me a letter wishing me happiness and ended with, "I'm glad you had the courage to follow your heart."

6

THE LIU FAMILY LIFE

FTER 1936 none of Grace's letters are addressed to Mama. After Grace left, Mrs. Divine returned to New York for a short time, then lived with different sons, moving from place to place, and grew increasingly more dependent and difficult. She continued to correspond with Grace but usually through letters that were shared. From this point on, most of Grace's letters are addressed to her brothers Tom or Sam, with whom her mother stayed most often.

Tom and his wife Mary Hills Divine became Grace's touchstone with the family and this close relationship largely created this body of correspondence. Her desire to communicate her experience to her family, to be understood and not forgotten, stimulated by their response, provides the details of her unfolding story.

But at this point, none of the imminent changes in China were evident to Grace. She was absorbed in a world that was not only alien to her family but also alien to the nation in which it thrived. The bizarre nature of this foreign subculture within China is reflected in the picture she sent home in the 1936 letter. She wore to a costume ball, not a costume at all, but a Chinese dress. For her, she was almost as far from China as she had been in Chattanooga when she dressed up as Princess Ting Ling.

Grace's letter of January 31, 1936, begun at the opening of the last chapter and interrupted to tell of her Chattanooga family history, continues. In this letter we see that Ju-lan has nicknamed herself "Nini," using the last sounds of "Fuchina." From this point on, Grace refers to her daughter as "Nini" and to her husband as "F. C."

. . . It is snowing this morning and Nini has gone out with her rubber boots on with

Grace, Mrs. Holmberg, and Erika Ruas at a masquerade party at the French Club, Tientsin, 1936.

Amah to play. She is getting so tall. I think you would have a fit laughing if you could hear her talk now. Her Chinese is better than her daddy's. He speaks still with Shensi dialect but Nini speaks perfect Mandarin. But her English is so funny! It's not American English at all. It's British. She talks about the motor cars, tram cars and she has tiffin instead of lunch. She takes a "bahth" and says "cahn't." The other day F. C. asked Amah to hand him the paper and he used the Shensi dialect word for paper. Nini said, "Daddy that's not proper, you should say "chih" not "shih.""

I can understand almost any ordinary communication and I can talk too when I have to but I am very timid about it because I am afraid of saying something ridiculous. It's so easy to make a mistake. If you use just a slightly different tone, a difference so slight as to be imperceptible to an unaccustomed ear, you have changed the meaning entirely.

I am sending you a funny picture taken at a masquerade party at the French Club at about 3:30 in the morning. In the picture of three, the woman in the middle is Mrs. Holmberg. She is Korean and her husband is Danish. He is a director of the Water Co. and was the Danish Minister in Peking a few years ago. The picture does not do her justice as she is really quite beautiful. She has on an Arabian costume she got in Egypt. The other woman is Mrs. Ruas. She is part-Chinese and part-German. Her father was a Manchu prince who married the daughter of a German manufacturer during the time of the Empress-Dowager and was cut off from his family. So she lived all her life in Germany until she married and came to China. Her husband is a Frenchman and is an engineer in the Water Co.

We have all been very well this winter and I am almost fat, though I haven't got a double chin like the picture. The Chinese high tight collar makes it look like that.

The letter concludes with a rare adventure outside the safe world of the concessions. Grace goes with Erika Ruas, who has now become her constant companion, into the Chinese part of Tientsin. Erika's verve and ability to speak Chinese embolden Grace to try what she dares not do alone:

Yesterday afternoon Erika Ruas and I went to the Chinese city to see the preparations for Chinese New Year. I have never been in the Chinese City except in a car and you can't see very much that way. We went in rickshaws and then got out and walked thru the narrow crowded little streets. They were lined on each side with little markets, bazaars, and shops selling all sorts of New Years' decorations—gorgeous paper boats, fish, flowers, lanterns, and everything imaginable. Every few minutes a big firecracker would go off and make me jump almost out of my skin. Very, very few foreigners ever go there so everywhere we stopped, such a crowd gathered around we had a hard time getting out. Incredibly old-looking hags ran after us and wanted to tell our fortunes.

We went into an old temple. They were having a bazaar or market in the court yard. Inside, people were burning joss sticks and kowtowing to a big image of Buddha. It was terribly, terribly cold and our noses got stiff and our feet turned to blocks, but the cold air was delicious with the odor of baked sweet potatoes and roasted chestnuts. Every few steps there was a big round stove with something cooking. We bought a bag of hot, hot chestnuts. My! but they are delicious. They are roasted in hot charcoal and sugar and taste marvelous. I bought several things for Nini and Erika bought some things for her little boy. We had a hard time getting through the crowd without getting our things smashed.

There are no beggars in the Chinese city now. The Chinese Municipality has taken them all up. Those that are able-bodied are given work to do and those not able to work are fed and housed.

Nini and Amah have come in and Nini is eating her lunch of raw carrots, celery, spinach, and goat's milk and she talks to me so much I can't write.

Show the pictures to Sam and send the small ones to Tom and Mary Hills. Tell them to send me pictures of their children.

With lots of love to you and everyone,
Grace

Between January and June of 1936, change was in the air. The weather had gone

Grace's stylized photo, in the gardens of the Tsing Hua campus during the Lius' trip to Peking in 1936, marked the end of the semi-colonial era in China.

from cold to very hot, and the political climate was heating up as well. Grace heard only "rumors of trouble" and hoped the "hostilities" would not disrupt her trip to Peking. Six months earlier, students in Peking had demonstrated against Japan's encroachment in China. In this letter is Grace's first mention of the Japanese. Although she described it as too "complicated," it is an indication of how involved they already were.

Even Grace's style of writing and vocabulary were beginning to change, but for the most part, she still lived in a world of dress-up. She dropped into the envelope a sapphire ring and said she regretted the loss of the silver bracelet that she had placed in the last letter, wrapped in a hankerchief.

June 5, 1936
Dear Mary Hills,

I was so glad to get your nice long letter yesterday and hear all the news of everybody. I got a lovely long letter from Mary McCallie last week. My, how I hope she really will get to China! Little did we think that last year we were together at the G.P.S. that ten years later we would be in China.

This spring has been very cold and disagreeable, windy and dusty. But summer has come at last. Last week has been so terribly hot I haven't had the energy to make the least effort, either physical or mental, that wasn't absolutely necessary. Yesterday it was 105 degrees in the shade and 118 in the sun. Of course, if this were not a dry climate it would be utterly unbearable. But it's bad enough. Our apartment is very hot. It's small and right under the roof and the sun beats in on both sides, and the building is between two bigger buildings so most of the breeze is cut off. The other afternoon when I was out at six o'clock, the sun was still hot enough to burn.

We are planning to go to Tsing Hua the first of July. F. C. is going to meet some of his classmates there for a reunion. The rumors of trouble we heard two weeks ago have died down. If there are any hostilities, Tsing Hua is liable to be a rather dangerous place, otherwise it's lovely. It's almost right in the Western Hills, little mountains that rise right out of the plain a few miles from Peking. It is cooler there and will be a good place to pass the hot days. There is a wonderful dairy and library and swimming pool. I've lived in China two and a half years and have not been to Peking yet.

On Saturday I got Mr. Liu to take me to see Shirley Temple in "Captain January." I am not a Shirley Temple fan but I used to love the book when I was a little girl. Mr. Liu went under protest and when we got there and found the theatre just over running with children and their amahs, he was so annoyed. I had to laugh! It's very funny to hear all the little English and American children talking Chinese with their amahs. Nini talks Chinese altogether to Amah and some to her daddy but she always talks English to me. She knows quite a lot of Russian too as so many of her playmates are Russian.

Nini (center) with her Russian playmates.

Sunday afternoon we went to see an English picture (very slow and tiresome) and we met Mr. and Mrs. Lin in the theatre. We hadn't seen them for about two months because they live at Nankai University which is some distance outside the city. Mrs. Lin's name is Adeline—she is an American girl from Washington state. She is a graduate of the University of California. She met Mr. Lin there while he was teaching Oriental literature. She is a tall pretty girl very much like Julianne except she has black hair. Mr. Lin is a classmate of Mr. Liu's, a very brilliant man but small and quite insignificant looking. She is teaching at Nankai too.

We invited them to join us later at our favorite Chinese restaurant for dinner. Mr. Liu and I got to the place quite awhile before the Lins did (guests are always late to Chinese dinners) and I had eaten up nearly all the watermelon and sunflower seeds before they came. The seeds are dried and salted and you crack them with your teeth and eat the kernel and throw the shell on the floor. They are delicious!

We had a very good dinner. First cold chicken liver and duck with cucumber slices covered with Chinese sauce. Then the hot dishes—fried frog legs with bamboo shoots, shrimp with sliced chicken, chicken fried and glazed with sweet and sour sauce, meat balls wrapped in lotus leaves, a Chinese green vegetable called "tsin tsai"

Grace, F. C., and Nini in Peking, 1936

99

with bamboo shoots and onions, another Chinese vegetable "bo tsai" with celery and green peppers, mushroom soup, chow mein (noodles) with shredded ham, fish, rice, tea of course, and last the dessert—delicious almond soup. It looks like thick cream slightly beaten and tastes marvelous.

I wore my new Chinese dress, white silk with a tiny red stripe going crosswise. It is made in the latest style, very long, just escaping the floor, very short sleeves, the right side split up an inch below the knee and a group of pleats inserted on the left side that open up like a fan when I walk. With it I wore red satin sandals, red earrings, and a red lacquer bracelet. I love to wear Chinese dresses. They are very comfortable.

There is going to be a shift in mayors soon. The present mayor failed to please either the Japanese or the Chinese. The Chinese said he was too pro-Japanese and the Japanese said he wasn't pro-Japanese enough. It's all very complicated.

The bell in the French church next door just rang for twelve o'clock and it's time for Nini to come from the park and Mr. Liu to come from work. I hear Nini and Amah coming up the steps now so I will have to stop.

Give my love to Mama and everyone,
Grace

Pictures the Lius sent home from their trip to Peking, 1936: the Long Corridor and the Jade Belt Bridge at the Summer Palace; the Great Wall.

7

JAPANESE AND FLOOD

GRACE didn't expect the "rumors of trouble" to break out into war when her cousin Mary came to visit. Mary arrived in China in 1936 with her husband Robert (Bob) Ware, a lieutenant in the Medical Corps of the U.S. Navy. While Bob was assigned to the *U.S.N. Tutuila*, a gun boat on the Yangtse River, Mary and their baby son Lewis stayed in Hankow [Hankou]. Mary wrote to Grace that she would come to Tientsin the next summer when Bob had leave.

Meanwhile, Grace heard on the radio on December 12, 1936, that General Chiang Kai-shek had been kidnapped in Sian. The incident immediately spurred an international crisis. So threatening was Japan's designs on China that one of Chiang's own generals, Chang Hsueh liang [Zhang Xueliang], known as "the Young Marshal," spearheaded the kidnapping. His intent was to force the Generalissimo into resistance against the Japanese. If Chiang agreed, it meant not only abatement of his determination to exterminate the Communists but actual cooperation with them in a "united front" against Japan.

To the Young Marshal, Japan was clearly the greater threat. His own father Chang Tso Lin [Zhang Zuolin] had been assassinated by the Japanese in Manchuria in 1928, after which Japan had occupied Manchuria. His family had moved to Tientsin, where Grace socialized, not with the Changs, but with people who knew the Changs. The explosive situation was soon resolved on December 25, 1936, with a verbal agreement, at least temporarily, for a united national resistance against Japan. Madame Chiang, well known in America through her frequent coverage in *Life* magazine, interceded on her husband's behalf; Chou En-lai [Zhou En-lai] negotiated diplomatically for the Communists, and the Young Marshal willingly gave himself up.

The spring of 1937 was one of relative calm. A change of government in Japan reaffirmed a commitment to the status quo and the tension between the two nations seemed to be easing. But Japan's military presence in Tientsin was already evident. The Japanese concession, adjacent to the French and British concessions, was constructing a fortress-like "police substation" at its entrance. The reinforced concrete barriers covered with brick gave a formidable appearance to the already impenetrable compound on Asahi Road. If the police station wasn't warning enough, the presence of armed sentries in drab olive green dress should have been. But Japan had secured a truce in 1933 which allowed them to maneuver troops in North China without Chinese opposition.

Therefore, business went on as usual in the foreign concessions of Tientsin, like the other treaty ports of China in the mid-thirties. Industries prospered, transportation and communication lines were greatly improved, and the standard of living in the foreign areas was relatively high. In these protected zones, business could go on almost undisturbed by the ripples of civil conflicts. Even wealthy Chinese found that having a "safe house" in one of the concessions was like having money in a Swiss bank. The native city, already dirty and disorderly, became increasingly demoralized. The narrow, dusty roads became more deeply rutted by rickshaws, and only gourd vines covered the gray mud or brick walls of the one and two-story buildings that predominated.

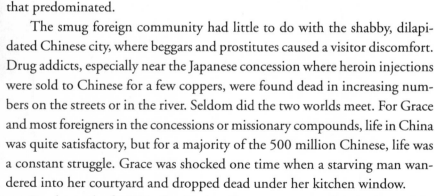

Nini and Lewis Ware, in front of the Water Works building.

The smug foreign community had little to do with the shabby, dilapidated Chinese city, where beggars and prostitutes caused a visitor discomfort. Drug addicts, especially near the Japanese concession where heroin injections were sold to Chinese for a few coppers, were found dead in increasing numbers on the streets or in the river. Seldom did the two worlds meet. For Grace and most foreigners in the concessions or missionary compounds, life in China was quite satisfactory, but for a majority of the 500 million Chinese, life was a constant struggle. Grace was shocked one time when a starving man wandered into her courtyard and dropped dead under her kitchen window.

By the end of 1936, the Nationalist government, headquartered in Nanking, ruled that a joint venture of Chinese and foreign capital must be registered in Nanking and have a Chinese majority of shareholders and board members. In addition, the Chairman of the Board, the General Manager and

102

the Chief Engineer had to be Chinese. Homer Lu had made several trips to Nanking to negotiate the transfer of the Tientsin Water Works, still a British owned company, registered in Hong Kong. F. C. had been brought to the company by Homer Lu, in order to have a qualified Chinese in position when the negotiations were complete.

When F. C. first came, the Water Works provided water only to a few concessions and parts of the Chinese city. After a year on the job, F. C. designed a plan to extend the water system throughout the city. He convinced the board in 1935 to let him build a modern filter system, which dramatically raised the supply of water available for use from the Grand Canal. After the filter system was installed, the Water Works' stock soared from $100 to $180 per share. By spring the company received a license to operate under the new structure, which would have supplied water to the entire Chinese city and all the concessions, except the British. However, these plans were not implemented because the directors chose not to spend the money necessary to extend the lines. F. C.'s plan lay dormant until after the Communists took over more than a decade later, and then the lines finally were extended.

Nini, Franklin Ruas, and amah in front of a water cart used before the water system was completed.

However, under the 1936 license, F. C. was designated Chief Engineer and Homer Lu the General Manager. Mr. Ruas was the Deputy Chief Engineer, and Mr. Holmberg, who supported F. C.'s hiring, remained a board member. F. C. had worked with Mr. Holmberg, Mr. Ruas, and Homer Lu since coming to Tientsin and his relationship with them extended beyond the workplace. They socialized frequently, and their wives and children were close.

The apartment on top of the Water Works was designated for the Chief Engineer. In March 1937, the Lius moved into what Grace described

Nini and Franklin outside the Water Works in the First Special Area.

Grace and Mary McCallie Ware, in the Water Works garden, 1937.

F. C., Nini, Grace, and Bertha Lu on a boardwalk at the pumping station in Tientsin, 1937.

as "one of the fanciest flats in the whole city." Grace was not quite settled by the time her cousin Mary McCallie Ware came. The spacious rooms were only partly furnished with a mixture of Western and Chinese furniture, some supplied by the previous Chief Engineer. But there was plenty of room for Mary to stay, along with her two-year-old son Lewis, called "Lolo," and his amah, whom Mary had hired in Hankow.

The apartment was located on Rue Fontanier in the French concession. To Mary, the street where Grace lived looked very European. There were wide paved boulevards, tree-lined sidewalks with street lamps and large Western-style buildings. A courtyard garden provided a good place for the children to play and the perfect setting for the two cousins to visit—if it had not been for the heat. Many of the foreigners in Tientsin and Peking got away from the heat by spending all or part of their summers in Peitaiho [Beidaihe], a seaside resort in North China. This foreigners' paradise was located near the mountains, only thirty miles from the end of the Great Wall, known as the gate to Manchuria. When Mrs. Holmberg heard that Grace's cousin had come, she offered her beach house in Peitaiho. Grace invited Mrs. Ruas and her son to join them.

When the three women, their three young children, Nini, Lolo, and Franklin, and three amahs set off for the beach at Peitaiho in late June 1937—it did not cross Grace's mind that they might be in the path of troops invading from the North.

July 5, 1937
Dear Julianne,

Is Mama staying with you now? She told me all about your wedding last October and said she would be visiting you again in the summer. I wish both of you were here now. Can you believe that Mary

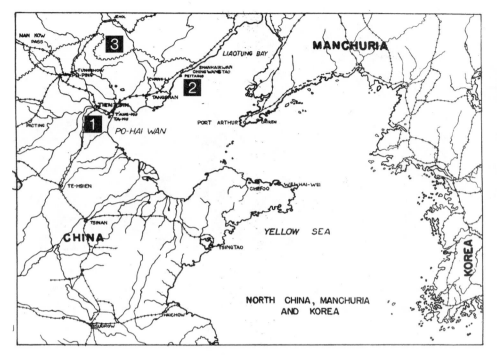

Map of North China.
1, Tientsin;
2, Peitaho;
3, the Great Wall.

McCallie is here! We are on vacation now at Peitaiho. It is the famous N. China resort on the coast. Peitaiho is the loveliest place on earth. All the foreigners from Tientsin come here because it is much cooler.

Since Mary arrived in Tientsin, she has caught me up on all the news of everyone. I had to explain to Nini that Lolo was her "second" cousin even though he is the first one she has ever met.

We are staying at the beach house of my friend Mrs. Holmberg. Her husband is on the board of the Water Works and is a very wealthy and important man. He is Danish and she is Korean. They have a beautiful house here with a wonderful orchard, the likes of which can't be found anywhere else in North China. The cherries grow as large as the apricots and plums. Every morning we have fresh fruit with sweet rolls and butter. I can have all the eggs and fresh goat's milk I want. In the afternoons we sit on the porch overlooking the sea and drink tea in blue and white tea cups. As soon as I see the shimmering white sand dunes, smell the tangy salt air, and hear the roar of the waves, I feel the "Balm of Gilead" come over me.

Right, the beach at Peitaho. Above, Nini, Lewis Ware, Franklin Ruas. Below, Nini and Lewis, donkey-riding.

My friend Erika Ruas and her son Franklin are here too. She is Chinese-German and is married to the French engineer at the Water Works. Mrs. Holmberg said we can stay for the whole month if we wish. The three children are about the same age and are just precious together on the beach. I'll send you some pictures when we get them developed.

Mrs. Holmberg's house has plenty of room for each family and the servants, plus the cook who stays at the house all year and tends the garden. I had to rest the first day here and was not able to go with Mary and Erika on an early morning walk. But by the next day, I was up at the first sign of the yellow morning light. We waded with the children ankle deep in the surf and stirred up a shoal of silver minnows, blue crabs, and all kinds of wonders which brought squeals of pleasure from everyone. The children caught hermit crabs and stood in awe when we found a huge jellyfish in the sand with tenacles almost three feet long. The most fascinating thing to them was watching the amah trying to kill a snake with a bamboo stick. The snake was eating a frog and each time the amah hit the snake, the frog would come out of the mouth, then the snake would re-swallow it.

I thought of you when we had tea at the hotel in Peitaiho. Some one was playing Cole Porter songs on the piano, "Night and Day" and "I Get a Kick out of You"—remember you used to kick your legs up while I sang. I haven't heard Cole Porter's music since New York and now I can't stop singing it.

Mary has gone to meet Bob in Peking since he just got off duty. She left Lolo here with his amah. After sightseeing in Peking they will come back and stay here for awhile. One night before she left Mary made a cherry pie from the big red cherries from the orchard. We didn't have the right equipment so she used a bottle as a rolling pin and rolled out the pie crust on the ledge on the porch. I wish Sun could have seen how she made that pie crust. I think it was the best I've tasted since being in China.

Last evening we climbed a steep cliff at the end of American Beach to watch the sunset. At that high point we could gaze upon the vast expanse of the jade green ocean and the serene blue sky in one direction and the spectacular panorama of the verdant green hills and purple-blue mountains in the other. We stayed there until the sun set behind the mountains.

There were several ships about a mile off shore—I couldn't tell what they were, only gray ghostly shapes. Yesterday was the Fourth of July celebrations. I don't know if the presence of the American and British navies makes me feel safe or nervous.

Tomorrow we want to take the children on a donkey ride up the Lotus Hills. There is a place where you can see the Great Wall. I'm not sure I can do this since I am expecting in October and I wouldn't dare risk bouncing around like that.

Please write to me soon. All my love to you and Mama,
Grace

Mary was in Peking when the Japanese attacked on the morning of July 7, 1937. She and Bob left the Peking station at six a.m., not knowing that only two hours earlier serious fighting had broken out at the Marco Polo Bridge on the Yongding River, just ten miles west of Peking. Grace heard it on the news. Japan had invaded North China and storm troopers were moving south from Manchuria. Rumor had it that they were burning down houses and butchering all along the way.

When Mary and Bob reached Peitaiho, they gathered up Lewis and left as soon as possible. F. C. met them in Tientsin and said he had sent a man to Peking to find out what the situation was. Within two days the Wares embarked on a boat for Shanghai where they transferred to a Navy vessel and departed for Manila.

When F. C. learned that the fighting had grown fierce and threatened to control the rail lines into Tientsin, he left immediately for Peitaiho to bring the women and children home. Grace learned later that they were on the last train to Tientsin before the Japanese took over the lines.

On hearing his sister was safe after the Japanese invasion, Sam Divine took the local newspaper a photo he had received earlier that year from Grace (depicting herself, Nini, and her amah). The accom-panying article quotes Grace's letter saying that conditions were peaceful, but "unrest and trouble are expected any moment." This article was published on July 30, 1937, but the trouble Grace foresaw had begun three days earlier.

NOOGA NEWS, CHATTANOOGA, TENN., FRIDAY, JULY 30, 1937.

Chattanoogan in War Zone

All seems peaceful here in Tientsin, wrote Mrs. Liu Fuchi, the former Grace Divine of Chattanooga, to her relatives here, "but there is an under-current of unrest and trouble is expected any moment." She is shown here in Tientsin with Ju Lamm, her 4-year-old daughter, and "Amah," her nurse. The former Chattanooga girl, her engineer husband, and their daughter are in the war zone. This picture was sent by Mrs. Fuchi to her brother, Sam Divine, of Chattanooga a few weeks ago. Her husband is manager of the waterworks at Tientsin.

At the Tientsin East Station, Japanese troops were already evident. F. C. carried Nini and told Grace and Erika to look straight ahead and walk fast. Franklin's amah held his hand and ran behind Erika. A sentry bellowed at them, but they quickly reached the International Bridge and crossed over. At the Rue de France a French guard checked them through without delay. They were safe inside the French concession.

The concessions were foreign territory and attacking them would have been tantamount to attacking France or Britain. Japan did not wish to invite the hostilities of these nations at this time and, in fact, used the opportunity of their preoccupation in Europe to make its move on China.

Peking surrendered without a fight. Tientsin was left undefended except for a paramilitary police force. Grace and Erika were anxious to see what was happening. When Grace heard there was fighting nearby, she and Erika hired two rickshaws and headed for the International Bridge, just across from the East Station. The whole area was deserted and had been sandbagged. As they approached, it got quieter and quieter. Suddenly a Chinese military policeman came running madly across the bridge. Shots zinged over their heads. The soldier fell dead. Grace's rickshaw driver stooped to dodge the bullets himself and gestured wildly for them to return: "Tai tai, bu shing! bu shing!"

When the bombing started on July 27, Grace and the other foreigners watched from their rooftops. At first the bombing was sporadic with simultaneous firings at different points throughout Tientsin. That night the Chinese attacked the East Station. The Japanese kept their stronghold on the station while the Chinese controlled the bridge, blocking access to the French concession. The concession responded with emergency measures and forbade entry of all troops bearing arms.

Grace's friend Adeline Lin came from

Japanese troops unloading at Tientsin station, 1937.

French troops behind barricades at the International Bridge.

109

The rooftop view in the concession as the Japanese bombed Tientsin, July 1937. Below, results of the assault.

Nankai University to stay with the Lius while her husband was away. Mrs. Holmberg was also there, along with F. C.'s niece, a student in Peking, who had fled that city and could not get home. All of them were on the roof that afternoon when the Japanese air force rained bombs continuously on government buildings and Nankai University. Great columns of smoke with bursts of flame were visible as incendiary bombs were dropped on Nankai. Mrs. Lin fell on Grace's shoulder and wept bitterly as she watched the destruction of the once-sheltered college. The pleasant campus, a few miles from the city with its lotus lakes and tree-covered pathways, had brought international acclaim for its impressive library, large academic buildings, and research facilities. Mrs. Lin claimed the attack was a ruthless purge for the anti-Japanese demonstrations led by students at Nankai.

The planes flew from bases only a few miles away, carefully hitting certain targets and avoiding others. Truckloads of dead were hauled through the city the next day. The fight for Tientsin lasted five days. By the end of the month, the Japanese controlled the whole region surrounding Tientsin and Peking. Students, youth, teachers,

intellectuals, and workers from Tientsin and Peking literally carried their libraries, belongings, printing presses, and other machinery with them as they trekked inland and resettled in the mountains or rural areas, joining the resistance.

Chiang Kai-shek made a new resolve for the "united front" and began to bomb Japanese warships off the coast of Shanghai, but missed and hit civilians instead. The Japanese used this attack as cause to retaliate with "all-out measures," and by December 1937, Japan had taken control of Shanghai and Nanking. The brutal Japanese raid on Nanking has been recorded in history as the "Rape of Nanking." The Nationalists were forced to retreat further inland to Chungking [Chongqing] and by October 1938 had surrendered East China—the most fertile farmlands, the most productive industries, and the cultural heartland of China.

The Communists, beleaguered by fighting both the Kuomintang [Nationalists] and the Japanese, were forced into a remote, poor district of north-central China in Yenan [Yanan]. In certain rural areas in North China, the Japanese campaign to "kill all, burn all, destroy all" aided the Communists in attracting more people to the resistance movement. They moderated their land reform practices in order to allow both landlords and peasants to fight the Japanese. "Chinese do not fight Chinese" was the slogan which pulled Chinese people together against the Japanese.

The foreign residents looked with dismay as Japan's undeclared war on China went unchallenged by the Western powers. The American forces pulled out of Tientsin in 1938. British troops remained until 1940 but yielded to most Japanese demands. Japan consolidated its control of China by creating a "puppet" government and plac-

American troops in 1937; the U.S. forces withdrew the following year.

ing Chinese collaborators in positions of power. Soon all businesses, ports, industries, transportation, and communication were under Japanese control.

Life in the concessions went on as usual, despite the fact that the sea around their island haven had completely altered.

Grace gave birth to a baby girl on October 21, 1937. The baby was named Ai-lien, or Ellen, after Grace's

grandmother. Nini later recalled her sister's arrival: "For the birth, Mother went to Dr. Ding's private hospital on London Road. She had two hospitals, one in the concessions and one for the poor in the city. Mother had been healthy throughout the pregnancy, so the fact that there was no anesthesia did not bother her. The labor was short and Ellen was born with a little red-tomato face."

At this time Nini started kindergarten at the Tientsin American School. Most of the students were foreign or mixed. "At first I didn't feel any different. I didn't know until later that this school was any different from the Chinese schools in the city. All the classes were in English; there was no Chinese at all. When it got colder, I wore Chinese padded clothing to school, and the foreign students snickered at me. But it didn't bother me; I was warm, and besides my best friend was half-Chinese, too."

Without actually attacking, the Japanese found other ways to exert pressure on the concessions in Tientsin. They tried to curtail foreign trade by eliminating all non-Japanese goods, retaining receipts from foreign customs, and replacing the Kuomintang fabi currency with a Japanese printed currency. The value of all currency fell rapidly. The Japanese controlled rail and river traffic, including the mail delivery—foreigners' contact with the outside world—which was sent by river tug to Tangku.

One day in mid-June 1939, Grace woke to find that what had once been a refuge for her had become a prison. In the night, the Japanese had erected barbed wire barricades at every entrance to the concessions throughout the city. The thousands of residents in these barricaded areas had to have special passes in order to exit or re-enter. At the checkpoints, steel-helmeted and bayoneted Japanese guards forced residents to fill out forms and subjected them to interminable delays. Likewise Chinese entering the areas, especially those bringing food and supplies—whether on foot, rickshaw, truck, car or horse—were held up and sometimes turned back. Chinese farmers or deliverymen waited patiently, sometimes two or three days, in sweltering heat.

The Chieh Yuan Pumping Station was in the native city and other substations were along the river or in other concessions. F. C. had to cross the barriers several times a day to supervise maintenance or attend to duties outside the French concession. Every time he crossed the barriers in either direction he was delayed, questioned, and subjected to humiliations. Every time he returned, however, he brought a vital resource to the family—information about what was happening outside the concession.

Nini's school was in the British concession and was backed up into the Chinese city. To get home, the children had to pass through the barricades and bow to the Japanese guards. "We didn't want to bow to the Japanese guards, so we slipped through a hole in the wall and ended up back in the British concession."

DESPITE THE invasion, the bombing, and even the blockade, Grace was still neatly sequestered behind safe lines. The forces of nature, however, were no respecter of the imaginary boundaries of national territories. When the floodwaters reached her door, Grace finally fell subject to the suffering of average Chinese.

The flood of 1939 was the worst in North China that anyone could remember, eclipsing that of 1917 and covering more than two thousand square miles. Five rivers flow into the Hai Ho River that passes through Tientsin. When the summer rains did not let up for days, the rivers swelled and swelled, moving massive amounts of water toward the city. Mud houses in the countryside simply disintegrated under the force.

Food, trains, and electricity were cut off. Millions died or were made refugees as the city prepared for the approaching waters, but no one was expecting the onslaught that occurred.

On Sunday, August 20, the flood waters broke through the sandbagged barriers into the concessions. People in the lower levels worked through the night to

Sandbagging the Hai Ho River.

remove furniture or personal belongings of worth. A parade of men, women, and children of all ages slogged past their compound in knee-deep, then shoulder-deep waters, carrying everything they could in bundles. Ponies from the Race Club were brought with cattle, pigs, and goats to higher ground. Nearly everyone in the British concession had to be removed to hotels. The French concession was on higher ground, especially at the point where it rose to meet the International Bridge. As the city streets turned into a Venetian-style network of canals, new enterprises flourished—

Floodwaters reached the base of the International Bridge and spilled over the sandbags into the streets.

shopkeepers improvised floating stalls, anyone with a boat offered it for hire, and catering services thrived for those who still had the means to cook. The foul, black waters were soon made intolerable with the stench of gases from dead and decayed material.

Grace wrote to her brother Sam during the flood. Everything about her letter shows distress—the paper is irregular and torn, the handwriting disorganized, words omitted, and pages stained or missing.

August 26, 1939
Dear Sam,

I enjoyed your letter very much. You and Mama are certainly marvelous. I got a letter from her at the same time I got yours, the first in ages, and I answered it immediately. But before I had a chance to answer yours, this last horror had descended on poor old Tientsin. I don't know why any one place should have to take such punishment. But compared to this flood everything proceeding has been a delightful picnic.

I hate to think that we complained one breath of the inconveniences before. This is death and destruction staring us right in the face.

A rather serious flood was expected, but not that the concessions and the city itself would be so devastated. There is not a dry spot in the British and Japanese concessions. Water from four to ten feet everywhere. And in the French concession there are about four or five dry blocks. That is, comparatively dry—the middle of the street and sidewalk. But our place is far from the dry area. There is more than six feet of water surrounding us. Of course the basement and the furnace room and coal room are completely submerged. All the first floor is flooded and the water comes up to the first landing on our front stairs and higher in the back.

Our court and garden is one big lake. Only the tops of the trees and grape arbor sticking out. The garage is full and the car covered. And from the roof as far as we can see the streets are like canals full of people on every kind of thing that will float—tubs, oil drums, big bamboo baskets, rafts, doors, beds, overturned tables, pieces of the pavement, boats of every kind from little homemade ones to big river junks. And whole families from old grandmothers to newborn babies together with the few household things they had managed to save—

This is the fifth day of the flood and I think the water has stopped rising. The smell is indescribable. For the first two or three days there was no bad odor beyond a slight fishiness. But the last two or three days had been like living over the most awful sewer on earth.

The magnitude of the flood was so unexpected that everything has been completely disorganized. Of course everyone knew there would be a flood and preparations were made and what the authorities thought were the proper precautions were taken. Barriers of sand—

August 31

This is the eleventh day of the flood. The water rose about four inches after I last wrote. Then for two days it stayed at the same point and day before yesterday started going down. It has now gone down about a foot and we all feel very encouraged and not so hopeless. Of course they say there are bound to be epidemics of some sort as the water recedes and everybody is trying to get cholera and typhoid injections.

I think I had better go back and tell you all about it from the beginning—fifteen days ago on Saturday the water started coming into the low spots of the concession. Everywhere at strategic points were three-foot barriers of sandbags and dirt. People who lived on low streets had bricked up their basement windows and doors. In the 1917 flood that everyone thought was so terrible the street that we live on had about two feet of water on it. So to make everything safe the windows facing on the sidewalk were bricked up and a two-foot wall was built on our top doorstep in [page torn] of the front door. A three or little more foot wall was built across the entrance to the court. All the yard and court is surround[ed] by a high wall, but about four feet up there are moon windows.

On Saturday night the south dike broke and the water started flooding the first special area (ex-German concession). We had been invited to have lunch on Sunday with the Ruases in . . .

The next three pages of the letter are missing. Nini and Franklin Ruas filled in the details of what happened.

On that Sunday, the 20th of August, the Lius had gone to lunch with the Ruases and then to a movie matinee of *Jesse James* starring Tyrone Power at the Empire Theatre in the British concession. Halfway through the film, the lights went out and the film came to a sudden, faltering stop. F. C. knew immediately what it meant—the floodwaters had reached the power station in the British concession. Being on lower ground, the British system was the first to fail. The water had caused a shutdown of all electrical machinery of the British pumps. The two men left immediately to rescue the failing system by connecting the British system to the main water system. In the sweltering heat, they sloshed through the putrid waters until after dark, locating and turning on valves that were already underwater, until the connections were complete, thus saving the British system from collapse.

The Empire Theatre under water in the British Concession, August 1939.

Grace and Erika quickly returned home to the French concession and found the amahs still in the park playing with the children. As they walked home, the children saw for the first time the water gurgling up into the drainage grids, sputtering and spewing, as if the system were regurgitating, before the dark waters emerged and began to flow rapidly into the streets.

116

THE JAPANESE commander of Tientsin had cause to suspect foul play. In 1937 Chiang Kai-shek had blown up the dikes on the Yellow River causing a flood that held off the Japanese advance for weeks. It was not likely that anyone had caused this flood but the Japanese were sure to prevent possibilities of sabotage from those in charge of the system. On the first morning after the floodwaters began to rise in the streets, the Japanese commander, riding a large brown horse, thundered into the Water Works' courtyard where both the Liu and Ruas families lived. The Ruases' amah was

in the courtyard with the baby, when suddenly the horse, not expecting a carriage to be in the way, was startled and reared up. The resulting noise and confusion brought Erika running to see what was the matter. The commander, still on horseback, demanded to see her husband. The cook watching from the back of the courtyard quickly ran inside to inform Mr. Liu and Mr. Ruas. By the time they arrived, a squad of Japanese infantrymen carrying rifles had reached the courtyard.

Tientsin residents had to pass through Japanese checkpoints even during the flooding.

From windows above, curtains partially drawn, the wives, children, and servants watched in terror as the commander pulled a long, silver Japanese bayonet and held it threateningly close to the two men as he barked . . . "if there is any interruption in services . . . or if the flood waters leak into the city's water . . . the first ones shot will be you." He waited for no response. When he had finished his threats, he roared out, leaving his infantrymen following in his muddy tracks.

During the ensuing days, the two men were gone for long hours and did all they could do to protect the water system from contamination. They knew how things were connected, but they had no control over the rising waters, and they did not know what would happen to the system after the power went out. Fortunately the Water Works pumping station was on high ground and heavily sandbagged, so no seepage occured.

During this time, Grace often went to the tap to check the water. If the tap water ran clear, she was relieved. But her nerves were wrecked as she and the children waited, helplessly, as the waters continued to rise. Ellen remembers, "The water was up to the first floor, we were on the second floor. I remember seeing boats from the bathroom window. Mother scolded us for playing on the stairs with buckets in the water."

Flooding at
Catholic and
Protestant
churches in the
concessions,
August 1939.

August 31, to Sam, continued

All the ground was covered even the concrete court between the front office which our apartment is on top of and the back offices. The men were still piling earth around the wall. The roaring from the front hall had gotten so loud we ran out to look again. It was horrifying. The water was apparently rushing thru the door in a torrent and was covering the first step of the stair case. We ran to the telephone and called downstairs that water was rushing into the front hall and up the stairs. Just then my rickshaw man came running in "Tai-tai, tai-tai, the water has come in the back door and is going in the cellar." We ran to the windows again. The water was pouring over the wall and thru the moon windows. All that work for nothing. Mr. Ruas had come in the meantime. He was forced to leave his car in front of the French Club about a half a mile away and wade thru the water the rest of the way—

When they saw it was hopeless and that the flood was so much higher than anyone had dreamed of, the men all left the court which was now covered with about two feet.

F. C. and Mr. Ruas came upstairs by a ladder put on the roof of the office porch to the cook's window. Before they came up, they turned off the electricity to avoid fires or short circuits. Fortunately we had a few candles in the house. But before the light went off we looked down the stairs and the water was coming up to the first landing.

When F. C. and Mr. Ruas got upstairs the water was rushing into the court and basement with such a roaring that we had to scream over it to be heard. I don't think I've ever been so frightened. The house was all dark but for a few puny candles and that awful noise of rushing water.

Then the street lights went out and we knew that the French power plant was under water. And they had taken such precautions to protect their engines. We sat around the dining room table with a piece of candle in the middle and another piece on the sideboard—

We were stunned; it had happened so quickly. Then I said, "We'll have to use the coal stove now." And F. C. said nobody had thought to bring the coal out of the basement and now it would be impossible to get it out. And then I realized that we would never be able to go to the French market and we had no vegetables and no eggs and no bread. All we had was twenty-five cans of evaporated milk, two cans of Quaker oats, seven cans tuna fish, two cans corn beef, two cans sauerkraut, one can tomatoes, and some cans of Del Monte juice, tomato, pineapple, grapefruit, orange, etc. Anyway we thought the children could get along awhile if we could make a fire.

By and by the water had stopped rushing in with so much noise and we went to bed in what seemed a very different world. I was afraid to sleep for fear the water would come all the way up while we slept. I got out of bed again and again to look out the window. It was a clear night with stars. The court and garden was a lake and the streets were rivers. I felt like Aladdin and his wonderful lamp—our house seemed to have been in the twinkling of an eye transported to some far place.

The next morning only the top of the car, which had been standing in front of the garage, was visible. The telephone house was full of water and the switchboard covered. Men were walking in the street with water up to their necks.

Well, here we were, no coal, no wood, no electricity, no boat.

The workmen who lived out in the lower places of the concession had brought their families in on the day before and now there were about ninety people—women, men, and children crowded into the back office rooms. The chauffeur's house which is in the garden was almost covered so he had to move into the office building with his wife, mother, and eight children. The first floor of the building is about four feet from the pavement of the cou—[torn page] and about three hundred dollars worth of rice and flour were stored there. It was partly submerged. They saved what they could of it.

That next morning was terrible. Our children were hungry and all the children in the back, I don't know know how many, were hungry and frightened and crying. F. C. had the men tear down the matting that covered the roof and court to protect it from the sun. There was not a stick of dry wood so we just kept on stuffing . . .

The rest of the letter is lost.

8

FAMINE AND WAR

ON SEPTEMBER 1, 1939, Germany attacked Poland and soon afterwards Britain and France declared war on Germany. As the waters which bound them to the fate of the Chinese subsided, the foreigners in Tientsin now found themselves enemies at home with those who had once been their compatriots abroad.

These transforming events happened at a frightening pace, leaving everyone shaken. Before the floodwaters had dried, the Japanese intensified the blockade. Barbed wire defenses were added to every barricade and to garrison posts along the railways, controlling movement to and from the city as well as within. Loudspeakers were installed at the barricades and turned on all the time, blaming the foreigners for the troubles in China. For the residents of the concessions, the shock of the outbreak of World War II was tinged with the deadening realization that their world was disappearing forever. The Japanese were doing what the Chinese had been unable to do for a hundred years—dissolve the grip of Western imperialism in China.

The prevailing concern the winter of 1940 was food. The flood had caused a famine that drove thousands of peasants into the city. The harbor was thick with sampans, long boats, junks, and rafts, tightly packed with refugees of all ages in starving conditions. Many of them came directly from the river into the concessions. The food crisis reached catastrophic levels. Imports stopped; grain was hoarded; supplies were turned away, and currency was invalid. The Japanese blamed foreign control; the Nationalist government blamed the communist-controlled countryside. And the Communists blamed the Nationalists for the spiraling inflation, doubling and redou-

Boatloads of refugees crowded into Tientsin.

bling monthly. Hunger fueled the fury of a world out of control.

When shiploads of flour arrived in March 1940, the flour became an object of speculation. Those who were wealthy enough to acquire large amounts stockpiled it, waiting for the price to go up.

With disgust for the new breed of "hoarders and speculators," Grace began to realize that the Chinese leaders did not really care about the conditions of the people. Her disillusionment was centered on the wealthy Chinese men who were now directors of the Water Works:

At this time when the poor were being forced into the city, some of the directors of the Water Works were hoarding flour and waiting until the price would go just high enough, then they would sell it. That's the way they did everything. They didn't care at all how many people died. There were too many Chinese anyway, was their thinking.

The scoundrels made money off these conditions and then they bought wives. One director told the board he must have a raise in his director's fee because he wanted to buy a new concubine, as he had seen a new girl and she was very fascinating. One would think that that would be nonsensical for a man to say how he might want to buy another woman—he might think it and do it surreptitiously— but then this was the thing to do. He didn't mind saying it out loud; he didn't mind that everybody knew it.

Grace felt overwhelmed by the distressing conditions on such a large scale. When she came face to face with one poor woman, begging for help, she responded instinctively:

There were so many poor people pouring into the city at that time. Of course, I wanted to give the beggars something—but if you dared, you would have a mob

122

around you—you couldn't get out. But one time I was walking home near where we lived, and there were not so many people around. A beggar woman came up— just a country woman, holding a baby in her arms, about the age of Ellen and another child was holding onto her jacket, just about Nini's age. She was so gaunt and looked so starved, and the baby was just a little bundle of bones. She wanted something. I opened my purse and got out a bill—I suppose it was a dollar bill. It might have been a five-dollar bill. I didn't even look. But nobody ever gave a beggar a bill! You gave a beggar a copper. Well, I handed her the bill. And she looked like she thought I was crazy. Maybe she'd never seen one. I saw a car pass me just at that time. So I hurried off. That car was a Water Works car and it had Water Works directors in it.

The next day my husband said, "Well, you have certainly created a scandal. Those directors saw you give the beggar woman a bill."

"I told you about it. I couldn't stand it. Those children were the same age as my children. So I just had to give her something," I said.

"But the directors said that they saw you give this woman a bill and that they were so angry. They said, 'We cannot afford to have a chief engineer with such an extravagant foreign wife who actually gives beggars a . . . a bill!'" He was laughing. "Well, this won't hurt them," he said.

But it did hurt . . . not the directors, of course, but Grace, and indirectly her whole family. The accusation of "extravagant" was an easy one to endorse since many of the customs that sustained her ordinary existence, such as drinking milk daily, were items of indulgence for Chinese. But the label was indelible and would hurt her even more in later years. While the directors were outraged by her "extravagance," Grace was repulsed by the sordid lifestyles of the wealthy, both foreign and Chinese. Nini recalled Grace describing a visit to a Chinese woman's home during this period:

She was the daughter of a warlord, who owned land in Tientsin. He had a house like a palace in the British concession. When he died, the huge garden surrounding the house became his burial ground and an enormous marble tortoise was built as his gravestone. His daughter wanted to meet Grace because she was looking for a husband who was an intellectual, not a rich man's son nor a businessman, and she knew Grace and

F. C. were connected to different circles. When Grace came, there was chaos in the house. She was told that the concubine had just run off with a lover and a lot of jewelry. The servants sat in the corridors on hard old antique chairs smoking opium. Grace was fascinated and horrified by the lifestyle. The young woman pleaded with Grace to find her a husband; F. C. later introduced her to an engineer, but he objected because she smoked opium. He said he wouldn't marry her unless she stopped smoking. She stopped and when they married, years later, one of their sons was in Willy's class in primary school.

At a time when foreigners were both envied and despised by the privileged class in China, Grace's presence muddied the waters for F. C. Being married to a foreigner and not treating her in the way a rich Chinese would treat his wife (and concubines) made F. C. incomprehensible to the other Chinese men who were directors of the Water Works. He was not one of them; he was not to be completely trusted. And yet he was not easy to cast aside. F. C.'s forceful personality and strong temperament made him formidable. They needed his skills to keep the company in their control, but his incorruptible character caused snide remarks and sometimes plotting. According to Grace, their way of getting at him was a traditional Chinese one, but not entirely unique to China.

They resented F. C. being a one-woman man. He would have to go to these directors' meetings sometimes. They would have them in restaurants or tea houses. They would deliberately try their best to get my husband to take a few girls. At one party they offered some money to any of those girls to get F. C., "Because he thinks he is a one-woman man so we will give you so much to get this man." That was supposed to be a huge joke.

F. C. would come home and tell me about these parties. One time he came home looking sad and said, "They had a new girl there, and she was only fourteen. They had just gotten her in some town. She must have been less afraid of me than the other old men, so she came and asked me if she could please sit by me. She said she was so frightened that I told her, 'All right. As long as I'm here, nobody is going to even look at you.'" And so she sat with him and told him her story, that she came from a poor family in a small village, that her father had had to sell her . . .

As early as 1937 the Japanese appointed one of their own engineers to work at the Water Works. Mr. Yasemoto was friendly at first and seemed to cause no harm. He offered to help F. C. carry out his duties. But while Homer Lu was absent, the other directors replaced him as managing director with another of the Chinese directors, more cooperative with the Japanese. Observing the division among the board, Mr. Yasemoto began to pressure F. C. into cooperating with him. The management support for F. C. that had once existed within the company began to dissolve dramatically.

For Grace and F. C., the aftermath of the flood was even more devastating than the flood itself, as Grace described in her letter six months later:

March 14, 1940
Dear Mary Hills,

I was absolutely delighted *to get your letter. Nobody has written to me for ages. Of course I can't complain as I haven't written to any of the family since the flood. I don't know why it is so hard for me to get a letter down on paper. I can write the most marvelous ones in my head.*

We have had many upheavals, trouble, worries, and so forth. But I am thankful our family have all stayed well, that is all but me. Since I have been in China I have been in better health than I ever was in my life. Up until last June when the blockade began and I began to get thin and lost my resistance to colds (but more about that later).

These past nine months since the beginning of the blockade last June have been a very bad time for Tientsin and especially the Water Works. First the blockade with all the terrible inconvenience and scarcity of food, then the dreadful heat of July and August, and then the flood! After that was over we all were as limp as rags. The children were quite pale and thin but not sick and they soon recovered when they were able to get outdoors. F. C. was exhausted but all right. But I hadn't been able to get any milk after the blockade started. The children drank canned evaporated milk but it was so terribly expensive that I did without any milk at all. And as I am very dependent on milk I lost more pounds than I could afford. The reason we couldn't get milk after the blockade is because all the dairies are outside the concessions. And the milk men weren't allowed to bring the milk in. And for a long time it was very difficult to get vegetables. And for a while no meat at all.

In November the Water Works got its first blow. Mr. Holmberg, one of the founders of the company and the first chief engineer, a former minister from Denmark and just then one of the directors of the company, had taken his seventeen-year-old daughter Dorothy to Denmark to put her in a university. He died there very suddenly of heart failure. It was a great shock to everybody. His wife is one of my best friends and he was one of F. C.'s best friends and a great help and support to the company.

After his death things began to go wrong. The other directors were demoralized and treachery and intrigue started. Homer Lu, the managing director, a very smart and able man and the one who brought F. C. here, was then on a six-month leave in the States on a very important mission, the purpose of which would be very unwise to speak of in these parts. He left in his place a man supposed to be very honorable and honest and his very good friend but he was really very weak and easily led and persuaded. So a very stupid and corrupt bunch of directors and shareholders got ahold of him and they accused Homer Lu in his absence of all sorts of things and at a directors' meeting voted him out and put another man in his place, a former schoolmate of F. C.'s, a lying, treacherous Chinese politician of the worst sort. Then they tried to get F. C. on their side. If they could win him, they were fixed, then Homer Lu could do nothing.

But of course he told them he did not choose to play their game and told them to their faces exactly what sort of swine they were. In the meantime they had turned the Japanese man who worked for the company against F. C. F. C. had always gotten along very well with this man (who was really a sort of spy for the Japanese army) and had been very wise in his conversations with him. This man now turned rabidly against F. C., accused him of being anti-Japanese (as of course he is) and demanded his pass (permit to pass barriers). So F. C. gave back his pass and resigned. But the directors were afraid for him to resign, it might mean a strike of workmen and technical staff and there was no one else who could do the job. So they refused to accept his resignation and gave him a four months leave.

F. C. appointed Mr. Ruas, the French engineer, to take his place outside. F. C. stayed at home and Mr. Ruas reported to him. So things went along until January when Mr. Ruas suddenly got a mysterious and violent pain in his leg.

He went to the hospital one Wednesday afternoon, they operated on his leg Thursday morning at eleven, discovered a deep abscess, and he died of blood poisoning at three o'clock Friday afternoon, January 12. It was a terrific shock to us, as F. C. and I and Mr. and Mrs. Ruas had been together almost constantly for the last four years. We lived together in Peitaho, they stayed with us during the flood and I don't think that there was ever a day that we weren't in their house or they in ours.

The day he died I had planned to stay in bed all day as I had caught a bad cold. But Erika (Mrs. R.) called me at eight o'clock from the hospital (a German-American hospital in the ex-German concession). She said Charlie was dying and she wanted me to come so I threw on my clothes and flew out as fast as possible. F. C. couldn't go as he couldn't pass the barriers without his pass. I have my American passport. I can't remember the details of that hectic morning. Only I know I went back and forth thru the barriers over six times and one time is no fun. I never get used to those dreadful faces and naked bayonets. It was very cold and windy and my teeth chattered. I knew my cold was getting worse but I couldn't help it.

Erika was seven months pregnant and almost out of her head—she began to vomit terribly and at twelve o'clock I made her come home with me. The doctor said they would telephone if there was any change. We got her two little boys and came home. At two o'clock the hospital called and told her to come. I went back with her. They said he wouldn't last long and we stayed with him until about ten minutes before he died. He died very very hard and it was dreadful to watch. I never saw anybody die before. I finally called the doctor and told him he must take Erika out of the room. She couldn't stand anymore. So they took her downstairs. And he was dead in about ten more minutes.

He was only thirty-five and looked as strong and healthy as a bull. The doctors were very puzzled and said they did not know what it was he had. Probably something he got during the flood when he had to walk in the filthy water. Erika and her children have been with us ever since. Last Sunday morning her baby was born, another boy. he weighs 8-3/4 lbs. and is marvelous. After Mr. Ruas' funeral my cold got me down and I went to bed for three weeks.

Homer Lu came back and now there is a fierce silent fight going on. Silent because nothing can be done above board on account of the Japanese, who would like nothing better than an excuse to take over the company. Now it all depends on which side wins. If the other side, then F. C. will go South and into the Interior. If our side, then he stays here and goes on with his work. The other side wants to keep him but he would not work for them. In either case I stay in Tientsin . . .

The contrast in the remainder of Grace's letter is remarkable. Despite the flood, the blockade, the birth of a child, the death of two friends, and all the political intrigue, social activities continued with an amazing sense of normalcy. At the same time that their world is crumbling around them, clubs continue to meet, people go to

F. C. (third from left), with a group of Water Works officials. Their western dress and casual poses on a tennis court show that notwithstanding the turmoil of the times, "normal" life went on.

church, children go to school, and Grace even begins to sing again:

. . . Tientsin is a very hard place to get well in once you get down. It's the most social place I ever saw. Either we are always going someplace or somebody is coming here. Everybody has to keep engagement books. So just as soon as I was better I started running again.

Did I tell you all in another letter that I had started singing again, not like I used to, of course, but people here think it's marvelous. I'm quite famous as a "prima donna" in Tientsin and another thing (I'm sure you will laugh or Tom will) I also have the reputation of being very "smart." People are always asking me if my clothes are imported. When I sang for the Women's Club, I wore a thin blue (powder blue) wool dress with a black velvet bolero and turban and white jade earrings and necklace. I sang Michaela's aria from Carmen, *Shubert's serenade, "Ave Maria" from* Cavallier Rusticana, *and four smaller songs.*

Last month on my birthday I sang at the big Rotary anniversary banquet and dance. I wore a black satin skirt and light red velvet basque with leg of mutton sleeves and a three-row crystal necklace and crystal earrings and a huge red flower on top of my head. I sang "The Kerry Dance" and "My Laddie," "Will You Remember" from Maytime, *Shubert's serenade, and a Rotary song to the tune of "A Perfect Day."*

Mrs. Walker, the wife of a very popular American lawyer, plays my accompaniments. Mr. Walker used to sing a lot when he was younger. And he still can sing. F. C. and I go there a lot and we have an awfully good time. Mr. Walker and I sing duets (they have all the opera scores nearly). Mrs. Walker plays the piano and sometimes Mrs. Hinke (wife of one of the American consuls) comes with her cello.

We have just lost two of our most congenial friends, Mr. and Mrs. Bakker, an American girl and her Dutch husband. They have just gone to Italy on leave and will be stationed in Shanghai when they come back. Of all the foreigners we know, F. C. liked them the best. How he and Andries (Mr. B.) loved their political discussions!

I forgot to say that at the Rotary banquet F. C. was there and when I went back to the table after singing my first group, everybody was laughing at him. They said he was so nervous he almost had a fit. I remember one time when I sang at the University of Tennessee and Tom was so nervous he wanted to crawl under the bench.

Nini is in the second grade at the Tientsin American school and is doing well. Her teacher says she is exceptionally bright and the best behaved child in the class. Nini is quite pretty and piquant-looking. But my little Ellen (Ai Lan) is a real beauty, the kind people gasp over. F. C. and I look at her and wonder how on earth she happened. F. C. adores Nini, but he can be quite stern with her if necessary. But Ellen just turns him to jelly. He

F. C. and Ellen.

almost tiptoes around her in awe. And her amah! She would take off her skin for Ellen. Consequently she is very spoiled. I have to give her all the discipline she gets and her amah and daddy think I'm very cruel.

One time when I had shut her up in a room till she got tired of screaming for something I wouldn't let her have, her own amah and Nini's amah both came to me to kowtow and knock their heads on the floor and beg to be allowed to take her out. They were wringing their hands and bowing and bowing and saying "Che che, Tai tai, che che, tai tai." "Please, please," (Tai tai means the "lady of the house.") I told them if they didn't go away and stay in the kitchen until Ellen behaved herself I would fire them both. F. C. was pacing the floor and wringing his hands, too, but I glared at him and said only over my dead body would anyone take her out until she stopped yelling. She finally did stop yelling and got as sweet as pie, but she didn't get what she was yelling for!

You see, Mary Hills, I have been carrying on about myself! I'm sorry Tom had to quit engineering but his insurance job sounds

Julia Divine and Mary Hills Divine, in a photo they mailed to Grace, on the street in Chattanooga.

good. The main thing, I suppose, is to have a job!

When I showed Tom's picture to one of the amahs and asked her if it looked like me, she said, "All same long face." Elinor looked fine in the picture, in fact, you all looked great, especially you. Amah said you looked, "All same little girl."

I wish Mama would write to me. I never know her address. I wrote a long letter and mailed it during the flood but she never got it. I suppose it got "drowned."

Nini is standing over me talking and asking what I'm writing and if I'm telling you anything about her. So I'm afraid I'm becoming incoherent and jumping around from one subject to another. I have just been out of bed two days after having the flu for nearly a week. The doctor said the flu wasn't serious but that I was very run down and must stop absolutely all my activities for the time being and do nothing but eat and sleep. And we were just in the midst of preparations for the Easter music at All Saints Church! It's Church of England and the rector is an Englishman whose wife was born in Macon, Georgia.

Have you read Lin Yutang's novel "Moment in Peking"? It's wonderful. Please write to me again, Mary Hills, and tell me about everybody. It's my fond hope that we can all come to see you one of these days. But I'm afraid I'd talk myself literally to death.

With much love to everybody,
Grace

Left, Grace with Nini and Ellen, 1940. Right, 1941, Grace with the girls soon before William's birth.

Crowds like this one gathered at the International Bridge when the blockade was lifted; in this case, the activity is an earlier French relief effort for refugees.

ON JUNE 21, 1940, the blockade was lifted. Immediately the roads were full of people on bicycles, cars, trucks, and rickshaws passing from one side to the other, reuniting families and resuming business. With the blockades down, F. C. was able to cross through the barriers and return to his position at the Water Works. But now everything had changed. Mr. Holmberg and Mr. Ruas were dead, Homer Lu had been replaced, and those cooperating with the Japanese were in control not only of his workplace but of all the city.

Grace's third child was born on May 16, 1941. Nini describes her brother's birth:

> Willy was born in Dr. Ding's hospital, too. He came so fast, he almost dropped on the floor. Dr. Ding caught him and announced, "It's a little William!" The name stuck, and we called him Willy from the start. His Chinese name was Wei-han. I remember when Willy came home, he was in a blue blanket and he stared at me and I stared at him. He became the favorite of the amah. She always liked the babies best but this one was a boy. Grace and F. C. did not show the Chinese preference for a boy—they were pleased to have a son, but not overly so.

131

Early one morning when Grace was nursing William in the back room, she heard F. C. anxiously hollering to her. She handed William to the amah and went forward to see what was upsetting him. Before she reached him, she heard a strange noise and looked out the window. Long rows of olive green trucks were moving down the street. Their engines groaned in low gear. Marching alongside, in helmets and rubber boots, were the dreaded Japanese soldiers. Even throughout the blockade and all the time the Japanese were in Tientsin, they had not dared cross the barriers into the concession. She did not have time to ask why they were pouring into the concession now.

F. C. was at the fireplace, feeding a roaring flame. "Quick, empty that drawer," he said. "Get rid of anything they could use against us." Grace grabbed letters and papers, without looking at them very carefully, and threw them into the fire.

It was December 8, 1941, in Tientsin.

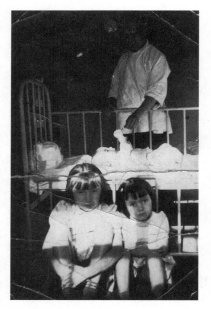

Nini and Ellen
at the crib of
baby William.

9

WORLD WAR II

FOR THE four years of the U.S. involvement in World War II, Grace did not hear from her American family, nor they from her. As an American trapped inside Japanese-controlled Tientsin, she escaped internment in a concentration camp by sheer luck. She wrote later that even though she had no way of knowing how the war was going, she never gave up her faith that the Allies would ultimately win. Finally, in the summer of 1945, the sight of U.S. B-29s lifted her hopes that the war was nearing an end.

Following the atomic bombings of Hiroshima and Nagasaki, Japan surrendered on August 14, 1945. U.S. forces in the Pacific were sent immediately to China to keep order until the Nationalist government, then in retreat in Chungking, could return and accept the surrender of the Japanese. The first marines in Tientsin found a forlorn city and a downtrodden population.

When the Third Amphibious Corps of the U.S. Marines steamed up the Hai Ho River to Tientsin in September 1945, a large throng was waiting. As Private Giles Brooks stepped off the dock, he was greeted by an American woman in the crowd who asked where he was from. When he replied, "Chattanooga, Tennessee," she responded, "I know a woman from Chattanooga and I will tell you how to find her."

He took the address of a Mrs. Liu but did not look her up until a week later. When he knocked on the door of the given address, a Chinese woman answered. Seeing an American G.I. at the door, she ran back inside calling out in Chinese. A moment later a young Chinese-looking girl, her hair in braids and wearing a dress too small for her, appeared at the door. She spoke in casual English, "Oh, hi, soldier,

Mrs. F. C. Liu, Former Grace Divine, Found Safe In Tientsin, Pfc. Brooks Tells Relatives Here

GOOD NEWS AFTER FOUR YEARS—Pvt. G. R. Brooks (center) last week brought news of Mrs. F. C. Liu, Tien-Tsin, China, to her family direct from that city, after four years of silence from Mrs. Liu due to her being at the mercy of the Japanese. Left, above, Sam Divine, Chattanooga, and right, Edward Divine, formerly of Chattanooga, who served in the Pacific war and witnessed the death of Ernie Pyle, which he was able to avenge on the spot. Divine entered the army at the age of 40, and his bald head entitled him to be known by the regiment as "Pappy," a coveted honor.

News of Grace's survival was received in fall 1945 but this article was not published until Giles Brooks returned home in February 1946. Brooks is pictured here with Grace's brothers Sam and Edward, now a war hero.

Marine Finds Ex-Local Woman, Given Up as Dead by Family

By W. G. FOSTER

Four years of anxiety over the fate of Mrs. F. C. Liu, the former Grace Divine, ended for the Divine family last week with the information that Mrs. Liu is alive and well in Tientsin, China.

stealthily around behind the shack housing the sniper and in spite of some trouble with wet matches set fire to the small building, jumping into a Jap foxhole, and covered the building, hoping to pick off the Jap when he was forced out. He was destined not to see the murderer, however, for as the flames devoured the house a hand grenade explosion inside indicated that the Jap had taken his own life.

Divine is officially credited with

come on in. We've been expecting you."

The girl, Nini, called to her father. When F. C. came into the room, Giles started to introduce himself. F. C. interrupted, "I know. You are the marine from Chattanooga. Our friend told us. We were hoping you'd come."

Grace was ill and unable to meet Giles Brooks the day he knocked on the Lius' door. But F. C. invited him back for dinner later in the week and told him to bring some other G.I.s. The Lius had little food or money so F. C. invited other Chinese who could help entertain the G.Is. Soon Giles and his buddies were frequent guests and there were many celebrations.

Before Giles Brooks's news of Grace's survival reached Chattanooga, another American also found Grace. Lloyd Hindman, chaplain for the U.S. squadrons entering China, had received a letter from Mary McCallie Ware, Grace's cousin who had fled China when the Japanese attacked in 1937. Mary asked her friend from the Navy to find out if her cousin survived. He asked at the YMCA if anyone knew her. According to Grace, the first person he asked was a friend of hers. Chaplain Hindman soon tracked down Grace's family and sent the following description to Mary on October 24, 1945:

Mrs. Liu has lost a great deal of weight, but other than that is in good health. She weighs only eighty-six pounds. She escaped being interned in a concentration camp by some miracle and was able to be with her family during all these years of Japanese occupation. Mr. Liu was fired from his job in 1941 due to the pro-Japanese interests at the head of the local water works. However, they have been able to live in a small apartment in the ex-British concession.

Their children are precious. Ju Lan, the eldest, is twelve years of age; Ellen is eight years of age; and the baby, Wei-han (William) is four years of age. The girls bear a strong family resemblance to Mary's people and the little boy looks more like his father.

Hindman wrote that the Lius were thrilled to have contact with someone who knew the family. Then he suggested to Mary "that the women in your family get together and send some clothes over, as the Lius are wearing the same clothes they had four years ago."

Before either of these chance meetings occurred, Grace had tried to contact her family but failed. In early September, when the first rescue team parachuted into Peking and came down to Tientsin by train, Grace received a notice that letters could go by air via the Swiss Embassy in Peking. She sat down immediately to write, and her letter was in the Swiss Consulate that afternoon. She waited but never heard anything back.

When Giles arrived, Grace wrote again. Giles sent her letter by the Marine Corps post. He addressed it to his mother in Chattanooga and asked her to deliver it to Grace's brother Tom. But Tom no longer lived in Chattanooga. Mrs. Giles found another "Divine" in the phone book and called him. Grace's brother Sam was so excited to hear that his sister was alive that he called the local newspaper before contacting Tom.

These photos taken by Giles Brooks were the first news Grace had been able to send her family since the U.S. declared war on Japan.

Grace's letter was the first word the family had from her since Pearl Harbor Day.

November 20, 1945
Dear Tom,

Four years is a long time and if I tried to tell only a part of what we've been through since I last wrote I would fill a book. I will say right away that we suffered none of the horrors that went on in other places. Tientsin was lucky and was, to the last, one of the best *places to live. In '42 we still had some of our own money and the cost of living hadn't yet become so impossibly high. But 1943–44 were the worst years for us. We didn't have any money and with eggs $140 a piece, milk $100 a glass and butter $6000 a lb., you can see we had to do without many things. For a large part of the time there was no fruit at all or it was too expensive to think of. For instance, one apple cost $100. The two years '43–44 are like a nightmare in my mind, of cold, never quite enough to eat, sickness and such weariness that I didn't know a person could be so tired and keep on living.*

In January '45, I applied through the Swiss Consulate for relief for myself and the three children, and from January through September that practically saved our lives.

During the first month of the war, I lost twenty pounds, and not only never gained it back but kept on losing. In '44 I weighed seventy-nine. Now I weigh eighty-six, and for the last nine or ten months I have felt much better and stronger but I look awful! F. C. is well but he looks much older.

In a later letter, Grace explained what happened after the Japanese came into the concession.

In 1941 just before Pearl Harbor, F. C. was fired from the Water Co. by the pro-Japanese management for refusing to cooperate with them, and also because he had an American wife. They said it didn't look good to the Japanese to have a Chief Engineer with an American wife. Homer Lu, the former managing director, had been replaced by two managers who collaborated with the Japanese, Ray Chang and Franklyn Koo. They came with a group of Japanese up into our apartment in January, 1942, and ordered us out of the place. Mr. Chang and Mr. Koo led the Japanese into my bedroom where I was putting Wei-han (then eight months old) to bed. The Japanese advisor wanted to see what of our furniture to take. We had to let go whatever he wanted. Mr. Koo told him that my beautiful Mongolian rug was company property. Those two men, Chang and Koo, sold or gave company shares to the puppet government [so that they could] live in luxury during these last five years.

They starved the workmen and held them down with the Japanese gendarmeries. Ray Chang informed the Japanese on Homer Lu, who had been his best friend, but when the gendarmerie went to take Homer they went at first to his concubine's house by mistake. She cried and carried on, allowing him to escape by a scant half hour. He has fled to the interior.

In 1941 they [had] tried every inducement to get F. C. to throw in his lot with them. When he refused and told them in a very plainspoken way what he thought of them in a letter to the Board of Directors, they fired him, with all the humiliating trimmings they could think up. They put up huge signs in every company office, trying to blacken his character and humiliate him.

A delegation of workmen came to F. C. and wanted to strike. Some wanted to assassinate Chang and Koo. F. C. calmed them down and reminded them that we were completely in the power of the Japanese and to fight and protest was worse than useless. They actually cried and one huge foreman, about six feet three and a few hundred pounds, just wept out loud. All the workmen and all the staff were intensely loyal to F. C. When we left the company, Chang and Koo refused to give us F. C.'s savings. Finally the Japanese advisor made them give him about one-half the amount. It was the Chinese traitors who fired him, not the Japanese.

In early 1942, all foreigners in Tientsin had been told to move into the British concession. By the end of February, they were required to register and wear armbands identifying the nationality of the wearer. Whenever Grace went out, she wore the red arm band with a black circle around the bold, black character for "America."

On March 28, 1942, during a sweeping dust storm, the British concession was handed back. In a formal ceremony in which the howling wind drowned out any words spoken, the Chinese collaborators, under the supervision of their Japanese leaders, formally accepted the territory for China. By mid-August foreign diplomats and professionals were loaded onto trains and sent to Nanking, and from there shipped out of the country. A short time later, all foreign residents remaining in Tientsin were rounded up and sent to an internment camp in Wei Hsien, Shandong province. The Tientsin prisoners were soon joined by those from Peking. In the course of a year, the Japanese had successfully orchestrated the ouster of foreign residents—that is, all but Japan's.

Grace's letter of November 20, 1945, continues:

. . . It just happened by a lucky chance that I was not sent to "Wei-Hsien," the concentration camp for allied civilians. In 1942 all "enemy nationals" registered with the Swiss and Swedish consulates. As we did not need relief at that time, I did not register with them. And that saved me, for it was from those Consulate lists that the Japanese Consulate

took the names of the people to be sent to the camp. I registered four times with the military, but they did not have charge of sending civilians to camp. I knew that I had been really "miraculously" overlooked, because with all their spies they usually knew everything.

I was so scared that they would see that I was there and that I hadn't been sent to a concentration camp that they would gather me up and send me. I was afraid to be seen on the street. So I just went into hiding. For one year and a half I never went outside our door except at night, disguised as a Chinese. I would cover my head with a black scarf and dress in Chinese clothes. Nini went with me. She would stop at each corner and check to see if it was safe. We went to see my friend who had T.B. and her daughter who was Nini's best friend.

. . . 1942 was one of the coldest winters I remember. We had to move out of our comfortable and warm apartment over the Water Works into a huge barn of a place. It was so huge we rattled around in it and when the wind blew, everything rattled. It was impossible to heat and we all nearly froze. It was the only place we could get because it belonged to Homer Lu. His concubine rented it to us and to my friend Mrs. Holmberg. Her daughter, Dorothy, came back from Denmark after her father died there in 1939. Mrs. Holmberg was just recovering from T.B., but her husband's death, the war, and troubles in Denmark, brought it all back. She coughed all the time and her voice was hoarse.

The children and I had flu and bronchitis for the rest of the winter. Willy was so sick that I carried him all the time. I tried to sing him to sleep in my arms, but I developed rheumatism such that I couldn't lift my arms. It lasted all winter.

In the summer we were lucky enough to find a very nice little apartment on Colombo Road. We live there still. It is divided into two flats; we live on the bottom and Mrs. Holmberg and Dorothy live above us. It is very easy to heat when there's any coal. Coal became so scarce that during last winter ('44–45) it practically disappeared, except a very little for cooking, at $100,000 a ton. Living through a North China winter in a house with no heating is something I don't like to remember. We wore padded Chinese clothes— long pants, gowns, shoes—everything padded. I wore a fur coat on top of that even in the house. And we never had any hot water. Our stove never got hot enough to heat the tank. Soap, even the worst, and it was all bad, cost around $200 a cake. So you can imagine how clean we were. Just about like the Mongols.

Nini began going to Chinese school during the occupation but Ellen, who was just approaching school age, did not get to start. She recalled later that both parents taught her at home. Her mother read her stories in English and her father began teaching her Chinese characters with brush. There was a field next to the house which gave them many opportunities for play. Ellen remembered, "My father didn't have a job so he was more at home then. We liked to play in the mud. He would make ditches and run water through the mud, like little water works. We played with the neighborhood kids, cops and robbers, adventure exploring, and especially catching grasshoppers. There were masses of grasshoppers, waves of them. They destroyed everything and darkened the sky. We played doctor and operated on them and found they had worms in their stomachs."

Our own money was gone by the end of 1942. It was impossible for F. C. to get any work unless he worked for the Japanese which, of course, we never considered for a moment. Later on, near the end of the war, he was able to get work with a conservation bureau, but up till then there was nothing to do but borrow where and what we could. We had some awfully good friends. Most of our friends though had gone to the interior. Of course, F. C. couldn't go and leave me and the children, not knowing what the Japanese might do to us. If my face were not so long and my nose so big, I might have gotten by, but there was no disguising my face!

There was no such thing as being careful with our diet. We had to eat whatever we could get. The cook had left because we could not pay him and there was no food. Sometimes I tried to cook myself but I wasn't strong enough. If I tried to do any kind of work that made me too tired I started running a temperature and had to go to bed. I was so afraid of getting T.B., because there was much of it here. We ground whole wheat and boiled it into porridge. We ate a lot of that. The flour was rancid but we ate it anyway, even with bugs in it. The children discovered that wild wheat grew in the field behind the house and Ellen got sick from eating too much.

F. C. and the children stood it all physically much better than I did. I just held on by the skin of my teeth. I began losing my hair. Last year in the spring my eyes just went to pieces, I think from lack of proper nourishment and vitamins. I couldn't read a word for three months and had to keep my eyes bandaged for several hours a day. I steamed liver in a jar and drank the juice with ginseng. It tasted like something the donkey made, but when I began taking that liver tonic and liver pills, my eyes got all right and I felt better in every way.

There were many epidemics of cholera, typhoid, and typhus. The children came through it all surprisingly well. They all had whooping cough at the same time. It developed into serious asthma for Nini. Last spring Nini had jaundice and an operation for chronic appendicitis. Willy had measles. Last year Ellen had typhoid for seven weeks. One day she went with Amah to get the rationed grain. It was hot and they had to wait in the heat for a long time while numbers were called out. Ellen complained of a headache and wanted to go back home but Amah would not let her leave. When she came back, she went straight to bed. I knew something was wrong then. She had a fever and was delirious. I was so weak during that time, I usually slept with her. We had no particular medicine. When I tried to brush her hair, her hair began to fall out and I had to cut it short.

The only official news the Lius had was from the *Peking Chronicle*, a Japanese controlled newspaper. It reported the Japanese victories which came in rapid succession—Guam, Wake, Hong Kong, and then Singapore. A large sign posted on the Empire Theatre read: "Singapore has surrendered!" The devastating news of Allied defeats was blasted from loudspeakers with strident militaristic music. Grace threw the newspaper down and stomped on it, yelling that it was lying. She never lost hope of the eventual Allied victory, but the wait seemed so endlessly long. The only scraps of hopeful news she could get were over somebody's hidden radio. News of the victory at Midway spread rapidly from person to person.

The "grapevine" was the usual means of hearing what was happening inside China. News of anti-Japanese activities in the countryside was smuggled like contraband into the city. Occasional fire between Japanese and the Communist Eighth Route Army could be heard just outside the city. Friends came by and brought news or F. C. took walks and spoke with others. In this way, the Lius were never completely cut off.

In 1944 Grace began teaching English in her home for income. Students were plentiful because the Japanese did not allow English to be taught in the schools. Most of her students were school-age but some were professionals or housewives who wanted to keep up their skills. She taught seven or eight hours a day when her strength permitted. Several of Grace's pupils, high school and college boys, escaped to the Interior. One student that she was particularly fond of disappeared one day. She worried sick about him. Years later, this student returned and told her that he had joined the resistance.

Another young man who came to the Lius frequently was overjoyed when he discovered that Grace was an opera singer. He had always wanted to learn to sing

Western classical opera and asked her to teach him. Using the techniques that her teacher had taught her, she had some success at coaching the young tenor. William remembered Grace's music lessons: "My earliest memory is hearing my mother sing with one of her students. He brought records and played them on the Victrola. I remember him singing 'Your tiny hand's so cold' while the Victrola played *La Boheme*. I was three or four years old and I danced while they sang."

Dancing and singing were revived after the G.I.s came. Grace's letter continues:

Since the marines came we have been having a marvelous time. They all looked positively beautiful to us after the occupation. How happy we were to see Giles Brooks from home! We have enjoyed him and his friends more than we could tell, and they have kept us supplied with candy, chewing gum, cheese, Woodbury Soap, tomato and grapefruit juice and things we haven't seen for years. And how F. C. has enjoyed Camels, Chesterfields, cigars, and Edgeworth pipe tobacco, after years of smoking what smelled like burnt peanut shells and incense. There are about six boys that we know best and they have met and been entertained in the homes of several of our Chinese friends. They are making a pleasing impression on the Chinese. I am very proud of these nice American boys. Giles is very popular and gets along with everyone, men, women, and children—and the way he is picking up Chinese is amazing.

I must stop before this letter gets too big. There are so many, many things I could write! I am trying to give you just a very general idea of what our situation was like, but you can be sure that we did not see the horrors of the occupation other people did. Remember I have heard nothing from any of you since 1941. Please make everybody write and tell me all that's happened.

With all my love to all of you,
Grace

Sam was the first to write back. When Grace received his letter, she was just sitting down to lunch: "I was so excited and my heart beat so fast I could hardly open it. But when I had finished reading it aloud to F. C., all appetite for lunch had vanished." After four years of silence, the news from home was both thrilling and shocking. She was delighted to learn that her brother Edward had become a war hero. He served in the Pacific and witnessed the death of the famous war correspondent Ernie Pyle on Iwo Jima, which he avenged in an act of heroism on the spot. But she was shocked to read Sam's cryptic note about her brother Robert, "just before he died on October 6." She knew nothing of how or why! And Tom—what had happened to him? Why had he left Chattanooga? And where was Mama?

By the time she wrote Sam back on December 11, her situation had improved. Both she and F. C. had jobs. Her cook and amah had returned. Food was available again, especially with supplies from Giles. But conditions in China were not going well.

The scope of the surrender was enormous. There were three million military and civilian Japanese in China. The Nationalist government was unprepared for reoccupying the vast country and had no means of moving personnel rapidly to fill positions vacated by the Japanese. The U.S. army flew Kuomintang commanders to sites to receive the surrender of the Japanese officers, but it took much longer for civilians to return. The management of utilities, banks, trains, and other essential organizations had to wait. Those assigned to leadership positions were chosen politically whether or not they had the necessary skills or knowledge. Often the same manager who had collaborated with the Japanese was retained. As the populace waited, shortages increased and inflation spiraled with two currencies in use. Grace described the dire conditions in Tientsin when she wrote to Sam on December 11, 1945:

Everything is in an awful mess. The new Mayor sent from Chungking is incompetent and stupid and too much like the old-time Chinese official. There are millions of necessary things to be done quickly and nothing is done but the silliest things such as turning some old temple into a memorial. And they have conference after conference and nothing is done but talk, talk, talk. F. C. simply can't stand that sort of thing. He is so practical and direct. He is a doer rather than a talker. I don't know how long he will stand it before he blows up. He is working for the Municipal Bureau of Sanitary Engineering now. In the Water Co. he was more or less his own boss so he is not used to waiting until some impractical official decides every little matter.

We are now waiting for Homer Lu, the legitimate managing director, to come back from the Interior and take the Water Co. over from the traitors who still have control of it. Then F. C. will be managing director and chief engineer.

I have a job too. I have been working for about two weeks at the Tientsin Transportation and Warehousing Bureau of the Chinese National Relief and Rehabilitation Administration (CNRRA). You know UNRRA, of course, the United Nations Relief and Reha-

142

bilitation Administration. The foods, medicines, and materials given China by UNRRA are distributed by CNRRA. I am English secretary to the directors and English advisor to the rest of the bureau. All the English communications go through my hands, and none leave until they have been okayed by me. I write all the important letters myself; those written by someone else I look over and correct. All of the corrected drafts of letters must have my signature before the Director will sign the typewritten copy to be sent out. Besides the letters I write a summary of letters, cables, telegrams, and reports to be translated into Chinese.

Dorothy Holmberg, the daughter of Mrs. Holmberg, who is very ill with T.B., is working with me. She is the stenographer and typist. Our boss, the director of the bureau, is a Tsing Hua (F. C.'s school) graduate of 1923. His English is not so very bad, neither is it at all good. So when he dictates to Dorothy in his Chinese-English I have to rewrite the letter in correct English. Then Dorothy types it. It's quite interesting and not hard, and I certainly like it a great deal better than teaching. It gives me a feeling of independence and importance that I really enjoy. But I don't feel good about leaving the children all day. With the cook and both amahs back, the children aren't neglected. I go home by "san-leur" (three-wheeled rickshaw) and see them at lunchtime. But sometimes I feel guilty about leaving them.

Ellen and William in relief clothes, with F. C., Fall 1945.

Nini is quite a big girl now. She lacks about an inch of being as tall as I and is a great deal fatter. She looks very much like F. C., but she also has a McCallie look. Ellen is eight now. She looks more like me. But she is a hundred times better looking than I ever was. She is really beautiful. F. C. says she looks like Mama. To my mind William looks like you [her brother Sam], although he looks distinctly Chinese with very black hair and almost black eyes. When he is well and plump he is a very good-looking little boy, but when he is thin, his ears look too big. The marines call him "Mickey Mouse."

Prices are so high now (higher than during the war) that although F. C. and I are both working we can no more than make ends meet. I will get $50,000 C.N.C.—that's $250,000 F.R.B. F. C. will get a little more maybe from the municipal job. Together we will have around a half million F.R.B. With that we can pay servants, house rent, food, milk, butter ($7,000 per lb.), but no clothes and no coal. Coal is nearly $100,000 a ton.

Nini's clothes have been handed down to Ellen and Wei-han. Mine to Nini and she has long ago worn out and outgrown my things. Nini has grown so fast I had to get her something the other day. The material for a Chinese padded gown and three yards of cotton coolie cloth to make a gown to wear over it cost me $50,000. The tailor would have been another $10,000, but one amah sews very well so she made them. She also has made padded shoes for the three children.

All these years during the winter I wore Chinese clothes, but now in the office I wear a knitted suit from 1940. It is absolutely the only thing I have left. I will be very, very pleased to get anybody's used clothes whether they fit or not. The Chinese tailors are very clever about making over old things. Everything we have has been made over out of something else.

The conflict between the Nationalists and Communists, despite the temporary wartime "united front," had not abated. From August to October 1945, the U.S. tried to mediate a settlement between the two sides, even bringing Mao Tse-tung and Chiang Kai-shek face to face, but with no success. In December 1945, President Truman sent his top negotiator, General George C. Marshall. In response to his leadership, both sides agreed to a cease-fire. A political consultative conference was convened in January 1946 in Nanking. Both sides sent high-level representatives. In addition to the Kuomintang and the Communist Party, other parties present included the Youth League, which had demonstrated for peaceful reconstruction, and the Democratic League, which advocated a centrist position of democratic reforms. The conference met January 11–31 and was widely reported in the national and international press. Basic terms were agreed upon: constitutional government, unified military, national assembly, and reduction of troops. Momentarily there was a glimmer of hope for China's future without civil war.

During this time, food prices rose daily with no central government to hold them at a reasonable rate. Prices increased fivefold between September 1945 and February 1946. The government response was to print more money, causing prices to skyrocket by May.

Grace wrote in a letter to her sister-in-law, Mary Hills, on March 8, 1946:

We're all glad they've come to some agreement. That is China's only hope. I am not a Communist and never could be, but the Kuomintang party is so corrupt that there would

144

be no hope for China if it stayed in complete control of the present government.

The food is not so bad now. We are getting plenty of very good eggs for two hundred dollars apiece. Meat, beef and pork, is plentiful at $2,600 F.R.B. a pound. Carrots, spinach, beets, Chinese cabbage, and onions are about the only vegetables. There's UNRRA flour on the market, so the bread is quite good again. Fruit is scarce and terribly expensive. The other day I paid $11,000 for four small Japanese oranges. $11,000 F.R.B. is somewhere around $1.25 U.S. Lately I have been buying black market grapefruit juice, pineapple juice, and tomato juice. It is only $5,000 or $6,000 a can and is much cheaper than buying the fruit. I think our diet has been greatly deficient in Vitamin C. Not long ago Ellen and Wei-han had a fever with swollen glands and red and bleeding gums. They got well when I gave them grapefruit, pineapple, and tomato juice.

Nearly every day some boys would drop in for lunch or supper. We spent every cent we could get hold of on food. Maybe it wasn't exactly sensible, but F. C. felt the same way I did. He never cared how many came or what it cost. He always said "Never mind, I'll get some money somewhere." And he did. We have some very good friends who have a great deal of money. I think F. C. used to tell them that it was their duty to help entertain China's allies!

Those boys had been in the Islands so long eating out of tins that anything fresh tasted wonderful. And I always had lots of vegetables and salad. You should see those boys eat carrots and spinach! They kept me pretty well supplied with coffee and sugar, and canned milk and cocoa, and they would bring the cokes along. That was just too expensive for me.

The truest sign that things had returned to "normal" was that Grace was singing again:

Besides my own parties we were invited to many others. The last one [party] we went to was a dinner dance given by the American University Club. It was held in the Astor House ballroom. General Rockey, General Worton, General Woods, and many other Marine officers were guests of honor. I sang "Carry Me Back to Old Virginny" impromptu! Paul Young, the UNRRA Director, was Master of Ceremonies and practically forced me to do it. I hadn't sung a note for several years, but he insisted so that it would have been embarrassing for me to continue refusing. There was a microphone and loudspeaker so it wasn't too bad.

We entertained nearly as many officers as we did boys, and quite often had them together. One night we came home from a dinner at the Banker's Club and brought a Major and a Lieutenant home with us. When we went into the living room there was one of the boys stretched out in a big chair sound asleep. He got up rubbing his eyes but not the least embarrassed over the "brass." A few minutes later a Private First Class came "busting" into the room with "Hi folks." They were soon all good pals.

Our apartment is small but very convenient for entertaining. The living room and dining room are together in one long room, and between the dining end and living end is quite a good-sized space for dancing. In 1941 we had a lot of beautiful things, nice carved Chinese furniture, bowls, vases, tapestries, etc., but what the Japanese didn't take the children have broken up, especially Wei-han. He is terribly hard on furniture.

Mrs. Holmberg and Dorothy live in the apartment above us. We moved here in 1942 and she has been in bed with T.B. for the last three years. She is not expected to live out the winter. A friend of mine died of it last spring. Two of F. C.'s friends died the year before. When people get T.B. here, they very rarely recover. Dorothy is twenty-three now and is getting married next week to a very nice young man in the Danish Consulate. Dorothy is exceedingly attractive. A Marine chaplain is going to marry them.

I simply must go back to visit all of you before much more time rolls on. The intention is firmly fixed in my mind, and I have hopes!

With love to everybody,

Grace

Interlude

HOW COUSINS VIEW THE WAR . . .
FROM TWO SIDES OF THE WORLD

The two cousins had met once, when Grace stayed in Chattanooga before she left for China in 1934. Both were toddlers then, Nini (Ju Lan) a year-and-a-half, and Elinor Divine, the daughter of Tom and Mary Hills, three. As toddlers would, they fought fiercely, with screams and tears, for the possession of a handcarved hickory chair that both wanted to sit in. After their "pitched battle" in which both "East and West wanted the same property," as Mary Hills characterized it, Nini was given the chair to take to China. (This is the chair that Grace accidentally left on board the Empress of Asia in her haste to change ships on her way to Tientsin.)

Nini and Elinor were teenagers as World War II came to an end. Concerned about her cousin's fate, Elinor wrote to Nini. She received the following letter in return. This letter, written in Nini's own hand (errors are included), provides a rarely seen view of the war and Japanese occupation in China from a child's perspective:

May 1946
Dear Elinor,

Thank you so much for your nice letter. I enjoyed it very much.

Now I am going to answer your questions. No, I don't remember you, but ma has told me about you and our fighting over the chair many times. I must have been very rude.

I am 13 year old, but I don't know what grade I am in, because I went to the Tientsin American school till the 3rd grade. Then in 1940 there was no more American school. Then I went to a French convent school. I learned French, English, Arithmetic, and Drawing. Then in 1942 the Japs made us move to the British concession. The house we moved into was a 17 roomed house not counting the servant quartars. Then I went to a chinese school. I had never been to a chinese school before, so I went to the 2 grade. Now I am in

147

the 6 grade. I am not in school now. I stoped in June 1945. I will go back next term. At that time all the schools were so dirty and full of flies and in the winter there was no heat besides 90 percent of the children had T.B. 5 of my classmates have already died of it.

All we learned was Japanese propaganda. They told us that the Americans were trying to invade china and make all the chinese into slaves. So Japan had sent her Army and Navy to help china because Japan like the chinese so much; and the Americans were so bad, oh dear, the Americans loved to cut off children's heads off and some of the Americans had two horns and oh yes the Japanese were our brothers. Oh they told such funny stories most of the stories sounded like fairy tales. We had to lea[r]n Japanese we all dint like it, so we all flunked in it, and the teacher dint care if we passed or not.

A chinese school is completely different from a foreign school. In China you don't read your lessons you sing them. We have to memorize all our lessons. I can memorize most of the books I have studied. I have not studied algebra yet, but we will have it next year. Besides arithmetic, I am learning how to use the chinese Abacus. When you use it you don't have to think. It is very convenient. My name in chinese looks like this [symbol]. Ellen's means Lovely Lotus.

I don't think you have seen a real Jap. I have seen them kill two people. One was a old man he could not understand what the Jap was talking about then the Jap got so mad he pushed the old man against a electric barbed wire and the old man fell down dead. The other was a a little girl about 8 years old. The Jap hit her right on the forehead she died also. It made me so angry I felt sick I wanted to pull his eyes out.

During the war there were lots of No. 8s. They have blown up many Jap factorys and Ammunition dumps. No. 8 means chinese guerrillas [Eighth Route Army].

I am 4 feet 11 1/2. You must be very tall. I have dark brown hair, dark brown chinese eyes, high cheek bones, a round face now you know what I look like.

My sister is 8 year old. My brother is 4 he will be 5 this May. I have a dog and a cat. Ma just bought me a pair of new shoes it cost $1,600 CNC. Dont you think that is very expensive?

Ma has been in china so long and she still can't speak much chinese. Even some of the marines we know can speak better than ma can. She says chinese is the hardest language to learn. The way you speak it the way you write it are not the same.

Tientsin is noting to look at. Its just a mud hole. Peking and Pei To Ho are beautiful places. I don't know any foreign children because ma says they are not nice people. all my friend are chinese.

I am glad you went to Florida and had a nice time. I hope everybody is well now. Hope you will write again.

With love, Ju Lan Liu

P.S. Please excuse my spelling—it is horrible.

P.S.S. Please don't use the address I wrote on the envelope its the old one. The new one is: 109 Chang Teh Road, 10th District, Tientsin, China

Grace had addressed her first letter after the war to Tom because she thought he was the most likely of her brothers to still be in the same place. But during the war, Tom had been offered a job with Holsten Ordinance Works in Kingsport, Tennessee, and then was transferred to the Tennessee Eastman Company, which was under contract with the federal government. He lived in Knoxville while he waited for quarters to be available at Oak Ridge, about twenty miles from Knoxville.

It was not known until after the war what Oak Ridge was. After the dropping of the atomic bomb on Hiroshima and, a few days later, on Nagasaki, the Manhattan Project was revealed. The top-secret operation begun in October 1941 was located in three huge complexes in remote parts of the country—Los Alamos, New Mexico; Richland, Washington; and Oak Ridge, Tennessee. Ninety-two square miles of ridge and valley woodlands of the Appalachian foothills was acquired as part of the Manhattan Engineering District.

A "temporary" town was carved out of red clay along the Clinch River in East Tennessee in 1942 to separate uranium in quantities large enough to make an atomic bomb. Tom was transferred there before the war was over but Elinor and the rest of the family did not move to Oak Ridge until after the war. Elinor's next letter to Nini includes some references to life in Oak Ridge, but more importantly it describes an American teenager's point of view after the war:

May 27, 1946

Dear Ju Lan,

I received your letter about a week ago and enjoyed it so much! The whole family read it and thought it was very *interesting!*

There are a lot of things I could tell you and I hardly know where to start! I think I will tell you something about my school. My school is rather new. It wasn't here last year but was just recently built. The buildings are mostly temporary because they are not going to be used very long. This week we are having lots of exams and things which I dread!!

Do you ever go swimming? I don't guess you have been since the war. That is one of our chief sports. I just love to swim! We also play tennis but we only have one racquet between the three of us, so that makes it pretty rare that we play.

The weather is very warm now. We had an early spring. It started getting very warm in February and has stayed that way on up.

(June 7th) June 4 was my birthday. I'm now fifteen. I got out of school on June 5 and we don't have to go back til September. I've been having a lot of fun since. Mother let me sleep till nine o'clock this morning but she says that I'll have to get up earlier hereafter because she doesn't want to fix two breakfasts.

Here in Oak Ridge all the houses are very much alike. Our house is just about the largest size they have, but even it isn't large enough! Grandma Juie [Julia Divine, Grace's mother, usually stayed with her sons Tom or Sam] has to stay in a little closet-like affair. My sister and I stay in the same room. Our kitchen is very nice and convenient, and there is a "utility room" where we do our washing.

You described yourself, so I will just describe myself. As you know, I am 5' 6." But I am not considered horribly tall here because lots of the girls are about my height. Most people say I look like Daddy, but I guess you don't know what Daddy looks like!! Anyway, I'm a little thin, my hair is dark brown and my eyes are blue. Maybe I can find a picture of me somewhere.

Oh, yes! I must tell you about our new kitty. The other day when I got home from school, Daddy was here. I asked him why he was home so early and he said, "I brought a little wild cat home," (in a very humorous tone). He pushed back the sofa and showed me a kitty. It was very cute. Daddy said that he found him at the office and took a fancy to it and chased it all around even though his employees were looking a little shocked. At any rate, he brought the kitty home. It is still too scared to come to us, and it won't eat unless our other kitty is around. I hope it gets tamer soon.

Do you have a radio? Do you ever hear any American Programs? We listen pretty often—mostly to dance music. I am now trying to learn how to jitterbug.

(June 9) Our little new cat disappeared. I guess it ran away. I can't think of anything else right now so I think I shall close.

Love,

Elinor

10

CHINA'S CIVIL WAR

THE FIRST months after the war were exhilarating. Letters and packages poured from Tennessee to Tientsin. But it was also a difficult time. Grace's eyes had been opened. The protected boundaries of her former life, which had once kept her separate from China's fate, had eroded during the occupation. She now saw China in a way that most foreigners did not. The story she had to tell was not one that the folks at home or the rest of the Western world, for that matter, wanted to hear.

"People then didn't want to hear what they didn't want to hear," was Grace's comment about the news correspondents that came to China to report on the conditions of the Far East.

One of those reporters, the young Seymour Topping, later became managing editor of the *New York Times*. When the young reporter arrived in Tientsin in 1946, he was invited to her home with a group of marines and other guests. "Oh, he made me so mad," Grace recalled in an interview. "He came to dinner and was asking everybody all sorts of questions. After he asked me a few questions, I could tell he didn't like the answers. He didn't say he didn't like them, but I saw that he didn't listen to what I said. I tried to tell him about the goings-on, what it had been like and what it was still like. He would turn and talk to someone else. He simply wouldn't listen, so I just shut up."

Years later Grace read Topping's book, *Journey Between Two Chinas*: "I didn't agree with everything he said, but he said it in such a way that I could accept his point of view. I wrote to him all the things I liked about it. I reminded him of our earlier encounter in China in '46. I said that I thought he was very arrogant and pig-headed because he wouldn't listen to me. But I read his book twice and think he did a wonderful job, and he wrote me back a very nice letter."

Beginning on April 9, 1946, Grace wrote three letters in a row over a ten-day period to her brother Sam. She was unable to mail the first two before some frightening things began to happen to F. C., which she described in the third letter and mailed them all together. She typed the letters at work on CNRRA stationery. When she started the first letter, the dinner parties were still in full swing. One hilarious episode was described to her brother, whom she knew would enjoy the humor of it. She was planning a dinner party for Major Snell, a Sanitary Engineer sent by the Army through UNRRA to work with F. C. on the sanitation problems of the city. She didn't get off work until six o'clock so she and Sun, the cook, had planned a simple buffet supper that could be prepared ahead.

But everything refused to go according to schedule—the stove wouldn't work, and the coal wouldn't burn. Sun's bicycle broke and he had to market on foot. So I left the office early and hurried home to help. We were having potato salad with celery, carrots, and beets, salmon salad (the salmon was a gift of a Marine), meat loaf sandwiches, bacon and lettuce sandwiches, cottage cheese and peanut sandwiches. I had ordered from the Victoria Cafe a lovely big cream cake, half-chocolate and half-white—It was beautifully decorated and tasted delicious. It cost $9,000 C.N.C., but that's cheaper than I could have made one, and what a lot of trouble it saved. We had American coffee and American sugar (also from the Marines).

When I got home I rushed like mad making the salmon salad, and oh yes, I forgot, the deviled eggs. Then I was going to mix some cocktails (very, very mild). I had some grapefruit juice, crushed pineapple, and about one-third of a bottle of gin (also presents).

But a little after six, a British couple came to call. They had been in the concentration camp at Wei Hsien and I hadn't seen them for several years, so of course, I had to drop everything and sit down and visit with them.

I prayed for F. C. to come quickly so I could dress and get all the last-minute things ready. He's very rarely later than six-thirty, but at seven he still hadn't come and the people wouldn't go and my supper guests were supposed to come between seven and seven-thirty. Finally when I was desperate I asked them to stay for supper. They had another engagement for the evening, so they gave up waiting for F. C. and left. But their staying so long had made me so nervous. I could do nothing right.

I mixed cocktails and dressed at the same time all over the house, one amah carrying my blouse, and the other putting on my shoes, while I poured the things together and mixed and stirred and tasted! I was already in a dither, and tasting the cocktails didn't make me any steadier. I am not used to drinking anything alcoholic, so I am easily influenced. Fortunately, all of the guests were late as well as F. C.

The party was quite a success and everybody had a good time, even the children and the dog and cat. Our flat is so small there's not place to stick the children away, so they are always underfoot.

Not only packages, but people from home made life constantly interesting.

Wednesday evening F. C. came home bringing a big six-foot, barn-door-shouldered boy. He said, "Here's another Marine from Chattanooga and he's graduated from McCallie School!" He had a letter from Anne McCallie telling him to look for F. C. at the Water Works. He had gone to the British Water Works and they gave him F. C.'s telephone number, so F. C. went by his barracks and picked him up and brought him home. His name is Jimmie Lail, and he's only eighteen, although he weighs 192 lbs. He's a very nice, sweet boy. Sunday night F. C., Ju Lan, and I took him out to a Chinese restaurant to eat Chinese food for the first time.

Ju Lan and I had a very exciting time trying on the clothes. I recognized the GPS uniforms immediately. They were just the same as when I wore them. Ellen could wear two of them and Nini the others. The white one and the turquoise one fit me exactly and I wore them to the office.

All the other skirts and sweaters fit Nini perfectly. But I can wear the green and white checked dress. It's a very good style for a very skinny person. It's disguising. It needs to be made tighter around the waist and the sleeves need to be shortened, but I couldn't wait to wear it so I just pinned it. How marvelous to have on something I haven't worn every day for the last five years! In fact, I have it on in the office now. I make all sorts of excuses to walk around the office to show it off. And I'm wearing it to a party tonight.

McCallie graduate Jimmy Lail came to visit the Lius in 1946. Bottom, the cover of the pocket guidebook Marines were issued.

153

A party for the Marines at Homer Lu's house. F. C. is second from left; Homer Lu is third from left.

The party was at Homer Lu's big house. Among his guests were high-ups in the Kuomintang who were involved in resettling Tientsin. With one exception—a foreboding reference to F. C.'s health—Grace's letter from the next day shows how much things had improved:

I went to a lovely party in the green-checked dress last night. Among the guests were the head of the Chinese Secret Service, who tends to the traitors, and Lieut. Gen. Yen of the 94th Army stationed in Tientsin. He brought a beautiful movie actress. After dinner she sang and I sang, and then there was dancing. I have danced so much since the Marines came that I am quite expert. I can tango, waltz, rumba, and most everything.

Last week I received a package containing a bottle of capsules. I don't know who sent it. The capsules are filled with a yellow powder which I think must contain vitamins. The bottle doesn't say what it is, just to take two after each meal. I have taken not half a bottle

Jimmy Lail took this photo of the Liu children, 1946.

yet and I feel very much stronger and more energetic. Please tell whoever sent it to kindly send me some more. It's doing me so much good. I was happy to get the wonderful Pet milk. It's been many a year since I've seen that.

The children are getting along much better now. Ju Lan is getting fat, and Ellen and Wei-han look brown and rosy. But F. C. who all during that last four years never got sick, now has developed some peculiar trouble. His left arm has gotten weak and slightly numb and causes him a great deal of annoyance.

My salary has been raised. I now get—at least, I got for March—$97,000 CNC. That's around $50 US. For April I will get $122,000 because the cost of living keeps going steadily up. F. C. is still at the Sanitation Bureau. The Water Works has not been taken over yet [with Kuomintang management]. Our crooked mayor is holding ev-

erything up. But it can't be very long now or there'll be no hot water this summer.

About my coming home—of course you must know how crazy I am to come, and as soon as possible. But F. C. must get firmly established in the Water Works first, get a strong hold on it, and the management firmly in his hands. Anyway, I am determined not to wait too long to come. I have my passport ready.

Please tell Mama or whoever to send me some more of those capsules.

Homer Lu finally returned from the Interior and resumed his position at the Water Works. F. C. rejoined him there and negotiations began to combine the Tientsin Water Works with the former British water company. However, before F. C. could get it properly organized with his own men again, he was faced with an intolerable situation.

The Tientsin Water Works had delayed in removing those who had collaborated with the Japanese. This inaction outraged the local citizens who had suffered under these "puppets." The re-occupation of the country was taking place in a way that denied the suffering that had been endured.

F. C. had hoped that Homer Lu would set the situation straight, but instead, Homer Lu delayed taking any action to clean house. Nini described Homer Lu's betrayal of F. C. and Grace's outrage:

> My father considered Homer Lu like a friend and he was always very loyal to friends. He would look after friends and give them whatever they needed in time of need. He treated Homer Lu like a friend even after he returned, at least at first. Homer Lu was the seventh child and was called Lu the seventh. As I can remember, his father had been an official at the time of the last emperor. How he got the money I don't know, but he was very rich. He had a wife who was quite educated, but he bought concubines whenever there was a famine. He bought them with flour and grain and didn't have to pay a lot.
>
> When the Japanese came to arrest Homer Lu, Jane, his concubine, wept and wailed and diverted the Japanese long enough for him to make a good escape. He fled to Chungking like a lot of rich Chinese because it was KMT territory. Grace liked her very much and gave her a name because she had no name. She called her "Jane" because she thought it was a

strong name, like Jane Austen. Jane was very loyal to Homer Lu and all through the Japanese occupation, she took care of his big house, kept his business going, brought up his children by his former wife, and took care of his half-brother.

When Homer Lu came back from Chungking, he brought along a new wife. He thought he would just return and take up as usual, but Jane would have nothing to do with it. Grace was disgusted with him at this time, but my father remained loyal to him. When Homer Lu returned he sided with those who had collaborated with the Japanese against F. C.

When father became ill, Homer Lu did not come to see my father or show any concern. We had no savings and no money coming in so my father asked to borrow some from Homer Lu. Then, while my father was down, Homer Lu asked for the money back. My mother was so angry that she got the money from someone else, took it over to his house during a party and threw it in his face and called him a skunk.

Grace's third letter to Sam in April 1946 explained why the first two were not mailed earlier. Her husband's sudden failing health reflected the stress that the family and, indeed, the nation were undergoing.

April 19, 1946
Dear Sam,

I haven't had a chance to get this letter mailed yet. I've been so worried and busy for the last week I haven't had time to tend to it.

Earlier I mentioned F. C.'s arm. It has turned out to be more serious than we thought. Not only his arm, but his shoulder and neck muscles on the left side start jumping when he gets the least bit excited or upset. Fortunately his blood pressure is normal (110) otherwise it would be exceedingly dangerous. We have fine doctors. Three of them are very intimate friends and know our circumstances. One is a nerve specialist. They all agreed that he smokes entirely too much. And they all said no tobacco, no alcohol, no coffee, no tea, no irritating spices, hot peppers, etc. He has to have injections of Thiamine chloride (B1) and other vitamins. The doctors say he must have a complete rest. He has been in bed a week now and his general condition is better. He looks more rested and his color is better. But he is very difficult to manage. He's so impatient. He's never been sick before and he doesn't know how to take it calmly and philosophically.

For the last two months he's been under a terrific nervous strain over this maddening, crooked Water Company business. If the mayor had been an honest official, and if Homer Lu hadn't been stupid and cowardly, one week could have seen the whole business finished. That's what everybody expected. But instead, this incomprehensible delay until a perfectly clear-cut, straightforward situation has become so muddied and ambiguous that the accuser has become the accused and the innocent has become guilty, so that finally a compromise must be effected.

Homer Lu is the former managing director appointed by the Government to take the Water Company from Ray Chang and Franklyn Koo, the two managers who collaborated with the Japanese and kicked F. C. out. They are the two who came personally with a group of Japanese up into our apartment in January '42, and ordered us out of the place. Naturally, everybody expected that when the Chinese National Government officials returned to Tientsin, people like that would be made very short work of. And they themselves expected it, too; but week after week passed by and nothing was done, giving the traitors time to take heart and get to the corrupt Kuomintang Government officials with their money and lavish entertainment.

Homer Lu has been back in Tientsin nearly two months. If he were a man of some character and courage, the situation would have been quickly settled. But he is too much the rich playboy with plenty of physical courage but no moral courage. By playing around and dilly-dallying because he hates to face a disagreeable task, he has given his enemies time to accuse him of corruption and using company funds. Fortunately, F. C. had saved at considerable risk a secret government document that proves Homer innocent of any misappropriation of company money.

However, Homer has had to compromise. The same corrupt directors are to stay on the Board, and Franklyn Koo is to keep his position of deputy managing director. The traitors are not only not being punished but are having their faces saved. And the mayor and director of public utilities will get a rake-off from both sides.

After four years of humiliation and poverty and suffering for the sake of a principle, to be still further humiliated by being compelled to go back to work under Franklyn Koo was more than F. C. could take calmly.

Sam, you can't imagine how corrupt the officials of the National (Kuomintang) Government are—from the bottom to the top, especially the top. The good men have no chance.

A capable, honest, straightforward man is something to be feared by the powers that be. Honesty is not the best policy. Dishonesty definitely pays much better. Efficiency gets you nowhere. In fact, to do things efficiently and with expedition is bad form. It is much better to delay and beat around the bush, to give everybody time to line his pockets—that is everybody who is high up enough to have access to the Government pocketbook.

And then there's the red tape! I know all Governments are more or less bound up in red tape, but for really expertly hampering all progress and completely discouraging any initiative and ability, Chinese red tape could make that of the Western governments commit hari-kari for shame. I work in a Government office and I know. Corruption, stupidity, inefficiency, and red tape strangle every effort for the good of the people and the country.

Lately I have read articles in the Reader's Digest *and* Life *by Congressman Judd, Henry Luce, and others whose names I have forgotten. And when they praise what the Kuomintang (Nationalist) government has done for China I could laugh. The present government will never be democratic. The Kuomintang officials who've been in power so long do not believe in democracy. Chiang's "Blue Shirts" are just like Hitler's "Brown Shirts," his secret police just like the Gestapo.*

The Kuomintang propaganda that is pouring from the newspapers, movies, and radio now is sickeningly like the Japanese and German propaganda we listened to for eight years. The U.S. newspaper correspondents who come out here and travel from place to place and stay a few days or a few weeks or even a few years, never really see the true picture. They are always on the outside and see only what they are allowed to see. I am on the inside and know what I am talking about.

I know of so many of F. C.'s friends, Tsing Hua schoolmates, graduates of American universities, as well-trained, capable, efficient a group of men as you could find in any country in the world, that are held down in mediocre positions because they would be a threat to those in authority. The present government would prefer to engage expensive foreign technicians than use the skills of educated Chinese.

I saw it happen right here in our office [CNRRA]. Our director was a capable and honest man with plenty of common sense, who could have run this Bureau with some degree of efficiency if he had been allowed to. But after two weeks, he was demoted to deputy director from director. No one knows why. And a stupid stickler for form and red tape was put over him as director! He is probably some Government "big-shot's" nephew or cousin.

Consequently, our whole outfit is a joke. There are a hundred people and five depart-

158

ments in the Bureau, and I don't think anybody knows what's going on. In the beginning, all English correspondence was kept together in one file. But the director decided it would be better for each department to keep whatever English letters concerned the affairs of each; and as some letters refer to several departments, nobody can decide where they belong. Consequently, when a certain letter is wanted, the whole office has to be turned upside down.

Personally I don't mind in the least running around all over the place to track down a letter I have to answer. But it certainly isn't efficient or the way an office should be run. Not long ago, after hunting for a letter for two days, I went to the director's office and told him he had better hire a detective to run the letter down, that I had done my best and I couldn't find it—he's such a stupid, pompous fool! I have talked to him very straight several times about the stupid time-wasting way the letters were handled, but it doesn't do any good. He is very nice and polite to me, but it just goes over his head and makes no impression. The deputy director could run the place with half the people and a hundred times the efficiency. So I don't bother about it anymore. When a letter finally comes to me, I write it or correct it and if it's three weeks late it's not my fault.

I think the United States will make a great mistake if they give too much money to help China without insisting upon and seeing to a complete revolution in the present National Government set-up. It is not democratic, doesn't want to be, and doesn't intend to be! It is completely in the grip of the Kuomintang party and the Kuomintang party is made up of and ruled by a certain class and type of Chinese, irrevocably hostile to any kind of true democracy. That type includes the big landowners, the big merchants, the militarists, and the old official type that ruled under the Manchus.

To them, a man's being capable, honest, and straightforward, and believing in methods that are not devious, circuitous, and obscure, mark him as an enemy. There is no place in Chinese officialdom for the qualities one usually thinks of as admirable.

A smooth, charming social manner, a glib tongue, the knack of suavely turning one's coat, absolute unscrupulousness about pocketing high sums of other peoples' money, and above all, the ability to out-crook the other crooks—these are attributes that make for success. Sometimes an honest man, if he is stupid enough, can get by very well, as the cleverer crooks can use him.

These people who control the present Chinese National Government will fight for the old order, whereby they can continue to amass their great fortunes, with every means in their power.

That is the reason they are in such deadly fear of the Chinese Communists. That is why they hated the Communists worse than they did the Japanese, and kept 80,000 troops, that might have been fighting the Japs, blockading the Communist territory.

I am not a Communist. I don't want to see China become Communist. At least I haven't hitherto. But all during those years when we were so completely under the Japanese fist and so cut off from all communication with the outside world, the Pa Lu (Eighth Route Army) was our only comfort. We knew they were not far away. We often heard fighting, and many young high school and university boys threatened with conscription by the Japanese disappeared into the country and were helped to escape into Free China by the Pa Lu. Several of my own pupils escaped in that way.

All during the last four years we have have taken comfort in the thought that somebody was nearby fighting for us. The Communists held the countryside so that the Japanese could never get the firm hold on North China they had on Manchuria. And they had practically nothing to fight with. Their best and most modern equipment was what they had captured from the Japanese. They got none of the American supplies sent to China. They lived so poor, not only the soldiers but the officers, even their highest officials.

When you compare the way the high Kuomintang officials live with their huge fortunes safely locked up in foreign banks, their palaces and motor cars, their selfishness, corruption, and hypocrisy, with the simple hardworking life of the Communists, you can see how we think they have been very badly treated since the end of the war. They were given no face, allowed no credit, for their eight years of fighting the Japanese. They were given no share in the victory. Their efforts and sacrifices were ignored. And Generalissimo Chiang asked for the Marines to come in and hold North China for the Kuomintang Government. They not only get no credit for all their years of fighting and no acknowledgement of their part in the war, but the Marines and the Nationalist Army actually used the Japanese to fight them and guard the railroads against them.

That is a disgrace to the Chinese Government. I hope General Marshall will not be fooled by the Chinese charming manners and delicious food and lavish entertainment that is dished out to him.

I just now looked at the clock. It's time to go home. I certainly did not intend to write a whole letter on Chinese politics; but I had nothing to do in the office this afternoon and as I was rather steamed up over this question I just took it out on you. I could write pages and pages more. I wish I were an American newspaper woman for a while and knew all I know.

The presence of the Americans, which should have helped the situation, was actually making it worse. In order not to reinforce the Communists, the U.S. forces sided with the KMT and often found themselves backing up the Chinese who had collaborated with the Japanese. Grace found such a situation intolerable. She read in the newspaper that one of the collaborators who had taken over the Water Works and kicked F. C. out was being placed in a position of leadership over the whole city. She couldn't tolerate it any longer. In a conversation toward the end of her life, she recalled what she had done:

I got so mad I didn't know what to do. So I went to the American Consulate and told the American Consul that I knew that man, that I had known him a long time, and knew he was a Japanese puppet, and I did not think it right that the Chinese people should be placed under such a person.

He replied apologetically, "Well, those things happen. Even in Europe, they had to use puppets . . . and well, what can we do? This is a matter of the internal affairs of the Chinese. As Americans we have no right simply to say what they should do."

I said, "Well, you know quite well, Mr. _____ that whatever you say goes. That if you tell this minister, they have to do it. You cannot fool me if you say, 'Oh, now it's the Chinese and they have to do as they please; we have nothing to say.' I know that's not so!"

"Well, we . . . " he hemmed and hawed. He said he didn't want to interfere in the city; it would get him in trouble.

And I said, "All right. I don't want to get anyone into trouble. But I'm not going to put up with this. I'm an American citizen and I know some people in Washington and I will write to them. I will write to Washington and I will complain. I will say what's going on here!"

"No, no, no, no. Don't do that. Don't do that. No, no. That's . . . that's . . . we'll think it over, and we'll work it out somehow or other," he stammered.

I replied, "Well, I don't mind writing at all!" and I left.

Then I saw a few days later in the paper that Mr. Chang had been replaced by someone, maybe just as bad—but I had won my point.

One of the young men working in the Consulate later told me, "I remember so well you laying down the law to the Consul General . . . We could hear you all over the place. The rooms had only temporary partitions so the whole office could hear. Everyone stopped and listened and were just about to die laughing."

I was stunned for I had no idea anyone had heard me.

BY AUGUST 1946, the political climate had changed dramatically. The agreements reached in the consultative conference earlier in the year had come to naught. Chiang Kai-shek had convened a national assembly as agreed upon but without democratic participation. Instead of building a coalition with the Communists, he had resumed fighting them. General Marshall succeeded in getting both sides to agree to another cease-fire in June 1946, but Chiang prepared for an attack on the Communists troops in Manchuria, while the Communists reorganized their forces. Both sides were preparing to fight, not talk.

Popular Chinese sentiment began to turn against the American presence. In Tientsin, student demonstrators protested against the American armed forces after an American G.I. raped a young girl. Grace observed that the G.I.s being sent to China in 1947 were different from those who first came after the war.

The first combat troops that came into Tientsin knew what they were fighting for. They just came from the islands where they had been fighting the Japanese. But they were taken out in December [1945] and sent home and a new batch was sent in. They did that two or three times. As new ones came in, they changed. They weren't combat troops; they hadn't fought. They didn't know really what the World War was about. They treated China like a conquered country. They treated the Chinese like the old colonialists had. So they got to be very unpopular. At first, they were greeted like liberators and welcomed, everybody entertained them. They were more concerned about the condition of the people. On the whole they were older men. But when the later batch arrived, they were no longer liberating us from the Japanese, instead they were holding off the PLA so that the KMT could come and take control. They were younger, new recruits, and they didn't have a mutual rapport with the people. They acted like conquerors.

There was a party given by one of F. C.'s classmates after the KMT had come back. There were some American officers there and some other Chinese. One of these American officers began to talk about how the Red Army hadn't done anything to help the KMT during the war. I was so angry. I said, "That's not true at all. The KMT ran away."

"They did not run away," he said. I told him that no KMT army helped us in the Japanese occupation. The Communists were the only ones who fought the Japanese and he shouldn't be fighting them now. He started saying that wasn't true. I replied, "You weren't here, we were." It started getting very hot. We almost had a fight, right there at the party. My husband was getting angry, too. He turned absolutely white and I thought we had better quit.

Grace began writing a letter to her aunt Margaret Ellen McCallie in June but did not mail it until August. Aunt Ellen had stayed in touch with Grace off and on since she had first accompanied her to New York on the train. Her own Ellen was nine and had been to school only one year, due to the Japanese occupation, the disorganization of the schools, and the fact that she had typhoid the previous fall and was unable to start. She and William were only one grade apart and started in a Chinese school.

By August, school was approaching. Her school teacher aunt lent a sympathetic ear to what Grace was experiencing in China.

August 1, 1946
Dear Aunt Ellen,

I started this letter in another room and at another desk, and when the directors [CNRRA] suddenly decided to move me I put this in a book and gathered up my belongings and moved. And I've been thinking all this time that this letter had long been on its way to you. You see, I'm still the same absentminded creature I always was, but I'm a great deal more energetic and useful. I am feeling quite well now and I've gained ten pounds, which makes me all of ninety.

We can get fresh milk now and I'm hoping to put on at least another fifteen pounds. The food situation now is not so bad. We can always get some kind of meat. The eggs have a queer taste but the vegetables are plentiful and not bad. And thanks to UNRRA we have decent flour. Now I can hardly bring myself to believe that I actually ate the awful bread made from that ancient, musty, wormy, and bitter flour.

I really don't know anything that's not expensive. Even for people with American money the cost of living is exceedingly high. We are spending over one million dollars C.N.C. a month. Apples are $13,000 a pound. Prices are out of all reason, and there's no *end in sight. Politically and economically, China is in a hopeless mess. Under the present government and its blind and selfish leaders there is no hope.*

And why should the American government back up with military and financial help a political party and a system that is crushing the Chinese people almost beyond endurance? The corruption and selfish stupidity of this present government are making it so impossible for anyone not a clever crook to earn an adequate living—many are being driven to suicide and Communism. If the government were thoroughly cleaned out and the people given a chance to live there would be no need to maintain huge armies to fight the Communists, or to keep the American marines in North China.

The government leaders are not fighting the Communists patriotically, for the good of the country, or for the sake of the poor people, but to save their power and colossal fortunes . . . There I go! Rambling off into politics.

To get back to my family affairs—we have Jimmy Lail to dinner at least once or twice a week. We are very fond of him. His McCallie school training certainly shows. He is getting to be such a big boy—he weighs 203 pounds now. Yesterday afternoon he invited us to see his baseball team play on the Ming Yuen field. F. C. and the kids went to watch the game.

F. C. has gotten much better this last month, in spite of his hard work. When he is free, to a certain extent, from worry and uncertainty, hard work doesn't seem to hurt him.

Jimmy Lail became a regular visitor to the Liu home, and invited F. C. and the children to watch his Marine baseball team play.

I am just now trying to find schools for the children to go to in September. It's not an easy matter. Ellen and Wei-han have never been to school and Ju Lan was out the last two years because the schools were so very bad during the war. About eighty percent of the pupils had T.B. Ju Lan will be ready for middle school this fall. That's about the same as high school. All the middle schools in the concessions are crowded and dirty, so we are thinking of sending her to the Keen School far in the Chinese City. It is a Chinese girls' school run by American missionaries. I know the principal and several of the other women. Most of the teachers are Chinese and even the American teachers teach in Chinese.

It is a good place to get a Chinese education in an orderly clean environment. Many prominent Chinese send their daughters there. It is so far, though, that she will have to live in the school during the week and come home over weekends. At first, I didn't like the idea of her staying away from home at all. But F. C. is very much for it. He said he left home when he was twelve and it was good for him. Ju Lan herself is anxious to go. She is not the "mama's baby" I was. In fact, she is only like me in loving to read and being lazy and messy. She is independent, saucy, and somewhat belligerent. She loves mathematics and works arithmetic problems just for fun as one would work a crossword puzzle. And I still use my fingers to add!

Last night we had a famous guest for dinner—Major General Chia Yu Hui, the Vice-Commander of the Chinese New First Army, that fought in Burma and India and is now in Manchuria. General Chia is on furlough in Peking, but he came down to Tientsin for two days to see F. C. and me and the children. He is F. C.'s oldest and best friend. They were together in the same class in school from the time they were seven until they were twenty-two. When they went to the states and General Chia went to the University of California and F. C. went to Cornell they were separated for there first time in over fourteen years. General Chia later went to Harvard. I knew him in New York. He is here very quietly. If the papers find out then he must be entertained by the mayor and the commanders of the 94th Army stationed here. So last night there was only another Tsing Hua classmate and his wife for dinner besides General Chia and my family.

But my boss, the director of our bureau who was appointed by the government, heard he was here and before we had settled ourselves at the table he came in with his wife and concubines and five children. Fortunately they had had their dinner, and some Chinese wine and coffee kept them occupied until we finished. But with eight children and four schoolmates who were together again for the first time in ten years, and two Chinese women whose tongues clacked like typewriters, it was not a very dignified and orderly meal.

We had plum pudding for dessert—an American-canned one procured by my cook from some mysterious place where he occasionally gets other things that I don't inquire too closely about. There was enough of the pudding for everybody, even the unexpected guests. But I didn't have enough cups and saucers and spoons. The neighbors were called upon for help and the dinner came to a very successful and satisfying end.

I don't suppose it is necessary to tell you that I am just learning to type. I am using a U.S. Armed Forces self-teaching manual. It's my ambition to become a good typist in due time.

Meanwhile, the political situation in China continued to deteriorate. On August

10, 1946, President Truman wrote a letter to Chiang Kai-shek informing him that his confidence was shaken: "A China disunited and torn by civil strife could not be considered realistically as a proper place for American assistance." For the next six months letters passed between Chiang, Chou, General Marshall, and President Truman but were followed with little action on either side for conciliation.

In January 1947, General Marshall declared that his mission in China had failed. The last American troops were withdrawn. The Chinese would have to fight it out themselves.

11

THE COMMUNISTS TRIUMPH

B Y 1948 THE exodus had begun. Before the year was over, Grace, like other
foreigners in China, had to decide where her future lay.

The conflict between the Nationalists and the Communists had been brew-
ing for over twenty years, but after the removal of the Japanese and General Marshall's
failure to create a coalition government, civil war broke out in earnest. On January 4,
1948, the writer of the "Week in Review" for the *New York Times* described the conditions that prevailed in China: "The military position of the Central Government
has worsened to the point where the Nationalist Army appears to have lost the initiative on all major war fronts . . . "

Although numerically superior and better armed, the Nationalist forces became
overextended as they pushed the Communists further into Manchuria. The Communists had primarily a pre-modern army, with no air force or navy of any kind, and
equipped largely by weapons seized from the Japanese or retreating Nationalists. But
they were mobile, highly committed, and suffered few losses. By 1948, the Nationalists forces had dwindled not only from defeats but also from massive defections.
Gradually the Nationalist army lost support not only from its own ranks but from
many civilians who once supported it—the intellectuals, professionals, students, and
workers of the urban centers.

As the civil war intensified, the conditions that Grace had described in her earlier
letters grew worse. Inflation flared into fantastic proportions. One U.S. dollar brought
$200,000 Chinese and changed again in the course of an hour. In early January, after
Grace completed a twelve-day stay in the hospital for a hemorrhoid operation, she

was handed a bill for $15,000,000 C.N.C. She wrote her sister-in-law, "Sounds a lot doesn't it? But in C.N. it doesn't mean anything."

America threatened to withdraw aid if the national budget of $9 trillion in 1947 could not be contained. In January 1948 the Nationalist government projected a $90 trillion budget for only the first six months. One price control program after another was scuttled, until in November the government announced a new series of economic regulations based on "accepting inflation as a recognized fact."

The Chinese economy was collapsing while corruption, speculation, and profiteering were commonplace. Taking advantage of the general collapse of the Nationalist government, the Communist forces reorganized as the People's Liberation Army (PLA) and moved forward rapidly, attacking transportation and communication lines. They first established control in the rural areas, then gradually surrounded cities in North China.

Life for the Lius grew more difficult as the civil war intensified. Frustrated by the bureaucratic mismanagement of CNRRA, Grace had stopped working. When the Water Works managers posted accusations against F. C., he quit, and then had to be called back because so many other managerial personnel had left.

Likewise, school conditions deteriorated. With inflation changing the value of money daily, the schools required students to pay tuition with sacks of flour. On the first day of school, Ellen and William had to take a rickshaw in order to carry the sacks of flour. Facilities were inadequate and resources dwindled as the year progressed. Grace wrote in February 1948: "Their school has practically no heating and in December and January the poor children had to sit in rooms of almost Arctic temperature. Their hands were so stiff they couldn't write. The teachers would take them out occasionally and run them around the block to limber them up a little. But they, the children, didn't seem to think anything of it. They've never known a nice warm comfortable school room so they don't miss it. I am the one who suffers for them."

Mail was sporadic. Letters were lost, and boxes of relief sent from home never arrived. Instability in the postal service caused Christmas to be delayed until February.

February 19, 1948
Dear Mary Hills,

The box has finally arrived! We got the post office notice day before yesterday, and yesterday morning F. C. sent a man to get it. They, the post office, had broken the box almost entirely to pieces and opened every package. They wanted to confiscate the nylons but Mr. Wu, the man F. C. sent, had some influence and argued with them. They said if we could prove they were a gift and not for sale we could have them.

Grace, William, Ellen, and Nini, 1948.

Isn't that idiotic? I gave your letter in which you described the contents of the box to Mr. Wu and he let them read it. So F. C. brought home the spoils yesterday afternoon.

The children were terribly excited and when F. C. came in the door with the box they nearly knocked him down. I'm afraid I was almost as bad. Nini and I nearly had a fight over the nylons. We've decided to share them. They're a lovely color—all the stockings you can buy here are still the old light shades. The soap smells heavenly. I've seen it advertised in the magazines but I've never seen or smelled it in the "flesh" before—I washed my hair with the shampoo this morning and it's wonderful even in our hard, hard water. I have my hair rolled up now. We're going out to dinner tonight. I'm going to take a bath with the "heavenly" soap and I'll certainly feel like a glamour girl smelling so good!

F. C. and Wei-han and Ellen are running the little train round and round the coffee table. Wei-han is jumping up and down and they're all three screaming and yelling. The little thing really goes fast. Nini and Ellen were making dresses for the doll last night and Ellen has already put the puzzles together. They've chewed up all the chewing gum and are just now finishing the Life Savers.

On the same day that Grace wrote the above letter thanking her American family for the Christmas presents, President Truman requested $570 million in aid for China. He stipulated that it was restricted to economic purposes, not military.

As Secretary of State, George C. Marshall had, up until now, withheld support from the Nationalist Government until they "put their house in order" (report to

House Foreign Affairs Committee). His previous stand had been opposed by the Republicans in Congress and by the Kuomintang in China. Marshall himself was seen by the pro-Chiang advocates as the chief stumbling block to all-out aid for China. But on February 21, 1948, Secretary Marshall reversed his stand and urged passage of Truman's request: "The rapid deterioration of China must be checked promptly for the world's good."

The ambassador to China, Leighton Stuart, had not given up hope for a unified China. In a last desperate plea, he declared on February 22, 1948, that the "best possible solution is still a coalition government of the Kuomintang and Communists."

Two outspoken advocates for increased aid were Bullitt and Judd. William C. Bullitt was a former American ambassador to Russia. He saw China as the key to resisting Communist world conquest. On March 3, he accused the U.S. State Department of "blindness and apathy" and urged Congress to grant outright military aid to Chiang Kai-shek. Republican Congressman Judd, a former medical missionary in China, urged not only military aid but deployment of U.S. armed forces.

As the debate over aid to China was thrown into bitter partisan wrangling, Henry A. Wallace, a third-party candidate for president, running in 1948 against Democratic Truman (for restricted aid) and Republican Dewey (for all-out aid), announced that he opposed *any* U.S. aid to China: "U.S. intervention has already cost the American people four billion in dollars and the friendship of several hundred million Chinese people, victims of a civil war we prolong by our support of the dictator Chiang . . . Sending money and military supplies to bolster reactionary governments against the will of their people serves the cause of reaction and war, not democracy and peace."

These political debates were well known to Grace from U.S. news reports available in China. She wrote the following observations to her sister-in-law in her February 19th letter:

I don't wonder that the average American is completely puzzled about the situation in China. When I read the things printed in American newspaper and magazines supposed to inform the American people of the truth of conditions, I wonder if the reports about different parts of Europe are as wrong or are interpreted as wrongly as those on China. Any investigator or fact finder who comes to China and is wined and dined and lavishly entertained by a certain party or clique naturally sees everything through the eyes of that party, unless they are very wise.

I think General Marshall saw a lot of truth and that's why he is apparently holding off the aid to China. He knows too well where the aid would go and that no amount of foreign help can stop this civil war!

Bullitt and Judd talk like crazy idiots. Maybe Judd is sincere and believes what he says, but Bullitt is just making a big noise to call attention to himself. All Chinese but the one group are hoping and praying that not a cent of American money will be forthcoming to help prolong the war. A decent government is the only thing that would stop it and that means the present government would have to be completely wiped out from top to bottom, especially top. The Chinese people have been sold down the river by the worst bunch of big-time gangsters in the world. But they are nearing their end.

What's coming after nobody knows, but the majority of Chinese, and there's an awful lot of them, are on neither side of this conflict so something may be worked out.

On March 30, the U.S. Senate approved $463 million in aid for the Chinese Nationalist government.

Despite U.S. aid, by spring it was clear to those in China which way the tide was turning. Rumors abounded over what would happen when the Communists took over. People associated with Chiang Kai-shek's government made plans to exit. Others with wealth or property calculated their risks. For the professional Chinese—those who had committed themselves to China's future, those educated abroad, or those married to foreigners—the decision was particularly poignant.

Nini summarized her father's quandary:

> F. C. was very patriotic. He believed in China. During the Japanese occupation when the Kuomintang collaborated with the Japanese and the Eighth Route Army [communists] were the only ones actually fighting against the Japanese, he began to be disillusioned with the Kuomintang. The Kuomintang returned to power in late 1945 or early 1946. All those who had fled, like Homer Lu, returned and they took over everything. Those few years were just a mess, lots of inflation, money lost its value. Students began to strike.
>
> By the late 1940s he was thoroughly disillusioned with them [KMT] and began to have sympathy with the Communists. But nobody knew for

sure what they would be like. There were underground rumors and occasional reports from occupied areas, but nothing was certain. American observers in the liberated areas often came to stay at our house and told us about the other side. They said things were very different, there was no corruption, people were working, there was land reform—but of course, they always ended by saying, "but they're communists . . . "

It got to a point where people like my father had to decide. They were professionals or intellectuals, unaffiliated, but it came to a choice and the only choice for patriotic Chinese was the Communists, even though people had many misgivings, doubts, and miseducation about them.

By the end of October 1948, the U.S. consulate sent letters to all Americans in the Tientsin and Peking areas stating, "As a result . . . of Chinese Government troops' crushing defeat, the U.S. consulates in Peking and Tientsin advise all American residents with unessential duties leave while transportation facilities still are available."

After receiving the letter, Grace went to talk with Sam Yeats, the U.S. Consul in Tientsin. William recalled her conversation with F. C. when she returned, and a subsequent exchange with their friend:

**Grace, Winter
1948.**

One day I had just finished my homework and was about to ask if I could go out to play when Nini suddenly shushed me and stopped me from speaking. I then noticed that Grace was talking to F. C. She had just come home from the American Consulate.

"They told me it was time to leave, that everything would be arranged for our passage and that you would be guaranteed resettlement. But I said I had to discuss it with you. I know I don't want to be a refugee without you." Grace said.

"It is impossible. If I leave now, no one is left to protect the Water

172

Works. I have worked so hard to build it. I can't just leave it to ruin." F. C. said.

I knew that my father had fought for the Water Works. But, now, the Kuomintang were fleeing, and he feared they would blow it up if he were not there.

"But what will happen to the children?" Grace glanced over at us and we pretended not to notice.

"We don't know what is in store for them, but this is their home. I don't believe that what is coming will be worse than what they've already been through."

"Well, we survived the Japanese occupation . . . " Mother didn't say any more but I knew she was not just thinking about the war but also the years after the war.

By the fall of '48, the exodus was in full swing. Many of my friends were leaving and there was a general feeling of uneasiness. Erika Ruas and her three sons left for France. Dorothy Holmberg, her husband and their new baby came to say good-bye. Dorothy was in tears. The last time she had gone to Europe, her father had died. She did not want to go back to Europe. Her husband's company had agreed to transfer them to Japan instead. Dorothy was holding her baby tightly and cried:

"At least Japan is close. I will be so home-sick."

"I know," Grace said sympathetically. So many of her longtime friends were leaving—in fact, almost all the people she had known since coming to China.

"Aren't you leaving, Grace?" Dorothy asked.

"F. C. and I have been talking about what to do. He feels he cannot leave, not now. We will stick it out."

"But, Grace, haven't you heard the atroci-

From left, Dorothy Holmberg, Mrs. Holmberg, Bertha Lu, and Grace. This photo was taken in 1940 on the group's last trip to Peitaho. All of these friends had died or left China by 1948.

173

ties under the Communists!" Dorothy exclaimed. She had recently seen their former boss from the CNRRA, where they both had worked after the war. He had told Dorothy, and she repeated it to Grace, that he was leaving with his wives and concubines because he had heard that the Communists would take all his property and divvy up his wives.

"Dorothy," Grace laughed. "The press has been saying such things for years. But think who is behind all that. And besides, unlike our previous boss, I don't have any property and F. C. has only one wife!"

For Grace the decision was not as simple as she made it seem to Dorothy. The air was electrified with anticipation. She, too, was gripped by fear and anxiety, intertwined with many layers of complex emotions. Her husband's decision to stay was clear. Her first commitment was to him, second to her children. If he felt he must stay, then she and the children would take the risk with him. But safety was not the only issue. For herself, she dreaded the thought of being a refugee more than anything else. While working for the CNRRA, she had seen the incredible desperation of families left homeless and helpless as a result of the displacement of war. She did not want to be one of them. Furthermore, returning to Tennessee as a refugee did not seem an option to her. What would happen to them there? She was determined not to be dependent on her American family for relief. If that is what they expected when she married F. C., she was determined not to let it happen. She had survived a great deal and could survive even more.

Further, Grace had seen China suffer for so long. She hoped for China to rebuild itself, a dream she shared with her husband. It was a dream whose fulfillment had been thwarted many times and was still unfulfilled. If her husband must stay, then she wanted to see for herself what was going to happen.

Grace was assured that somehow one could survive a civil war, no matter which side was victorious. She recalled that her grandparents had faced a similar decision. In 1863 when the Union army was advancing on Chattanooga, they had to decide whether to stay or flee. They had been warned to leave and were concerned by rumors of what would transpire when the "Yankees" came. Shells screeched overhead, and their friends fled, urging them to get out before the trains stopped running. But her grandparents had stayed in Chattanooga throughout the Civil War. She had heard their story as a child, but she had never felt it so deeply as she did in 1948, facing another advancing army. Years later she found in her grandfather's memoirs the following description:

> Everything was in commotion. The excitement was deep. Citizens were leaving on every train, going South, and the very air seemed surcharged with the electric flashes of the coming storm. Great and powerful forces of the Northern army were hemming Chattanoga in on every side, and it was not known where and when the thunderbolt would fall . . . I did not intend to go one foot away from my home, but . . . we knew not what those dark days had in reserve for us . . . With fear and trembling we looked . . . to the capture of Chattanooga by a victorious army that counted those of us that were here as nothing but rebels.
>
> . . . At length came the fatal day, the ninth of September, 1863. The Confederate cavalry withdrew about nine o'clock in the morning and about ten a.m. streams of Union soldiers, the first we had seen, came pouring in. Not a child was harmed, not a woman insulted, not a man was killed. It was a triumph of civilization . . . We remembered how all through the ages . . . the capture of a city by a victorious army meant not only pillage, but death to men, outrage to women, worse than death, and the destruction of everything the conquerors could not use or carry away. But here was a peaceable occupation of a city without any violence or outrage of any kind.

BY LATE 1948 the Communists controlled most of the North China countryside surrounding Tientsin and Peking. Chiang Kai-shek, in an attempt to stop further infiltration of the Communists, declared martial law. But the Nationalist army withdrew hurriedly. In their retreat, they often destroyed property rather than leave it in Communist hands. The approaching Communist army sought to allay fears of the remaining citizens and to protect property from further destruction. They distributed circulars to local citizens in advance of their arrival in Tientsin. F. C. received the following notice. Grace saved it and later had it translated:

The Tientsin ening Journal

天 津 晚 報 英 文 版

TIENTSIN, SATURDAY, DECEMBER 11, 1948

G.Y. 2.00 per Copy

Assembly Asks Security Group To Reconsider 12 States' Membership Bids

PARIS, Dec. 9.—(USIS)—In a series of regulations approved at a plenary session on Wednesday night, the UN General Assembly called upon the Security Council to reconsider the applications of 12 nations for membership in the United Nations. Particular emphasis was placed by the Assembly on the applications which have been vetoed by the USSR, after having been approved by the required majority of the Council's members.

The assembly asked that the council review the Soviet-vetoed bids of Austria, Ceylon, Eire, Finland, Italy, Portugal and Transjordan, along with the applications of Albania, Bulgaria, Hungary, Rumania and the Mongolian People's Republic, which would get the necessary majority when brought to the Council.

Prior to voting, the Assembly heard U.S. delegate Benjamin V.

Martial Law Throughout China Declared By President Chiang

Mme. Chiang Seeing President Truman About Aid For Nanking

WASHINGTON, Dec. 9.—(USIS)—President Truman declared, in reply to questions at his press conference today, that Madame Chiang Kai-shek is coming to see him about aid for China.

He and Mrs. Truman will have China's first lady and Mrs. George C. Marshall, wife of the Secretary of State, as guests at tea on Friday afternoon. Asked whether he would have other talks with Madame Chiang, Mr. Truman said that remains to be seen.

Concerning Argentina's Foreign Minister, Juan Atilio Bramuglia, who also has an appointment with the President on intensified their study of possible emergency measures.

Thus far about 900 of more than 5,000 Americans in China have left the country in response to the Embassy warning to leave unless there were important reasons to stay.

About 30 American business and industrial concerns were represented at a meeting Monday in New York city. A State Department representative was

NANKING, Dec. 11.—(Reuter)—President Chiang Kai-shek last night declared martial law in the greater part of China still remaining under his control.

The President's order, effective immediately, is aimed presumably at checking Communist infiltration and "subversive activities" in the area and cities of Peiping, Tientsin, Tsingtao, Hankow, and Wuhu.

Areas unaffected are Taiwan and the Western Provinces of Singkiang, Sikang and Tibet.

In issuing the order, President Chiang Kai-shek acted on emergency powers granted him by the constitution.

Meanwhile, the Legislative Yuan approved Chinese Postal and Telegraph censorship measures, it was learned here.

CHINESE WAR SITUATION

The Tientsin Evening Journal, December 11, 1948.

November 1, 1948

To Executives, Technicians and Laborers:

After the liberation of Manchuria, our armies will proceed to capture Tientsin and Peiping, which are already surrounded. The time for liberation of these cities draws near, so we should offer some advice with the hope that you accept it.

Oppressed by Chiang's government, the people cannot breathe. Industry cannot flourish. The people cannot make a living. We think you have endured much suffering. Those who care not for the welfare of the people will be despised by them.

176

Final victory will be to the armies of liberation together with the people. Within the past three years we have not only firmly maintained our liberated areas, but have enlarged them. We have formed our own government based upon democratic principles. Now Peiping and Tientsin are soon to be liberated. Do not fear. Do not depart. Do not allow lawless elements to commit acts of sabotage to installations. In obeying these precepts you will not only preserve the fruits of victory but will also have had a part in the revolution.

If factories are destroyed, the workers' means of livelihood are likewise destroyed. If you should find persons destroying property, advise them to cease. If they still do not desist, find out who their leaders are, keep the list of names, and we will punish them according to the provisions of 'martial law' first promulgated October 10, 1947, and reissued November 1, 1948, after we have entered the municipalities.

The dawn of the new day is near. Maintain your factories intact.

Further instructions were included and signed by Chu Teh, Commander in Chief, North China People's Army of Liberation and Peng Teh Hwai, deputy commander.

William and Ellen in new coats, 1948.

The story of the exodus is told by William from the perspective of a young boy:

The winter of 1948 was cold and dry. I was seven years old and was in Grade Two, which made me a veteran now, after the first traumatic year of entering primary school and dealing with the nickname of the "Big Nose Boy." Since I never liked to get to school early, I walked at a slow pace noticing everything along the way. Ellen, age eleven, had gone on ahead to meet her school friends.

The Liu family, 1948. This was the last formal photo taken of the Lius before the advent of the new society.

The usual twenty-minute walk to school was dragging into half an hour. I first stopped in front of the big house across the street where the huge poplar trees were shuddering in the cold. The big tough leaves had already fallen and one could still find a few crammed in the corner where they had not been swept away. The dog wasn't barking and not a stir could be seen in the house. Well, Kong and his family have really left, I thought, remembering the times I had come here to play with my classmate under these trees. We pretended we were at sea in a pirate ship and the rustling of the poplar leaves providing the sound effects of the waves. Their silence now reminded me of the bewildering change that had been going on these past few months. Everybody had been in a stir.

"The Communists are coming!" Kong had said, his eyes as round as the black marble we used to fight over. Kong's father was a high ranking official, with a wife and two concubines, one of which was Kong's mother. "My father says they will kill all of us, even the children."

I meandered up another block and came across the compound with four buildings forming a square with a six foot wall around it. The usual hustle and bustle on this compound was muted, only a bored-looking servant at the gate. From time to time, I had been inside with Nini who often came to visit her friend. Those who lived here all belonged to the family of a Manchu prince, who came to Tientsin to live after the Emperor Pu Yi was driven from his palace in the early twenties. I wondered where they had gone. I did not ask but only nodded my head when the servant greeted me with: "Liu Shaoye (Young Master Liu) is going to school."

Then a few doors up was the home of one of Mother's best friends, Bertha, who was the widow of one of Homer Lu's brothers. We were always glad whenever Sun came in and announced that "Mistress Lu" had come to visit. Bertha was a warmhearted lady who giggled often and was dearly loved by our whole family. Now she was somewhere on the high seas. Mother could not see her off at the docks, so she had sent Sun to give Bertha two of Mother's lemon-meringue pies. Bertha also took with her two of our beautiful Persian kittens. I still had a difficult time imagining Aunt Bertha carrying two pies and two cats as she "fled" on a boat to Taiwan.

A few more steps and I could see the Min Yuan Athletic Grounds. Something strange was happening there. I saw not the athletes marching in formations, with cheering crowds in the bleachers where Daddy took us nearly every Sunday afternoon to see the soccer and baseball matches. Instead I saw soldiers milling around and guards keeping any passersby away from the various entrances to the grounds. Although I was curious, it was getting late and I quickened my steps to our school another block away.

"Wei-han! Wei-han! Over here!" Ellen, with her two classmates, was waving at me. They were standing on the edge of a big crowd of students; none seemed to be going through the gate of our school. As I approached them, I could see some soldiers standing guard at the gate and many more soldiers on the school ground, some even at the windows of the second floor classroom.

"What's going on?" I asked in a hushed tone.

"Don't you know? They said that martial law has been declared and our school has been requisitioned."

"What is martial law? What does it mean?" I asked, confused. I was scared by the presence of the soldiers and the unfamiliar words.

"Stupid second grader," one of her friends taunted me. "They are going to use our school as barracks to fight the Communists. Schools will be closed and people are not allowed to go out at night."

"What about school?"

I still could not understand what they were saying.

"Attention students! There will be no school today," one of the teachers was shouting through a paper megaphone. "You will be notified when school will start again. Please go home now."

The People's Liberation Army distributed this communiqué throughout Tientsin before occupying it.

PLA Notice to People of Tientsin
December 15, 1948

Be calm.

Tientsin is surrounded, and victorious armies are on the march. Make your decision now between destruction or cooperation. The following precepts are addressed to all our brothers:

1. We will be responsible to protect lives, property, and liberty of all classes. Don't listen to rumors or propaganda.

2. Our army will protect the citizens' industries, factories, and private holdings. We will not interfere with private enterprise, banks, shops, and warehouses, but they are to continue business as usual.

3. Kuomintang government factories etc. will be investigated and put in order. Bureaucratic capitalists will be assimilated into the democratic government. Should private capital be involved, it will be recognized as such and put to the good of the democratic government. Accounts, sketches, and plans must be preserved. Those who assist in their preservation will be rewarded. Present workers will continue in their usual employment and be paid as usual.

4. Directors, managers, presidents, superintendents, professors, teachers, priests etc. of public works, schools, universities, hospitals, churches, museums, post offices, and recreation centers will be protected and will continue work as usual.

5. With the execution of leading criminals, Kuomintang municipal officials, police, 'pao chia' etc. will not be detained provided they do not take up arms and resist. If they obey the orders of the Army of Liberation and the democratic government, protect property and do not shelter criminals, they may be placed in new government positions.

6. All foreign consular staff members and foreign residents who obey the orders of the democratic government, refrain from damaging the government, and from sheltering war criminals will have their property, etc., protected.

7. Both before and after the Army enters the city, all the people should maintain order. The good will be rewarded; the bad will be punished.

8. Our Army will not extract even one needle or a piece of thread from the people.

Carry on your work well. Do not cause unnecessary disturbance. Be calm.

signed: North China People's Army of Liberation

In a daze, the children walked away in small groups quietly and hesitantly, in sharp contrast to the usual exuberant caper when they were free from school.

"Are you going home?" I asked Ellen.

"We might go to Wang's house. You better go home and tell Ma what has happened."

Before I left, I turned around and took another look at the school. How strange it looked, full of stern-faced soldiers, quiet, ghostly, in the long shadows cast by the early morning winter sun. Strange as it might have seemed, none of us had any inkling that when we returned to school, it would be another era.

SUN, OUR cook, was just mopping the living room floor when I got home. Mother looked up surprised from her unfinished breakfast. Before she could say anything, I blurted out, "Martial Law, Ma, and no more school."

"So it is coming closer," Mother said, sounding worried. "Daddy hasn't called from the Water Works. I hope he doesn't have to go to any of the pumping stations outside the city. I wish Nini were back home."

Nini was then at a boarding school run by missionaries in the Native City, beyond the ex-Japanese concession. Mother sighed. It was just a little over three years since the Japanese had surrendered after the horrors of the occupation. The uneasy peace was coming to an end.

Had they made the right decision, the decision not to flee, not to evacuate with the other Americans, not to be refugees? I knew my parents had had many discussions on this. It was one of the recurring themes of their life and had had horrendous consequences the last time around. It was not a decision they made lightly.

And soon there wasn't any time to worry about whether or not they had made the right decision to stay. The battlefront was approaching rapidly and the outlook was grim for the KMT.

Another communiqué was issued by the People's Liberation Army (PLA) right after the KMT government declared martial law and the schools were closed. The circular tried to reassure the citizens of Tientsin that the transition would be a peaceful one. My father received a second message at work, as did other company leaders.

THE PUMPING stations of the Water Works were outside the city. Our family always heard the news first because the workers there kept in touch with F. C. at all times. Each phone ring, day or night, would signal some crisis caused either by the retreating troops, bomb explosions, or injuries of workers by the mines planted by the KMT.

Our cook Sun became terrified to go out at night. The retreating troops were press-ganging able-bodied men into service of the army and once he barely escaped. Other families had been storing food and supplies for the past few months now. One day when I visited one of my school-mates, I found that their family had stacked sacks of flour in front of the window facing the street, creating a bulletproof wall and a source of food supply. But my family never thought about such practical things. Sun still had to go out to buy food daily. Food was getting very scarce as the peasants and the farmers fled their villages.

Then, suddenly, another ring of the phone—the Deputy Chief Engineer, Mr. Tuan, had been taken away by the KMT soldiers. F. C. searched all around the city to find him. He finally found out that someone had reported seeing Communist signals being fired from one of the pumping stations. The KMT had arrested Mr. Tuan, holding him accountable. After much negotiation at the KMT Headquarters, F. C. was able to secure Mr. Tuan's release.

One day the water main was blown up. The KMT planes, trying to bomb the PLA, dropped bombs instead on their own troops and disrupted the water supply to the city. My father was called out in the night to try to repair the big pipes. We woke up the next morning with black smoke blocking the sun, and we heard that the KMT had set fire to the villages surrounding the city to create a "no-man" zone so that it would be more difficult for the PLA to sneak into the city.

During these frightening days and nights, Grace worried sick about F. C.'s safety. She tried to remain calm with us when F. C. was gone and tried not to show anxiety when he was home. But all of us were conscious of waiting for the phone to ring with another crisis. We frequently gathered around the radio to listen to the Voice of America, but we could only get the official KMT radio station and it only broadcast "victories," with no hint of the impending defeat.

As the battle around Tientsin grew nearer, attempts to sabotage and destroy the Water Works and other public works also intensified. The Water Works was F. C.'s life, and he was determined to save it. He was constantly working with the other workers to protect the facilities. Come what may, there was no turning back. The People's Liberation Army was already at the gate. The streets were deserted. Then the bombardment started.

12

THE PLA ARRIVES

F ATE, AND her love for Liu Fu-chi, had given Grace a front row seat to witness the victory of the People's Liberation Army over the Kuomintang. She described the incredible events in her memoir for January 15, 1949:

The clear, icy blue sky and bright sunshine made it one of North China's beautiful midwinter days. But a biting wind was sweeping down from Siberia. It rattled windows, shook doors, and dashed through the deserted streets taking with it all the rubbish it could gather. Standing on a chair at my dining room window, I tried to peer over the courtyard wall and look into the empty street, listening to the unnatural silence between gusts of howling wind. With the bombardment going on outside the city for the past month, I had grown accustomed to the rumble and roar of gunfire; now the silence was eerie.

Suddenly there was the sound of running footsteps and three deserters came racing into my line of vision, throwing off whatever they could of army uniforms and desperately trying to pull on some civilian clothing; another second and they were gone, leaving the discarded uniforms lying in the middle of the street like dead birds. Two stray dogs came along, sniffed at the uniforms and went their way. The gate! I thought. Had F. C. bolted the gate when he left? Deserters could be desperate!

Early this morning F. C. had left me alone with the children and I was expectantly looking for him out the window. Yesterday he had received a phone call from the Deputy Chief Engineer saying that the fighting had reached the pumping station outside the city; the pumping station was intact, having sustained some shots. The PLA would be entering the city the next morning. Our part of the city was still under siege. Rifle shots, popping in the distance, then the frightening swish and scream of a shell and the boom of an explosion shook the window.

Abandoning my perch, I joined the children and tried to appear calm and unworried. Nini, just turned sixteen, sat with a book open on her lap. Across the room from her, I also pretended to read a magazine, staring blindly at the print, waiting for the next shell to scream its way over our heads or hit the house.

The two younger children playing cards on a low coffee table in the middle of the room appeared absorbed in their game, but at the sound of the explosion, Ellen, now eleven, dropped to the floor and seven-year-old Wei-han gave a gasp, covered his ears and shut his eyes in a painful grimace. This annoyed his big sister.

"Stop it!" she snapped.

"I don't like to hear that noise," complained Wei-han.

"Make him stop it, Ma."

"Oh, Nini, let him hold his ears, it doesn't hurt you."

"It makes me nervous."

Suddenly the terrifying shriek of a shell apparently speeding straight at us brought us all to the floor, eyes shut tight and hands over our ears. A deafening explosion shook the whole house, and all the windows burst open. Cautiously I opened my eyes. I was alive, the house was still standing and the children were looking at me shocked and wild-eyed.

The cold wind was blowing through the house. My magazine was fluttering in the wind but there was no other sound.

"Quick!" I said, "Help me close the windows."

Nini and I went from room to room shutting out the freezing wind. The dead silence between the anguished howls of wind gave me the uneasy feel of something holding its breath, getting ready to spring. The street beyond the gate had a shut-up and waiting look.

Then I heard the gate open and footsteps! Before I had time to panic, Wei-han cried, "It's Daddy! Daddy's here!" And as soon as F. C. had entered the front door Wei-han pummeled questions at him, "Did you hear the big guns, Daddy? Did you see the explosion?"

Ignoring him, F. C. came straight to me. "Are you all right? Were you very frightened?"

"Of course I was! Who wouldn't be? But we're all right. Did you see what was hit?"

"No, I couldn't tell. I came as quickly as I could. They don't seem to have hit anything. But the explosion blew out a lot of windows. There's broken glass all over the streets."

"What's going to happen now, Daddy? Why have they stopped shooting?"

F. C. now looked at his son and said, "I don't know what's going to happen. I don't know anything except it's not over."

Something had hushed the big guns. The foreboding silence continued.

"I'm hungry," blurted Wei-han. "Let's eat."

I almost laughed. He was used to having lunch when his father came home, but today nothing was routine. The city had been surrounded for days and no food was coming into the city. Sun had not even attempted to make his usual trip to the market.

"There's nothing to eat," Nini snipped at her brother. "You'll have to have sardines."

"But I don't like sardines!" Wei-han objected.

"Spoiled brat! Don't complain."

"You know there's nothing else in the house," reasonable Ellen tried to placate him.

Despite the uselessness of my actions, I went to the kitchen to see what kind of lunch Sun and I could put together. I was glad to have the semblance of normalcy. Sun sat on his kitchen stool hunched over the table apparently doing his accounts. The amahs sat quietly in a protected corner of the kitchen which had no window on the street. But it was already too late. We would never eat that lunch.

Rapid shots not far off sounded like the pop-popping of hundreds of strings of New Year's firecrackers. The gunfire was interspersed with loud explosions. Food was forgotten. I hurried back to the living room.

"Machine guns," explained F. C., "and hand grenades—coming this way. Listen—they're coming right down this street."

The children ran to the window and Nini climbed up on the window sill. She wanted to see what was coming down the street.

"Come away from that window!" shouted F. C. "Bullets can come over the wall into the room."

He herded us into the windowless corridor under a cement stairway where stray bullets couldn't reach us. The staccato barking of the machine guns and crashing explosions of hand grenades came closer and closer until it seemed that the battle was directly in front of our house. I held tight to F. C. with one arm and to Wei-han with the other as the choking smell of gunpowder began seeping in.

Gradually the sounds receded up the street and when the noise of battle seemed safely in the next few blocks, the children ran to the windows. Nini, being the tallest, climbed up on the window sill and hollered, "Ma, come look!" I expected to see nothing but an empty street. I stood on my tiptoes and could barely see over the six-foot wall in front of the house.

What I saw startled me. Stretching from curb to curb and as far up and down as I could see, an army was marching. The sound of the tramping feet was so blended with the noise of the wind that it created the impression of a phantom army surging silently on, wave after wave. It was more hair-raising than the shooting.

I felt compelled to see for myself, but unable to see over the wall and with the children on the window sill, I turned, as if driven by some deep impulse, snatched up the nearest coat, which happened to be a spring coat—it was very cold and I was bareheaded, wearing only a house dress and spring coat—I unlocked the door and without saying a word, without thinking even, rushed out. I was surprised to find the courtyard gate unbolted. I pushed it open—and suddenly a bone-piercing gust of wind with a strong smell of gunpowder snapped me to my senses.

There before me stretched a whole army of fur-hatted soldiers, maybe eight abreast, going down the street. The Attila-the-Hun-type hats they wore were huge, with long-haired ear pieces, suitable for Siberian winters, reminding me of Daniel Boone's cap, flapping in the wind. The padded leggings and padded overcoats disguised their bodies beyond any semblance of arms and legs. All sorts of things hung over them—not only machine guns draped across their backs, and pistols, knives and hand grenades at easy reach, but across their bodies were strapped pots and pans, shovels and poles, rakes and all sorts of ropes.

I was so close that I could have reached out and shaken hands with any one of them, but not a one turned or looked at me. It must have been astonishing to see a foreign woman on the street, but no one broke discipline. At first their wild fur hats flapping in the wind had a strange and savage look. But when I saw those eyes under the fur hats, I realized they were just young boys, maybe none older than seventeen, eyes sparkling with excitement and cheeks red and chapped.

I looked around—there was no other courtyard gate open, no other person on the sidewalk, no faces at the windows—only me—face to face with the People's Liberation Army.

13

EYEWITNESS TO REVOLUTION

SOON AFTER the PLA marched down Grace's street, Chiang Kai-shek resigned as president of China, on January 21, 1949, and two days later Peking then surrendered without a fight. While the Communist army gathered its forces on the northern banks of the Yangtse River, waiting to move further south in the spring, the administrative arm focused on creating a provisional government in the North. To avoid the disasters that faced the Nationalist government after its return to power in 1945, the Communists maintained strict orders to occupy the cities of North China peacefully, to keep businesses and industries operating, to reopen schools and hospitals, and guarantee safety as much as possible. Food and fuel were stabilized and stockpiled supplies made available. A new currency, called the *renminbi*, was exchanged for gold, silver, foreign currencies, and the despised, fluctuating CNC notes. Orders were issued to round up but not to harm former KMT officers and soldiers.

Mail service soon resumed and Grace received back issues of American magazines. In the January 1949 issue of the *Saturday Evening Post,* she saw an editorial cartoon of a pitiful figure of a Chinaman, representing the "Chinese people" sitting on a heap of rocks in a barren waste, with the smoke of burning cities in the distance. Out of the sky descended a hammer and sickle just about to cut off the head or beat out the brains of the "Chinese people." The cartoon stirred her to pick up pen and paper.

Grace's letter to the editors of the *Saturday Evening Post* in April 1949 was a ten-page description of what she experienced immediately after what the Chinese called the "liberation" and what the West called the "Communist takeover." The details of this letter were in such contrast to what the American media was portraying about China then that Grace sarcastically wrote: "It would seem that one has a clearer view of things from a ten-thousand-mile distance. We here in Tientsin are perhaps too close to see what is going on or too close to interpret it properly . . . After three months of observing the Chinese Communists, I wouldn't have the least worry if it weren't for the things I read in the American magazines."

Not sure of mail service out of Tientsin, Grace sent it through a friend to his brother in Hong Kong and told him to send it to the *Saturday Evening Post*. When it got to Hong Kong, a lot of people read it—one was the editor of the *China Digest*, which was an English publication favorable to China. The next thing Grace knew it had been reprinted all over the world . . . Singapore, San Francisco . . . wherever there were overseas Chinese. One of F. C.'s engineers studying in Paris at the time said he read it there in English and French and Chinese.

The editorial cartoon on the left spurred Grace to write the *Saturday Evening Post* in April 1949. The cartoon on the right appeared in 1950.

Tientsin, April 22, 1949
Editor of Saturday Evening Post
Philadelphia, Pa.

Dear Sir,

. . . It's now three months since the Pa Lu Chuin *took over the city.* Pa Lu Chuin *is a sort of nickname for the communist army; it means literally "Eighth Route," and* Chuin *means army. And what follows is my personal version of the plain truth about things here in Tientsin before and after the advent of the* Pa Lu Chuin.

All my years in China have been lived in an anti-Communist atmosphere. Tientsin is a cosmopolitan port city; the home of foreigners of all nationalities, rich Chinese landlords and businessmen, the families of old warlords who had squeezed whole provinces dry; wealthy officials and bankers—a hotbed of anti-Communism. We were steeped in anti-Red propaganda. The Chinese Communists were godless, murdering, torturing, thieving, liberty-suppressing bandits, and before December 1941, I took it all to heart and was one of the most convinced of antis. But the Japanese occupation cured me of swallowing any kind of propaganda whole, for I heard the Japanese turn the Americans into all sorts of human fiends, and from that time I take all propaganda with a large dose of salt.

When it was clear that it was only a matter of a very short time before Tientsin and Peking would be in the hands of the Communists, there ensued a hectic scramble to get out on the part of those afraid of what might happen when the Communists took the city. We determined to remain in our own home and face whatever came—hoping it wouldn't be too bad! We expected to have our way of living perhaps radically changed. We expected to be behind some form of an "Iron Curtain." We'd heard much of the Communists' anti-American feeling and I thought it likely that things might not be altogether pleasant for Americans. We'd heard that everybody would be forced to work and all would have to eat the same sort of food. One friend of mine, a wealthy young Chinese widow, flew to Formosa because she'd been told that Communists did not approve of widows or idle women and she was afraid she would be forced to marry some comrade and set to hard labor.

I expected that American books and magazines would probably be banned and that surely no more American movies would be shown. I expected to have to give up my American coffee and American tomato, pineapple, orange, and grapefruit juice and V-8! . . . that my children could no longer drink Borden's Hemo and irradiated Pet milk. It was a dreary prospect but it couldn't be as bad as the Japanese occupation we'd lived through and almost anything was better than being a wretched refugee!

My first sight of the Pa Lu Chuin was not reassuring. Dogtrotting down the street about one-half hour after a fierce street battle took place just on the other side of our garden wall, the square, squat, fur-hatted soldiers had a savage look. But when the line halted and the soldiers leaned against the wall "at ease," I saw their faces, and the horde changed before my eyes into a crowd of jolly, red-cheeked Chinese boys, laughing, scuffling, and kicking at each other like schoolboys on a lark. Any fears I might have had of a fierce, ruthless, conquering army evaporated.

Nini, in a later interview, picked up the story of what happened immediately after the Pa Lu came into their neighborhood and Grace impetuously rushed out to see them:

> When mother ran outside, the cook was horrified and called to F. C. "Tai-tai is going outside, going outside!"
>
> F. C. said, "Let her alone. They won't hurt her."
>
> In a few minutes we all ran outside, first us children, then father, and the cook and the amahs. The soldiers stopped and had a break and it was very cold. They sat along the wall on the other side where the sun was coming down very brightly. The cook was so polite. He offered them some hot water and things, but they refused.
>
> Willy began prancing up and down mimicking the soldiers marching. I was afraid that maybe they thought Willy was fighting them so I called, "Stop it, Willy." He came back and stood with us.
>
> We lived in a very upper-class neighborhood with bankers and industrialists—who were all afraid. Our neighbors came out slowly into the streets. About two or three o'clock, the soldiers had gone and the shooting had stilled. Everybody came out and chatted, wondering what the next step was. People were even more friendly to each other than usual, after so many days of staying off the streets and imagining the worst. One neighbor had sandbagged up his door, because he was afraid of the fighting. When the soldiers came, he refused to open up. All the neighbors came by and shouted at him that it was all right, everybody was safe and the fighting was over. Finally he took away the sandbags and opened his gate.

The PLA came back in the afternoon and searched each house for KMT soldiers. One neighbor had an officer who had gone in the day before and changed all his clothes. I had seen how the KMT soldiers had acted, looting like bandits, and I had seen how the Marines had acted sometimes. The PLA commander, when he found the KMT soldier, treated him nicely, tried to console him, even carried his bundle on his back, and was saying, "Now don't be afraid. Nobody is going to hurt you. Come along. We'll go along with the rest of them." This gave me a big impression. And then later, when more KMT soldiers and dependents were rounded up, they were all weeping and complaining, and the PLA soldiers were consoling them and helping them. It was almost funny.

Grace had one encounter with the PLA in her bedroom:

When I stayed out on the street watching the PLA, I got chilled. I was shaking and couldn't get warm. So I went to bed with a fever. I was in bed when the PLA soldier came back to search. The cook came in my room and whispered politely, "Tai-tai, there's a comrade here." He learned quickly to say *comrade*. "He wants to search the house for deserters. They're picking up all the KMT soldiers that were left behind or hiding somewhere."

I said, "Well, of course, take him around, Sun."

"Well, he wants to come in here,"

"Certainly. Bring him in. Let him come in, look in the closet, under the bed—anywhere."

So then I looked at the door and I saw a big hat, a big fur hat coming around the corner, and two round eyes peeking out at me, two red, red cheeks like apples. He looked just about fifteen years old to me. And so the cook very politely told him to come in and said I wasn't very well. I smiled and said something, I don't remember what, in Chinese. Then he tried to tiptoe and he had on these enormous boots. I tried not to laugh. He walked through the room on booted tiptoes into the bathroom and the other rooms. I told him to look in the closet and look all around so he would be sure that there was nobody hiding. He just went all around, made the circuit, and then went out, still tiptoeing in those big boots.

193

Ellen remembered other details:

Afterwards the soldiers stayed with the families. They stayed in the hallways, wherever there was room. No soldiers stayed with us, but many, maybe a whole platoon stayed on our street. The first thing they did was to sweep and clean and straighten things up. I asked, Why don't they put one in our house? We have a hallway. We have room. Was it because of the foreigner? I wanted to have one because I often saw when I was walking down the street that these soldiers were so useful. They swept the court-yards, they made the fires; they took care of the children. I saw many of them walking up and down the street, carrying a baby or strolling a baby. One day I went past a house, and I saw the *Tai-tai*, the lady of the house, just leaving and she was saying to the soldier who was holding the baby, "Now you feed it at such and such a time and do this at such and such a time." We had never seen anything like it. No one believed it.

They only stayed a short while, but what won over the people was the army's discipline and the contact between soldiers and the people. You can talk and talk and talk, but what means the most is the contact. Any-thing borrowed was always returned, anything broken was always paid for. Kids in the neighborhoods took to them like they were heroes. We watched them in the stadium practicing climbing, drilling, crossing a swinging bamboo bridge they had rigged up to get ready for the south. The stadium was full of kids watching the soldiers. They stayed for a few months before the next big battle came and they left, before the weather became warm.

In Grace's letter to the *Saturday Evening Post,* she referred to the English civil war as described in Macauley's *History of England,* one of the few books she had to read during the Japanese occupation:

Since that day we've had plenty of opportunity to observe this amazing army that has something of Cromwell's Ironsides and something of M.R.A.—The Moral Rearmament Association! There have been as many as four hundred thousand soldiers in the city at once. They come and go; as some go out to the south, others come in to take their places.

They are not quartered away off somewhere in barracks but are billeted on the people. Nearly every family with extra room has a few soldiers. Most of the people we know have or have had them at some time or another.

Of course not many people are overjoyed at having soldiers billeted in their homes, but there's not much grumbling, and no one can complain of the soldiers' behavior. They all seem kind and courteous and good-natured. There's no stealing in the army—no liquor and no "wimmen"! Any soldier caught going into a house of prostitution would be shot. I heard an American say it was the first chaste army he'd ever seen and it got him down. As Lord McCauley said of Cromwell's army, "In that singular camp, no oath was heard, no drunkenness or gambling was seen, and during the long dominion of the soldiery, the property of the peaceable citizen and the honor of woman were held sacred." Only the "no oath" clause would not apply to the Pa Lu—swearing is too important a part of Chinese conversation.

Every morning at 5:30 insistent blasts of a police whistle sound up and down our block for about ten minutes. Then all the soldiers in this neighborhood gather in a field two doors away from us and start the day with calisthenics and song. During the day when they are not working or drilling they play in all the vacant lots, fields, and playgrounds. They play basketball, practice broad and high jumps, and swing like monkeys on bars. In the Ming Yuen field they have built tall structures and ingenious contraptions that they have to climb over and around and down to perfect their agility and balance. It is marvelous to watch what they can do, how far they can jump and all sorts of gymnastics. They run across a high narrow slippery plank that is kept constantly in motion. They run back and forth on a swinging log, and they practice scaling walls and dropping from the top.

There's a great deal of singing and dancing that the children enjoy enormously. The Pa Lu have taught all the children in the city how to do the "Yang Ko"—the Rice-Planting Dance. It is much like ballet in that a song is acted out in movements that have meaning such as drawing water from the river, planting rice, sowing and picking cotton, reaping grain, etc. When my children are home the house is filled with the sound of dancing feet and singing voices. My small son, imitating the clash of cymbals with his hands and chanting the onomatopoeic "ch'ang, ch'i, ch'ang, ch'i," dances the Yang Ko through the house with the verve of a soldier going to battle, while my daughter practices the inspiring song and dance in which the growth of the revolution is pantomimed, from the farmer's reaping and sowing motions in the field to the soldiers' bayonet charge like a ballet dancer. The movements are beautiful and, at the same time, very strenuous for exercise.

They kept some of the KMT prisoners in the old Empire Theatre. One time when I was passing that theater, I saw them—several hundred sitting outside the theater with the PLA singing revolutionary songs. In the evening after their early supper, the Pa Lu gather in squads in the street and, led by a combination of cheerleader and orchestra conductor, they fill the air with lusty, vigorous, joyful harmony. It's quite an experience to pass through street after street of singing soldiers.

. . . Our pre-liberation fears have not materialized and there's no change in our way of living so far. If there is a curtain, it certainly is not iron, for I've received my February and March [subscriptions to] Good Housekeeping, Ladies' Home Journal, McCall's, The Woman, Your Life, Journal of Living, *and an assortment of movie magazines. My husband has received literally stacks of engineering news records, and the doctors are getting their medical journals and the journals of dietetics and nutrition. I've gotten mail from my home in Tennessee and from Formosa and Shanghai. I am still buying Chase and Sanborn and Maxwell House coffee, Hemo, evaporated milk and all the juices! I even bought two cans of Wesson Oil yesterday, the first I've seen for nearly ten years. Somebody had been hoarding it all this time! Our diet has not changed; our wardrobe has not been altered; we visit the same places and see the same friends. That is true of most of the people I know.*

American movies are still being shown. I saw Frank Sinatra and Jimmie Durante in "It Happened in Brooklyn" last week. Two rows of Pa Lu soldiers sat in front of us and enjoyed Jimmie Durante enormously, and we were enormously amused at the little Pa Lu who couldn't make up his mind whether or not to put his bayonet back on his rifle during the intermission. He finally decided to put it back on in case some emergency should arise. The great decision made, he relaxed and had a good time gaping at the "big city" audiences.

Those who had the most difficult time adjusting to the changes were the ones whose livelihoods were the most dependent on previous conditions. Grace described her own neighbors and associates in the letter to the *Saturday Evening Post:*

Only a very few have anything to complain of and they are probably getting only what they deserve. Money shops have been closed and speculation stopped. Things look dark for the bankers and many of the private banks have closed. Bankers and brokers, speculators and owners of shops that catered to the wealthy are very unhappy, but they are by no means

196

suffering; they can't go on making a lot of money. I must confess that their plight arouses no compassion in my bosom!

Take our landlord, from whom we rent our flat, for example. He comes from a very wealthy family and is the manager of a bank. He married three wealthy women—one at a time though as he is a rather decent sort—and his eldest daughter married a grandson of Yuan Shi-kai [President of the first Republic 1912–16]. So he is connected with big money in every direction, but his bank is folding up and he is terrified and has taken to his bed with high blood pressure and what he calls a nervous breakdown—not just because of the bank, for he never even pretended to be able to live on his salary as bank manager, but because he feels the foundations slipping out from under the only way of life he has ever known. That is the case with many of his class. They have not been mistreated or even bothered, but they feel that their day is done. Some of them feel lost and unhappy and some have the good sense to try to adjust to changing conditions.

I was talking to a clever Cantonese export-import man the other day and I asked him just what did he think of the situation in a business way. He said business wasn't so good; nobody was making any money, but seemed to be just getting by. However prices were more reasonable, ending the leaps and bounds that had made everybody nearly crazy for the last few years, and money was worth something again. He had no complaints; he had done a piece of business with some Communists from Manchuria the day before and said it was the quickest deal he had ever transacted. They gave him a check, he handed over the goods. He sent the check to the bank and he got his money immediately. Formerly, he said, red tape would have strung out that business at least a week. He was cheerful and optimistic and declared he was truly thankful that he had not run off to the South.

. . . One evening last week we had dinner guests, Mr. C. and his wife from Peiping. Mr. C., who has a Ph.D. from Columbia, is a former Central bank of China man who was sent to Peiping several months ago to be a financial advisor to General Fu Tso-yi. His wife, a Stamford graduate, taught economics in a Shanghai school. Both are now in the Communist People's Bank in Peiping, working with wholehearted enthusiasm in the Research Department, and had come down to Tientsin to inspect the factories, flour, and textile mills and other industries.

They were late for dinner because she had been so far out in the Chinese City going over a cotton mill. A girlish looking woman of forty-four, and so tiny my five foot three towered over her, she came in with slacks on under a long Chinese jacket, dusty shoes and hair wisped from the wind. But her eyes were sparkling and her face beaming with satis-

197

faction at having found some of the factories producing even more than formerly and also at seeing what a friendly spirit there was between the "old" people and the "new" people.

The relationship between the "old" people and the "new" people, that is, between those who had already been there and the new Communist representatives, was not always so friendly. Lacking trained personnel to run the cities, the challenge to the new regime was to gain the cooperation of the educated, technical, and professional people as well as urban laborers. A team of military representatives were sent to each workplace to manage the transition. These recruits were usually drawn from the PLA forces who were young men from rural areas of northern China.

F. C. had a rather hard time adjusting to the new managers at the Water Works:

To all business, except the strictly private, to the schools, public works, and industries, two, sometimes three or more, political workers called "military representatives" are assigned by the Military Commission that has charge of the City Government at present. These military representatives are sometimes green young country fellows without any experience in dealing with a large city's established organizations, and ignorant not only of the city but in a large measure, of the rest of the world. Situations arise that they cannot handle and they create unnecessary complications.

In the Tientsin Water Works there are ten of these military representatives. Their leader is a young man such as I have described. He is zealous for doing good and means well, but he made the mistake of doubting the work of the General Manager and Chief Engineer, who is a Shensi [Shaanxi] man. Now the Shensi pi chi [pi qi] (disposition) is notoriously stubborn, independent, and hot-tempered, and besides this man is a Cornell graduate and learned his waterworks trade under Allen Hazen in New York City, which means the ultimate in waterworks training. So while the Assistant General Manager and Secretary stood palefaced and horrified, the Shensi pi chi blew up; the table was pounded and the military representative was treated to a thorough dressing down.

Then not waiting to see what effect his speech had on the comrade, the furiously angry man left the place. He did not know what serious consequences his action might have but he said to his wife, "They can shoot me, hang me, or cut off my head but no so and so farmer is going to call me a liar."

His wife watched him go away to work the next morning not quite sure whether or not she was ever going to see him again. At noon he came home beaming, his pi chi unruffled and serene. The Communist representative had come into his office all smiles and apologies, "You know," said the young man, "we are just tou bau tze [tu bao zi] *(country jacks). You must be patient and teach us so we can study and learn* (hsueh hsi [xue xi])*."*

I know this is a true story for it is my husband who is the General Manager of the Water Works. From that time he has been treated with the greatest respect by the comrades.

Nini remembered this incident and added,

F. C. was the kind of person who would make a lot of enemies. He had a strong sense of right and wrong. He was very outspoken and would shout at people, but he never held a grudge. He was also very stern with the engineers he worked with. He was born in a large Chinese family, but he didn't remember much of his own family life. He had very little feudal family influence, but still he would think he should be stern sometimes. When he came home from work, he would bawl us out. But then he would forget it and in general he was very democratic.

He didn't have such a bureaucratic notion as he would have had [if he had been trained] in China. In America he worked on a construction site. That was important in shaping his ideas—there was more contact with the worker. Americans were so practical. They did things. An engineer in China was an intellectual and Chinese intellectuals never did anything. F. C. worked very well with the workmen. He used to say that no matter how dirty they may appear, he would drink out of the same bowl, eat the same food, hang out with them. This was very unusual.

F. C.'s conflict with the peasant leader was not merely of class differences—F. C. was also from the interior of China, and his accent showed his origin. His anger was at being told how to run the water company by someone who knew nothing about it. He had suffered for years under leadership that knew less than he did and his tolerance had grown thin.

Soon after the incident with the military committee in charge of the Water Works, the Lius were visited by the head of the Public Utilities. Mr. Ching had the responsibility for making the system work for the whole city. From his perspective, Liu Fu-chi was in a critical position, but F. C. was known to be difficult and principled. Mr. Ching needed F. C.'s cooperation for a grand vision. Grace said, "Last night we had a most interesting session with the man responsible for not only the Water, Light, Power, and Tramway Companies but for all the factories. He is a Whampoa [Military Academy] graduate and has been a Chinese Communist Party member since 1927. He told us that the Water Works will finally put into effect the Extension Works Plan. This plan was made by my husband in 1935, but he was never able to carry it out. But now it looks as if some honest intelligence and common sense have taken control and things are going to be accomplished in China at last."

Mr. Ching explained to F. C. that it was the policy of the new regime in nationalizing some of the important industries to purchase them from the former owners, even the former board members. He asked F. C. to help negotiate purchase of the Water Works before the expansion project was put in place. This was to be the first citywide water system designed and built solely by Chinese from products made in China. Such massive public projects were among the first developments begun in the cities while land reform remained the primary focus of rural areas.

Grace described her husband's work that began in 1949 in an article entitled "My Husband is a Model," published in *China Reconstructs* in 1953:

> **During the first years after we came to Tientsin in 1934, long before he became chief engineer of the Tientsin Water Works Company, he had designed and blueprinted plans for extension work to increase and improve the city water supply. At the time until after liberation, only about forty-five percent of the people of the city had piped water. In districts where the workers lived, people had to use water straight from the river or dirty ponds, and there were frequent outbreaks of waterborne diseases. Fu-chi's early plans provided for the gradual extension of pipelines to every part of the city, gradually eliminating the use of harmful sources of water.**
>
> **But those plans stayed locked away in a safe for fifteen years. The former Water Works directors and Kuomintang officials, concerned only with lining their own pockets, could spare no money for service to the people.**

William described the family's outings in connection with his father's work during this period:

F. C. used Sundays to visit and inspect the various work sites while the project was under construction. The family often tagged along for the outing. The Hai Ho project and the Chieh Yuan Pumping Station were located in the countryside northwest of the city, nearly an hour's drive from the city center, in the area outside of the old foreign concessions. The drive to Chieh Yuan Pumping Station was through narrow and tortuous lanes, filled with throngs of pedestrians, bicycles, and rickshaws. The chauffeur-driven car (an occasional jeep) often caused a sensation, with people peeping and pointing at the car and commenting on the strange foreign woman and children inside.

I went off with my father nearly every weekend, watching F. C. confer with the other engineers and workmen. It was huge, as large as a college campus, with sediment basins, like little lakes, and piles of sand to filter the water. To me it was like a giant park; I loved to play in the sand piles by the huge sediment tanks and climb on the gigantic concrete pipes.

When father and I walked through the village on the West River bank to the work site, bystanders would point at me and whisper, "Look, a little Russian boy!"

F. C. would laugh and say, "What Russian boy? That's my son."

In the early fifties, very few visitors went to China, and so when they saw my "big nose" they assumed I was Russian.

Grace continued in "My Husband is a Model":

One Sunday afternoon Fu-chi took the whole family out to the Hai Ho construction site while the work was going on. Around the Hai Ho pumping station all was intense and bustling activity. Wei-han went off with his father to watch new pipes being laid in trenches while the two girls and I climbed up on the old reservoir embankment to locate the source of the singing and chanting we heard. From there we saw the singers below—hundreds of workers, digging away in the new basin, pushing small cars full of earth over miniature tracks. Bright red stars on their shoulder-wide straw hats were dashing in the sun.

From our height we could look down at Fu-chi standing by the pipeline in a characteristic pose with feet planted wide apart and looking broader and shorter

than ever beside the very tall, lanky, Shen Ta-nien, one of the engineers.

"I could tell Daddy a mile away," laughed Nini, "just by the way he stands. He looks so determined and unbudgeable!"

Fu-chi called to us to come down and see the new pipes. These tall white cylinders arranged in rows while waiting to be laid in trenches were an impressive sight and were the pride of the whole Water Works. Knowing the story of how they happened to be made, I could fully sympathize with the feelings of the worker I saw proudly patting the smooth white sides of the pipes.

F. C. was very proud of the reinforced concrete pipes his Water Works teams made locally.

The making of these low-pressure pipes of reinforced concrete is a good example of the new way people have begun to work and think and cooperate after liberation. Several hundred of such pipe sections were needed. They could not be bought in China and were too expensive to import. When Fu-chi suggested that the Water Works make their own pipes, opinion was divided. Such pipes—each section was eight feet long with an inside diameter of four feet and a five-inch wall and weighed around three and a half tons—had never been made in China. Was it possible that they could be made without modern machinery?

Failure could waste a lot of time, effort, and money. Many meetings were held to discuss the idea thoroughly. Fu-chi and the engineers were confident of success and discussed everything with the workmen and painstakingly explained exactly how it could be done. The Party organization appealed to Party and Youth League members to be courageous and take the lead in helping others to break away from old conservative backwardness. After a few pipe sections were made and tested under pressure, the whole company was seized with enthusiasm. Everybody wanted to help—even the clerical workers went out to Hai Ho and dug trenches, mixed and carried concrete, and helped to bind and wind the steel. The pipes were a great success.

14

SCHOOLING THE CHILDREN

GRACE had long worried about her Amerasian children growing up in a semicolonial and semifeudal society with all the hatred of the Chinese toward foreigners and the entrenched racism of the Europeans toward Chinese. Now, with one child in middle school and two in primary school, she faced a new regime with heightened uncertainty of the treatment and education her children would receive. The character of school life was of the utmost importance to her.

According to Nini, Grace had pretty set ideas of how to raise interracial kids:

> Tientsin was a semicolonial, harbor city, therefore it had the worst elements of both cultures—comprador Chinese and imperialist foreigners. Her fear was that children like us, half-half, can very easily take the bad from both cultures. She spent a lot of time, at least with me, reading—always Western classics, that way I learned what was best from the Western culture. As our father was Chinese and we lived in China, she thought we ought to take the Chinese part more, that we shouldn't be left straddling a fence, you might say. I think my mother's viewpoint was correct. Since you live in a society, you're part of that society and you must have your loyalties to one or the other. You must know what you are. We stand with China, with her people.
>
> Yet the good part of having another culture is that it leaves you broader-minded. You can get the benefits of the good things of another culture.

THE YEARS immediately following the Communists' rise to power were greatly welcomed after years of exhausting, harsh and uncontrollable conditions. Grace's husband and children fared better. Their workplace and schools became productive and their health improved. Grace wrote: ". . . If I had to choose one thing that impresses me above all the others, I would say it was the revitalization of the schools—the injection of vigorous new life into the dead, dried-up, conventional Chinese educational system . . ."

The choice of schools had been difficult before liberation with the schools divided by nationalities, languages, class backgrounds, and religious instructions. After Nini's first experience in the Tientsin American School before the war, Grace and F. C. chose only Chinese-speaking schools for Ellen and William.

Grace's description of the schools is presented in an article in the *China Weekly Review* in December 10, 1949, entitled "An American Tells of her Children's Education in New China."

Since the liberation of Tientsin on January 15, nine months ago, we have been gradually learning to live a new life—We feel that we are living where history is being made and where great things are taking place under our very eyes . . .

I feel left behind and passed over by a whirlwind that has swept my children out from under my undoubtedly too-hovering wing—the children I used to coax out of bed, whose lessons I had to supervise and for whom a tutor had to be engaged occasionally. All that is a thing of the past. They now get *me* out of bed, and they must do their share of tutoring.

When my twelve-year-old daughter says she must be in school before seven, I set the alarm for six; but she is usually up before it rings. And why does she have to be at school at such an hour? She is on patrol duty! My daughter wears on her coat a shoulder patch bearing the Chinese characters "Fu Wu." That means she is on duty serving the school and her fellow schoolmates—watching to see that the small children do not get hurt, that the schoolyard fights do not become too violent, and that wastepaper and trash are not thrown on the floor or in the yard.

She is also the "tzu chang [zu zhang]" (group leader) of her "hsiao tzu [xiao zu]" (small group or unit); a group of three boys and three girls of the same class who meet to discuss their own and each other's shortcomings and how to "kai kuo [gai guo]" (change). But the most noteworthy and useful thing about the "hsaio tzu [xiao zu]" system is the help the pupils give each other. Those who excel in their studies must help those who are having difficulties. The group pulls together and solves its problems whether scholastic or disciplinary. It is excellent training in teamwork and cooperation and automatically does away with much of the old selfish striving for individual superiority.

A few weeks ago I had a very instructive talk with my eight-year-old son. He is the deputy group leader. Their "hsiao tzu" has nine children. I asked my son to tell me about their "tan pei hui [tan bai hui]" (a meeting in which the children speak out honestly concerning their misbehavior in school).

"Well," said he, "everybody says what he has done that wasn't right. Then each body says he must do what to make him remember not to do bad again." (His English is a somewhat literal translation from Chinese.)

In other words each child imposes his own penance and carries it out immediately. I asked my son, "And what did you say you had done that wasn't right?"

"I talk sometimes while the teacher is teaching the lesson." For that misdemeanor he penalized himself five extra pages of "big letter writing" (writing about one and a half inch square Chinese characters with a brush).

"And did you do it?" I asked.

"Yes," he said, "I must do it."

"Do they all do what they say they must do even if the teacher is not there?"

"Of course! We say we do what, we must do what"—directly from the Chinese: "Wo men shuo shen mo, wo men i ting tso shen mo."

In answer to my question about the books they are using now, he said, "Now our books are much better than before. Now they teach us good things."

When I wanted to know what sort of "good things," he got one of his books and translated several small stories for me and explained the lesson each taught. Here first is the countryside—all the able-bodied adults are hard at work in the field, the children are carrying food and water to the workers, and the old grandpas and grandmas are sitting taking care of the babies or making shoes. Each has a job according to his strength and ability. As my son explained it, "Even the little people and the old people can do something useful. Nobody must be lazy!"

Then comes the story of the ants and the dead dragonfly. One ant cannot move the least little part of the big creature, but when hundreds and thousands of ants combine all their tiny efforts, short shrift is made of the great dead body and it is soon stored away for the ants' winter food.

"You see," explains my small instructor, "one person cannot fight the Kuomintang all by himself, but many, many people together have much strength and the Kuomintang is soon finished."

Perseverance and persistence are illustrated in the next lesson. The rain of many years has worn a hole in the stone step and persistent filing has abraded away a piece of steel to the fineness of a needle.

William internalized these lessons: "Every time my mother would read books to me, I would ask her what was the significance of the story. Everything had to have a meaning. When she read *Treasure Island*, I asked who were the good guys and who were the bad. In this book, the good guys are the squire, the doctor, and the boy. And the sailors and the workmen were the bad guys. Yet in school it was different. I couldn't see how landlords could be good guys. Grace thought it was amazing that we were being taught not only to hear the story, but to think about it and ask questions."

Grace pondered these lessons intently. She recognized that the "bad guys" and the "good guys" were intended to be the KMT and the PLA, but at the same time, the stories carried values of hard work and perseverance that were not so far from her own upbringing. She decided to withhold judgment and see how these lessons were carried out in practice.

The girls' middle school, where sixteen-year-old Nini boarded, was about twenty minutes away by bicycle. Nini would rush home in the afternoons to collect extra food or items and listen to the five o'clock news on Voice of America then rush back to school, dressed in a black, padded-cotton jacket over wool slacks and Chinese padded shoes. Grace's article described Nini's experience in the former non-Catholic school for upper-class girls after liberation:

The same class of girls attend the school but they have ceased to be languid "hsiao chiehs [xiao jie]" (pampered young ladies). They have become energetic, hardworking, hard-playing, enthusiastic school girls who run the school themselves in a most progressive, democratic way.

Shortly before liberation, the KMT troops occupied the school, and left it in

Nini's class visiting a worker's home. Nini is standing at the far right.

an almost ruined condition. In one part, all the windows were broken and the floors torn up. The part that wasn't damaged was left filthy. After liberation the damage was repaired, and the superintendent called for volunteers from among the students to clean up the place. A surprising number turned up willing to work but many of them had no idea how to launch an attack on the really appalling filth, and they wandered around aimlessly flitting dust cloths about. Although somewhat of a "hsiao chieh" herself, my daughter was not a complete stranger to house cleaning. She organized a squad of the most enterprising of the young ladies and they rolled up their sleeves and went to work. They took home blistered hands and aching backs. But they went back every day until the job was done. Now they take great pride in the "slick" appearance of their school. On holidays they wash the windows and scrub the floors and desks with hot water and washing soda.

Judging from my daughter's spirited reports, school life is more interesting than ever before with something exciting always going on. Earlier in the fall there was the election of the school committee with its week of election campaigning. The girls took a lively interest in making campaign speeches and composing slogans extolling the virtues of their candidates . . . Out of thirty candidates—three from each of the ten classes—fifteen were elected by vote to make up the school committee. The girl with the highest number of votes was chairman of the committee, the girl with the next highest, the vice-chairman. Of the remaining thirteen, each became the leader of one of the school groups or units, such as: the recreational activities group—taking in athletics, singing and dancing; the social workers' group—in charge of the small school for the very poor children of the neighborhood, taught by the girls themselves; the co-op group; the inter-school relationship group; the class "hsueh hsi" (study) group; and eight others. One of these fifteen girls is later elected to represent the school in the All-Tientsin Schools Union.

On the school grounds there is a wall the girls call the "Min chu ch'iang [min zhu qiang]" (the Democratic Wall). Here a girl can paste up any complaint, protest, or suggestion she pleases provided she signs her name to it. When the pupils do not like a certain school policy and paste up enough protests with valid and reasonable arguments, something must be done to change the objectionable policy.

Interviewed more than two decades later, Nini said, "We went to school, but our school was reorganized. Nothing changed, and everything changed. The outside was the same, but the essence changed. The teachers were the same, but we were taught completely differently than before. We learned new songs, the meaning of liberation. It was more interesting, more exciting. We had never had folk dancing and singing in school, but now we did. I learned to play the waist drum. You could air your opinions in the student union more freely than before. Teacher/student relationships were quite good at this time. It gave us new ideas. There were lots of new ideas. We heard them on radio, at school, in the newspapers."

UNDER THE command of General Chen Yi, the Communists crossed the Yangtse River in April 1949. Meeting little resistance, they captured Nanking, the former capital of the Nationalist government, on April twenty-third and Shanghai in May 1949. With amazing speed, the Communist forces moved west and south, consolidating their hold on the country as Chiang Kai-shek's forces evacuated to Formosa. In late September, Mao Tse-tung, leader of the victorious army, assembled in Peking a "Political Consultative Conference," echoing the name of the body instituted by General George Marshall in 1946 and giving the appearance of finally succeeding in establishing a democratic coalition government. At first, the consultative conference bore representation from many different parties, although they were outnumbered by the Communist party representatives. This body elected the members of the central government of a united China, with Mao as the chairman. They also declared October 1, 1949, as the date for celebrating the founding of the the new nation and gave it the new name of the People's Republic of China, to distinguish it from the first Republic of China founded in 1911.

The largest parade celebrating the founding of the People's Republic of China took place in Peking. Miles and miles of happy faces marched past Mao and the other Communist leaders in front of the Gate of Heavenly Peace at the entrance to the once Forbidden City. Smaller parades, but no less glorious in celebration, took place all over China.

Grace described Nini's part in the October 1st celebration parade in Tientsin:

Nini's school distinguished itself in the huge thirteen-hour parade celebrating the establishment of the new government last month. On the night of the big celebration parade, around 1 a.m. some reactionary element attempted to create a disturbance in what they thought was a weak spot. A gang, thought to be KMT sympathizers, tried to break through the marching column of girls and their Yang Ko groups. But the girls stood firm and fought back. Some of the girls were knocked down and my daughter, one of the twenty-six Yang Ko dancers, was hit on the shoulder and knocked unconscious. Carried to a nearby ambulance, revived, and sent immediately back to the school; she suffered no worse injury than a bruised nerve in her shoulder. The disturbers were quickly subdued by the armed postmen who came to the rescue of the girls.

Wearing her arm in a sling all the next week, my daughter was smugly proud of herself. Now she could swap parade stories with her father who once in 1919 couldn't sit down for a week after getting "whammed" across the seat of his pants by a soldier's rifle butt during a striking students' parade in Peking.

Indeed, Grace was the only family member who did not fare well in these months after liberation. What she did not yet know was that she had tuberculosis. The dreaded disease which had killed Mrs. Holmberg and many of the family's best friends during the war had now taken hold of her. It was only diagnosed later, but during this time, just when she was wanting to be active, she found herself confined to bed. She wrote in a letter to her brother in 1950: "The children are well and F. C. is well and weighs

209

165 pounds! But I have had a lot of asthma and bronchitis again, just like last fall and early winter. It has kept me confined to the house more than I like and I'm much too thin again."

Because of her confinement she relied even more upon her husband and children for knowledge of the transformation taking place around them. In addition to their experiences, she was still actively engaged in learning all she could about the new society. She read and studied all that she could to interpret what she was learning. She found herself often writing to dispel what she read in Western publications. The following description of Tientsin was sent to her brother in January 1950:

Six months or so ago the Voice of America was quoting "China Experts" as saying that the Communists could never run a big city, that they would run the cities into economic chaos, etc. Just to mention one thing, the city has been literally cleaned up. The streets which have been in dreadful repair since the 1939 flood have been repaired, old eyesores (tottering buildings, garbage dumps, etc.) have been removed. Garbage boxes are never left standing, overflowing with garbage on the sidewalks for days, but are taken away every morning at 6:30. In the summer it used to be a nauseating sight to see in front of the courtyard gate, beggars, mangy dogs, and flies swarming over the odorous garbage boxes.

And to see the traffic, that hopeless China traffic, efficiently and kindly (none of the Kuomintang kicks and blows) regulated is a marvel to behold! The Kuomintang police-men used to kick and beat the rickshaw men and still the traffic was a hopeless snarl. Perhaps it's not as picturesque and "so typically Chinese" as formerly but it's a lot safer.

A few weeks ago, neighborhood cleanliness campaigns were held all over the city. The police inspected all the courtyards, kitchens, and servants' quarters and the cleanest places had red stickers stuck on the door and dirty places got black stickers. We got a red sticker! The accumulated filth of decades was raked out of some places.

Now that the railway lines are open and clear from Peking to Nanking to Shanghai and from Peking to Canton, we can get food from all over the country, things we haven't had for years. For instance, I didn't taste an orange for eight years and now they are coming from Canton and Szechwan and we eat up a dozen a day!

I have to laugh when I hear over the radio and read in American magazines and papers things that are supposed to have happened in Communist China. Our friend who came back here from Formosa said he heard over there that F. C. had been put in prison, and another friend from Hong Kong was surprised to see Life, Time, Newsweek, Saturday Evening Post, Reader's Digest, *and* Ladies' Home Journal *in our living room. He'd heard in Hong Kong that the Communists had stripped the houses of furniture and allowed no imperialist literature to be read. There is not and never has been from the very entrance of the "Pa Lu" Army into the city any force, or any terror, nothing but the most Christianlike kindness and patience I have ever seen—a lot more than I would have under the circumstances.*

By the end of 1949, almost a year after the advance of the People's Liberation Army into Tientsin, conditions had improved so dramatically that Christmas could once more be celebrated at the Liu home. No longer in hiding. No gifts from the U.S. marines. No more boxes sent from Tennessee and delivered too late. Salaries were stabilized and money had value. It was the first time in William's life that the family had been able to celebrate Christmas.

Grace described the celebration in the letter to her brother:

We had a wonderful Christmas—the best since 1940. F. C. has had an eighty percent increase in salary and we just splurged. He bought Ellen the bicycle she's wanted for a long time and Nini a black lamb jacket and two books she'd been begging for—"Les Miserables" and James Body's story of the American Revolution, "Drums." Wei-han's heart's desire was various and sundry small items among them a set of Chinese story books. I got two beautiful pairs of nylon in a lovely dark shade, an American wool rose colored scarf, plum colored silk-padded satin jacket lined with silver grey silk. F. C. bought himself three new shirts—collar 16-1/2!—a pair of new shoes and two new gay neckties.

Christmas Eve we had a dinner party—our family and five guests made a table of ten. Our guests were a doctor and his daughter (Nini's best friend), another doctor and his wife (my best Chinese friend), their little son, and a young man from Shensi (F. C.'s province). We had roast duck and apples—duck to the Chinese is like catnip to cats, they almost roll in it—but we had braised chicken for me and Ellen and Wei-han because we do not like duck. For dessert we had "pa pao fan [ba bao fan]" (eight precious rice), a glorified rice pudding containing raisins, lotus seeds, dates, walnuts, lichi, a sweet bean puree, and several other ingredients. I made a luscious eggnog with eggs, sugar and whipped cream, the kind you eat with a spoon. It tasted so exceedingly good that we all ate a lot, fairly licking the bowl clean.

Nini went to midnight mass at the Kung Hsang Chapel with our Amah, a Catholic, and her friend and schoolmate, a Presbyterian! Nini is at present a weird combination of Catholic and Communist, she's pro-American, anti-Russian and a very enthusiastic supporter of the Chinese Communist Revolution. But she's got plenty of sense and nobody can tell her what she must believe.

Drinking eggnog and attending midnight mass at Christmas did not fit the Western perception of what was happening in China in 1949. The description of her daughter as both Catholic and Communist must have shocked Grace's family back home. To them both Catholicism and Communism were equally intolerable—and to proclaim them so forthrightly as a parent was unthinkable. When Grace said, "Nobody can tell her what she must believe," she was speaking not just for her daughter, but for herself.

After the so-called fall of the "Bamboo Curtain," Grace's communication with her American family grew more and more tense, while antagonism between China and the U.S. increased. Before the next Christmas, the two countries were at the brink of war.

15

SLIPPING OF FAMILY TIES

THE KOREAN conflict brought America to the brink of war with China. And while General MacArthur pushed toward the Chinese border in Korea, Joseph McCarthy was busy on the U.S. Senate floor raising a list of "known Communists," most of them associated with China in the State Department. As anti-Communist fervor flamed in America, Grace was in the "belly of the beast," writing home as passionately of America's wrongs as Americans spoke against the evils of China.

Grace's communications with her family became strained in the early fifties. Her letters became longer and more strident. She was frustrated because, from her great distance, it seemed that the torrent of anti-Communism which bombarded her brothers swayed them more than the eyewitness experiences of their own sister.

By 1950 Grace had been in China for sixteen years without returning home. Adding her eight years in New York, she had been gone from Chattanooga for twenty-four years. Sadly, she realized that she did not really know the adults her brothers had become. In a poignant letter, Grace began to wonder about their lives and the things she had missed. At first, she blamed herself for the loss of communication:

January 5, 1950
Dear Tom,

I haven't heard from any of the family for more than six months. I wrote Sam early in the spring and got a rather prompt reply asking me to write only about my family and not about China. He used to write me so faithfully and now I haven't heard from him for such a long time. It's true that during the summer months there was a lot of confusion about the mail to and from the States, but for several months now, mail has been coming straight to Tientsin.

I know I've been very bad about writing. I am lazy still and prefer thinking my letters in my head after I go to bed rather than getting them down on paper and mailing them. Sometimes one doesn't write because there's not much to write about and sometimes there's too much. Mine is the latter difficulty. To pick just enough to put into a letter out of all the upheavals and interesting events we have been experiencing is not easy and I can't sit down and write only ordinary family events.

I often wonder what you are like now. The last time I really talked to you was 1926, you were getting married—the year I went to New York. Remember packing your trunk in the Jones' house and the white kitten went up in the attic and got her paws black and came down and walked on your clean white shirts? As far as I am concerned you are still a boy of twenty-four. I know nothing about a middle-aged man with grown-up children. And we used to be pretty good friends and thought just alike. But twenty-four years lived in such different environments have probably made a difference in our thoughts and ideas.

I often get myself mixed up in my mind with Mama now. I look so much like her— my hair is getting noticeably gray and my cheeks have hollows. And I have to argue with Nini so often the way Mama used to argue with me. In many ways Nini is very much like the girl I used to be. She always has to be hauled out of a book and prodded to her studies, and she never wants to dress warm enough or eat properly—where is Mama now?

America's attitude toward China was split at the time between two very differing points of view. President Truman issued a statement declaring "disengagement" as the official U.S. policy: "The United States Government will not pursue a course which will lead to involvement in the civil conflict in China . . . [or] provide military aid or advice to Chinese forces on Formosa." Dean Acheson replaced George Marshall as Secretary of State and his report on China supported Marshall's view that the Nationalist army had "disintegrated" because the Chinese people had no faith left in the Nationalist regime. Further American aid would be pointless.

Even though high officials knew the Marshall/Acheson analysis to be true, the "hands-off" policy was not accepted by others, some of whom had strong ties to the U.S. media and Congress. The "China Lobby," as the advocates of U.S. aid to Chiang Kai-shek came to be known, attacked the Chinese Communists as pawns of the Soviets. The argument of Soviet domination of the world, made through magazines like *Time* and *Life,* owned by Henry Luce, son of missionaries to China, had a powerful influence on American thinking and foreign policy.

In December 1949, Mao had gone to Russia, his first trip outside of China. His protracted negotiations with Stalin had limited effect and eventually resulted in a bitter split between the two nations. But this split was not yet evident as Russian advisors returned with Mao to China, adding to an illusion of alliance with Russia which spurred dread of a Communist world bloc.

Grace's letter of January 1950 blasted this assumption:

All this yip yapping in the American press and over the "Voice of America" news broadcasts about "foreign domination" in China . . . is complete nonsense. The two hundred much advertised Russian advisors visited Peking, Nanking, and Shanghai and now have apparently evaporated into thin air or returned to Russia. Nobody sees or hears anything further of them. The only one I've heard of in Tientsin is a Russian woman— Chinese born—who is helping out in customs. They say she's marvelous at statistics.

F. C. went to Peking with the Director of the Public Utilities (a former Communist General) and met the Deputy Mayor of Moscow and the Moscow Water Works engineer. F. C. said the Deputy Mayor of Moscow was a pleasant, witty fellow who talked of the marvels of the Ford plant in America, and the Water Works engineer was quite impressed with F. C.'s Allen Hazen background and expressed desire to visit the Tientsin Water Works if he could get permission from his "higher ups." About a month later, after a visit to Shanghai, the engineer did stop off in Tientsin a half day. F. C. took him, accompanied by some Municipality officials, to the Chieh Yuan pumping station, where he was shocked at the thick, "muddy soup" of the Grand Canal that had to be changed to clean drinking water. He was impressed with the American-type rapid filters that F. C. had designed and built; and when he saw the clear, clean drinkable water flowing over the weirs, he delivered a lecture to the Municipality officials standing around about the difficulties and hard work attending the miracle of obtaining pure water from such a source. He ended with the Russian equivalent of "good, very good" to F. C., thereby giving that already complacent person much face.

Naturally I'm pro-American and dislike the Russian propaganda we've been subjected to for the last few months, although I know it's mostly for Russian and American consumption. It's annoying but nothing to worry about. The Chinese "lau pai hsing [lao bai xing]" (ordinary citizen) just shrugs it off. Stalin would have to have an army a hundred times bigger that the one he's got to force anything on the Chinese. They don't force easy! They have more "resistibility" than any people in the world, I think. The people in the street greet Stalin's and Lenin's pictures with "Here come the poor old Russians!" followed by expressive Chinese vulgarities and much laughter.

At the height of the propaganda furor, Russian classes were started in most of the schools, but Russian was elective and had to be paid extra for while English is required. In Nini's school at first there were eighty teachers and pupils who signed up for the Russian classes. It gradually dwindled to forty, then twenty and now Nini says there are only five or six faithful ones who go merely to save the Russian teacher's face.

. . . What a waste of time and money, to say nothing of human life, it was that the powers that be in the U.S.A. made up their bright minds that Chinese Communism was synonymous with Russian aggression. That false idea led to the stupid and unprincipled U.S. policy toward the Chinese people. If those in authority in the U.S. had not been, and remained, adamantly hostile to the Chinese Communists whom the people were backing, and had not been determined to bolster up the enemy of the Chinese People, cynically disregarding the wishes and welfare of the Chinese People—there would have been no exaggerated Soviet propaganda in China and Mao most probably would not be in Moscow now. Heavens, I hope you were able to make that jump. I get so wound up and involved I forget which sentence I'm on.

I listen to "free" nations' broadcasts and read "free" nations' papers and magazines and I compare the plight all the "free" nations are in with the almost unbelievable progress that China has made in the short two years that the Chinese people have been really free—free from all foreign imperialism and ancient Chinese feudalism!

For the first time in hundreds and hundreds of years, China has a government that has the interest of the people at heart—and forsooth, the United States does not approve of it! Well, that's just too bad, for it is here to stay—

We were glad to hear the other day President Truman's very emphatic announcement of his "hands-off" Formosa policy. What a mess of trouble those antiquated old dodos Hoover and Taft would like to precipitate.

The China Lobby's cry—"Who lost China?"—presumed that someone in America was responsible for China turning Communist. They targeted State Department officials and sometimes Truman himself as "soft on Communism."

On February 9, 1950, Senator McCarthy flaunted before the press a list of 205 "subversives" in the State Department as being known members of the Communist Party and shaping U.S. foreign policy. His press conference set off a wave of national hysteria and "Red baiting" which led to a witch hunt that flamed the rhetoric of the Cold War and mirrored the practices he condemned.

The conflicting forces in America soon weighed upon President Truman, who commemorated Washington's birthday with an impassioned speech on freedom, democracy, and the right to self-determination—from the American perspective. Grace heard the speech over the radio and immediately wrote her brother:

February 23, 1950
Dear Tom,

I am writing this at 7:30 in the morning. Ellen and Wei-han left for school about ten minutes ago. F. C. hasn't gotten up yet and Nini is still sleeping—her spring holidays aren't finished yet. The house is very quiet, but my thoughts are far from quiet, for at seven o'clock I listened to President Truman's Washington's Birthday speech broadcast on the "Voice of America." And it stirred me up to more anger than I've known for a long time.

He talked of freedom from oppression, freedom from coercion and force, the freedom of a nation to choose its own form of government. And he ended with the words, "freedom and justice for all."

As I listened to the nice sweet words that flowed from the radio I got hot with indignation and I wanted to yell back at Mr. Truman, What nation spent billions of dollars trying to force the Chiangs and their Kuomintang government on the Chinese people, although acknowledging how rotten he and his regime were, although admitting the knowledge that the Chinese people were sick of them and had repudiated them? What nation still refuses to the Chinese people the right to choose their own form of government?

Mr. Truman warns the world against Communism and the Soviet Union. I have lived under Communism for a little over a year and I have seen and heard of none of the dreadful things with which the press and radio frighten the American people morning, noon, and night. There's no "iron curtain" here—we hear the A.F.R.S. from Manila and San Francisco, the "Voice of America" (so called, I'd hate to think that it really spoke for the American people) from New York, the BBC and Radio Australia every day, several times a day. I read the Reader's Digest, Life, Time, Newsweek, *the* Saturday Evening Post *and the N.Y.* Times *and I don't wonder that Americans are jittery!* . . .

After retreating to Formosa [Taiwan], Chiang Kai-shek began bombing the harbor of Shanghai, then Nanking, in 1949–50. The bombings had the backing of the United States navy and were supported by U.S. aid to Chiang. Grace heard that the bombings were coming closer to Tientsin. Her letter to her brother continued:

The Shanghai air raids have caused death, destruction, and misery. Nanking was bombed yesterday, and Formosa announces they're building a new air base on an island only four hours by air away from Tientsin. So the city is getting ready, antiaircraft guns have been placed in different parts of the city, the windows of all the houses are being pasted with strips of paper to help keep shattered glass from flying all around, dark curtains are hung over the windows and we are just waiting, hoping we won't get any of the "American aid to the Nationalists on Formosa." As far as Mr. Truman's warning against the Soviet Union is concerned, our greatest danger of death and destruction comes from the U.S.

Do you wonder that I don't appreciate Mr. Truman's noble sentiments? To talk to the Chinese people about "freedom from coercion," freedom from force and oppression to the Chinese when they all know that American bombs dropped from American airplanes using American gasoline have killed whole families in Shanghai—and not Communists either—is doing the cause of American Democracy no good. If Tientsin is bombed, the Water Works and Power Company will certainly be targets. Naturally I thought the bombing of Shanghai and the killing of perfectly innocent civilians was dastardly, but the prospect of Tientsin being bombed at any time now selfishly upsets me a great deal more, because I might be one of those innocent civilians or my husband or my children.

Well, my house is no longer quiet, so I will have to bring to an end this outpouring of my indignation on your innocent head. I hope you got my other letter. If we don't get bombed I'll write you a more cheerful letter next time.

The cheerful letter never came. Grace's brothers thought she had turned against her American family. To Grace, it seemed that only her sister-in-law was still willling to listen:

April 18, 1950
Dear Mary Hills,

Your letter made me feel very happy. In the first place because it was so interesting and full of news of people I love to hear about; and in the second place I was delighted with your attitude and relieved that you believed that I meant what I said and also knew what I was talking about.

I am writing to you because you are the only one of my rather numerous connections that has expressed the slightest curiosity as to what has been taking place in China. Although it is of such great importance to the whole world, no one has been interested enough to even comment on things I've written in my letters. Your one letter asking for information was the only one that showed any desire for firsthand information on a great historical revolution and rebirth.

I think you don't realize what an iron or rather "brass" curtain there is in the States. The ordinary American citizen is kept just as ignorant of the truth about the rest of the world as they think the Russian people are. The American press and radio are pretty tightly controlled. Americans are carefully "protected" from knowledge that might bring about a better international understanding and a peaceful solution to the present unnecessary world complications. I will tell you just a few instances of proof of this fact—instances that I know personally. I was naive enough a year ago to believe American papers and magazines would like to hear the true story. Well, I know better now.

Last summer, after listening to a particularly vicious and nasty broadcast by the "Voice of America," I wrote a letter to the N.Y. Times. *I did receive a reply and got my letter back. They said they regretted their inability to use the material I had sent. I wrote to* Life. *They printed part of my letter in an issue of the "International" edition, but followed it of course, with a "slap down" and refutation by the editor who evidently knew more than I did! I wrote another to the* New Republic, *but even such a liberal paper as that was afraid to print it. Finally I wrote to Edgar Snow [author of* Red Star Over China*], and he had my letter printed in the* Nation *last November, of course with all reference to himself cut out. The last of January I wrote a short letter to the* Washington Post. *To my astonishment they printed it—probably because I said I knew they wouldn't. Several days later the* Post *printed a letter from the director of the Bureau of Far Eastern Information who "put me in my place." He said I had to write that letter in order to avoid the "miserable existence" of every American in Red China!*

Characteristically of Grace, she decided it was time to educate herself. She was in a unique position to read the literature of both sides. She wrote to her sister-in-law of her observations:

Concerning the American people's distrust of the Soviet Union, I will tell you a little of my own experience on that line. Although I knew they were lying and distorting the truth about China, I believed they were telling the truth about Russia. The true facts in China were in front of my eyes; Russia was far out of sight. Like most people, I never questioned the dreadful things I heard. Gradually I began to see how inconsistent my attitude was . . . I made up my mind not to be a political illiterate any longer. I bought an armful of Lenin, Stalin, Marx, and Engels and went to work. And I meant really work. I found the going very difficult at first, but I read and reread and studied until I had gone through seven of Lenin's most important works—they're small—and one big one of Stalin's, some Marx and Engels and then the History of the Communist Party of the Soviet Union, *and then back to Lenin again. Now it was much easier to understand. . . . Next I got out my old* Reader's Digests *of the last ten years, also old and new* Saturday Evening Posts, Life, Time, Newsweek, *and* Colliers *and I studied diligently and with an open mind and critical eye every article on Russia. And I made discoveries that completely changed my ideas on the Soviet Union and the menace of Russian imperialism and aggression. I found discrepancies and contradictions galore, deliberate tampering with quotations, fixing them up to mean what they don't, a half of a sentence put together with the half of another, sentences and phrases taken from their context and made to sound altogether different. But in the '45, '46 and early '47 issues there were articles more favorable to Russia [because they were our allies in the war against Germany] . . .*

It would take a big book to tell you all my mental comings and goings, but this is where I am at present—I believe at least three-fourths of the things told against Russia are false. Maybe one-fourth is true; the Russian communists have probably made great mistakes, as the Chinese communists admit they have and as they most likely will again. But I think . . . the people of the United States and the people of the entire world have more to fear from whatever very powerful element is in the States that is backing this "Cold War" than from Russia.

Because of the bombings of Shanghai, the foreigners remaining in that city could not leave. The last ship out left in September 1949. Another ship had been promised by November but Chiang's bombings and his blockade of the Shanghai harbor had prohibited the boat from entering. By April 1950 the remaining non-Chinese in Shanghai were told to go to Tientsin to catch the *General Gordon* as their last chance to leave.

April 21, 1950

    The city is in a pleasant dither of excitement. All the Shanghai foreigners are pouring into Tientsin to wait for the "General Gordon" which is coming to Taku Bar. One or two parties have been straggling up separately for the past few weeks, but now they are coming wholesale on every train. The hotels are overflowing and many are staying with Tientsin friends. Tientsin shops and eating places will certainly make money for a few days. Fortunately for the Americans, commodity prices are down and the American dollar still up, so I think there will be an orgy of buying.

    Last Saturday F. C. and I were invited to dinner to meet some of these people. Everybody was "overcome" when one of the women and I each discovered the other was from Chattanooga! Can you believe it? Her name is Jenny Lea and she had been teaching in the Shanghai American school for three years. She had come up from Shanghai with Mr. and Mrs. Douglas, an American newspaper man and his wife. She seemed to know all the McCallies, Cousin Eula, and my old school friends. She said she would look everybody up when she got back, especially my brother Tom, and tell about seeing me well and happy in this "unhappy land" (quoted from Dr. Jessup's report).

    Another thing causing excitement in the town is Laurence Olivier's "Hamlet" which is on for eight days. Nini and Ellen went yesterday afternoon. Hamlet is Nini's favorite "piece of writing." She came home in ecstasy and got out her copy of Hamlet to read her father the most effective passages. Wei-han insists on seeing it because it has a "kuei" (ghost) in it. F. C. will take him tomorrow. I will have to miss it as there is too much smoking in the theatre and I can't stand, or at least my bronchial tubes can't, that tobacco-laden atmosphere.

    F. C. and I have never had time to become bored with each other. The years have gone by so fast, and exciting event has trod on the heels of exciting event to such a degree that we've never had time to settle down to being an old married couple.

    I have got to stop before I write you a small book. When I write with a pen I get tired, but writing on a typewriter is like thinking with your fingers. You think, and the thoughts flow throughout your finger tips and on and on—

16

THE KOREAN WAR

THE 38TH parallel was drawn across Korea in 1948, separating the Republic of South Korea and the Democratic People's Republic of Korea to the north. On June 25, 1950, North Korean troops crossed the 38th parallel and marched into South Korea, overrunning the country in a few weeks. President Truman responded by shifting U.S. troops from Japan, and fifteen other nations joined suit under the auspices of the United Nations' newly formed international forces. On June 30, the U.S. announced it would give all necessary military and economic aid under the leadership of General Douglas MacArthur. Army reservists were called up in America.

By August the U.N. forces in South Korea were having little success in regaining territory. On September 15, U.N. troops under MacArthur's command swarmed ashore at Inchon, winning back Seoul and moving on toward the 38th parallel. Confident from the victory, MacArthur told Truman that he could be finished by Thanksgiving—but his optimism had not counted on Chinese intervention.

Mass rallies throughout China called for defense of Korea against U.S. aggression. Thousands volunteered in a wave of patriotism. When U.N. troops captured Pyongyang, the capital of North Korea, on October 19, Chou Enlai threatened Chinese involvement if MacArthur proceeded to the Yalu River, the border between China and Korea. Hundreds of thousands of Chinese volunteer forces moved toward the border. Despite warnings, MacArthur continued to press toward the Yalu. Heavy fighting took place under the worst winter conditions. By January 1951, the U.N. forces had been driven back to Seoul.

Grace's letter of that month reveals that she is bedridden after having been diagnosed with tuberculosis, which she had had for some time. But her own health is of less concern to her than the war:

January 17, 1951
Dear Mary Hills,

I am writing in bed so I can't use my typewriter. I'm now left with only a pencil—the children have "borrowed" all my pens.

I've been in bed for two and a half months—resting, and have nearly another month to stay. I felt so well and energetic during the summer that I really didn't expect any asthma last fall, but with the first cool weather it hit me more viciously than I've ever had it. The ephedrine and codeine I had to take in order to breathe destroyed my appetite completely and the asthma exhausted me. So I lost eleven pounds in six weeks. When I started having a very high fever around the first of November, I got carted away to the hospital for all sorts of tests. An X ray discovered very tiny spots of T.B. up in the region of my shoulders. I had two shots of streptomycin a day, and after the second day my temperature was normal and has remained so. I stayed in the hospital twelve days. The doctor said I was not infectious and no danger to the family. After I came home I had four more weeks of streptomycin. The doctor came every morning and gave me a concentrated shot—the equal of the two a day I had in the hospital. The shots are rather painful. I feel restless now in bed, because I feel perfectly able to get up and go about my business. F. C. scolds and fusses so when he sees me up that I wait until he's out of the house and I get up and listen to the radio.

I've been wanting to write to you for a long time, but I have hesitated. Not having heard from either you or Tom since I wrote last I have thought that perhaps you didn't think it wise to have any further communication with Red China.

The instigators of this frenzy of war preparations in America and Europe do not fear attack by Russia. It's something else they fear entirely—and they want to strike before it's too late. The Korean strike was a bad miscalculation and has increased their madness. The U.S. administration is taxing the American people billions of dollars to create weapons of destruction when nobody wants to or intends to attack the U.S.A.

The way the U.S. government has acted in Korea, it's practically taking over Formosa, and the bombing of Chinese on Chinese territory in Manchuria has been the last touch, the final "chemical" agent needed to bind a mixture of many different elements (Catholic, Protestant, Buddhist, business, workers, intellectuals, rich, poor, all kinds) into one Chi-

223

nese People, solidly and enthusiastically supporting "Aid to Korea and Resistance to Imperialist Aggression." For all Chinese understand now from where this aggression comes—from the big financial Empires interlocked across national boundaries—and at present with the power concentrated in the U.S.A.

The effect of the Korean War in China galvanized the Chinese people in the same way that the common enemy of Japanese aggression had created a "united front" in earlier years. Use of the war as an internal propaganda tool was immense. First it gave the Chinese reason to praise the heroes of the war, those new young revolutionary volunteers who had held off a great power, far superior in military technology. Movies, speeches, novels, and plays, acted out with music and song, praised the brave soldiers. Secondly, the war also gave the Chinese clear evidence that the U.S. was a hostile enemy, no longer a friend. The evils of U.S. imperialism were trumpeted as broadly in Chinese propaganda as the evils of Communism were in America.

The Korean War also rid China of its remaining foreigners. The "Resist America and Aid Korea Campaign" resulted in the closing down of foreign businesses, searches for spies, and arrests of foreigners for possessing radios or firearms. By 1951 only a few foreigners remained in China.

One American couple that stayed were Bill and Sylvia Powell. Together they published an English-language magazine called the *China Monthly Review*. Since there were so few foreigners left in China to provide stories in English, Grace found an eager outlet here. From 1950 until the magazine finally closed in 1953, Grace wrote several articles for the *Review* about her observations of life in Tientsin. In addition, Grace often sent articles from this magazine home to the family to give them broader exposure to points of view other than her own. She wrote, "I am sending you an American magazine published in Shanghai. The publisher, John William (Bill) Powell, is a China-born American. His father started the magazine twenty-five or thirty years ago. The elder Mr. Powell was tortured in a Japanese concentration camp, lost both his feet and died about a year after he was released. The magazine will tell you some of the truth about the China situation that the American press is never allowed to tell."

From the outset of the Korean War there were differences between Truman and MacArthur, but their differences intensified as the war escalated. January to April 1951 witnessed the heaviest fighting. Truman advocated a "limited Korean war."

MacArthur wanted to attack bases or bomb supply lines in North China. MacArthur conferred independently with Chiang Kai-shek, thereby positioning himself in opposition to Truman's authority. MacArthur accused Truman of supporting "those who advocate appeasement and defeatism in the Pacific."

On April 11, 1951, Truman stunned the nation by firing General MacArthur as commander of the Pacific forces.

Meanwhile, Senator McCarthy's purges on the State Department had spread. No one was exempt from suspicion. The "liberal" media came under attack. From newspaper reporters to Hollywood actors, anyone could be called to testify. In cities and small towns throughout America, fear gripped the nation. Many were arrested or investigated on the basis of "leftist" comments or membership in targeted organizations. Careers were ruined and lives disrupted.

During this period, Grace's brother Sam received a letter from the government with an enclosed form asking him to identify any family members living in Communist countries. Frightened and uncertain what to do, Sam sent the letter to his brother Tom, who was still working at Oak Ridge. Tom's job had changed after the war from procurement to public relations. One day, Tom received a call from the local newspaper asking about a man who had been taken into custody by the FBI. His arrest coincided with rumors of a Russian spy ring and leaking of top-secret scientific information. These two incidents during the Korean War heightened the family's fears that by writing Grace they could be accused of leaking information to Communist China. Merely receiving her inflammatory letters worried the family, and it was clear that Grace could not limit her correspondence only to domestic news.

Grace wrote the following letter at the height of the McCarthy era, at the most controversial point of the Korean War. The physical appearance of this letter reflects the intensity of her feelings. It is fifteen pages typed, single spaced, from edge to edge of paper, every empty space filled with handwritten notes, emphasis added through underlining and exclamation points. Grace wrote this note at the top: "Nini typed most of this for me but she rebelled toward the end—said her fingers were sore."

The letter was written to her sister-in-law in response to her questions to Grace. But it was hard for her family to read, not just because of the small, close type with no margins, but because of the obvious emotion with which Grace wrote these words from inside China.

April 20, 1951

Dear Mary Hills,

 I was surprised to get a letter from you from Washington. And you had just been listening to the Senate discuss foreign policy! Well, I must say that the gist of your letter sounded very much like the Voice of America.

 I am feeling much better, practically well, if it weren't for occasional bouts of asthma. However, I still spend most of my time in bed as we are having a raw cold spring and I want to be very, very careful. When the weather is really warm I will go out for an Xray to see if there's any T.B. left, I don't think so, as I don't feel in the least like it.

 Now, I think I had better get down immediately to your questions as they will require rather long answers. To answer them all fully is a big order, because you seem, to my mind, to have everything completely higgledy piggledy.

 The anti-American feeling in China is against the government, the rulers, not the people. American imperialism is a very real and menacing thing. You are thinking of imperialism in terms of the old British imperialism, literally taking over countries openly as colonies. That is not the American style. You say that the U.S. did not want to annex China and Korea. It didn't, not in the manner you have in mind. But think of this—why did the "powers that be" in America spend billions of dollars and do everything short of sending in U.S. troops and making an all-out invasion, to keep Chiang in power? Marshall, the other generals, and the State Department knew all about Chiang and his government, even before the war was over . . . they acknowledged that the Chinese people had abso-lutely turned thumbs down on Chiang and his gang. . . . but the U.S. went right on trying to force Chiang on the Chinese people . . .

 If the Communists had not been armed, and the people with them, Chiang would have won with American money, American equipment, and would have ruled China as a puppet of the American government. And China would have been to all intents and purposes a colony while the U.S. could pose as a benefactor and reap rich rewards from the ground-down Chinese people. You may think this is an exaggeration, but you weren't here in the first three years after the war. You couldn't see how the Americans "took over"; they owned China!

 I do not think that the American People are unanimous in their approval of the Government's imperialist policy. I think most Americans are completely fooled by the pro-paganda that is constantly being repeated in different ways, and through different agen-cies. They read it in short stories, novels, jokes, advertisements, news items, editorials, articles on various subjects, hear it in movies, sermons, lectures, and over the radio.

. . . You say it is not clear to anyone in America just why the Chinese took up the fight in Korea. Until I remind myself how little most Americans know of the Far East, its history or geography, its races and their relationships, I am inclined to retort sharply that you must know people who are not able to put two and two together and make four. There are two vital reasons why the Chinese had to go to the aid of the Koreans. The Chinese and the Koreans are close kin and are very much alike, much more alike than Chinese and Japanese. Its very difficult to tell a Korean from a Chinese. There's only the narrow Yalu river between China and Korea. During the war many Koreans joined the Chinese 8th Route Army (The PLA) to fight the Japanese and many Koreans fled from Japanese. So there is the natural sympathy and desire to help one's brother when he is attacked by a much larger nation, or by a whole "gang up" of nations.

Now remember that Korea and China are as close as Canada and the U.S.A. . . . so wouldn't China be slightly simpleminded to busy herself "living successfully and peacefully in her own country" while a country whose government was openly and adamantly hostile to the Chinese government was sending a large army with super-equipment, accompanied by vast naval and air power nearer and nearer her border, until at last forward units stood on the opposite bank and looked over into China only a few hundred feet away?

The Chinese could see the flames and smell the smoke of the burning Korean villages. But that wasn't all. For a long while, planes had been coming over every day, bombing and strafing Chinese territory and killing and wounding Chinese people, sinking Chinese fishing boats and killing Chinese fisherman. If a hostile army attacked Canada or Mexico and brought their artillery to the American border and sent their planes daily over American territory killing and wounding Americans, I'm sure Washington wouldn't sit quietly saying, "We won't notice them and perhaps they'll go away."

. . . You say the Chinese are "killing us." Just what would you expect them to do, when "we" come with our super-weapons and "our" so many "rounds upon rounds of death" from our huge naval guns and "our" round-the-clock bombing with incendiary bombs, and napalm, that jellied gasoline—marvelous invention—that burns alive, turns to "pillars of flame" everything, women, school children, and babies, the old and the sick, in villages far behind the lines? Do you think killing American combat troops is something worse than that? After all, the American troops were sent to Korea with every modern death-dealing weapon for the express purpose of killing Koreans. It is quite inevitable that

227

some of them would be killed in turn. A great many Chinese have been killed, too. War is not a tea party. Somebody always gets killed! But for those who order behind-the-lines bombing of villages, schools, of all buildings, of anything that moves, for those who are responsible for the massacre of countless civilians, for the wanton destruction of homes, civilian industries, and the campaign of frightfulness and horror worse than Hitler's, I cannot say with you "Father, forgive them, for they know not what they do." For that which they do is deliberate, and they should not be forgiven.

. . . Just think a minute. Whose armed forces, whose air force, whose navy is in the Far East? . . . Just what country is actually dominating the world?

Now, about writing to the Senators, as you advise. I used to be naive and believed people really wanted to hear the truth. But I found out that they really don't. Most people only want to be confirmed in what they already think, in what suits them to think. I've written the truth about China many, many times, but the truth doesn't fit the official policy, it's most definitely not what America wants to hear. Now if I should write about how dreadful it was over here, and what a miserable existence I live, as an American in Red China, they'd eat it up—I couldn't write fast enough.

. . . Your last question is do I not believe in God anymore? Well, just whose God do you mean? Do you mean the God of the Protestant Church where I used to go every Sunday? It was very strange when I came to China and went to church with Chinese people where missionaries preached. When I heard American missionaries teach and talk to the Chinese about God, they made their God so American. Somehow the American God of the American missionaries never seemed right for the Chinese.

I certainly don't believe in the God Americans pray to to keep them safe and comfortable while American bombers hurl hundreds of thousands of tons of bombs and napalm on Korea, killing countless women and children and old people, even changing the courses of rivers and shape of mountains with ceaseless bombing.

I could ask you—Do the American people believe in God anymore? Since the Korean war started, I've not read in any American paper or magazine or heard in any American prayer or speech over the radio any condemnation of the inhuman bombing of the Korean civilians and their homes. Even in your letter you say "they are killing us," not a word of the Korean mothers and babies, little boys and girls burned alive by napalm. The utter hypocrisy of the American policy talking of the sacredness of the human personality and human dignity, the evils of Communism and Russian and Chinese aggression! What's happened to the American people? They've lost their moral conscience and moral sensitivity. Every country has protested against these atrocities and barbarities against innocent people. But American complacency in the face of MacArthur's terror bombing makes me think that the American conscience has dropped dangerously behind the conscience of humanity.

For the well-off Americans, I think their religion and their belief in God is a sort of magic formula that they hope will keep them and theirs out of trouble and discomfort. For those for whom this world is a "vale of tears," their religion is an escape into a future land of everlasting happiness. If the Christians would take Christ's own words literally and act upon them . . . Christianity would be an alive and efficient force instead of the dead and hypocritical thing it has become! It seems to be no longer a power for good. The so-called "Christian countries" are planning to bring horror and death to the world. It is the greatest Christian country in the world that has atom bomb bases in the East and the West. It is from the Christian countries the threats of horrible death are coming.

. . . Don't think I've gone entirely "anti-American." I haven't, but from this distance I can see that the U.S.A. has gone off on a dangerously wrong path.

But I still do have faith in the American people. I believe what I read somewhere the other day, "The future doesn't belong to Senator McCarthy and the armaments trusts. It belongs to the people." I'm counting on that.

I think America is the most beautiful of all countries and the spring and fall in Tennessee is such weather no people in any other part of the world ever get to see. Two things besides my family I miss in China, the lovely, lovely climate and real honest to goodness buttermilk. I have plenty of sweet milk, but nobody here seems to know how to make good buttermilk. When I crave some terribly, I let my sweet milk clabber and beat it with a fork—but it's not quite the same.

Well, I certainly have taken up enough of your time. You are probably a busy person, but you can easily see that I have nothing to do but sit in my bed and scribble. I did appreciate your letter, Mary Hills, and your questions. And if I've answered some of them with asperity (Mama loved that word!), it's not aimed at you, but at the whole awful situation. I hope you will write again, and if you feel like taking me down a peg or two, go ahead. I love to argue.

So you and Tom are grandma and grandpa now! I guess I'll have to wait some time for grandchildren. Seventeen, thirteen, and ten are pretty far from the marrying age.

F. C. has just come back from Changsha in Hunan province where he went to fix up their Water Works. It's very far away. It took him three days and three nights on the train to get there. He had to cross both the Yangtse and the Yellow Rivers, and he was terrifically impressed with China's bigness (never having seen anything but Peking, Tientsin, Nanking, and Shanghai before), with the plentiful crops and, as he said in his letter, "Our wonderful people." He came back bringing four beautiful umbrellas with pictures and writing on them (Changsha is famous for its umbrellas), a big bunch of writing brushes, another Changsha specialty, and some multivitamins for me.

I am sending you some more magazines and a great bunch of clippings. Read them if you have time. Even if you don't agree at all, and even if they make you angry, at least they will give you some insight into and understanding of the other side, and that's never a bad thing to have—even to argue against it.

I hope you write to me again with more questions, and I hope you and Tom will both interest yourselves in political affairs. Those things are left too much to the politicians. Every American citizen should take a fine and vital interest in politics—what is more important than the way your country is run?

With love to both of you,
Grace

As the Cold War escalated, the world became divided into two camps. Both sides began stockpiling weapons of defense. On May 12, 1951, the United States detonated the H-bomb, the world's first thermonuclear device. The H-bomb was so massive it needed an atom bomb to set it off. Its destructive power was one thousand times greater than the bomb dropped on Hiroshima in 1945.

The U.S. Congress continued to side against Grace's China. The February 1, 1952, edition of the *U.S. News and World Report* stated: "The U.S. is now pumping supplies and dollars into Formosa at the rate of nearly a million dollars a day to build up the Chinese Nationalist forces . . . "

August 11, 1952
Dear Tom,

I have put off writing this letter to you for many months. I don't enjoy talking of unpleasant truths. I know it's unwelcome and most likely will be dismissed as propaganda.

But my conscience won't allow me to keep still about what I know to be true while the American people are being convinced by brazen lies and deceit that they must go to war against a dreadful evil—an evil so awful that they must run the risk of their own and the world's destruction.

The premise of those who urge war and preparation for war is completely false, therefore all their conclusions are false. The newspapers, magazines, and radio are working overtime to keep the people befuddled, inactivated—to make them feel helpless, frightened, or fatalistic . . . I hear the "Voice of America," the Armed Forces Radio Service from Tokyo, Radio Australia, and BBC from London EVERY DAY. I heard the Republican and Democratic conventions over "VOA." I recently read an editorial in Life *on "The Terror in China." It gives a malicious and deliberately distorted and false picture of China. The truth is just the opposite. The* Reader's Digest, Saturday Evening Post, Colliers, Time, *and* Newsweek *are full of lies and concocted slander. . . .*

I have lived now for three and a half years under a Communist-led government, and the false lie-inspired prejudice I had has been swept away. I have seen the wretchedness and misery due to abject poverty wiped out of China. The former starved and ragged are now adequately fed and clothed. Hovels have been replaced by decent houses. Miles of swamps have been filled in and dumping grounds leveled, cleaned, and planted to make beautiful public parks where thousands of workers and the former scorned "coolie" can enjoy their holidays. Illiteracy is being wiped out at an incredible speed. The whole country is teeming with constructive activity.

The Chinese people have been given faith in themselves, dignity and self-respect as human beings and as Chinese. They are free with a freedom they never dreamed of before and that doesn't exist in the U.S.A. Freedom from hunger and cold, freedom from fear— of the future, of war, of depression and unemployment.

The Chinese people are proud, happy and enthusiastic, and have such love, respect and gratitude for Mao Tze-tung, the government leaders and the Communist Party, that man, woman, and child would rise like one *to destroy anything that threatened to "liberate" them from those to whom they owe their new life.*

This I see with my own eyes and hear with my own ears. During the last year and a half, F. C. has traveled from the northeast to the southwest and through central China and he was filled with not only enthusiasm, but with awed amazement at the marvels the people with the help of the government have accomplished.

Now, I've told you the truth! Whether you allow yourself to believe it or not is another matter. If you use your brains and think a few reasonable, considered, independent thoughts, instead of thinking what you're told to think, what you're supposed to think, you cannot help if you are honest, seeing the truth of the present world situation.

. . . An aroused American public opinion can still control government action! Smugness and conceit as well as ignorance of the rest of the world's people give the average American a dangerous contempt for other people and an entirely misplaced *belief in his own rightness.*

I hope you are all well. I am better this summer. My Xray showed no activity, so the T.B. is arrested. But I must be careful. I haven't heard from Sam for ages. Perhaps my letters became somewhat bothersome to him. I am sending you some clippings and some magazines. I hope you get them.

Truce negotiations began in the Korean War in July 1951, but like the war itself, dragged on for two more years, ending finally in July 1953, with the same 38th parallel as the boundary between the two countries.

The Cold War had extended its grip. The void between Grace and her family was as great as the ocean between them. Contrary to their assumption that the Chinese Communists had "rung down the Bamboo Curtain," thereby prohibiting mail to and from China, it was, in fact, Grace's family in America that stopped writing.

The letter of May 1, 1953, just before the end of the Korean War, is Grace's last extant letter home. In the letter, Grace made it clear that she sent and received mail from other people in other parts of the country. It was only her family that did not respond. She pushed the point further—that other countries had well recognized China and its achievements. As far as Grace was concerned, news of her family and news of the country were one and the same. For Grace this was an exciting time. F. C. was at the pinnacle of his career in 1953. He was invited to Peking to view the May Day celebrations. As he watched the joyous parade of China's accomplishments, he had never envisioned such glory even in his earliest, most idealistic days. Grace was angered and dismayed that her own family would cut her off.

May 1, 1953
Dear Tom,

What's the matter with all of you? I haven't heard a word from Tennessee since last spring. Doesn't the post office there take mail for China? I hear often from other parts of the U.S.A.—New York, Pittsburgh, Chicago, Connecticut, Oregon, Minnesota, and California.

May Day parades have been going past the house since eight o'clock—it's now eleven. From where I sit I can see the beautiful huge silk flags, red and gold, pink, lavender, blue, pale yellow, turquoise, jade green, coral, so many colors! And such a noise of singing, drums, and cheering. A bigger noise is coming in from Peking over the radio. F. C. went to Peking yesterday afternoon and is now seeing the parade together with other labor models from the reviewing stand. Also on the stand are about one thousand visitors from all over the world—Poland, Czechoslovakia, Bulgaria, France, Finland, Sweden, Germany, Australia, Mongolia, India, Indonesia, Burma, and other places whose names I didn't hear distinctly.

We are all well. I was sick during the fall and half the winter, but I feel fine now and weigh more than I have at any time since before the war (1941).

I hope all of you are well.

Love,

Grace

The last word that Grace heard from home was a letter from Sam in 1954, informing her that her mother had died. Grace did not write back.

17

F. C., MODEL WORKER

IN A 1953 issue of *China Reconstructs*, the Chinese government's English-language magazine, Grace wrote an article entitled "My Husband is a Model." The "model workers" of China were considered labor heroes, and in the early fifties were elected by fellow workers. The recognition was initiated by the government as a way of encouraging hard work at all levels. She wrote:

One evening in October 1951, F. C. came home and told us in a manner he tried to keep calm that he had been elected one of Tientsin's "model workers." This unexpected announcement left the children and me quite speechless for a few moments. Then came whoops and cheers from the children. My pride and pleasure were expressed only a little less vigorously. In New China those people chosen to be model workers receive great honor. Their experiences and methods are read about and studied all over the country and they are looked upon as examples to follow, to learn from, and to emulate.

Soon I noticed the girls looking thoughtful. "Well," said Nini, "this means that we three have got to be better students. "

"Yes," Ellen agreed, "we can't be just 'pretty good' when Daddy is a 'model.'"

Ten-year old Wei-han then became quite sobered by the thought of the responsibility that devolved upon all of us as members of a model worker's family.

"Why did you get elected a model worker, Daddy?" he asked. "You didn't invent anything."

"No," F. C. said, "I didn't invent anything. I just used my head a lot and worked

234

as hard as I could." The pride in his eyes belied his casual tone.

Then he explained to his son: "The Hai Ho extension project which we finished this spring meant that all the two million people in Tientsin could have plenty of clean, safe water. And building a strong water tower for Hsinhsiang [Xinxiang] meant that the people there could afford a modern up-to-date waterworks plant. So I got elected a model worker because my work is helping the people to live a better life. Understand?"

The children and I were familiar with the two projects Fu-chi mentioned. For years, the one on the Hai Ho River had been a favorite family topic. Now it has been carried out. The new government has put a great deal of money into the Water Works and the original plans have been considerably increased to more than double the capacity of the existing water supply.

A large new reservoir (sedimentation basin) holding one hundred million gallons of water was soon built along the Hai Ho River, and a reinforced concrete pipeline was laid down through which the water flows by gravity to be filtered and purified at the main pumping station more than a mile away. Pipelines are being extended to every district in the city, providing clean, safe water for the nearly two million inhabitants of Tientsin.

A clean water supply was essential to improve the basic standard of living and to develop industrially. While still working on the Tientsin Expansion Plan, F. C. was called on to advise other cities. Grace's article continued:

While the Hai Ho project was still under way, the municipal authorities of Hsinhsiang, Honan [Henan] province, asked F. C. to design a waterworks for them that would be within their budget—that was a bit of a challenge. A steel or concrete frame water tower would be so expensive that it would leave very little of Hsinhsiang's money for the rest of their waterworks.

F. C. remembered the ancient brick tower-like structures that are still standing in various parts of China. Some of them are as much as eight hundred years old and well-preserved. "Surely," he thought, "that's durable enough!"

He did a lot of research, reading on the old towers, discussing the proposition with his engineering staff and especially with the older workmen, and they all decided that they could build a brick tower just as well as the ancients could. So

235

The Lius in 1953, with the responsibility of a model worker's family.

Hsinhsiang now has a brick water tower and enough money left over to build a small but very modern, all automatic waterworks plant—one that is run easily by the girl superintendent, a former normal school teacher of chemistry, and her two assistants.

Lacking access to modern machinery, F. C. had to design ways to build the equipment with Chinese parts and labor as well as to train workers in mechanical and technical skills for maintaining and running the expanded system. Developing the personnel to run the new systems was an accomplishment equal to building them. F. C.'s experience of learning on the job as a construction worker in New York had prepared him to work closely with his workmen and to create ways in which they could learn from practice.

Early in the winter of 1952, F. C. started on the new purification plant for the Tientsin Water Works. This plant, with mechanical filters having an output of twenty-five million gallons of water a day and automatically operated by electric and hydraulic mechanisms, was a complicated project. Its like had never been done in China using all-Chinese resources. Many factories cooperated with the company's engineers in designing and making all the elaborate equipment.

Workmen had to be taught and trained to read complicated drawings, weld steel tanks, lay complicated pipings, use slide rules, install automatic apparatus, and make steel pipes from steel plates made in China.

The workmen were divided into groups. Each engineer took charge of one and after work hours would give his group some fundamental technical instruction in the line of work they were doing. The engineers worked closely with the workmen. As the workmen began to acquire technical knowledge, they gained a more intelligent understanding of the work to be done, became more enthusiastic, and felt ready to tackle any difficulty.

The entire project, including a big mixer and coagulation basin and the handsome four-story building housing mechanical filters, automatic equipment, pipe galleries, and a large chemical laboratory, was completed in ten months.

The overall accomplishments of the newly trained work force inspired Grace to write the following conclusion in another article entitled "Workers Become Engineers" (*China Monthly Review*, July 1953):

They know that the building-up of new China industrially depends in large measure upon them and their fellow workers all over the country. Just this initial step in technical education has been enough to show them what they are capable of doing when they begin to acquire scientific knowledge. They have caught a glimpse of what it will mean when all China's innumerable workers are skilled technicians.

It is an exciting and inspiring vision!

In the construction that took place in the early fifties, F. C. traveled throughout China, helping other cities design and build modern water systems and advising factories on water supply problems. Once when he was in Sian [Xian] near where he had grown up, he looked at the new construction happening everywhere, including the newly completed Lanchow-Sinkiang [Lanzhou-Xinjiang] railway—it was spring and the peach orchards were in bloom— and told Nini later that it made him very proud to see his country moving forward so rapidly.

F. C. with engineers and workers at the control panels.

Grace wrote in the *China Reconstructs* article that she delighted in the positive changes she noted in her husband's *pi chi*:

While he was working on this [Water Works expansion] project, F. C. always came home late, long after the family supper, and although he would be tired, we often talked over the day's happenings while he ate. We all sat around him at the dining table and would discuss his problems and difficulties and sometimes have very heated arguments. Although inclined to be hot-tempered and stubborn, F. C.

The Water Works expansion project, 1952, included a sedimentation basin holding 100 million gallons.

had learned to take honest, objective criticism [so] that none of us, even the youngest, hesitated to speak out when we didn't altogether agree with his views or his attitude.

What a change from the old days when constant frustrations and fruitless conflicts within a strangling environment made F. C. so irascible and difficult to get along with! Arguments then usually led to recriminations, tears, and hurt feelings all around. Now the exhilarating sense of freedom and the joys of accomplishment that liberation had brought were giving him a new disposition—in many ways making a new man of him.

F. C. wearing his model worker medals, with PLA soldiers, 1953.

All his best qualities—his clarity and honesty of thought, his real kindness and feeling for people, his creative initiative and tremendous capacity for work— could now grow and expand. Traits I never saw in him before began to show—a new humility and patience along with a new kind of self-assurance and the ability to impart his own knowledge to others.

In 1953 when F. C. was elected model worker for the third year in a row, his citation acknowledged that he had "saved the government more money than can be counted." I thought of those years of frustration in the old China. When he was a student at Tsing Hua, he had chosen engineering as a way in which he could best help China; he went to America to study at Cornell and stayed four extra years for practical work in hydraulic and water engineering. When we met in New York, he shared with me his hope that some day his training could be put to use by the Chinese people. At last his dream has been realized.

As a Model Worker for three years, F. C. was invited to Peking to view the May Day celebrations that Grace described in her 1953 letter. His accomplishments, not only in Tientsin, but throughout China, were soon to be recognized with an even higher honor and responsibility. But for the meantime, it was F. C.'s family that kept him from having "too much face," as Grace recounts in the following episode:

Not long after he became a model worker, F. C. had to make his first radio speech. When he left for the broadcasting station he denied stoutly that he was the least bit nervous, but the family waited around the radio in our dining room with dry throats while "special model Liu Fu-chi" was being announced. And then we heard a perfectly strange voice roaring out into the room, speaking faster and faster until when it stopped with a final roar, we were all out of breath. When we recovered from shock and amazement, we all burst out laughing. When Fu-chi came home, grinning sheepishly, we told him teasingly that he might be a model worker, but he was certainly no model radio speaker!

Assembled Model Workers, 1952. Liu Fu-chi is seated, fifth from left.

18

IN A CHANGING WORLD

T O ACCOMMODATE the increased numbers of children attending school, many schools temporarily used facilities the foreigners had abandoned. Ellen's middle school was housed at the former horse racing course. The place where the social life of the British and other foreigners delighted in gambling and games, drinking and parties during the heyday of the semicolonial period, now housed not one but two schools. Located outside the former concession, it took Ellen forty-five minutes of fast walking to get there. The makeshift surroundings did not interfere with Ellen's having an active social life in the middle school years, as she recalled in a 1970s interview:

> They made all the horse stalls into classrooms. We played in the walk-
> ing yards, in the mud, in the creek during breaks. We were often late
> coming to class. Once I was in the mud and kicked my leg and my shoe
> flew into the creek. I got reprimanded for that. We also played in the hay
> in the barns. We had a lot of fun out there. Then in midyear we moved to
> our new designate school. I worked hard on my lessons. I liked [to learn
> how to run] machinery. We took field trips sometimes to factories and
> workplaces. At school I played basketball and high jumping and running.
> I was not bad in sports. I represented my school in the relay races. I liked
> high jump quite a lot. We used gymnastic horses to jump over. We still
> went to the Water Works on Sundays with F. C., but not so often. We had
> more of our own lives then—school, friends, other activities.

As the literature of the revolution began to emerge, Ellen read Ding Ling's *The Sun Shines over the Sanggan River* and other novels praising the heroic peasants, or diaries of optimistic, fervent young cadre: "In sixth grade I started to read Chinese novels a lot. Some were liberation stories and occupation stories, fighting the Japanese, about the underground during the occupation, and some were about land reform. And there were Soviet novels about fighting the Germans, and some old Russian classics. I still read some English stuff, like Shakespeare, but in Chinese."

The next year four new schools opened and Ellen moved to another middle school, but there were so many middle school students that the school operated in shifts. Ellen and William attended the same school but in different shifts. The school was built near Nankai University in a former cemetery whose graves were moved so new housing could be built.

William attended the early shift. Each morning he would walk from their house in the former British concession, which was now incorporated into the city as a whole, through the graveyard to school. For him the transition to middle school was not an easy one:

> I finished primary school in 1953 and then went into junior high. That was a very bad experience for me. I was twelve and had been in the same school for six years. My primary school was more or less like home— when I first started primary school they called me the little foreign boy or "big nose" boy. I made an effort to fit in. I didn't want to dress in foreign clothes or let my father take me to school in the Water Works car. Soon I was just one of the kids and I didn't think about differences anymore. When you start junior high, you are a complete stranger. Twelve-year-olds are the naughtiest anyway. The first few weeks were terrible—kids teased me a lot. When the kids teased me, I'd get upset and my nose would bleed. Once when I got really upset, my nose bled and I had to walk home in the cold wind through the cemetery. I didn't have anything to stop up my nose but my school things, and then the blood came out of my mouth. When I got home, Grace was upset. She told Ellen to talk with my teacher. The teacher talked with the class and told them to stop teasing me. After a few weeks it got to be okay again.

Nini in school,
1954.

Being older, Nini took problems in stride better than the two younger children: "We had some conflicts at school because we looked different. Some people were nasty, and we got teased about being 'foreigners.' Sometimes I let things pass. To me, it was not so very deep. It was always just something I lived with. I have always found that if you are not snobbish and don't hold yourself apart, people very quickly forget about differences. But Ellen didn't let anything get by. Ellen was a little tiger. She fought back with fists."

William soon had many friends and one in particular, Kelin, shared his love of books, movies, and Western music:

Kelin and I were very interested in cinema. We went to movies after school and discussed the film techniques as an art form. There were Russian films and still some European ones around. One Saturday, I told my mother I was going to study for an exam at Kelin's house and Kelin told his mother that he was going to study at my house. We met at the cinema and watched films all day. We did okay on the exams so no one ever found out.

We went home after school and listened to Beethoven. We listened to music on the radio and attended concerts. There was a great promotion of art right after the liberation and that is how I got interested in the violin. My father got me a violin and I took lessons.

We all liked to read. During these years my mother used to read us novels like *Ben Hur*. But when she was sick, Nini read to us. Nini was a great storyteller. She would read us books like *Les Miserables* and *Wuthering Heights*. Sometimes she read them in English, sometimes she translated them into Chinese. I think I got my first literary education from Nini. My friends would come after school to listen to her. It motivated us to read ourselves and to learn English.

We all thought we should do well and work hard in school because F. C. was a national labor model. It put a responsibility on the whole family. Ellen was very good in school. She was a model student and was a leader in the Young Pioneers. I got in the Young Pioneers too, but I was always too undisciplined, always talking in class, too individualistic. At least that was the criticism the teachers gave me. There was quite a lot of homework. Sometimes we would study on our own and sometimes we would meet at someone's house and study in a group. In our textbooks were stories about the anti-Japanese war and landlords and political things. Even our group study and support for homework was political. It was all mixed together.

During Nini's early high school years, she too was interested in learning everything she could about the political changes in China:

The [Korean] war was still going on, and we became a part of the effort. There was a lot of political study in the classroom, maybe two or three hours a week. In student groups and youth league we studied current events and the movements that happened. We had a movement to keep prices down, and an anti-counterrevolutionary movement. Many students volunteered for work in the more newly liberated areas. I wanted to volunteer, but I was too young. They wanted senior students.

But as Grace's health became worse, Nini took over more responsibility at home:

In the early fifties, when F. C. was traveling a lot, I think my mother might have been somewhat lonely. Grace was sick about eight months every year. I think she may have been in a weakened condition during menopause. We didn't know what to do. I stayed out of school most of two years to take care of her. We still had one amah and our cook, but I took care of Ellen and Willy.

During that time, Grace studied. She always had her bed piled up with letters and magazines and books. At first she couldn't understand the Marxist language. She talked with my father about what she read. They were both going through the same process, I suppose. They would discuss books and things they read. We'd discuss the books with them and talk about political events in China. Both my parents were very democratic that way. Whatever was happening or being talked about, we were always let in the conversation. We got to know their opinions and why they were for or against things. And we began to form our own opinions.

During this time when F. C. was often traveling and Grace was sick, William was quite independent. Most of his time was unsupervised, except when Nini took charge. But he lived with a constant lurking fear each year when his mother was sick through the long winter months:

> One of the fears of my childhood was that my mother would die. Asthma is an awful thing. It sounds like you are dying. Nini took care of Grace and she took over disciplining me. She was quite a holy terror. I was much more scared of her than my parents. She would yell at me: you must do this, you must do that—she always thought my parents had spoiled me too much, so she was going to set me straight—"Don't make noise when you eat! Don't breathe through your mouth! Stop howling! Don't drink so much tea!"

By the time she was out of high school, Nini had her own strong opinions. Her ardent commitment to the new China grew from her awareness of the need for change. She had seen the extreme poverty and harsh conditions early in her life. Since the time of writing the letter to her cousin in America after the war, she had seen many changes and her ability to communicate them improved. Grace encouraged her to write. In May of 1952, at age nineteen, Nini wrote an article for the *China Monthly Review*, describing the changes she witnessed in her neighborhood:

> To give a picture of the liberation, let me describe the suburb in which I live. Formerly the wealthiest people of the city lived here, in mansions fortified by ten-foot walls, electrified wire, and protected by huge dogs. Outside the walls, the garbage boxes invited the explorations of beggars and stank to high heaven in summer.
>
> Ashes were dumped carelessly into an empty lot; here the poor children would play and root about for burnt-out light bulbs and other treasures. Street lights were scarce, and after dark in winter thinly clad women workers hurried home through the pitch blackness, clutching their infants and empty lunch boxes.

One night I saw a woman standing at the gate of a mansion as big as an ocean liner, which belonged to one of Tientsin's worst traitors. I shall never forget how she cried and raged against the owner, cursing him, his forefathers and descendants for the wrongs he had done her.

But since that day when the PLA came through, knocking on doors and calling out, "Don't be afraid, countrymen, this is the PLA!" my neighborhood has changed almost beyond recognition. The mountains of ashes and garbage are no more; nowadays, a bell rings every morning, the residents bring their garbage containers to the street, the refuse is carted away, and the containers are taken back again. Empty lots are filling up with new buildings, lumber yards, playgrounds.

At the spot before the big gate where the poor woman stood cursing the traitor, the student union cultural troupe performed a dance to welcome the World Federation of Democratic Youth Delegation. The traitor, to everyone's relief, has been tried and shot, and his huge house is a hostel which has sheltered the Panchan Lama and the Korean people's delegation, among others.

Many more street lights relieve the gloom at night, and in warm weather groups of people gather under them to sing or talk over current topics and problems. The workers still hurry to and fro, but no longer in haggard silence; they are warmly dressed and well-fed, and many, in the evening hours, carry books as they laugh and chatter on their way to night school.

I know many more people of the neighborhood than I used to. Mrs. Wang is our group leader. The old man who is always in a hurry is our street representative, Mr. Pai. The neighborhood meetings have created a real community for us at last.

Some of the conversations in the Liu household in the early fifties were about land reform. F. C. was among the urban professionals asked to serve on the land reform work teams that fanned out across the countryside. According to Ellen: "F. C. was away a lot during this time helping other cities design and construct waterworks. Nini and I went to fetch him from the station when he came back. We heard a lot of things from him about landlords and peasants. He came back talking about how

245

poor the people were, the cruelty of landlords and a lot of things we had heard in school, but hearing it from your parents is more convincing. He talked a lot with Grace about what he had seen, and we heard the conversations."

The atrocious poverty of China's rural areas had been a recurrent theme of literature on China since Pearl Buck's *The Good Earth*, published in 1931. For its time, Buck's novel was a welcome break from the previous portrayals in Western literature of Chinese as devious, sinister, or inscrutable stereotypes. The Pulitzer Prize-winning book played a major role in reshaping Western attitudes toward China, but it was disparaged by Chinese intellectuals, like F. C. He resented the superficial image of China as a helpless peasant—the very image that the American press had manipulated to rationalize adverse policies toward China.

One American observer of rural land reform was William Hinton. Working for the U.S. State Department under the United Nations, he was sent to observe a land reform team in Changchuang (Long Bow Village) in Lucheng County in Shansi province in 1948. His notes became the basis for his book, *Fan Shen: Documentary of Revolution in a Chinese Village*, which was published in 1966. He met the Lius when he was working at Lutai, a state experiment farm outside Tientsin.

Mr. Hinton joined the table conversation at the Liu household. He and F. C. explained the land reform process to Grace—that to shake up the deeply ingrained feudal system, outside help was necessary from land reform work teams. These teams of five to twenty-five people were made up of a broad mix of Chinese, representing different classes of society, many of them from urban areas. Involving urban professionals like F. C. accomplished two things at once: it created a representative group to address the imbalances of the old feudal system and it educated the urban elite about the problems in the rural areas.

IN 1954, F. C. was asked to head the Institute for the Design of Urban Water Supply and Liquid Waste Treatment. He was made responsible for water-related aspects of urban development throughout the whole of China. This national position required that he leave the Tientsin Water Works and move to Peking where he would work directly under the central government. This was an exciting development for F. C. and Grace, but because the move would require new schools for the children and other practical changes, the family decided that F. C. should go ahead to Peking while Grace and the children prepared for a move. The move never materialized.

19

THE DEATH OF F. C.

F. C. WAS in South China climbing a mountain with a team of workers when he ran out of breath halfway up and told the others to go on without him. When he returned home, he was busy with his new responsibilities as head of the national water and sewage intiative and ignored the warning signals for a while.

When he was in Peking, F. C. smoked with everyone else at the office, but when he came home to Tientsin, he quit. The family noticed that he was short of breath and wheezing. F. C. joked that since Grace, Nini, and William all had asthma, he was just catching up with them. But Grace was worried. She had seen these symptoms before and had even written to her sister-in-law in April 1950:

F. C. was the heaviest smoker I ever saw. It was only when he was sound asleep that he did not have either a pipe, cigar, or cigarette in his mouth. It distressed me so I could hardly stand it, yet I sympathized, and understood his apparent need for it. The Japanese occupation and the year and a half immediately after was a time of almost unbearable strain. But I also knew he was literally killing himself with tobacco. I talked, I argued, I begged, I pled, I threatened. I was just knocking my head on a stone wall.

Whenever I heard a woman say, "I made my husband stop smoking" or "I don't allow my husband to smoke so much" or sometimes from a friend, a trained nurse, "Grace, why don't you stop F. C. from smoking like that? It's very bad for him," I would say in desperation, "Please, please, tell me how one makes a husband obey. I've tried everything short of hitting him in the head with an axe."

Finally nature stepped in and scared him so bad that he's never touched any form of

247

tobacco since. He had five doctors and they all attributed an inflammation of a nerve in the right side of his brain to excessive smoking. Tobacco constricts the blood vessels and the nerves are thereby cut off from their proper supply of blood. His whole left side was affected with numbness and spasmodic jerking, he walked like a drunk man, and his speech was thick. The doctors said, "No smoking, rest in bed, milk, eggs, tomato juice, multivitamins, and vitamin B." The inflammation cleared up in about three weeks and the distressing symptoms disappeared, but F. C. was not very well for four or five months after. He had a stomach ailment that looked like appendicitis, and two or three bouts with something like flu. He gradually regained his health and strength and for the last few years has been quite well, only now he's too fat—160 pounds and only five, six and a half!

F. C., 1952.

But his resumption of smoking had exacerbated the earlier health problems. In mid-1954 Grace made F. C. go to Dr. Chang, a friend of theirs who was a renowned lung specialist. Dr. Chang had worked for the Peking Union Medical College before starting his own practice in Tientsin. According to Ellen: "The doctor took Xrays which showed that one of his lungs was completely black, but he told us only that [F. C.] had water on his lung. The doctor began a treatment to clean the water out, then sent him back to Peking, without informing F. C. of the seriousness of his condition."

When the trouble persisted, F. C. went to the Russian Red Cross Hospital in Peking for observation and continued to work from there. As the weather got colder in October 1954, Grace was unable to travel but sent William to check on his father at the hospital. William recalls:

This was the first time I went to Peking by myself. I was thirteen and in my second year in junior high. Before I left home early that morning, Mother gave me a letter she had written to Daddy, a bag of food from Sun and a list of books to buy at the foreign language bookstore—as I was going out the door, Nini shouted at me, "Don't forget the books!" "I know, I know," I shouted back, "*War and Peace* and *The Red and The Black*. I won't forget!"

To be able to take a day off from school and go to Peking was quite an exciting endeavor for me. Peking seemed much more Chinese than the foreign section of Tientsin that I had grown up in. That Daddy was sick did not seem to be a serious concern then, as he was always very strong and hardly ever had a day of illness as I could remember.

When I got to the hospital in Peking, I was told that F. C. was having a meeting with his colleagues and would not be able to see me until noon.

I left the hospital and went wandering in the bookstores in the Wangfujing area. While looking for the books that Nini wanted, I found the Chinese classic *The Journey West*. My father and I both loved this story and used to read it aloud together. It was compiled during the thirteenth century and described the Monkey King's journey to escort the famous Tang Dynasty monk to India to bring Buddhist sutras back to China. We used to laugh at the hilarious events that satirized the societies hundreds of years ago. They reminded us of people and events around us. The same was true for books by Jane Austen, which we read out loud. These classics are all timeless. One of us would burst out laughing and would say, "Listen to this . . . Isn't it just like so and so." If the passage was in Chinese, we would translate it into English for Grace. I bought *The Journey West* and

Grace, by the wall of the house where the Lius lived before F. C.'s death. This photo of F. C. is from about 1953.

249

F. C. with William, age 14. This is William's last photo with his father.

took it back to the hospital with me, hoping Daddy would enjoy laughing again.

When I arrived at noon, the meeting was just breaking up. I recognized two engineers that Daddy had brought with him to the Institute from Tientsin and saw others I did not know. Daddy said to those present, "Ah, here is my son with goodies from home." Daddy looked fine. With a white coat on, he looked more like a doctor then a patient. "Let's have some lunch. I have another meeting in the afternoon."

He had lunch brought to us in his room. While we ate, he asked me about school, about Nini and Ellen and about Grace. He said he was very impatient to get out of the hospital. Although he was working full time in the hospital, there was still a lot he could not do. He read Grace's letter, wrote a note to her and told me he would be back to visit in a couple of weeks. When I left the hospital, the others were already returning for the afternoon meeting.

When summer came, Grace recovered from her asthma and bronchitis, but F. C. did not get any better. He returned to Tientsin to see Dr. Chang. The family did not know what was wrong. William described the frightening way in which they learned the cause of F. C.'s troubles. It was a very hot and humid day in early July 1955:

> The heat was very oppressive and a thunder storm did not alleviate the heaviness in the air. Right after supper, Mother said that Dr. Chang had called to say that he needed to speak to her about Daddy. Mother asked me to accompany her and, all the way there, she was unusually quiet and nervous and hardly said anything to me.
>
> When we got to Dr. Chang's house, he was eating watermelon and asked if we would like to have some. Both Mother and I refused, and I sat at some distance from them while Dr. Chang talked to Grace sitting at the dining room table, where he continued to eat the watermelon. I could

250

not hear what was being said, but I watched him smugly slice up the melon while talking to Grace. He'd take a bite, juices running down his chin, then spit out the seeds, all the time spitting out his words as well. Grace sat there with her face turning to stone. I watched and waited. They then got up from the table and came over to me. Dr. Chang said that he would drive us home.

As we were getting into the car I asked Mother, "What is the matter with Daddy?" She answered in a very low voice, "I will tell you later."

Fortunately it was a very short ride. We left the car, passed through the courtyard. No lights were on and it was completely dark. As we groped our way towards the front door, I asked again: "What . . . what?"

"Daddy has lung cancer," came the quiet answer.

"How . . . how long . . . "

"Three to six months . . . "

Mother took a deep breath and gave me a quick hug.

I shuddered.

"Don't say anything to Daddy," she said.

We pushed open the door and went in.

There was only one lamp on and Nini was reading by it. She looked up. When she saw Grace's face, she got up from the chair and went with Grace into the bedroom where Ellen was. I stayed in the living room and sat down in the chair Nini had just vacated. I could hear Ellen crying. I didn't know what I felt—all my insides had turned upside down.

Grace was very angry when she found out that Dr. Chang knew F. C. had cancer a year before but didn't tell her. If we had known early enough perhaps we could have done something. . . . By the time he told her, it had spread throughout his body. Dr. Chang told her that there was nothing she could do for F. C. except alleviate the pain. He suggested that Nini learn to administer morphine injections. We talked into the night. How could we just keep him at home and let Nini inject him with morphine! We decided to ask the Water Works company for help.

The next day Nini talked to the management of the Water Works, and they immediately arranged to have F. C. taken to a hospital that specialized in cancer treatment. They hired two nurses around the clock.

Nini and Ellen took shifts, so that one of them was always with him day and night. Grace was not feeling well, so I stayed at home with her at night and brought her to the hospital every morning.

In interviews in 1979, the children recalled the last few weeks of F. C.'s life.

NINI: F. C. talked to me and to Ellen, but I don't think he said any of this to Grace. He said first he wanted to be cremated. That was new in China. He had designed the first crematorium in Tientsin because the Public Works Department didn't know who else could do it, so they asked him. Second, he said that we should not wear mourning. Chinese used to wear white for death.

Then he said always look forward, never look back. He had had a great life and he was able to realize his life's dream. To Ellen he said that Chairman Mao was the greatest man in the world and to always follow his teaching. He said that he did not worry about us and that he knew the government would take good care of us.

ELLEN: He was in a lot of pain. It was very hot and, of course, there was no air conditioning. The hospital brought a big tub of ice to put under his bed. We were young, and didn't know quite—we never saw anyone dying. Then one day the nurse said, "Are you prepared for anything that might happen?" His hand was turning blue, and he went in and out of consciousness.

One night I was there with him alone. There were empty beds around him and he was awake. He said, "It's late, why don't you go to bed."

Later on he called me. I went over to him, but he didn't say anything at first. Then he said, "Why are you here, why are you up so late?"

This happened several times.

In the morning around seven or eight I went back home and Nini came.

WILLY: Nini went early to the hospital to relieve Ellen. Then Grace and I went to the hospital not long after eight o'clock. When we arrived,

Nini said to Grace, "I don't think there is much time left. I better notify people." We walked toward the bed, F. C. was having a hard time breathing and his eyes could not focus. Grace put her hand on his hand, and he held it and tried to put it to his lips and had a difficult time doing it. As he kept trying, tears rolled down Grace's face. She could only murmur, "No, no . . . "

Nini came in. She took one look and beckoned me to the window and said to me, "Mother needs some vitamins. Could you go to the drugstore and get her some. Go past the Water Works and tell them Daddy's situation is extremely serious."

I did not know whether to leave or stay. Nini said, "Go!"

I took a last look back at the room and left.

After I bought the vitamins I walked quickly to the Water Works. I went to see the chief engineer who had taken F. C.'s place after he was transferred to Peking and said to him that my father's condition was very serious. Just then someone else walked into the office. As soon as he saw me he said, "What time did he pass away?"

I must have looked stunned as the words echoed in my head.

"He doesn't know yet," another disconnected voice sounded somewhere beside me.

I got up and walked out in a daze with the words "pass away . . . he doesn't know yet" ringing in my ears.

When I reached home, Grace and Nini were already home and there were half a dozen people sitting in the living room, people from the Water Works and some friends of the family. I didn't know where to go. Just then the door to the bedroom cracked open and Ellen, who had been sleeping, poked her head out and whispered to me with a smile, "Who are all those people?" I blurted out, "Daddy died." The light in her shining eyes dimmed and without a word she slowly closed the door.

ELLEN: You think it will never really happen. Even later, we thought we would hear him coming home for lunch. We never did cry in front of each other. We held everything in ourselves, and didn't let it out to each other—but it was a shock for Grace.

It was decided that the funeral would be too much of an ordeal for mother as it would be long and all in Chinese. Nini and I represented the family and Willy stayed home with Grace.

F. C. was very well-known and had worked with people in all walks of life. The funeral was attended by a great number of people. It was organized by the Water Works and his colleagues made speeches. The funeral procession was a street block long. People lined up to say goodbye. Then the body was taken to the crematorium that he had designed.

News had quickly spread of F. C.'s death. Some of his former classmates and friends wrote or came to visit. Rensul Yang, a Tsing Hua classmate who had studied in the States and visited F. C. and Grace in New York, came down from Peking and stayed with the family for a couple of days.

He and other friends told Grace that living without F. C. in China would be difficult—now was the time for her to consider returning to the States. But Grace would not hear it. She felt strongly that F. C. wanted his children to grow up in China and be part of the new China. To honor him, she would do whatever she had to do to carry out his wishes. She had no idea what it would mean to live out this commitment.

20

GRACE CHOOSES CHINA

F. C. DIED September 1, 1955. The cancer that took his life also took from Grace her beloved companion of the past quarter century, a man she loved so much that she chose him and his world over her own career, culture, and even family. She wrote in her memoir of being reunited with him in New York shortly before they married: "All doubt and hesitation were gone now, for both of us. I knew that this was the one man I wanted now and forever to live with and be with, to face life with whatever the years might bring." And the years, beyond her wildest imaginings, had brought life rich in tragedy and triumph. She and F. C. had survived separation, war, flood, famine, and revolution. They had raised loving children in both Chinese and American traditions. They had seen F. C. rise to the top of his profession. Throughout all, they had remained devoted to each other, friends and lovers. But now he was gone.

In the days to come, writing became Grace's outlet. Cut off from her family—her mother, her brothers, her sister-in-law, her older aunts—restrained from expressing her feelings even to her own children, Grace chose to express her grief, her sorrow, her shock, her despair—to an older woman across the ocean.

Harriet Eddy was eighty-two years old and stone-deaf. Grace had never met her. Harriet lived in Palo Alto, California, where she had retired after working for the California library system. She had seen Grace's articles in the *China Monthly Review* and had written to her, beginning a correspondence that was warm and personal. A few weeks after F. C. died, Grace poured out the news to Harriet:

Tientsin

September 24, 1955

My dear, dear Harriet,

 This is a letter I hate to write—I hate to see the words down on paper. But I cannot hide from reality and I feel very close to you and very sure of your love, sympathy, and wise understanding. My summer was a nightmare of anxiety and suffering. For nearly half a year I could see that F. C. was not improving. During the heat wave of July, he became much worse and the doctor was forced to tell me that what we thought was pleurisy was incurable cancer of the lung. F. C. never knew what he had and after six weeks in the people's hospital he died on September 1st.

 I did not know that last fall the Central Government wanted to send him to Moscow, but the Soviet doctors in the Soviet hospital in Peking, where F. C. stayed for nine weeks, said that the Soviet Union did not know how to deal with such an intractable condition except to keep the patient as comfortable as possible. Everything that could possibly be done for him was done up to the very last. The Government ordered from Hong Kong at great expense a British preparation made from a Japanese medicine that kept down the worst pain, so that it was not necessary to keep him drugged with morphine. He was fully conscious most of the time. He had five doctors and two special nurses and one of us stayed with him all the time, never leaving him alone with only a nurse.

 Though he never knew he had cancer, during the last week he began to realize that his illness was fatal and he told me to be prepared for his death and to face the future with confidence. He said he had had a full and satisfying life especially during the last six years when he was able to do much work for China's industrialization, and he had hoped to do much more, but if he had to go now, he had no regrets—he had a good and wonderful share of life. He spoke of the children's future in a socialist world and told them always to live as Chairman Mao had taught the young people and children to live.

 He did not—noticeably—lose weight until the last few days, but he had difficulty in sleeping, increasing difficulty in breathing, and hated to eat, all of which made him nervous and exhausted. For the last two days he had to have oxygen to relieve the terrible heaviness of his breathing. The growth traveled from his left lung to the right lung and then to the stomach and liver, under the left armpit and around the neck and then finally to the lining of the brain. The morning he died and the night before, he recognized no one and kept calling for old schoolmates he hadn't seen for twenty-five years. But I think he knew me although he didn't speak to me or look at me. For an hour or two before the end he held on to my hand and kissed it repeatedly. He could then no longer talk.

The whole terrible six weeks had so benumbed me that I had the sensation of standing aside and watching myself go through some kind of fantastic scene. It all seemed so impossible, so utterly impossible that F. C. had gone out of my life forever.

Since then constant physical activity—washing, ironing, sweeping, scrubbing, and cooking—is helping me overcome my first frantic desperation and despair. I have to keep myself reminded of the thousands of thousands of women all over the world who have faced the same thing, and worse, so bravely and firmly.

The children are so good and considerate that I cannot oppress them with any excessive grief. Fortunately I have no asthma this fall, thanks to a Chinese medicine, and I can keep active. The government has been very generous and if we live very economically, the government money will be enough for about eight years, until all the children have finished the university and can work. I have dismissed both my domestic helpers and we are moving to a smaller place. I am a good cook and the girls are learning; and we—

I was interrupted and now I don't remember what I was going to say. The only time I regret my cook and Amah is when I want to write a letter and have no time. Otherwise I'm very glad to be kept too busy to think.

To make our expenses as small as possible without cutting down on essentials we are going to have to cut out some items that we could afford on F. C.'s salary—We are now planning to move out to Sian within the next year. That is F. C.'s old home where there are quite a lot of cousins. Sian is the gateway to the Northwest—the new frontier—the cradle of ancient Chinese civilization and now one of the newest industrialization centers. F. C. was out there a year ago in the spring and he said it was beautiful and fast becoming a modern city, and with a much better climate than Tientsin and Peking.

I must stop now and get lunch for Wei-han and Ai-Lien (Ellen). Nini eats in school. We are going to have To-fu (bean curd) cooked with tomatoes and green peppers; eggs with Chinese sauce and Kan fan (dry rice). Very simple but good.

Dear Harriet, I know you are a wise, brave and useful person. I hope you will write and help bolster up my courage, I have confidence in the future and I've nothing to worry about. But my joy, enthusiasm and interest in life are gone—and I know that is a wrong attitude and a selfish one. I try to combat it with all my might and I think I succeed in at least not burdening the children and the people around me. But here I am burdening you!

With love and thanks,

Grace

Grace had no idea at this point what lay ahead of her. She had had little experience with managing money or budgets. William, only fourteen when his father died, was worried over how the family would survive economically:

During the first two weeks, we were too stunned to think about the future. He died when he was only fifty. We didn't know how to manage financially. When I was about twelve years old, I wanted to put some money in the bank for savings. My father said, "What for? Are you going to be a capitalist?" He was the great provider and we were not supposed to worry about practical things. It was an intellectual's attitude—that money was not worth anything and you should not worry about it. That was okay for him because of his highly valued skill. F. C. had one of the highest salaries but he spent all he had. Our cook's salary was as high as a university graduate's. As far as I know, we had no savings at all when F. C. died.

Now twenty-two, Nini was already used to being in charge:

Grace stopped eating for quite a while after F. C. died. I had really a tough time to make her eat and get her back. It was a terrible shock for her. We didn't have much money, so I suggested we move. We lived in rather an expensive place. I knew that how we lived was not what you call Chinese normal. Even when my father was alive, we talked about it—he said he couldn't have such a high salary for too much longer. I wanted to go to work. After liberation it was new for women to go off to work. It was exciting for me and my classmates to work for China and have economic independence. There was a policy that allowed children to be hired by the same workplace when a family member died, so I went to work for the Tientsin Water Works.

When F. C. died, the Lius still lived in the house into which they moved during the Japanese occupation. It was the same house where they lived when the PLA came marching down the street, where they entertained the U.S. marines after VJ Day. It was a simple Spanish-style duplex, with tile roof and stucco walls, located on the edge of the former British concession. It was not very large by Western standards, but it was for Chinese. It was rental property and the landlord exacted a good rent. F. C. had never bought a house or acquired property as the wealthy Chinese around him had.

It was Chinese policy that the workplace handled pensions and responded to the family's needs. So it was the Institute in Peking, and not the Tientsin Water Works, that actually was responsible for F. C's pension. According to William, the family was unprepared for what happened:

A representative from F. C.'s organization in Peking came and said that the government had decided, in honor of F. C.'s contribution to the state, to give the family one year of F. C.'s salary. Since that was customary and since F. C. had such a high salary, he probably considered that a generous offer, although some people expected them to do much more. But then he went on to say that to honor F. C.'s memory, Grace should eschew her former extravagant ways and really live like an ordinary Chinese. They had heard how extravagant she had been and that the family was lazy and had not taken good care of F. C.

I was too stunned to know how to respond. He did not know Grace at all. He had never seen us, had no relationship or history with the family. What could he mean?

Many undercurrents of feelings and resentments made life very difficult for Grace after F. C. died. There were many built-up resentments against F. C. and Grace. F. C.'s principles and hot temper had made many enemies over the years. Some resented F. C.'s role in nationalizing the Water Works. Other upper-class Chinese had never felt camaraderie from F. C. They expected F. C. and Grace to prefer Western tastes and extravagant styles, but they always looked down on these indulgences. Some of these people resented F. C.'s high profile and felt that he had gained it only by catering to the Communists.

Grace was always blamed for keeping F. C. from being truly one of them. He did not do the things that Chinese men of that class did away from their wives. They always accused her of being extravagant, even if it was just "different." Anything that was different from their ways was criticized.

259

The people in authority over F. C. thought it was his foreign wife that made him draw such a high salary. They assumed that it was F. C.'s wife that kept him from joining the Communist Party and from being of like mind with them.

I felt that Grace was being punished, for being who she was. She was being blamed because they thought she was the reason that F. C. wasn't totally "Chinese."

The first thing Grace did was to take care of the cook and amah. Wang nai-nai had already retired and returned to her home. Grace paid the other amah and reluctantly dismissed her. Then she wrote a letter of recommendation for Sun Pao-san and he got a very good job with the Finnish ambassador and moved to Peking. The children began looking for another place to live, one they could afford.

ELLEN: After school, I went to the house bureau and checked out houses. Friends helped us arrange a swap for a new place. We checked out the place we moved to--it was light and sunny and quite nice. We went and scrubbed it out, cleaned it up. Grace was in bed; after we moved she remained in bed for a while. I did the shopping and Nini cooked the meals. We moved to a house that was shared by other families. To Grace it must have seemed like a tenement, so many people in the same building, sharing things, no servants. To me it was just like how all my schoolmates lived.

WILLY: So in early November, two months after F. C. died, we moved to our new home—two rooms in a huge dilapidated mansion shared by seventeen families, most of whom were blue-collar worker families. The building was built in the grand style of the twenties and had belonged to an aide of the "Young Marshal" Chang. It was a big square building, like a mansion with a courtyard and a wall around it. There were three floors and a half basement with windows. Several families lived on each floor, and each family had one or two rooms. Two families partitioned the parlor and one lived under the stairway. Each floor had a bathroom and a faucet. People bathed outside, or in their rooms with a pan. From the basement to the third floor, each family had a small coal stove, for heating and cooking, placed in the hallway in front of their doors. Whenever anyone started their stove, the smoke from the kindling and the coal would go up the stairwell and permeate each room in the building.

We were fortunate—we had the two nicest rooms in the building with a door in the middle and we had access to a balcony which looked out over the courtyard and street and was shared by three families. We had a room that opened onto the balcony and an inner room that opened to the hall. The outside room had big double-glazed windows and a fire-place that wasn't working. It had wooden floors and high ceilings, but the high ceilings just made it harder to heat. The rooms were bright and clean, an oasis from the hallway. Unfortunately the smoke still poured in whenever some family started their stove.

The four families on the second floor where we lived shared one toilet and a bathroom with a faucet and a sink. The bathtub was filled with someone's coal. Of course there was no central heating or hot water. We had to heat water on the coal stove for both bathing and laundry.

Before we left our old home, we had to sell most of the furniture, our refrigerator, and the stove with an oven. We all had to learn how to start a small coal stove, to keep it going and cook on it.

None of us knew how to cook. Chinese cooking takes a lot of work for the uninitiated—just lighting the stove was a challenge. You first put paper and kindling in the stove, then you put soft coal on top and light it from the bottom. You put a funnel on top of the stove if it does not have a chimney to draw the air through and the fire to catch. The "soft coal" is easier to ignite but produces a tremendous amount of smoke. When the soft coal catches, you put the normal coal on top. We actually used a coal brick which was pressed into a round tube with holes in it like a beehive. The whole process produced a lot of choking smoke that made your throat and eyes burn. Sometimes we'd bank the stove at night so we didn't have to make it everyday and sometimes the stove went out a couple of times a day and we'd have to make it all over again. Imagine seventeen families lighting stoves at once! Grace learned rather quickly how to do it, but the smoke was very hard on her.

As the weather started to turn cold, we were at a loss as how to keep warm. One of the extravagances that Grace had been accused of was that she had always kept her home too warm and used up too much coal. Since she had such bad bronchial asthma every winter, we had always kept our home warm and we did not know of any alternative, not being used to having all the padded clothes on at home. During the day, Grace liked to stand on the balcony and watch the street activity. Even in winter she would wait on the balcony for us to come home from school.

One day about a week or so after we moved, I came back from school and found Mother standing on the balcony in the cold with her coat and scarf on—looking very pale and shaken.

"Ma, what happened?" I asked in alarm.

"Oh, I nearly asphyxiated myself with the coal stove," she replied, rubbing her head. "It felt so cold that I brought the stove in from the balcony and then closed the door. It did keep me warm for a while, but then I started to get a headache and felt woozy. I suddenly realized it must be the stove, so I moved it back to the balcony and opened the doors wide to get in as much fresh air as possible."

Our neighbor Mrs. Wang asked me what had happened and when I told her, she shook her head and said, "You poor things, you didn't even know that you can't put a coal stove inside a room without a chimney. Go get those chimney pipes tomorrow and I will help you put them up."

Mrs. Wang shook her head again when she saw us trying to cook on the small stove. She shared the balcony with us and heard us fussing over it. She ofered to cook for us and said, "I have to cook anyway—it is no trouble cooking for two families."

Mrs. Wang was in her late thirties with three daughters between the ages of eight and twelve; her husband worked as an janitor in a hospital. From then on Mrs. Wang cooked for us and her husband brought his big industrial size mop and cleaned our floors every other day. That made our lives a lot easier as none of us objected to having simple meals. At first Mrs. Wang refused any compensation for her work, but we insisted on paying her; it was only a fraction of what F. C. had paid Sun and Amah.

NINI: When we moved, it put her with a lot of people. The neighbors immediately came over to help. They were very kind and I think it sort of got her out of herself. I think that did a world of good for her.

Immediately she learned more Chinese. She understood more than she thought she could. She knew she talked like a foreigner so she was hesitant to speak in Chinese. But she really understood quite a lot. Grace was able to converse, in halting Chinese, with Mrs. Wang. While washing and drying the dishes, they would talk about what was going on in the neighborhood. If Grace found something very difficult to understand, she would ask one of us to interpret for her. Mrs. Wang would tell about what the neighborhood women studied in their political study group and Grace was quite impressed with how much the ordinary housewives were learning about the theory and practice of the new society.

Mrs. Wang was from a landlord Protestant family, high school educated. Her husband, we learned later, was a former KMT security chief, and an interpreter for the Japanese. He was born in a poor peasant family in the Northeast, didn't get along with the stepmother and ran away. After liberation he went to find his family. His wife came to Tientsin. When he returned he turned himself in and confessed his past deeds. After that he became a hospital cleaner and worked conscientiously.

Mrs. Wang was also the neighborhood representative then, and was involved in many community events. She represented our house in the neighborhood meetings and would bring us news and ask our ideas and opinions. They might meet up to two or three times a week, whenever things came up. Because the society was constantly changing, the people had to catch up with the changes. New things cropped up everyday and we had to talk about how to deal with it, how to face it.

After moving, Grace discovered the lives of ordinary people and their way of handling everyday affairs that she had never been a part of before. Here she found an entirely different world from what she had known before. Over time she became fascinated with what she learned from the women in her neighborhood, especially from her neighbor, Mrs. Wang. The following excerpt is taken from an article Grace wrote in 1956, entitled "Election Day in Tientsin"—

One day Mrs. Wang and I were doing the dishes on the balcony. She always had some amusing story to tell.

"I've been at a meeting all afternoon," she said, handing me a bunch of chopsticks to dry.

"What was it this time?" I asked, knowing that she was our neighborhood representative and always had interesting stories.

"I talked to the housewives today about the election for people's deputy. The lau tai-tai (old ladies) have the funniest reasons for disapproving of some candidate. For instance, one old lady said, 'No, no, I don't like him at all! He didn't speak to me on the street the other day.' And another one said about a woman candidate, 'I don't think she would make a good people's deputy. She drove my chickens out of the courtyard once.'"

Mrs. Wang saw much to laugh over, but she took her duties very seriously. She worked hard to give even the most backward women some knowledge of the importance of the elections . . .

When election day for district representative arrived I watched the women of our house gather in the courtyard, and I could hardly recognize them! They were making a great occasion of the trip to the ballot box and were wearing colorful dresses and jackets, flowers in their hair and makeup!

Mrs. Chi, from upstairs, for instance—a bright jacket, red flower in her hair, and lipstick had transformed the thin sallow-faced women that I was used to seeing every day in black trousers and jacket.

Mrs. Wang was also wearing red flowers, lipstick, and a pretty new gown. They all went off in a group to vote for the five candidates they had approved. These five deputies of our neighborhood, together with the deputies of all the other neighborhoods of our district, made up the district people's congress. Tientsin's twelve districts formed the Tientsin Municipal People's Congress. Thus, the members of the city government were first elected in neighborhood zones . . . I didn't know much about these things until after my husband died—when we moved into a real neighborhood. Everyone was in a group: either you were in a school or a factory or a neighborhood organization. In this way, I saw ordinary people learning to participate and becoming leaders. . . .

That winter of 1956 was the coldest the Lius could remember since the Japanese occupation. Grace learned to keep on layers of padded winter clothes like all people in China did during the winter. The house was always cold, but this also had its good side: lessening the contrast between the inside and the outside prevented Grace's children from catching colds. But Grace suffered in the cold room where she stayed all day. All her energy had to be spent on keeping warm, keeping alive. Even so, she was healthier than she had been in many years. Perhaps it was the changed conditions which contributed to her health, but just as likely it was her determination.

The idea of a trip to Sian had been growing in Grace's mind for some time. Well-meaning friends tried to discourage her. She was told that few people, even those much hardier than herself, would undertake such an arduous trip. But she wanted her children to know their father's roots and thus their own Chinese side.

So less than a year after F. C. died, in the summer of 1956, Grace and her children embarked on the roots-seeking journey to the West Liu Village in Shensi Province, one hundred and fifty miles from the ancient city of Sian, in the very heartland of China.

The following account of their trip started out to be an article—from which an excerpt was published in the *New World Review,* October 1956—about traveling on the new Lanchow-Sinkiang Railway, one of the most difficult engineering feats undertaken in New China. But Grace expanded her account into this longer and more personal description for her memoir. She had initiated the trip for the children, but by its end, it is clear that the journey was for her. She traveled not only into the heartland of China but into her own heart, to the reason that she had come to China and then chosen to stay.

In August 1956, my three children and I were on our way to the ancient West Liu Village in Shensi Province. I was taking them to visit their father's birthplace where their ancestors had lived for hundreds of years. Coming from the port city of Tientsin with its conglomerate population and foreign atmosphere, to the old family village in the lower Yellow River Area, the cradle of Chinese civilization, my children would see and learn something of their Chinese heritage.

It was just seven years after the founding of the Chinese People's Republic and although the tracks of new railways were hourly spreading and advancing all over the country, there were still far too few railway lines, cars, engines, and railway

personnel to handle comfortably and effectively the unprecedented crowds of people traveling in China. Traffic was especially heavy on the lines going to the Northwest to the oil fields and new industrial cities and to the land being settled by pioneer families. To anyone unused to traveling it was a daring adventure to join even for a few days—this surging advance into China's fabulous Northwest.

I knew it would be a physical ordeal for us as we started traveling just as the majority of the people, workers, and peasants did—on "hard seats," with no sleeping accommodations. But it would be an experience that I needed to bring me into closer contact with the Chinese *l'au pai shing* [lao bai xing] (literally, "old one hundred names," ordinary people).

Our plan was to spend a week with one of the Liu "sisters" (cousins of the same generation) in the Shensi capital city of Sian which as ancient "Changan" was the capital of one of the earliest dynasties of China. From there we would travel under her guidance to West Liu Village.

We left Tientsin with much conflicting advice and confusing information. Some friends thought we were very unwise, in fact, "absolutely crazy" to attempt such a journey in the hottest part of the summer, or to think of going to a village that could be reached even after two days and a night on the train, only by ox-cart and foot. But others were enthusiastic and thought it the wisest thing we could possibly do.

From the railway-ticket office, we received vague information on very important points and, of course, ran promptly into what seemed to me at the moment a catastrophe—we missed our Sian train in Peking! All because we hadn't been told of some formality that had to be gone through when changing trains. To such inexperienced travelers as Nini, Ellen, Wei-han, and I this was a dreadful blow, especially as the Peking ticket office seemed utterly indifferent to our fate, even saying that there was no place on the next Sian train, four hours later.

The waiting room we were in was jammed—every seat was occupied and every inch of floor space, except the lanes where people were lined up to board the next outgoing trains, covered with bags, bundles, baskets, and small children. Perhaps we would have to wait here until morning—twelve hours. Our one seat was piled with luggage and we had just room enough to stand.

However, we were not left long in our wrath and dismay—the station police came to the rescue. The courteous young man in the new summer blue and white police uniform who had inspected my traveling permit as we entered the Peking station now came with an anxious face to see why we had not gotten on our train. When he heard our story he said, "Never mind, we will think of something." In a little while we had our tickets for the next Sian train and were settled in four seats in another less-crowded waiting room. For the next few hours I relaxed and observed my fellow travelers.

I envied the composure, calm confidence, and good humor of these hundreds of peasants, workers, and their families, army men and women and students. Those having many hours to wait were as practical and unselfconscious as if they had lived all their lives in a railway station. Bedding had been unrolled and whole families had gone to sleep on the floor, which was kept clean by frequent sweeping and mopping.

I saw a soldier take out his wash basin and give his face and neck a good scrubbing. A group of cadres sitting on their bags were reading and eating watermelon seeds, carefully putting the shells back in the sack. One opened a bundle and changed his shoes and socks.

Though undoubtedly most of them must have been hot, tired, and uncomfortable, I didn't see any cross faces or hear any quarrels; no one looked angry and upset as I had a little while before. By the time the same policeman came to tell us that we could get on the train, I was feeling ashamed of my biting remarks about the whole railway administration and the ticket offices in particular. Nini's reminding me of how the country's rapid development had necessitated sending great numbers of people over widespread distances, before the railways had become able to do the task expertly, made me ready to be more lenient with the railway and its faults.

We met more negative aspects of present-day railway travel in China, things that needed and were getting criticism. But compared to rail travel of twenty-two years ago when I first came to China, I found that the positive outweighed the negative. For one thing, I appreciated the railroad's one hundred percent safety record when we crept across the wide expanse of the Yellow River, crossed deep gorges, ran along steep hillsides that sometimes "slipped," and went through low-lying plains that had been recently swept by a hurricane. At every station the train was gone over from end to end by repair crews.

It was comforting to look out just anywhere and see the faithful and vigilant track-walkers. The citizen track-walkers spaced themselves at unusually close intervals wherever there might be danger. These civilians protected the trains from the kinds of attacks that F. C. had known as a young man. In his student days this trip was so dangerous that he attempted it only twice—once to go to Peking and once to return.

At intervals during the daytime the pleasant voice of a young woman announced stations over a loudspeaker, called the passengers' attention to historic places and famous scenic spots, advised mothers with small children, and gave some simple rules of hygiene. Every half-hour or so a man come through with a broom, then a mop—the cars were never allowed to become littered.

Perhaps I was the only passenger who did not enjoy the noisy Chinese opera that poured through the loudspeaker between announcements and hygiene talks— as far as I am concerned the continuous playing of music from Chinese operas on trains is definitely a negative point!

Our car was full of railway workers, going out to work on the Lanchow-Sinkiang Railway which had then already reached Yumen, China's biggest oil field, and in a few years would connect with the Soviet Union's Turkestan-Siberia railway; or to the Lanchow-Yinchuan section, which cuts through the Great Wall to reach Yinchuan, a major wool, hide, and skin trading center in the Northwest. Several village woman with their children were going to join oil-field and railway-worker husbands in Lanchow and beyond.

A short, stocky young engine-driver, his tall pretty wife, and their three small children sat across the aisle from us, and we were soon old acquaintances. "Papa," as we nicknamed the young man, was a marvel of efficiency, energy, and good-heartedness. He took wonderful care of his family and, like a mother bird, was always feeding them with chicken, preserved eggs, steaming bowls of noodles and vegetables, apples, and melons. He helped all the passengers around us with his many useful ideas about how to arrange bundles, bags, and children so as to use every bit of space. He soon found out all there was to know about us and passed on the information to other interested passengers. He, in turn, told everybody about himself and his job and what a wonderful healthful and beautiful country it was where he was working in the mountains beyond Lanchow. He had already been there and had gone back to his old home near Peking to get his family. His wife said she knew it would be a good place to bring up children.

From daybreak until dark we never tired of watching the amazing scenery.

Fantastic terraced hillsides, like huge red and green layer cakes, cave dwellings carved out of red hills, and toy-like villages perched on mountainsides flew past the windows. Something entirely new had now appeared on China's landscape—the wide-stretching collective farm fields of corn, cotton, millet, and soybeans, instead of the patchwork of tiny fields of the old days.

We made frequent trips to the diner to relieve our cramped legs and backs. The diner was open and full all day and most of the night. The people who ate in the diner were the same people who made up the passengers—it was a curious sight to me to see a peasant family eating in a railway dining car—such a thing was inconceivable in the China that I entered in 1934.

The food in both the diner and in the stations was a decidedly positive point for the railroads. Formerly no one with the least idea of hygiene would dare to buy anything to eat in the stations. But now the vendors were dressed in white coats and caps and their wares were packaged and wrapped and carried in glassed-in carts. Some places famous for their roast chicken did a rushing business through the car windows. We bought two—deep-red brown, with a special flavor and tenderness. Even our vegetarian Wei-han ate not only all his share, but a great part of mine while I was absorbed in the scenery.

After two days and one night, we reached Sian three hours late. Tracks had been washed out in a place or two by hurricane rains and had to be repaired. Eighth Sister Liu met us at the station and we spent an exciting time in the beautiful old city—more beautiful, I think, than Peking—once the capital of ancient China, and now in 1956, a bustling young frontier gateway to the great new developments of the Northwest.

Now, Eighth Sister told us that our journey had only begun here. She would accompany us to the township of Fu-ping, a small county seat about a hundred miles from Sian. There we would stay overnight with Fifth Sister (another cousin) and go the next day another ten miles to the village.

Approaching Fu-ping station, we saw the small city with its ancient wall and moat, perched like a medieval fortress on top of the hill facing us. Wheat, millet, and corn fields were flourishing all around for this was fertile countryside. We went down the slope from the station and climbed the road leading up to the city gate. To the right of the road a little river meandered down the hill, and beneath a splendid eight-hundred-year-old bridge of white stone, small boys were catching

river crabs. Beyond the river spread a thriving vegetable garden.

We walked across a brick causeway and through the big city gate. There we were met and welcomed by Fifth Sister and her husband. Their house near the gate was built right up against the city wall; in fact, the city wall served as one of the walls of the house. The children were delighted to look over the wall that was common to both house and city and see down into the moat.

Nini, left, Ellen, second from left, and William, far right, with cousins from Xian. Photo was taken in Summer 1953 when the cousins visited Tianjin. William is wearing the tie of the Young Pioneers.

We spent the afternoon sightseeing around the city. I think all the children in the place and many of the adults, too, came along with us. I was quite a sight to see myself—a foreign visitor who was actually a relative of one of their neighboring families!

One of the places we visited that afternoon was the school where Third Uncle Liu had taught for many years. In the school yard we saw a memorial stone carved more than a thousand years ago honoring some ancient hero or, more likely, a scholar. As a young boy Fu-chi had attended this school under his uncle's tutelage. My hands lingered a moment on the stone that he had undoubtedly touched.

The next morning the ox-cart arrived to take us to the village. This type of vehicle must be of unknown antiquity—in Bible times, Abraham and Sarah would have ridden in such a thing. It was an open box on two huge entirely wooden wheels. A light wooden framework had been added to the top and sides, covered over with some kind of cloth. The wooden surface on wooden wheels was entirely without springs of any sort. The cloth covering protected the travelers from sun and rain, but nothing would protect them from being bumped and shaken to bits.

The ox and his owner were a well-matched pair. The huge red ox was magnificent and had a calm ponderous dignity that was truly impressive. The driver, a strong young peasant whose red-brown face flowed with health, was Eighth Sister's own brother. He was the farmer of the family. His younger brother was to be a schoolteacher like his father, our Third Uncle. Eighth Sister was going to be a doctor and was a student at Sian Medical School. She is the one that F. C. had stayed with when he visited here. She had been worried then about his condition.

My son, fifteen-year-old Wei-han, sat up on the driver's seat with the driver. Most of the time, the driver walked beside the ox to encourage him over the rocks and ruts. The rest of us, my two girls, Eighth Sister, and I settled ourselves as best we could on the floor of the cart—and away we plodded! The extreme slowness of the pace somewhat mitigated the severity of the jolts and bumps.

We soon came to an almost dried-up riverbed where tiny streamlets of water trickled through stones of all sizes. After being shaken across the dry rocky bed, we came to a place where the water was deep and wide and swift. When the ox found the going difficult, the driver told the younger ones to get out of the cart. They gleefully took off their shoes and socks, rolled up their pants, and waded through. I wanted to do the same, but in China when you're over fifty you must be treated with great respect, so I had to submit to being carried over in the treacherous cart.

By and by we came to a beautiful place. We were going down a long tree-shaded lane which stretched as far as the eye could see. It was lined on both sides with tall trees, many of whose branches met over our heads. It was a very beautiful, peaceful scene, so why, then, did I have such an eerie feeling when I looked up into the branches?

"Ma!" Nini exclaimed excitedly, "this must be the place where Daddy saw the heads hanging from the trees."

The type of cart Grace and the children rode to West Liu village.

Yes, that was exactly what was running through my mind! We were all familiar with the description of this place and we all had a vivid mental picture of a little boy running for dear life, pursued by some fantastic horror.

271

It was a gruesome tale from my husband's boyhood. He was going home to the village from his school in Fu-Ping one late afternoon. He was taking his time along the old familiar 'road when, on tree branches just ahead of him, he saw human heads hanging in the breeze. After one frozen instant he covered the remaining miles to the village on wings of terror. At home he heard about the capture and execution of marauding bandits. Their severed heads hung up in the trees along the roadside were supposed to discourage other bandits. But I don't think that banditry was thereby any lessened.

At last we were nearing the end of our journey. The sky had clouded up and rain was beginning to fall. Just ahead we saw the village veiled in a fog of drizzle with wispy curls of smoke floating reluctantly from noon-time cooking. As we rolled ponderously along toward this scene with its misty look of an old Chinese painting, I felt that our mode of approach was well suited to an ancient place, wrapped in the peace and calm of the ages.

This old West Liu Village, less than ten miles from Fu-Ping, lies in fertile country nearly a hundred miles south of the poorer and harsher countryside around Yenan. Because the land is fertile, the village has not been so poverty-stricken and ground down with hardships as those farther to the north. But we knew that it had many times known violence and terror. The Mohammedan region was not far away and the eight-hundred-year-old village history records its partial destruction several times in raids during Mohammedan rebellions.

In the Liu family after the last big raid there were only three cousins (called brothers) left as heads of the family. My husband's father was one of them and the father of the present head was another. But those times were long over by 1956 and the Hui people (Mohammedans) and the Han people (Chinese) were, on the whole, peaceful and amicable neighbors, as some of the curly-haired and big-nosed cousins bore evidence.

The big ox knew when he was home. He stopped with determination in front of a door in a wall. We all hurried out of the rain through the wall door into a small front garden. From there we entered a house where Third Uncle, Third Aunt, and other relatives, including our ox driver's wife and small child, welcomed us.

The old Liu home was built around a courtyard rather like a Peking house—the courtyard wasn't a yard at all but a shallow green-tiled pool. Under overhanging eaves a narrow porch or walk ran around three sides of the pool. As in most Chinese houses, the kitchen was at the front on the right of the entrance. I never did find out how many rooms the house had or how big it actually was.

Ellen and I were given the room my husband's mother had occupied—the very room where F. C. was born. It had been a year since F. C. was struck without apparent warning by a fatal illness, after a year's fight for his life during which time everything possible was done to save him. He died in the midst of work of great urgency, the work to which he had dedicated his life.

And now it was a solace and comfort to my spirit to be here in this room where he was born and in the house where he had played as a small boy. I could feel the continuity of generations that is so strong in China. Its eternal quality helps to soothe and heal the sharp pain of individual loss.

That night as I lay next to my daughter, watching the candlelight flicker on the ceiling, I imagined that candlelight had flickered the same way on the ceiling when my husband was a baby. I could imagine his young mother holding him. How did she feel in that flickering light? Did she not wonder what would become of him?

He had loved his mother devotedly and when he was older realized her great strength of character and broad-mindedness. At the time he left home, F. C. did not know his mother's story, but he heard it many years after: She had been a slave girl in a great landlord family in the south of the province. The mistress of the family loved the little slave girl and brought her up like a daughter. At the proper age, the mistress saw to it that she was married to a respectable man of a good family and came to live with the Liu family of West Liu Village.

His father died a short while before F. C. was born in 1904, leaving his young widow with a two-year-old daughter and a baby son. The little boy was brought up under the Confucian discipline of his three uncles. It was his uncles who decided that he should be sent to Peking, that education was his only hope.

I thought of the thirteen-year-old boy leaving home, leaving his mother and sister, leaving the village that he had known to go to school in faraway Peking. Setting off down the road, over which we had just traveled, did he turn one last time? Did he see her standing by the door in the wall? F. C. told me that before he left her, she told him not to think of her or to think he must be ruled unduly by the demands of the family—but that he must make his own life when he got out in the world.

By leaving in 1917 at such an early age, F. C. escaped from the more pernicious

273

side of the Confucian, feudal, patriarchal family system with its veneration of authority and its downgrading of women. But he took with him the best of the moral training and discipline from his uncles, the love and devotion of his mother, and the noblest of Chinese character from the people of the village.

At Tsing Hua a new world opened up to him. He stayed at Tsing Hua for eight years, meeting boys from all over China and forming close friendships that lasted his entire life. Those friendships extended to me and the children and are still a source of comfort and happiness to us.

In the summer of 1925, just after his graduation from Tsing Hua, F. C. made the long trip back to West Liu Village for the first time in eight years. It would also be the last time before he left for America in the fall. Grown up now and traveling with a group, he found the trip safer and he had no alarming experiences along the way.

But a totally unexpected blow awaited him. He learned on his arrival home that his mother and older sister had died. His uncles had not told him because by Confucian tradition he would be bound to return to the village and perform the last rites as a son. They feared that he would not graduate and waited until his return. The sudden news of his mother's death shocked him into a realization that he was utterly alone in the the world.

There was one last duty that, as an only son, he must carry out. His mother's coffin was still unburied, waiting in the village temple for her son to perform this last rite for his mother—he must go to the temple and sleep beside her coffin every night for a month and he must go alone . . .

Grace never finished this portion of her memoir. We can only imagine the emotion she felt that night in the candlelight, sleeping in the room where her husband had been born, thinking of the young boy, wondering how his mother felt when her only son left home, and identifying with the young man, sleeping beside his mother's coffin, alone in the dark, having no family, no home to return to. Grace had become his only family. Like him, she had left her home and now had no family to return to. She was utterly alone in the world, except for her children—his children. They were her family and China was her home.

21

A CADRE IN THE WORK FORCE

I F THE CHINESE revolution were a symphonic score, the first movement would
end here. Up till now it had been, in Grace's view, a rousing and compelling
march, with the different sections of society playing their parts in the great Chinese socialist transformation. After liberation, China had engaged in a patriotic surge
of progress that F. C. had hoped for in his youth. The success of those early years led
the nation into an ebullience symbolized by Mao's daring dive into the Yangtse River
in the summer of 1956. He proudly boasted his robust health at age sixty-two as well
as that of the emerging productive nation.

In 1957 things were good in China. Attitudes were opening up, evidence of
which could be seen in the more colorful fashions, a variety of art and cultural forms,
and more learning—even foreign languages were encouraged. In May 1957 Mao
proposed an openness to new ideas. The march changed for a moment to a light and
airy melody, befitting the warm spring weather and Mao's expansive words: "Let a
hundred flowers bloom . . . a hundred schools of thought contend."

The Hundred Flowers movement in the spring of 1957 had something in common with the Prague Spring of 1968. Both were heady bursts of open expression in a
previously restricted environment. From May 1 to June 7, 1957, an air of openness
pervaded the country. People were encouraged to speak their own views "on what are
fragrant flowers and what are poisonous weeds" as long as their criticisms and grievances were intended to strengthen and not weaken the socialist transformation and
the leadership of the Communist Party. With some persuasion, individuals gradually
responded, tentatively at first, and then with enthusiasm—in newspapers, magazines,

circulars, open forums, posters stuck to the walls, and big rallies. The movement, *ta ming ta fang* [da ming da fang] in Chinese, literally meant "big chirping, big letting loose."

The students of the May 4th Movement of 1919, who had criticized China's backwardness and attacked its institutions and leaders, were now middle-aged teachers, doctors, lawyers, writers, artists, managers, scientists, and engineers. Many were attracted to Mao's revolution because of their patriotism and their hope for China's progress; some had even returned to China from abroad. Many earned positions in the new government and contributed to the nation's rapid development in the first years. They created an uneasy tension in an ideological revolution.

Some members of the central government feared a rebellion as had been seen in Poland and Hungary in 1956. When the aired grievances, mostly by the educated class, went as far as challenging the very authority of the Party, it became too threatening to the nation's leaders. Those who had spoken out were labeled dissidents or "rightists," and an anti-rightist campaign set in. First, the rightists in the Party were set straight, and then a rectification campaign spread throughout the nation.

With an urgent need to galvanize the political energies of the nation, Mao announced in the summer of 1958 the next movement to speed up development. The Great Leap Forward proposed a fantastic goal—to surpass Britain as an industrial force in fifteen years. The vision of plentiful foodstuffs from agricultural communes and self-reliant industries in every village was the expression of the "continuing revolution." Mao was counting, once again, on concerted human willpower to boost the economy.

The momentary light melodies of 1957 ended abruptly, and another march began, in a higher key with a deeper, stronger drum beat.

GRACE RETURNED from West Liu Village with renewed commitment to her husband's memory, to her children, and, through them, to China. Soon afterwards, she was offered a job to polish the English proficiency of a group of men and women from the Tianjin Foreign Affairs Bureau. Although contact with the West was limited by 1956, there were occasions when the Foreign Ministry needed cadres who were skilled in English. Grace gladly accepted the offer. It not only gave her extra income, but made her feel useful and took her mind off herself.

These students were well-educated. They came to Grace's apartment in the former mansion for their lessons. They sat on the balcony that she shared with the Wangs or on the bed or on borrowed chairs. Since these cadres already knew some English, they identified topics and talked about things that were important and relevant to them. As her students gained greater fluency, Grace learned more about China. It was a mutual exchange.

She also became aware of the specific problems that the students faced in learning to speak English. These insights led her to develop a teaching style based on conversational English. But when the rectification campaign set in, the cadres quit coming to Grace's house for English. Grace was disappointed. She had grown fond of them, and she missed having something to do. But more importantly, she was beginning to develop as a teacher.

To be a good teacher, one must first be a good pupil.—Mao

During the early 1950s the nation's need for teachers was enormous. Through a friend Grace heard that Nankai University was expanding its offerings and looking for new English teachers. William described her interview appointment with the head of the English Department:

> The head of the department, Professor Li, was a Chinese intellectual of the old school—white-haired, distinguished, well-poised, and professional in his manner, with a round face and well-manicured hands. We learned before she went to see him that he had been a student of Lu-Xun, the most famous of China's writers of the twentieth century.
>
> Grace told me that in her interview Professor Li asked her when she had come to China. When she answered 1934, he replied, "Ah, that is the year I published the first Chinese translation of *Jane Eyre*."
>
> Jane Eyre was one of my mother's favorite books. She had always been interested in the Bronte family and replied, "Did you know that Charlotte Bronte wrote that book, or most of it anyway, in only three weeks?"
>
> "Well," he said, "it took me considerably longer to translate it."
>
> They had a good laugh. I think that broke the ice. They began to talk about their experiences. He had started teaching at Nankai the same year

that she came to Tientsin. During the Japanese occupation he told her that he had gone with other teachers and students into the Interior. Grace had heard about the students and teachers who had carried their books and equipment and set up in the hills until the war was over. She told him that she had watched the bombing of Nankai from the roof of her building with Adelaide Lin. He remembered the Lins who had taught at the university in the thirties. He was glad that so much of the damage caused by the bombing had been repaired. They had many things to talk about. When Grace left that day, Professor Li gave her a copy of his book which she always treasured.

Grace began teaching at Nankai University in the fall of 1957. She was hired initially as a part-time, temporary teacher of second-year English students.

The difference that working for an institution, instead of teaching in her home, made in Grace's life at this point is best explained by her description of her former cook, Sun Pao-san, in an article she wrote for the *New World Review* in 1959:

It was lunch time at the "Willow Forest" sanitarium for T.B. patients. The stout, middle-aged man in white cap and gown was not one of the sanitarium doctors. He was the head cook—and had just shown us over the spotless big kitchen and introduced us to his assistant cooks, one attending a huge cauldron of meat sauce—for noodles—and another frying fish. "Sun Pao-san, the cook, is very famous," I was told. "Cooks from all over China come here to learn from him."

Four years ago, when we started living on a smaller scale after my husband's death, Sun Pao-san went to the Finnish Ambassador's family in Peking. Here he managed the other servants, planned the meals, even the big dinners, receptions, and official banquets, and ordered all the food. His wages were high.

Some time later he came to see me. He had gained considerable weight and was looking prosperous. He told us about the famous people he had seen and served at the ambassador's big parties and banquets.

"Well, Sun," I said, "you must feel very satisfied and pleased with such a job."

"No, Tai-tai," he said, "I'm not. I know it's a good job. I never thought of getting so much money before. And the Ambassador and his wife are good to me. But I don't feel happy there."

"Oh, you'll feel different when your family moves to Peking," I said. His wife and eight children were still living in Tientsin.

"No," he said. "It's not my family. It's just that I feel left behind. I'm making money. I get to see interesting, famous people. I live comfortably; my family is comfortable. But"—and his voice rose—"I'm not getting anywhere. I'm not learning anything. The whole country is going ahead on a new road. Everybody is studying and learning new things. But I am standing still, learning nothing, belong to nothing—just a cook in a private family!"

"But Sun," I reminded him. "The pay in government places is quite low compared to what you are getting now. Your family couldn't live so comfortably."

"I don't care," he said stubbornly. "I'd rather live hard and feel that I was going ahead with all the people than to live easy and feel the way I do now."

After a month or two he came back, much thinner.

"I'm working for an institution, now," he told me. "The Willow Forest T.B. sanitarium for workers. It's hard work and the pay isn't much, but I feel I'm really living and learning. We have meetings all the time to discuss our work and how to improve it. And in our study group I'm learning politics and international affairs and what's going on all over the country. And"—smiling proudly—"I belong to the opera group! And I have sung in performances in the biggest theater in Tientsin."

"So you're not sorry you gave up the fine job in Peking," I said.

"Never!" he declared. "Now I'm in step with the whole country."

The next time I saw him was in the late summer of 1958. He had regained much of his former stoutness. The union, he said, had long ago had his wages raised to almost the amount the Finnish ambassador had paid him. He had become a labor model and had been sent that summer for a ten-day vacation to Peitaho beach, the summer resort only for foreigners and rich Chinese in the old days. His opera group had given several performances in Tientsin and he sang a leading role.

He had come this time to ask me a favor. He wanted some American recipes, especially pies and salads. He told me that he was training cooks from all over China.

The next time I saw him was in the sanitarium dining room. When we said goodbye, I shook hands with a man who was no longer just somebody's servant. He had become a person with dignity and honor.

When Grace went to work at Nankai University, she was no longer just someone's

Grace, when
she went to
work at Naikai
University,
1957.

wife, nor just a foreign woman teaching at home. Now she belonged to an organization; she had a role, a professional life, and colleagues. She was now a cadre in China's huge socialist work force. In essence, after twenty-three years in China, she had finally become a participant, not just an observer, of Chinese society. But as a participant, her actions and her words were no longer accountable only to herself.

Nini described the change she saw in her mother at this time:

It must have inspired Grace spiritually a great deal because she worked so terribly hard those years. At the beginning it was a few hours a day, then she went every day. Everyday Grace would get up at 5:30 to go downstairs to the breakfast shop and buy fresh, crisp donuts which we ate with pancakes and soy milk. She would come back by the time we were all up. She would tend the stove, heat the soy milk, and we would all eat together. She was healthier than she had been for a long time. After F. C. died, Grace started using Chinese medicine for her asthma. We read in the paper that this new medicine, with arsenic in it, was doing good for people, so she and I took it for a while. I think it did some good, even for me. It made us feel very "hot," as the Chinese say.

After their breakfast together, each member of the Liu family set off in different directions. Nini went to the Water Works as F. C. had for so many years. William and Ellen each walked about forty-five minutes to different high schools. Grace took the bus to work, a thirty-minute ride followed by a twenty-minute walk. Sometimes, if the weather was good, she walked all the way. When the weather was bad, the twenty-minute walk from the bus stop to the university could be challenging. In the winter, knife-sharp gales from Siberia swept down across the iced-over rice paddies and the campus lotus ponds. Grace, who barely weighed ninety pounds, often had to hold on tight to a tree or lamp post or be blown aloft in the piercing winds.

As the demand for English classes increased, Grace's courses did well and she soon became a full-time teacher. It didn't take long for Grace to notice that the style of teaching at the university was quite different from the conversational approach she had used with the cadres at home. The traditional approach to teaching English in China was based on grammar and translation. The professors lectured in Chinese, the students answered in Chinese. Although they were studying English, they did not communicate in English. The teacher gave a detailed description of the grammar in a certain literary text. The students would translate the text from English into Chinese, or from Chinese into English. They took pages and pages of notes in Chinese and analyzed each passage thoroughly. William described his mother's early encounter with the results of this system:

> One night Grace was grading some papers at home and she sighed out loud. "Ma, what's the matter?" I asked.
>
> "It is so unnecessary," she moaned. Then she read to me what one of her students wrote. He had just come back from Peking where he had seen an English-speaking group with an interpreter from the Foreign Ministry. The interpreter was having a difficult time. Grace's student was very embarrassed for her but he couldn't help her because his English was no better. He was very upset because he had worked so hard for many years and he knew that the interpreter must have worked even harder.
>
> "My student feels that it is his fault. But it doesn't matter how hard he works, the problem is not his—it is the way he is taught. He can read—he can even analyze the structure of a sentence better than I can, but he can't speak. I asked a senior student the other day what time it was and he could only point at his watch—yet he had just come out of a class where they had been diagraming sentences from T. S. Eliot. Imagine that! What a waste of time! "
>
> The next day Grace explained to her student why it was not his fault. A period of teaching reform was just beginning to take place at the university. Word got around that Grace was

Nini worked at the Water Works, Ellen and William were in high school, 1957.

criticizing the department and especially the old professor whose name was also Li, but he was not the head of the department. It did not go over very well with the long-time professors in the English Department.

By early 1958 the whole nation was engaged in "study and criticism" as part of the rectification campaign. At the university, teachers met in groups for discussion. The meetings were intended to be a time to correct one's way of thinking and style of work, both in and out of the classroom. William continues:

> It came up in these meetings what Grace had said. Grace's criticism caused quite a stir. Some of the students and even the younger teachers agreed with Grace, but the grammar-translation method had been used for years and many of the professors were wedded to it. It was the way they had learned. They had built their reputations teaching this way. And many of the students liked the old approach as well because they were good at it. They felt accomplished when they dissected a sentence in Hardy's *The Mayor of Casterbridge*. They felt inadequate and embarrassed if asked to actually speak. Consequently, Grace was criticized. She was told it was wrong to talk about someone behind his back.

Talking behind someone's back was a question of incorrect political behavior, not one of bad manners. In his 1937 essay, "Combat Liberalism," Mao had written that in the process of "active ideological struggle" it was considered a manifestation of liberalism "to indulge in irresponsible criticism in private instead of actively putting forward one's suggestions to the organization. To say nothing to people to their faces but to gossip behind their backs, or to say nothing at a meeting but to gossip afterwards." Changing this kind of behavior was what Mao called "shedding one's bourgeois skin."

Part of the process of shedding one's bourgeois skin was self-criticism. Self-criticism was intended as an opportunity to point out your own errors and set forth ways in which you sought improvement. "Criticism, self-criticism" became the proscribed process for political discussion groups which Grace had become part of at the university. The method, based on Marxist-Leninist analysis, required that people examine their own class backgrounds to understand the ways they had been taught to think and act that were prescribed by their class background. The goal was to break from one's class and to achieve a truly proletarian world outlook.

After each political segment, it was standard practice to write a self-criticism. Grace's "Summary of My Thoughts" was written at the end of her first year at Nankai.

Grace Liu
August 14, 1958

I began taking part in the political movements after "ta ming and ta fang" and the anti-rightist struggle—just before the first teaching reform movement. It was the first time I'd ever taken part in political meetings; and during the movements that followed I have gained a great many benefits, although a large part of the time I have been uncertain and confused as to what was being said.

First of all I have learned to estimate myself somewhat more correctly. Formerly I was inclined to overestimate myself in some ways while feeling inferior in others. Because I was a foreigner, couldn't speak Chinese, and had never taught in a university before, I was sensitive, lacking in confidence, suspicious, and easy to feel hurt. This bourgeois, individualist sensitivity is, I realize, only the other side of pride and conceit. These feelings are egoistic, individualistic, and completely bourgeois. I have long known this intellectually, but it is only since joining in these collective political discussions and criticism and self-criticism that I see the way to overcome this self-centered attitude—criticism and self-criticism and the discipline of collective endeavor.

Because I have read and studied Marxist-Leninist literature for several years, I thought I saw things from a working-class standpoint, and that I was very successfully shedding my bourgeois skin! But the criticisms, ta tze pao (big character posters) [da zi bao], and collective discussions have shown me that just studying Marxism-Leninism doesn't automatically give one a working-class standpoint. I still have many bourgeois feelings, reactions, and attitudes.

During the first movement this year, before the Spring Festival and holiday, I received practically no criticism, but even some praise, and was in danger of being very satisfied with myself. But one incident during the combined meetings in which the students criticized the teachers shocked me out of my self-satisfaction. My student asked me for permission to repeat my remarks to him about Mr. Li and T. S. Eliot, the English poet. It was very painful to me to have to consent. I did not want to appear before everyone as a person who talked behind the backs of my colleagues. So I came face to face with a very ingrained bourgeois ze yo zhu i (liberalistic) [zi you zhu yi] trait involving both hypocrisy and dishonesty. Later on [the Chairman of the Department] Professor Li criticized me in a ta tze pao [poster] for criticizing other teachers behind their backs instead of publicly in meeting or in ta tze pao. These two incidents caused me to do some very serious thinking. I didn't like to say straight truths to a person's face, especially to someone who was polite and friendly to me. I felt it would be unpleasant and embarrassing. So I excused myself by thinking one ought to be tactful. To talk behind one's back I excused by thinking it a very human failing that most everyone indulged in. But I've come to realize that it is not a *human* failing but a typical bourgeois trait that can be overcome when one's standpoint is changed.

Many students thought it their responsibility to point out their teachers' shortcomings toward building this ideal. There were several ways to do it—to address the teacher in class, to bring it up in a political discussion group or to write big character posters, called *ta tze pao*. Anyone—student or teacher—could write any comment or criticism in bold Chinese characters on large sheets of newsprint-like paper and post it on a wall. Grace's summary continues:

The several ta tze pao [posters] that the students put up for me showed up other subtle bourgeois traits that were so easy to overlook in one's self. Peng Tze[Zi]-mei gave me a shock when he said I'd made a serious mistake in political outlook in one of my classroom exercises. How could that be, I thought. He must have misunderstood the English words. But when I had his criticism translated several times to me I had to admit that he was right. I had turned the story into a dialogue for the students to practice. My dialogue of the two workers was a far less severe indictment of capitalism than O. Henry's story. Especially to students not so familiar with English, my dialogue actually sounded as if I were softening the evils and the suffering caused by capitalism. This has taught me that I must be vigilant in everything I write and say, so that no bourgeois attitudes creep in. I hope the students will always be very sharp in their lookout for any kind of errors in my teaching and warn me immediately.

There are two other questions on which I've only rather recently begun to realize my wrong way of thinking. They are the question of my salary and the question of security—that is having a position as a regular teacher.

Up until only a month or two ago I have considered that unless I am paid a salary every month I do not have enough to get along on. My reasoning has been this: I am fifty-seven years old and not strong physically and I have been afraid to lower my living standard any further for fear of getting sick or breaking down in some way. However, even without my salary from Nankai, we still have, counting my daughter's salary, more than most working people live on (between seventy and eighty yuan a month). Then am I really standing with the working class when I say it's impossible for me to live as a working-class person? I think that this is only a superstitious fact that I and my family can't get by on this amount. I must dare to break old habits and learn to live as a working-class person. I know that to work hard and enthusiastically in a collective social environment is conducive to health and long life.

I have also feared a lack of security. Not to belong to any organization, to be engaged only by the hours of the month, to be temporary or expendable, had made me fearful of the future when within the next two years I have used up the last of the money given me by the government when my husband died. But this attitude—does it not show a lack of faith in the Party and People's Government? Why should I fear the future for myself? If I have a real socialist mentality, if all my interest and efforts are concentrated on doing my utmost to help build socialism and bring about the ideal state of the future, would there be room in my thoughts for concern over my own individual future?

In the next part of her report, Grace criticized her own teaching. She admonished herself for her inexperience, not planning systematically, lack of direction, and being indulgent rather than firm with the students. In a spirit of being "open and receptive to criticism" she volunteered to sit in on other teachers' classes, especially the teachers she had criticized. She also invited them to sit in on her classes and offer their criticisms on her. Finally, she suggested overall coordination and planning with the other teachers. Grace concluded her summary, "I feel that I have reaped a real harvest from the parts of the rectification campaign that I have taken some small part in and have made some progress in the liberation of my mind from old selfish ways of thinking."

Before F. C. died, he told Nini and Ellen that he was not worried about them; he knew that the government would take care of them. But he could not have foreseen the changes that were ahead nor the difficulties that Grace would be facing.

22

THE GREAT LEAP FORWARD

I N THE SUMMER of 1958, fearful that the economic reforms proposed by the soon-to-begin Second Five-Year Plan would not reach the goal of surpassing Britain's industrial output, Mao decided that the whole nation needed to be mobilized. He had always relied on the voluntary, heroic outpourings of the masses—like the volunteer soldiers of the Korean war and the peasants taking charge of land reform; it was the power of the human will and determination of the spirit that created the "revolutionary fervor." Hoping to renew political enthusiasms and to step up the pace of socialist transformation, Mao announced the Great Leap Forward.

The Great Leap was intended to carry out the ideal communist society almost overnight. Collectivization instead of individual ownership and effort would be the key. The agriculture cooperatives would be collectivized into communes. Private ownership of land or business would be replaced. Men, women, and children would share work, food, and pay. No incentives other than selfless devotion would be necessary.

Another reason for the Great Leap was that the relationship between China and the Soviet Union was splitting. It did not fully crack until a few years later but the shifting could already be heard. The Chinese people drew confidence from their emerging independence, the realization that none of the great foreign powers had conquered China—not the British, the Japanese, the Americans nor, now, the Russians.

A bumper harvest in 1958 fueled the nation's enthusiasm, and a massive outpouring of industrial activity resulted. By late 1958 hundreds of thousands of back-

yard furnaces were melting any metal that could be found in a frenetic effort to increase industrial output by one-third and reach an unprecedented target for steel production. Initial statistics revealed fantastic increases and it seemed that the nation would reach a "high tide" of production through mass effort.

But, indeed, steel cannot be made in back yards. And charcoal cannot fuel a national industry. Families and villages cannot change their very structures and functions overnight. And personal initiative needs rewards. Not only did impossibly high targets and bad management figure into the failure of the Great Leap, but bad weather added disastrous results in 1959, '60, and '61. Indescribable famines were the tragical legacy of the Great Leap.

Nini was working at the Tianjin Water Works during this period. Nini had been going to the Water Works all of her life and knew most of the people, the workmen and the managers. She ate lunch in the canteen and supper too when there were meetings at night. At first she did filing in the technical department and then mapping. This was where she met her husband:

> My husband Enhua and I worked in the same room. In China you become quite close to your colleagues. In addition to meetings, we both

Nini (seated, far left) with her work team at the Water Works. Enhua is fourth from the left on the back row.

belonged to the Youth League. In the League we helped carry out the production plan, and if there were social movements on, we helped promote the movements. We did a lot of study, reports, and lectures. We were given tickets to go hear certain people talk. We had amateur plays, singing groups, and dancing. It was very lively and social—I helped with backstage decorations and things like that—it was lots of fun.

About two years after we knew each other, maybe in 1958, we went out together to a movie. At that time, it was fairly common for young people to date, go to movies, etc. But the first time we really got to know each other was during the "anti-pests campaign." Sparrows were considered one of the pests because they ate grain—so we went out in teams early in the morning to keep the sparrows off the ground. We hit pots and pans and gongs together to make a loud noise. The sparrows could not land and they eventually dropped down exhausted and died. Enhua and I went up on a roof to scare them and after we were there someone took the ladder away. We were stuck there together for a while, so we talked.

Enhua was my group leader in 1958, so we were thrown together a lot. I was attracted to him, and thought we might get married. One day he asked me if I would want to be closer friends (a closer friend is a future husband or wife). It was like a proposal. I wasn't so very surprised. I said yes right then.

We got married in 1959 during Chinese New Year. I had to register early because I had lost my cloth coupons. If you got married, you got extra cloth. We had no ceremony, we just registered in the security bureau, the police station. They asked us some questions, we signed the papers. We each got a license. We had a small supper with our two families to celebrate. Things were getting hard to get during this time, and we wouldn't have enough for a big party.

We moved in with his family. They lived in the native city outside the former concessions. There were two families living in a courtyard. It was a long room with a bedroom on either end, and the main living area in the middle where the cooking and eating happened. We had to get water from way down the lane. My mother-in-law had a very strong character, and I learned a lot from her. She had bound feet and I learned a lot about

Chinese women in the past. She didn't like my father-in-law at all. They didn't get along. My husband didn't get along well with his mother or father either. When he was around them, he changed. He said he couldn't help it, but when he walked through the door he felt different.

Food became much scarcer in 1959. Rationing began then. There were many discussions about who would get how much. It was decided by how much people ate as a rule. I didn't eat much then, so I had one of the lowest rations. I had about twenty-six catties a month, eight ounces of grain a day (mostly corn meal). There were not many vegetables. We began pickling parts of the veggies we used to throw away. There was only a few ounces of oil a month, maybe two ounces a month. Very little sugar. Coal was also scarce. Once food is scarce, everything is scarce. Each region had its own quota depending upon how much food was available. It was better for us in the big cities than in the countryside.

People got sick a lot more from lack of food. Work was at half pace—the Party told people to rest a lot because there wasn't enough food. We ate in the canteens more often because there was a little more available and it was prepared to make it seem like more (more water in the rice, mixing in lots of bran, etc.).

The first sign of malnutrition is swelling, so everyone was checked for swelling and enlarged livers. People who were malnourished were given extra food. At the Water Works we went out as a group and collected certain kinds of edible summer weeds. Everyone was in the same boat. Our leaders too were on the same rationing. We could see them suffering with us from the effects.

Our family went on those rations and we'd never been that hungry before. Grace discovered that she could eat a little cornmeal. She had been allergic to it during the occupation. I got swollen and my liver was too big.

Babies born in those years were quite weak—we were all in it together. There was very little black market or "going through the back door."

Our work at the Water Works almost stopped. We went to work everyday, but we just sat around and talked. People were too weak to work, and the leadership kept saying don't work, take it easy.

In the latter part of 1962, we began getting duck eggs. There were more vegetables, a little more meat, and oil. Grain rationing gradually increased until I was getting thirty-one catties.

In 1961 my husband and I moved back with Grace and Willy because I was quite sick at times, and it was so far to my work where we had been. Willy and my mother slept in the inner room, and my husband and I slept in the outer. We all took care of each other.

My husband went four hours every night to school for six years. He learned civil engineering. He came back around 11:30. On Sundays, he was at school half a day, home half a day. Often we just passed each other in the hall. It wasn't so hard on us. We had no children then.

ELLEN FINISHED high school in 1958. Grace and Willy were in Beijing when notice came that Ellen had been accepted at Harbin Industrial Institute. Nini helped Ellen prepare beddings and clothes for cold weather. Harbin was a city far to the north, in what was formerly Manchuria, a city once controlled by the Japanese and then by the Russians. The scientific and technical program at Harbin Institue had been set up by the Russians but the Russians had already withdrawn their teachers by the time Ellen arrived. Ellen explained the connection between Russia's withdrawal and the Great Leap:

In Tientsin there hadn't been many Russians, so we didn't notice much change. Some places like Harbin knew what was happening much more because they had to readjust to the Russian withdrawal. The Russians took all their blueprints and plans, teachers and experts with them. The Russians had been at Harbin beforehand setting up the program. But even by 1958, the Russian experts and teachers had withdrawn from the school, so the Great Leap was partly from necessity too. It all came out in 1962, at the conference in Bucharest—the Russians stood up and denounced the Chinese. The Albanians defended us, but the Russians withdrew aid and other materials. Anyway, this was the first we knew that the Russians had withdrawn from China completely.

It was a five-year course. We had a lot of basic courses: mathematics, machinery, drawing, physics, chemistry for three years. My major course was precision instruments. The courses were hard. Almost all my time went to my studies. My first year was at the beginning of the Great Leap, so we did things like making iron and steel. We set up stoves on the sidewalks. I was in a group making coal into charcoal. We went to school with black faces from making charcoal. In the higher classes, the students did experiments and had their own factories.

The arts did a great leap too. Everyone was performing in these small groups. We did everything—singing, plays, performances, things we made up ourselves. I sang in a group and went around to the workers and students and did small performances. There were eight girls in my dorm room; three of them came from the same high school I did. We four, more or less, hung together. We all took the same courses together, and we knew each other well. There was quite a lot of mutual help. The ones who were better were always tutoring the worse ones. I always planned my vacations going home, and it was always a big occasion for me.

We ate a lot because we were doing so much work. I came back fat the first year. There was still plenty of food then. When it got really cold, we wore double scarves on our heads, and masks on our faces when we went out. But inside we had double [glazed] windows, with wood chips between the cracks. We had central heat, steam heat, radiators. We had physical training in the morning. We did ice-skating for fun. I did some competitive running, long distances.

When food got scarce the next year, outside activities were frowned on. We mostly studied. Everybody was run down because of the lack of food and because it was so cold. The teachers didn't give many assignments. They wanted us mostly to stay in bed and not do much to use energy. Everybody had a ration, so we were only a little undernourished. It was forbidden to do hard work or gymnastics. We learned Tai-Chi at that time; it's quieter, builds your body up, gets the oxygen going without using so much energy.

In 1962 things started getting a little better. The grain rations were slightly higher each time. The students had more rations than others.

I met my husband Rei-sheng in my classes. I didn't much notice him

Ellen and
Rei-sheng,
freshmen at
the Harbin
Industrial
University,
1958.

at first. He spoke loudly, but he was in another group. He had been a worker before so he worked in the factory, showing people what to do. I was making the charcoal. I suppose he noticed me. A year or so later we became more friendly. He was our class leader—then later a kind of assistant to the teacher because he had work experience. We studied more together then.

Rei-sheng described his first impressions of Ellen: "The first time I saw her, she walked into a big lecture hall with a couple of hundred other students. I almost gasped. She was so beautiful that I was afraid to look at her. She never wore make-up or put on airs but she stood out from the other girls. She had a gentle manner yet she seemed tough. When the other students knew I was interested in her, they taunted me, 'Who do you think you are to go after the most beautiful girl in the school?' But some of the authorities in the Party warned me that her mother was an American and it would taint my record, especially since I came from a working-class background. But I disregarded them both. She was so serious about her work I was afraid she wouldn't talk to me. Then I was assigned to be her group leader—so I offered to help her in her studies."

Ellen continued:

I wasn't thinking of getting married. I wanted to do my study, and I didn't want to be bothered by all these things. Some boys in college wrote letters to me, or bothered me, but I didn't like it. I suppose everybody else noticed his interest before I did. Some of the classmates teased him about me and then I noticed that with other girls he was at ease, but with me he was a little bit stiff. I knew him for more than a year, and I knew he really had feelings for me and I for him. He's capable, very outspoken, he's not at all devious or tricky. He says what he thinks.

You can't get married in the university, but we knew we would later on. I didn't want to think about it then. Sometimes we went out together, boating on the river in boats which we rented by the hour. We studied together sometimes. He was half paid to work, and so he was busy.

Before we graduated we had to work in a factory. I went to Shanghai and to Sian. I went back to my father's old home when I was there. They asked me if my fiancé's family had any money. I said no, but neither do I. Why should I pick somebody for that reason? It was feudal thinking, that you should marry for the best match financially. Rei-sheng's father died when he was a boy of four or five. He had a mother and a brother. They lived in a village in Shantung province and grew vegetables for the city.

After you graduate from the university, the government finds you a job. Factories request workers from the labor bureau. Then they assign each factory a certain number of graduates from a particular school. The graduates decide where they want to be, but you might not get your choice. Because Rei-sheng and I were engaged, they tried to assign us to the same place. I was designing precision instruments for weights and measures, and most of the jobs for my kind of work were in Beijing, and that's where we ended up. Beijing was the closest I could get to Tianjin, so I was happy to be assigned there.

Rei-sheng and I worked in the same city, but very far apart. I lived in a dormitory in the science institute. We saw each other on Sundays. I didn't want to get married just after I came out from school. I wanted to start working, do the job well, and spend time on other things. Then he went to study in another factory outside of Beijing for about half a year. When he came back, we were married. He was nearly thirty and I was twenty-seven.

Our wedding was very simple. Our colleagues were there. No family was there. You take a letter of identification from your workplace to the police station and they give you a marriage license. We all went back and bought some candy and cigarettes for our colleagues and sat around for a while. Our colleagues said some words and did a simple ceremony. My husband had an extra room in his dormitory, and I stayed there on weekends, and then went back to work during the week. It didn't change my life much, being married.

Ellen and Reisheng, 1962.

293

23

TESTS OF COURAGE

WHEN ELLEN went off to college and Nini lived with her husband's parents, William and Grace were alone in the two rooms of the big mansion. William helped to get the water from down the hall and start the coal stove in the mornings. Their balcony became a familiar place, especially in the summer, for William's friends or Grace's students and sometimes teachers from Nankai. Study groups met in her home and she would ask the students how they thought they could learn better. Grace studied at night and read everything she could get her hands on about linguistics and the teaching of English.

William recalled that on these evenings he learned things about his mother he had not known before:

> My friend Kelin and I would be talking and studying in one corner and Grace would be reading in another. She was always there to help us if we didn't understand something, but she really knew how to concentrate. I would have to call her several times, "Ma, Ma, MA, MMAAA!" before she would hear me.
>
> One day Kelin and I wanted to read *Gone With the Wind*. I had heard Nini talking about it but Kelin had never read it. I started reading it to him in English, but he wanted to know everything, so I read it in English to myself and said it in Chinese to him. I really noticed the language that way—Southern expressions like "Now don't be so mean and hateful to your sisters" fascinated me.

"Ma," I said one night after Kelin left, "this is the first book I've read where the people in it talk like you!"

I guess I began to contemplate my mother's origins in a different way. She often talked about her upbringing so that it was part of our upbringing too, but it had always seemed unique to mother. I began to realize that there were certain language, culture, values, and history that she shared with others. Of course, we children knew that, but in China the subtleties got lost in the generality of being a foreigner. To everyone outside the family, she was just "the American Mrs. Liu."

One day we were listening to a radio broadcast from Shanghai. A Chinese soprano was singing "Depuis le jour" from the opera *Louise*. Her voice was clear and lyrical, with such emotional resonance that I was touched deeply and commented when it was over:

"That was remarkable!"

Mother said, "I used to sing that."

"You did! But it is very difficult," I said, thinking I knew so much about opera.

"Not really," she said. And then she began to sing—in a subdued voice, but with perfect pitch, she sang what I had just heard. I was dumbfounded. I knew that her lungs were shot from years of asthma and coal dust, but it was apparent that her voice had been trained. For the first time I realized that my mother could have had a very different life had she not met my father. But I also knew that she would make the same choice.

GRACE READ everything in the Nankai library that related to language-teaching. When she exhausted that source, she began to search periodicals and recent publications; these led her to a network of linguists around the world who were developing new approaches to the teaching of English. She wrote for information, textbooks, and

William, right, with his friend Kelin.

manuals. While she conducted her research, teaching at the university did not change much. In a interview years later, Grace described what she did to change the way English was taught:

In 1961 I was very distressed. I saw there really was no hope for the students in learning English. About this time, Chen Yi, who was the Minister of Foreign Affairs, gave a national talk to students at a conference, noting that the Foreign Ministry could not even find enough interpreters for diplomatic situations. This was embarrassing for China. By pointing out the backwardness of the teaching of English in China, he called for educational reform.

I was fascinated by what he said and agreed completely. In my excitement, I sat down and wrote him a letter—ten typewritten pages. Can you imagine! I suggested to him that there was a way to change it. I had read all the books on linguistics and the teaching of English that the library had. So I made some suggestions about how to reform the teaching of English. My thoughts were based on "practice before theory."

I talked to the Chairman of the Department, Professor Li, and to the other teachers. I tried to convince them of the need. I told them that it was against Chairman Mao's teaching which said that theory must serve practice. I quoted his essay, "On Practice"—practice comes first; then you use theory to go back and guide the practice. The aim is practice, not theory. Theory is the guidance but you must apply it to practice or what is the use of theory? If your theory isn't proved right in practice, then you throw your theory out.

That is how language should be taught—You should not first teach the theory (grammar) then try to let them piece up the language with the theory (grammar). They should get exposed to the language first (the way it is spoken) and learn some practical things, and then use some grammar rules to sum up what they have already learned.

[Chen Yi] gave the letter to the Minister of Higher Education in Peking who sent it to various universities and experts to have it evaluated. Then the Minister of Higher Education wrote to the university saying that these reforms should be supported. During this time I heard from a well-known linguist, Lu Shuxiang, of the Language Research Institute at the Academy of Science, who encouraged my approach. I wrote to him the next time. He talked to the Minister of Higher Education again. And so it went. It took a long time to "trickle down."

But I still had to fight for it [at Nankai] because the conservative professors had vested interests in the old way. They had learned that way—they had gained their reputations on the old way—so they did not want to change. And some students did not want to change either. They didn't want to really practice English because it showed their deficiency.

Some of the younger teachers became involved with me. We studied all the materials we could get our hands on. The education minister of Australia sent us some materials; they had made a new book based on this approach and they sent it to me. We also got textbooks from England and from America about the structural approach. It was the way things were being taught then outside of China, but China had been cut off for so long. We began to use some of these methods, but we had to adapt it to the Chinese situation—we changed the dialogue to reflect what the Chinese students do in their daily lives.

Several of Grace's former students and teacher-trainees—some still teaching at the university—were interviewed in 1998. The comments below are representative of what they recalled about their early years with Grace Liu:

Grace Liu was very enthusiastic, very aggressive about English teaching. We were young teachers, most of us recent graduates of the university. We formed a group, a work team. It was something like a training group. At first we met in her home, later at the school. We read articles from journals and periodicals around the world, such as *English Language Teaching*. We did not know about these things before. We learned that there were different kinds of methods based on different theories. This theory based on practice and emphasizing the spoken language was very suited to us. We used pattern drills. The drills were based on the structure of English, like this:

Give me the *book*.

Give me the *pencil*.

Give *him* the pencil.

Grace Liu would give us the pattern, then we practiced it—then she added a call word, like "him." We would insert the call word in the appropriate place and make a new sentence. It was quite efficient. Then we would use it in the classroom with our students. If we had problems in the classroom, we discussed it in the group. We improved the method as we went along. Eventually, we compiled a textbook for other teachers—a manual of these sentence patterns—and adapted the content to the Chinese situation.

Before, we had learned English through translation and grammar—that is, only through our eyes; now we could learn it through our ears and speak it readily. We immediately put into practice what we learned. It was quite fresh at the time, exciting. We could speak English better and teach students in a new way. This changed everything for us.

In a letter to a friend in the United States in May 1962, Grace described her work at the university:

I haven't written to anyone outside the country for a year or more. I have been, and am, very busy. I am still teaching at Nankai University and all my thoughts and attention are absorbed by the work I'm doing because it is new and rather difficult for me. My actual teaching work is not only heavy but we are breaking new ground in teaching methods. We are trying to break with the old time-honored methods of language teaching that have prevailed here for the last fifty years or so. It isn't easy and requires infinite patience, work, and study. I've never studied so hard in my life, not only teaching methods, teaching psychology, teaching English as a foreign language and language teaching in general, but for the last year, descriptive linguistics both British and American—they don't altogether agree! I'm very interested in Prof. Charles Fries work in the English Language Institute, Ann Arbor, Michigan. I've been studying his "Teaching and Learning English as a Foreign Language" and his "Structure of English." Right now I'm "plowing" through a book by a University of Texas professor. It's really too technical for me but what I can understand of it is very interesting. This year I've made my own composition course based on my recent studies. The old method was so unscientific, time wasting, and useless.

We've had to combat some pretty die-hard attitudes in our English department, but just this term we've gotten the head of the department convinced that we must make some radical changes, so things are going more smoothly. The students are delightful to teach, so intelligent, diligent, and eager to learn! Most of them come from peasant families from as far away as inner-Mongolia and Canton, and some are overseas students from Indonesia, Malaya, and Burma.

We've been having a pretty hard time for the last three years. I'm sure you've heard plenty about it. Although accounts in the U.S. are exaggerated there is no denying that things have been and are pretty tough! But we've turned the corner and things will now gradually get better.

I've been hearing about the remarkable women's movement for peace in the U.S. from Sylvia Powell and Harriet Eddy. It seems things are really stirring. Maude Russell sent me the "China's Case" chapter from Felix Greene's book. I haven't seen the rest of the book, but he certainly did a good job explaining how the Chinese people feel. I can testify to the absolute truth of it! I haven't written anything for the N.W.R. since my October 1959 article [Sun Pao-san's Story in the New World Review*]. I simply have no time.*

I go to Peking to visit Anna Louise Strong occasionally. She says she's getting ready to write a new book but she didn't say what about . . .

Grace was still in touch with friends outside China even during the Great Leap. Her infrequent correspondence was primarily with women. Most of the women that she mentioned in this letter had interests in her or in China and were active in educating others in the States. Harriet Eddy, to whom Grace had written after F. C.'s death, was a lifelong member of the Women's International League for Peace and Freedom, founded in 1915 by Jane Addams, a well-known American social reformer. Even after she went blind, Harriet was an avid correspondent with friends and members of peace organizations throughout the world.

Maude Russell had been the YWCA secretary in Changsha, China, before the war. After she returned to the States, she organized the Committee for a Democratic Far Eastern Policy and published the *Far Eastern Reporter.* She was a well-known lecturer and attracted large crowds on college campuses.

Anna Louise Strong was an American correspondent who had visited China many times. Her personal interview with Mao Tse Tung in August 1946 became famous but made her infamous in America. In the interview, Mao first used the phrase "paper tigers" in reference to American imperialists. She continued to live in China and write, as a guest of the Chinese People's Friendship Association. Grace and William went to visit her in Peking about twice a year—that's where they were when Ellen received notice of acceptance at Harbin.

Sylvia Powell was the editorial assistant to her husband, Bill Powell, publisher of the *China Monthly Review* in Shanghai, for which Grace had written several articles. Sylvia was called a "Communist propagandist" by the U.S. passport office after she wrote an article for a Portland newspaper criticizing the U.S. for its support of Chiang's blockade and bombing of the Shanghai harbor in 1950. When the Powells returned to the States after the magazine closed down in 1953, they were accused of treason and sedition and were put on trial in 1956. It was the magazine's coverage of the Korean War and accusations of U.S. use of biological warfare that caused the greatest threat. When the Defense Department refused to release documents, a mistrial was declared in 1959 and all charges were dropped.

Along with Harriet Eddy, Sylvia was active in the Women's International League for Peace and Freedom. Harriet Eddy had sent a copy of Grace's letter about F. C.'s death to Sylvia. In 1956, the year Sylvia's trial for treason began, she wrote back to Harriet: "[Grace's] courage gives me courage."

GRACE'S COURAGE was tested again in 1962 when she was diagnosed with breast cancer. The story of how she faced and survived radical mastectomy is told by all three children.

NINI: Grace began getting weak and tired in the winter of 1962. She would sigh very heavily. I first thought maybe her T.B. had come back. She wasn't getting much protein because of the food rationing. Finally I suggested we go to the clinic for tests. On the way there she told me she had a lump in her chest and had had it since 1958. I was shocked but I saw that she was frightened so I didn't ask her about it. I tried to reassure her. She was pale, and I knew she was scared.

She said that she hadn't told us about it because we were still in school and she thought it would be too much for us after F. C.'s death. At the clinic we were told she needed to go to the cancer hospital for further tests.

WILLY: When Mother and Nini came back from the clinic, they were both very pale. "Ma might have breast cancer," Nini said to me, "we must take her to the Bone and Tumor Hospital." My heart dropped into the pit of my stomach. It was the nightmare coming back again. It brought back that hot and humid summer night, watching the face of the doctor spitting out watermelon seeds, telling her the news that her husband was going to die. It had been more than seven years now, and it was in the dead of winter, but the feeling of doom came back upon me.

None of us could swallow a bite that night at suppertime, none of us could imagine what the outcome would be. Nini tried to cheer us up saying that since Mother had felt the lump in her breast for a few years now, it must be benign. She went on to say that breast cancer was operable and the Bone and Tumor Hospital had a good reputation of treating breast cancer.

When they went to the hospital the next day, they were very fortunate to get to see a specialist, Dr. Wang, who lived right across the street from us. He gave her a thorough checkup. After a week of tests, Dr. Wang was ready to do the biopsy and if it turned out to be cancerous, to do a mastectomy immediately.

I went to see her the night before the operation. She appeared to be calm and cheerful, but I knew she was really scared, staying in the same hospital where F. C. had died and to be struck down with the same disease.

When she saw me with a book in my hand, she asked what I had brought for her to read. I told her I had brought Charlotte Bronte's *Villette* to read unless she wanted to sleep. She said she wasn't tired although they kept her busy all day with a hundred and one tests. She remembered reading *Villette* to me a few years ago when I still had difficulties in reading. Mother had a wonderful reading voice. Although reading often made her cough and sometimes brought on asthma, she always insisted on reading to me as she felt it was important for me to appreciate the spoken language.

That night before her operation, we talked about Lucy Snowe, the main character in *Villette,* and her experience as a foreign teacher teaching English in Brussels and some of the humorous situations she got herself into. Mother told me she had read the first chapter to the young teachers she had been training and that they were so fascinated that they all went to the library to borrow a copy of the book. When I left the hospital and went into the cold winter night, I felt less fearful of what might come.

The next day, our worst expectation came true: "Carcinoma," they said, and it must be operated on immediately.

NINI: I was with Grace when she came to from the ether. She mumbled and giggled, she didn't know what happened. They wanted me to be prepared in case they needed a skin graft, but they didn't need me because she was so thin they just sewed her back up. Later that day, the head nurse told me that they took a lot out—it had spread to the lymph nodes. "These cases," she said, "might live another five or ten years."

Ellen was at school in Harbin, and we hadn't told her. Willy was at school and came in the evening. My husband was at work. A neighbor and I were there all day waiting for Grace to come out. That night my husband came and relieved me, and I went home to sleep.

She was always complaining in the hospital, wanted to do everything herself. She pulled her tubes out and would go to the bathroom by herself . . .

With determination, she recovered fairly quickly. Three days after the operation when Willy and I went to visit her, the doctors where examining her; they were treating her very gingerly as if she were a delicate old lady who had just had a major operation. One doctor asked her if she could raise her feet. She looked at him and then kicked her leg all the way over her head. The doctor was so startled he screamed and Ma laughed so hard the pain in the wound brought tears to her eyes. The doctors talked about it for days. They had never seen a sixty-year-old lady kicking her legs over her head, not to mention one that had just had a radical operation. She was already exercising her arm. I came in one day to the hospital and she was leaning against the radiator holding her arm up, using her body to push against her arm.

Big tears were rolling down her cheeks. I asked her what she was doing. "Oh, it hurts like hell," she said. A week later, they took the stitches out. She regained full use of her arm eventually.

When it came time for Grace to move to another room, the hospital assumed that a foreigner would want privacy and better accommodations. But Grace said she wanted to go to the general ward, a room with about ten or twelve other patients. The hospital staff said it was too crowded there and she would not be able to rest. But she insisted. Grace spent the next two weeks in the general cancer ward of the hospital. In Chinese hospitals, there is a lot of activity, families visiting, patients helping each other, sharing food. When anybody gets depressed, others try to console or cajole them. People get to know each other quite well and compare how they are doing. Grace thought this atmosphere would be good for her. She did not want to be left in a room alone. She got quite friendly with the other women in the ward. The people there kept her very much occupied. There was always a bunch of doctors around her bed. They all wanted to practice their English so she had quite a few impromptu classes for the doctors. Her students or other faculty would come and they would talk shop. She was never left out of things.

The women patients around her all had had mastectomies. One of them was an old country woman from the suburb of Tianjin. She told Grace that she had to sell her pig to pay for her operation. Her son came to see her every day and brought her food from home, which she shared with Grace and that helped her appetite. There was a woman judge on one side of her and a school teacher in her thirties on the other side. We got to know them quite well. Since they all had their operations about the same time, they went through radiation and chemotherapy together for the next whole year. Every time she went for either the radiation or chemo treatment, we would see her "old gang" again. The old country woman did not like to exercise her arm and she was amazed at the progress Grace had made. Grace encouraged her to keep on using her arm, regardless of how painful it was. The school teacher told the others how she dealt with the nausea caused by the radiation and everyone compared their white blood cell counts and the burns they had to suffer. The judge's cancer returned around the end of Mother's treatment and everyone supported her when she had to have another operation. The camaraderie with these women was the real secret to Grace's recovery.

303

Grace, her children, and her son-in-law, Enhua, in Summer 1963, after Grace's breast cancer surgery.

ELLEN: I was having my exams when Grace had cancer. Nini wrote me a letter saying that Grace was going into the hospital and could I come back as soon as possible. I was very worried. I finished my exams that day and started home. By the time I arrived, Grace was out of the hospital.

During the summer of 1963 Willy and I took Grace to the hospital to get radiation treatments when Nini was working. I think we went once a week. She felt weak, out of breath, and her white blood cell count decreased some, but she was able to continue the treatment. She wasn't discouraged. She was quite satisfied with the treatment. She was also reading a lot of American health books and magazines, like *Prevention*, which friends sent her. She took lots of vitamins, large doses of vitamin C. She would talk about what she read. She believed in vitamins. She was always trying to get us to take more vitamins. But we thought that if you weren't sick, it didn't make much sense.

WHEN GRACE finished her last chemotherapy treatment, the university offered her a place on campus to live so she wouldn't have to travel so far back and forth. She and Willy moved to the campus in early 1965. The move was good for Grace. She was close to her work and in the middle of things. The air was much cleaner and the noise less. There were large lotus ponds surrounded by willows and Chinese locust trees with paths that wandered through the campus in a park-like atmosphere.

Grace and William had a nice little bungalow in a grouping of faculty housing. There was plenty of space with two main rooms, a bathroom, a kitchen and plenty of storage space. They were surrounded by trees. Across a field from the bungalow was the main university building. Behind the bungalow was the main road to the campus. There were lots of comings and goings as both students and faculty moved to and from campus. Grace liked to watch people and bicycles go back and forth on the road to classes.

The school gave her a lighter load while she recuperated. She continued training the young teachers, and many of her reforms were being supported. William began working in the language lab and helping Grace write the teachers' manual. Nini came twice a week to visit and was usually there on weekends. There was enough food to eat again and the country seemed to be on the upturn. Both of her girls were married to good men and she had survived cancer. The reward for all she had gone through came the moment she saw her first granddaughter. How pleased Grace was when Ellen brought her newly born baby to visit in May 1965. The air was warm and flowers were in bloom. The lotus ponds were beginning to turn green again. She was a grandmother and her life, at last, had an air of calm and normalcy.

Grace proudly displays her first grandchild, Ellen's daughter, Hui, May 1965. Below, William, Ellen, and Hui on the Nankai campus, May 1965.

305

24

THE CULTURAL REVOLUTION

F ROM HER window at the back of the bungalow facing the main road of Nankai University, Grace first saw the bands of students from the nearby high schools storm in angry mobs onto the campus. Starting in the summer of 1966, wave after wave of marauding students passed before her window, their shouts growing more fierce, denouncing the bourgeois authorities at the university.

The drastic policies of the Great Leap Forward which had brought the nation to the brink of starvation were moderated by 1965, but the push and pull of the political tide continued unabated. Some leaders had reacted by urging more gradual reforms and less revolutionary approaches toward economic and cultural development. Others pushed for an even greater proletarian vision of the revolution and criticized their opponents as taking the capitalist road. A wave of rhetorical attacks against "reactionary bourgeois capitalist roaders" began to move through the Communist Party and soon spread throughout the nation.

The split in the leadership occurred after the split with the Soviet Union. By the early 1960s, the Soviet Union had completely withdrawn from China at a time when threat from the United States intensified. The U.S. involvement in Vietnam to the south created tension on the border of China and fear of possible escalation. In October 1964 China sent a warning to both by testing its first atomic bomb.

In the sway of opposing opinions, criticism of the nation's policies emerged most fiercely in the arts. Disturbed by the growing trend among artists and writers to criticize the leadership, Jiang Qing, a former actress before she became Mao's third wife in 1939, was appointed to head up the cultural revolution group in 1966. Advocating more radical and socialist policies of cultural development, her crackdown on the "bourgeois ideology" of the arts soon spread into education.

The education system itself was criticized for not following the government's policy of promoting workers and peasants. At the crux of the system, the barrier which determined who would be educated and who would not, was the college entrance exam. Grace explained in an interview years later how the college entrance exams were unfair to those from worker or peasant backgrounds: "If they selected students based on the traditional examinations then the students from intellectuals' families got into college and those from worker and peasant families did not. So the Cultural Revolution began with the debate on abolishing the college entrance exams. By 1966 many students from worker and peasant backgrounds had entered the colleges and found the whole system discriminatory. In the spring they began putting up wall posters and criticizing the authorities and policies of the university. This attack made others in the university feel that the very standards of the educational system were being threatened."

By the summer of 1966, schools and universities were shut down, classes canceled, and teachers and authorities of the university targeted as "reactionary bourgeois intellectuals." In some places the fighting became fierce. The more radical students issued red arm bands, becoming then known as Red Guards.

The Great Proletarian Cultural Revolution was officially announced by Mao from the Gate of Heavenly Peace (Tiananmen Square) on August 18, 1966. Mao's wife, Jiang Qing, stood on the stage with him. Her presence at the parade signaled which way the nation was heading. A massive, awe-inspiring parade of China's youth passed before Mao as they shouted "Ten Thousand Years" and called him the Four Greats: "Our Great Teacher, Great Leader, Great Supreme Commander, and Great Helmsman." Throughout the summer and fall of 1966, Mao reviewed millions of youth through Tiananmen Square, empowering them to a level of zeal surpassing what had been seen before. Mao gave fuel to the fire by directing the students' rage not just toward the bourgeois authorities at the universities but toward "revisionists" in the leadership of the party itself.

All schools came to a standstill as the revolutionary struggle became foremost. Students swept away anything that represented the "Four Olds"—old culture, old custom, old habit, old ideology. In the name of sweeping away, old street signs were taken down and replaced with revolutionary names, art objects were smashed, pos-

Grace and
William at the
beginning of
the Cultural
Revolution.

sessions confiscated, temples or old buildings destroyed. High school students as well as those from universities traveled across the country by train and stayed in hostels for free. They visited sites of the revolution, such as Yenan and Shaoshan, Mao's birthplace, and saw parts of China most of them had never seen before. They met other students and felt an excitement that overcame the crowded conditions or lack of food or accommodations they faced.

The tide of revolutionary fervor moved across the nation and left almost no one untouched. Starting on school and university campuses, the attacks spread into the society as a whole, the main targets being the educated and managerial class. Wanting to demonstrate their revolutionary superiority, students attacked anyone who in their opinion retarded the revolution or had associations with "bad" family elements—former KMT, landlords, capitalists, those who had affiliations with the West or were educated in the West or intellectuals in the broadest sense. Managers, doctors, administrators, teachers, government officials, and authority figures at any level were dragged before jeering crowds or humiliated in public. Many were exiled to the countryside or driven to suicide. Once labeled as bourgeois authorities, they and their families could be ruined forever.

The first sign Grace had that the student attacks had spread beyond the campus was the same day that the great parade took place in Beijing. The day began innocently enough, as William recalled:

On August 18, 1966, I took Grace into town to get a "perm," the last one she would ever have. After that "perms" were too bourgeois and went out with the other "olds." On our way back to campus, we stopped to see our friend Bernice Ko, a Chinese-American woman who was married to a Chinese gynecologist. The Kos lived in a big, gracious house with a lovely garden, a house filled with antiques and equipped with every Western luxury. Two days after our visit, Red Guards ransacked the house, smashing vases, slashing pictures, and carrying out furniture. The young guards screamed at the Kos, "Bourgeois monsters!" then took what they wanted. The house was sealed off and the Kos were left on the street.

Then we heard that Dr. Fan, a respected pediatrician that Grace knew, had come home one day to find his wife dead, apparently beaten. In an abortive suicide attempt, he leapt from a window and was permanently crippled.

Our colleague, a professor of Russian, a mild-mannered man had jumped to his death from a fifth story window after the humiliation of being paraded publicly as a criminal. His mistake had been to tear up his diary. On the inside front page of that diary, as in all Chinese diaries then, was a picture of Chairman Mao. The scraps of that picture had been found in his wastebasket when the guards ransacked his house.

From our small bungalow on the west side of the Nankai University campus, Grace and I saw our colleagues being paraded up and down. Some wore placards identifying them as "reactionary academic author-ity." Grace gasped one day when she saw old Professor Li, the chairman of the Foreign Language Department, his hair shorn in a grotesque manner, doing manual labor, some meaningless task of moving heavy rocks from one place to another. Grace knew that he had a heart condition and wor-ried that the stress would be fatal. We also saw other colleagues in the Foreign Language Department lined up, forced to bend over and get their entire heads shaved except for a strip down the middle, or chunks snipped out at random. Dunce caps or a waste basket were placed on their heads before they were paraded outside, with slurs and threats, and sometimes with fists and heels. The student guards yelled at them, "Smash the dog heads of the traitors."

We watched as high school Red Guards made a huge pile of "bour-geois and revisionist" books—and that included all Western literature— and set them on fire in great bonfires. The smell of burning books seeped into our windows and their soot fell around us.

I knew that Grace had only a vague notion of the danger of those days of sweeping incriminations. I had repeatedly warned her to be cau-tious of what she said and wrote. I even tried to censor her letters, which had, in turn, incensed or amused her. Grace had always spoken her mind and had never had any fear of expressing herself. She had learned through the last few years to be careful of what she said, but I could tell that her patience was growing thin in recent months.

Grace and
William in
Beijing, with
visiting
teachers from
Britain, during
the second
year of the
Cultural
Revolution,
Spring 1967.

When the revolutionary students fanned out across the countryside, everyone remaining on campus, including me, had to participate in building a monument to Mao. We mixed concrete, dug a huge foundation, and sorted black stones from white ones. One day right after the construction of the statue, Grace and I took a walk around the campus. The statue stood on a pedestal in front of the main classroom building. The whole thing was four stories high. It was a conglomeration of stones and concrete. None of us knew how to build a statue, nor did the construction leaders. Grace commented to me on how hideous it looked and that this was what people put on tombs. I soon forgot about it and had no idea she would mention it to anyone else.

So much of the rhetoric was absurd to her, like calling Mao "the Greatest of the Greatest of the Greatest of the Great Leaders." That was redundant, she insisted, with each added "great" you diminished the meaning of the first one. But an English teacher's grammatical corrections were not appreciated in this fanatical environment.

BY THE END of 1966, the students had split into battling factions. While one

310

group attacked the "bourgeois intellectuals," the other claimed the more radical stance. Encouraged by the *People's Daily* on January 1, 1967, to "launch a general attack on the handful of people in the Communist Party who are taking the capitalist road," the second group attacked members of the party itself and called themselves the "revolutionary rebels." They labeled the other faction the "reactionary royalists" because they protected the party. The two factions began to fight among themselves, each calling the other "counter-revolutionaries." Grace described how she viewed the conflict between the opposing factions of the student guards:

The two sides began quarreling, and the fighting got fiercer. The leaders in the party did not want to be criticized so they instigated one bunch of students against the other bunch. First they debated with loudspeakers. When one side got loud, the other side got louder. One side had ten loudspeakers, so the other side got ten loudspeakers. Then, of course, when you fuss like that, you are bound to get into fist fights. So they got to fighting with sticks and clubs. Brandishing nightsticks, they fought each other long into the night, loudspeakers blaring, "You are wrong!" "No, you are wrong!" With sticks and fists, they staged battles in open fields in Gilbert and Sullivan comic operetta style that settled no issue. The campus was a battleground. It was like a fight you would go see on the athletic field. I went and watched several of them. It finally got so bad, the government had to send the PLA in to stop the fighting. I heard them coming—what was that sound, I wondered. Three thousand PLA walked onto campus and parted the fighting students down the middle. They came with the little Red Book and shouted, "Chairman Mao said to fight with words, not with sticks."

25

GRACE'S ARREST

B Y FEBRUARY 1967, the PLA had quelled the campus disputes temporarily and called for classes to resume. Local factions became their own authorities on how to carry out this revolution, most often accountable only to inflammatory rhetoric. The disorder continued at a bewildering pace throughout 1967.

In August 1967 a burst of anti-foreign resentment was stirred up in Beijing. Red Guards ransacked and torched the office of the British *charge d'affaires*. Radical students took over the Ministry of Foreign Affairs, and Chen Yi, the Foreign Minister, was taken prisoner. He was the one to whom Grace had written about reforming the teaching of English only a few years earlier. Before becoming Foreign Minister, Chen Yi was commander of the Third Army, leading the PLA forces to victory across the Yangtse in 1949. Now he was under arrest by students.

The few foreigners still remaining in China, mostly in Beijing, were brought under investigation. Anyone with contacts outside China was suspect for espionage. Letters and papers were searched for clues to information that could be leaked or personal contacts that could be detected as a network of spies operating within China. Grace had a friend who taught German at the Foreign Languages Institute. Olga Li was a Swiss woman, divorced from her Chinese husband, living with her three adult children in Beijing. Grace and William often stayed with her when they went to Beijing and corresponded in between visits.

The storm of the Cultural Revolution had been raging for a year and a half before it finally arrived at the bungalow. It was a cold night in January 1968, William remembers:

It was after midnight. I was awakened by a knock at the door. I came out of my room shivering, wondering who could be knocking at such an hour.

Through the glass panes in the door, I saw half a dozen people standing in the small yard, some in the shadow and some clearly etched in the bright, icy moonlight. The closer ones were recognizably college-aged Red Guards. In the back were two adult-looking shadows with military bearing. My heart stopped.

I turned. Grace was coming from her room, securing her robe. "Who is it, Willy?" she asked.

I could not answer. I could only think: So they have come for us!

She saw them through the glass and said, "Open the door, Willy."

Six heavily bundled people stomped in, the cold night air rushing in with them.

"These comrades are Red Guards from Beijing," said the more mature-looking one, who seemed to be from the campus Security Office. He was addressing himself to Grace, "It seems you have friends who are involved in counter-revolutionary activities and espionage." The other guard, a young one who had been identified as from Beijing, interrupted him and said gruffly, "We need to ask you some questions. Put on your clothes and follow us!"

Grace hardly ever went outside in the coldest months and did not have time to fully dress. As we walked along the path between frozen lotus ponds, the piercing wind hit us in the face and nearly took my breath away. She coughed. I looked anxiously at my mother. She showed nothing, only shook her head, her face pale in the moonlight.

One of the Red Guards walked ahead and two followed. The others stayed behind to search the house. The silence of the night was broken only by the crunching sound of our footsteps on the icy path and the wind whistling through the bare branches of the trees.

Beyond the lotus ponds, we came to a group of dormitory buildings and were led into one of the rooms in a dorm, where there were four or five bunk beds with some students sleeping in them. We were told to sit on a lower bunk and wait. The room was freezing and the concrete floor

313

numbed my feet. A student sleeping on one of the bunk beds woke up and looked at us with bewilderment. Nobody said a word.

It got colder and colder as the minutes ticked on. Thoughts raced through my head—which of our friends in Beijing had gotten into trouble? Had we said anything or had we written anything that might incriminate us? Fear turned my stomach into a block of ice. I looked again at mother. She appeared uncannily serene as she smiled at the sleepy student.

I had told Grace over and over the importance of being cautious, but I had the feeling that we were already implicated. I could not imagine why Red Guards had come from Beijing.

After an hour of waiting, we were taken into another room in which there were only some chairs and a table. Those who had been searching the house had returned. Two of the Red Guards and two men from the security force sat by the table on which were piled stacks of papers and what looked like bunches of letters.

"We think you know very well why we brought you here," said one of the Red Guards from Beijing who spoke fairly good English. "We have dug up some heinous espionage activities from the Beijing Foreign Language Institute. Your friend, Olga Li, has been passing valuable information to the Swiss Embassy. A lot of the information was gathered by you. You must confess your crimes or you will be dealt with severely."

Grace looked shocked. "That's nonsense," she protested. "Olga would never do anything like that. And I don't have any information of any kind to give to anybody."

The Red Guards looked at each other and smiled smugly. "We have all the letters you wrote to Olga. The ironclad evidence is in your own handwriting. We are only testing you to see if you are willing to confess and give up your criminal activities."

"I only wrote about myself and my children," Grace said indignantly. "How can that be a criminal activity?"

"So you used your children to gather information and then reported what you found out to your foreign friends in Beijing, didn't you? Who else did you supply information to?"

Grace showed anger welling up in her chest, but she quickly choked

it down. She began to realize what happened to her might have repercussions for Nini and Ellen and their families. Taking a deep breath, she said, "Since you have my letters, you must know that I did not say anything that could cause any harm to the country."

"You reported in detail what had happened on campus and in the city. What about the letters we might not have? What did you report in them?" snorted the other Red Guard. The questions continued until daybreak.

We trudged back over icy ground to the house, stunned by the wind and the badgering interrogation. The stove in the bungalow had gone out, so it was freezing cold inside. We stood with our overcoats on and looked around. The drawers had all been pulled out and their contents strewn across the room. I felt violated and immediately began trying to put things in order around the room. As I did so, I tried to order my thoughts and construe any meaning from the events. I was searching for anything that would give me a clue. It seemed that only our letters were gone. Other papers were still there. Grace, on the other hand, didn't move. She just stood there with her coat on and then she mused, like a teacher who had given a tough assignment, "They are going to have a lot of reading to do! It might improve their English."

Then she sat down, not even trying to clean things up. "Poor Olga," she muttered. "I hope she's all right."

"What could they be taking so seriously?" I asked, trying to figure things out. "We haven't done anything wrong. You didn't say anything objectionable in your letters, did you?"

"Of course not! You always read everything I write."

I paused, afraid to admit it: "Not to Olga."

I had seen no reason to read Grace's letters to Olga. They were good friends, both without their husbands; they talked about their children, events of the day, woman-to-woman sorts of things. What incriminating things could she have written in letters to Olga?

The investigation dragged on until spring. The Red Guards from Beijing returned home, and a faction of Red Guards from Nankai were put in charge of the investigation. The leader of that group, a Red Guard

315

from Nankai, called T., was one of the students with a "good" family background, meaning from worker or peasant families. He had recently graduated from the university and been hired back as a young teacher. He saw an opportunity here to demonstrate his revolutionary zeal and to further his position on campus. He took a small group of students to Beijing to investigate what the Beijing Red Guards had brought to their attention.

During this lull in the investigation, Grace never left the house. Once you are labeled, no one dared have contact with you. Colleagues at the office stopped talking when I walked into the room. We talked with no one on or off campus except Nini. There was only silence.

The silence came to an end one morning, towards the end of April. The willow trees were just turning green, and the dreaded yellow dust was blowing down from the Gobi Desert. I had just arrived at the Foreign Language Department when T. entered the room and approached me.

T. was a thin young man with small eyes and a large mouth which appeared to be frozen in a perpetual sneer. He was followed by a pretty, plump girl, another Red Guard, whom I recognized as a second-year English student before classes were canceled. Although T. was one of the English teachers, he spoke to me in Chinese.

"I want to talk to you about your mother. Come with me," he demanded.

They headed me back the way I had just come. As we walked, he informed me that Grace's actions were much more serious than anyone had thought. They constituted crimes against the Party, against China and its people. She would be taken into custody immediately for further investigation until all her crimes were exposed.

He continued, "Although you aided your mother in many of her criminal activities, you are still young and have grown up in the new society, under the red flag; therefore, you are being considered as those who are educable. If you will clearly draw the line between yourself and your mother and do your utmost to expose her anti-revolutionary activities, there is still hope for you to become a new person. Of course, if you should follow in your mother's footsteps, you will end up an enemy of the people."

I did not hear half of what he said. I was wondering where were they going to take her and what were they going to do to her. How much abuse could a frail sixty-seven-year-old woman endure?

Grace was at breakfast, sitting at a little table peeling a hard-boiled egg when I arrived at the bungalow with the two Red Guards escorting me. Two more Red Guards, a man and a woman, and a man from the campus Security Office arrived at the same time. T. gave the orders. The two Red Guards who had just come seized "foreign agent" Liu. The others went ransacking through the house again.

"Where are you taking her? She needs . . . " I stammered. It didn't sound appropriate for me to say she needed her vitamins daily.

"She is in the hands of the people now, and she will be dealt with as the revolutionary committee sees fit. You must think about your own sins now!" T. exclaimed.

"But what has she done?"

"You know very well what she has done. Her accomplices have all confessed, so all your evasions will be in vain. Start right now to expose all her evil deeds before it is too late for you."

Two Red Guards stayed to keep an eye on me and prevent me from having contact with anyone. For three weeks, these guards, whom I had known as English students, watched me and refused to tell me what was happening to Grace. During these long days, they demanded that I write down all the connections our family had or had ever had in China or abroad, the nature of the connection, and the nature of our recent contact. It was a staggering thought. I knew that confessions had to be thorough and complete. Self-righteous restraint or non-cooperative silence could be punished cruelly. If I didn't cooperate they might seek out Nini or Ellen. What could I do?

One day, my guards did not show up. I was relieved just to be freed of the usual tedious tasks. But by afternoon, when they still had not come nor sent any message, I became alarmed. I feared that something had happened to Grace and they no longer needed me. But I had no idea where to go to find out and I dared not leave.

Around ten o'clock that night, the loudspeakers positioned at every corner of the campus suddenly came to life. An angry and agitated voice shouted over the public address system: "Revolutionary Comrades, we have won a big victory over the enemy! We have triumphed in catching an American spy hiding on our campus! This evil monster is also a vicious counter-revolutionary that opposes the Communist Party and our Great Leader and Supreme Commander, Chairman Mao! . . . All revolutionary comrades will gather at the Great Auditorium tomorrow morning to repudiate the heinous crimes of Grace Liu!" The announcement was repeated every ten minutes for an hour.

The angry voices, echoing and bouncing off the buildings, mixed with the howling spring wind left me in mental torment all night. I could not fathom what had happened to my mother.

The next morning, my jailers returned to escort me to the denunciation rally. They wanted to show me how enemies of the people are dealt with. As we walked to the Great Auditorium, I was shocked to see big character posters denouncing my mother, the hideous words written in bold black Chinese characters, "counter-revolutionary American spy." The posters had been plastered on both sides of the main road leading into campus and over the big gate.

The Great Auditorium doubled as the students' dining hall in normal times, but it had been converted into the stage setting for the almost-daily denunciations. It was large and cavernous, so that every sound echoed back and forth, repeating again and again the error of your ways. A crowd of nearly five thousand gathered that morning in the large room. There were two other targets of the "repudiate and struggle" meeting that day, but Grace Liu was the premier exhibit.

To make the greatest impression on me, I was put on the front row, as close to the stage as possible. Since the accused were already held prisoners, the meeting began on time, just as announced.

"Down with Grace Liu," roared the Red Guard on stage, as an opening call.

"Down with Grace Liu,'" the crowd chanted back. The litany echoed across the large hall.

Up on the stage, two young women guards brought my mother for-

318

ward, holding her by her arms, one pushing her head down, the other pulling her arms up. If only I could see her eyes I would know if she were all right. But in that position I could not see her face.

"We are here to repudiate this heinous American spy and counter-revolutionary, Grace Liu!" shouted the leader. His voice was amplified on the P.A. system. I knew that meant it was being blasted over loudspeakers all over campus.

Some in the crowd rose to their feet and raised fists in an aggressive gesture of condemnation as they shouted agreement.

I looked up at the frail figure onstage. My mother weighed less than ninety pounds, and she was all but swallowed up by her loose-fitting Chinese-style, red corduroy jacket and full-legged, dark blue trousers. It was the same outfit she was wearing the day she was arrested. She did not make a sound or look up. Now and then, her head would involuntarily bob up and one of her guards would punch her on the ear to force it back down.

I had been through enough of these public denunciations in recent months to be reasonably certain that her life was not in danger. Still, I was frightened. Her health was not good and anything could happen. Around me, the shouting grew louder.

"Long live Chairman Mao!"

"Down with the traitor!"

"Long live the proletarian dictatorship!"

My mother was bent over with her arms stretched backward, in the position the Chinese called "sitting in a jet plane." She remained expressionless.

Then the speaker enumerated the crimes of this unrepentant American woman—she was a spy, leaking information to other foreigners. She was a reactionary bourgeois authority, poisoning the minds of young students with Western culture and values. She was a counter-revolutionary who opposed the leadership of the Communist Party and dared to ridicule the "Four Greats" of Chairman Mao.

"Listen to this woman's words: What did she say about our revolutionary warriors?" The speaker's voice grew louder. "This belligerent Ameri-

319

can woman dared to call the Red Guards 'hooligans' and 'rascals!' She said they should be thrown into a frying pan and fried!"

The crowd roared.

I could not believe my ears. Grace had no way of knowing what was being said and I doubted she had said these things.

"Furthermore, we have it in her own handwriting, in letters she wrote to a foreign agent in Beijing, that she called the monument we built for our beloved leader a tomb. If it is a tomb, then she wishes our Great Leader Chairman Mao dead!"

The crowd jumped to their feet with raised fists and shouted over and over again, "Protect Chairman Mao with our lives! Smash the counter-revolutionary Grace Liu!"

I was breathless. They had found a crime worse than teaching bourgeois culture. Now I realized there was no hope for her. Speaking out against Chairman Mao was a crime punishable by death. I knew people had been executed after being accused of saying things like that. Whether she had said it or not, I feared this was the end.

While the roaring was at a frenzy, the other two criminals were brought before the crowd. One was a former Party secretary of the university accused of being a traitor, and the other a counter-revolutionary professor. In precisely two hours, as though anger and emotion ran by time clock, the denunciation rally ended.

As if they had not been humiliated enough, the three accused were forced to walk through a sandbox of dirt and manure to reaffirm their status as sub-humans, before being pushed offstage and led away. The speaker's words were still ringing in my ears—"They will be dealt with severely!"—when I tried to get up. But I couldn't move. I was paralyzed. It was like a nightmare, I tried to get up, I tried to reach her. But I couldn't do anything. The distance between me and her—although in reality only a few feet away—was a vast chasm of blackness.

Suddenly a sharp whack on my shoulder stunned me into reality. T. and another Red Guard grabbed me from behind and hissed in my ear, "Grace Liu is an enemy of the people! You will be dealt with the same way if you follow in her footsteps."

My two jailers escorted me back home and told me to continue to write denunciation material about Grace to show that I had drawn the line and was on the side of the people. I just sat and stared at the walls wondering what was going to happen to Grace, to me, to my sisters . . .

I had not seen Nini since Grace was arrested and I worried about what might have happened to her. Nini had already suffered during the height of the fighting between the Red Guard factions. About a year earlier, she had come to the campus when she was eight months pregnant. We were all excited because it had taken Nini seven years to get pregnant and in those years she had had several miscarriages. She had been extremely cautious with this pregnancy. As the birth approached, Grace was looking forward to having a grandchild close by in Tianjin and gave Nini advice to be careful in the last month.

On her way home—she and Enhua still lived in the old mansion where we had moved after F. C. died—as she left the campus, she was hit from behind by someone riding a bicycle. She was knocked down and didn't even see who did it. By the time she got home, she was hemorrhaging.

Enhua rushed her to the hospital, which was only three blocks away. The doctor examined her and told them not to worry. He said that the baby still had a strong heartbeat and that they would perform a Caesarean operation to save the baby. But the hospital, like all other institutions during that time, was also caught up in the battling factions. While preparation for the operation was under way, the loudspeaker in the hospital came alive with shouts:

"Revolutionary comrades, the Reactionary Royalists are protecting the capitalist roaders in the Party. They are unwilling to give up their power. We Revolutionary Rebels must seize the power from them! Come immediately to the office of the head of the hospital! We must break down the door! "

The operating room doctor and nurses stopped their preparation and ran out, leaving Nini on the operating table, not knowing what was happening. Enhua was kept outside waiting, pacing up and down smoking cigarettes as he worried what was happening to her. No one would answer any questions or help them. Nearly three hours later, when they came back to the operating room, they could not then detect any heartbeat from the baby. The Caesarean was performed but the baby was dead.

Nini was released from the hospital and came home. She kept her feelings to herself. Enhua called me to come. She was resting in bed when I got there. As soon as she saw me, she began to cry. With tears rolling down her face, she sobbed softly, "I miss my baby. I miss my baby."

As I waited alone in the bungalow, I did not know that Nini was also being implicated. Immediately after Grace's denunciation, posters went up at the Water Works with slogans that Liu Fu-Chi was a bourgeois reactionary authority, tainted by Western "influences" and Western education. Nini's husband Enhua was a leader of one of the production units at that time and he tried to argue with the Red Guards, but they threatened to go to his house and arrest Nini. Enhua left immediately but by the time he got home, the Red Guards were already there. Nini had been found burning English magazines and newspapers. She was afraid that they would be used against her, but before she could flush the ashes down the toilet, the Red Guards had burst into the house. Her actions made matters worse because they accused her of trying to destroy evidence of spy activities. Enhua tried to stop them. He argued that they could still read the words in the print and see that these were harmless magazines. But they did not listen.

No one came near me for another two days. I was kept completely isolated. Finally on the third day, T. and his assistants returned. T. said that Grace's attitude was still not good, but she had confessed to some of her crimes and that she would be allowed to come home that afternoon to continue writing her confession. T. went on to warn me, "If you do not help her to confess her crimes, both of you will be severely punished. You must not have any connection with your co-conspirators and, if anyone should contact you, you must report them to us immediately."

That afternoon, two women Red Guards, both of whom I recognized from the Foreign Language Department, brought Grace back home. She looked paler and, if possible, even thinner. However, she did not look frightened or even depressed. She told me that she had been kept in the girls' dorm for the three weeks and was interrogated every day by a group led by T.

"The accusations were so ridiculous that I could hardly contain my laughter. They accused me of wishing Chairman Mao dead because I had written to Olga that the statute of Mao the students built was 'sepulchral.' It was made of black and gray stones, and I remarked that black and gray are colors used for monuments or tombs of people. T. said in a pompous tone, 'I know "sepulchral" means tomblike. I looked it up in a dictionary, so don't think you can use sophistry to hoodwink the revolutionary warriors.' He twisted his face to show how much he hated me. But I repeated what I had said in the letter—I told him that Mao had specifically said not to make statues and carry out personal worship and that the Red Guards were going against his wishes to build the statue. They were the ones building a monument to him as if he were dead."

I never dreamed she would argue with T., certainly not by quoting Mao. "How did he respond?" I asked.

"He sneered back at me and said, 'We Red Guards built the statue out of our love for the Great Leader. How can you, a class enemy, understand how we feel? It shows just how much you hate Chairman Mao.' I told him that I understood it quite well. I had been in China before the liberation and I knew how unjust the system was and I supported the revolution wholeheartedly. I don't guess it mattered one bit what I said because he twisted everything I said to mean the opposite."

"He said you confessed. What did you confess to?" I asked.

"I didn't confess to anything. No evidence turned up. He had no case against me for a crime so he kept saying I had a bad attitude," she laughed.

As light as my mother's tone was, the situation was quite serious. As soon as someone is denounced as a class enemy, all rights are suspended. As I expected, the next day people came to our house and asked why were we, the class enemies, living in this nice house while the workers were still living in small rooms. So within a few days we were driven out of our bungalow and into a small room in a house on the other side of campus. The house belonged to a former party leader of the university who had also been denounced and was forced to give up some of his rooms.

The room was about ten feet by ten feet. We crammed into it our small beds, a table and book shelves which we had to stack on top of each other. There was no chair and no place to sit other than the beds. We shared a kitchen and a toilet with others under the staircase. We could not take all our things, but we did take our books. I moved them stack by stack on my bicycle. They had never been confiscated. The book burnings had happened early, before Grace was a target, and had been carried out by the high school Red Guards who overlooked her. The university Red Guards were interested in other issues and so by the time the revolution swept into our home, nobody was interested in confiscating our books.

Instead of being destroyed, Grace's books had been protected. Since Grace had many of the textbooks and research materials important to the English department, some members of the department had approached her early on and offered to put some of her books in a safe place "until the storm blows over." Furthermore, Grace continued to receive boxes of magazines, periodicals, and books from abroad even during the Cultural Revolution. The Tianjin Customs Office knew her well and had always given her special permission for receiving printed materials provided there was no anti-China propaganda in it. They knew these supplies were for the young teachers that Grace was training. William tells of an incident that took place during the first time he was under surveillance by the Red Guards:

> Two weeks after the Beijing Red Guards came, packages arrived from a friend in America who usually sent them to us—full of recent *Saturday Reviews* and contemporary novels. Both of my jailers were former English students. One of them asked to "borrow" the copy of Arthur Hailey's *Hotel* and during the day, while I was supposed to be writing my denunciation materials, he would ask me to explain various English idioms he encountered in the book.

While Grace and William were restricted to one small room, their books and magazines played a significant role in their survival. William's description of their experience under house arrest continues:

We were each given fifteen yuan (less than $3.00 U.S.) a month to live on which just barely kept us alive. I cooked on a small "beehive" coal stove. Fortunately it was summer so we did not need to light the stove for heat. The only time I left the room was to go out to get food. I did not set foot off the campus and I never spoke or looked at anyone for fear of implicating them. Once she was denounced, no students or colleagues dared to contact us. We did not know what was happening to Nini and Ellen or any of our friends. The only faces we saw were the sneering faces of the interrogators. T. came several times a week when he was on campus and then he would disappear for several days. We heard later that T. or members of his group were tracking down anyone in China who was connected to us.

During these times when they were busy tracking down other people, mother and I were left to ourselves. To keep ourselves busy, we would read or do crossword puzzles. It didn't take us long to go through our last shipment of *Saturday Review*s. When we finished the crossword puzzles and cryptograms in these, we made up new ones for each other. Mother would make one for me and I would make one for her. We had a dictionary when we got stuck. This activity filled the long hours and was good vocabulary practice for me, but it produced a jumble of scribbling with suspicious-looking numbers and letters all over them. I joked with Mother, "We better destroy these as soon as we solve them or our jailers might suspect that we are devising some kind of secret code."

Of course, whenever we could, we read. There was one book Mother really wanted to re-read. She told me that this book was so enthralling that once her grandfather McCallie had picked it up and couldn't put it down. The old reverend didn't believe in reading novels, but one day he found this book lying on the table—he picked it up to see what one of his daughters was reading and it began, "It was the best of times, it was the worst of times . . . " He read it all the way through and when he returned it to her, all he said was, "Don't leave books like that lying around." I could easily identify with *A Tale of Two Cities*—the story of those that were swept into the French Revolution. "If you were facing such a situation," Grace asked me, "and you suffered, then did it mean that the revolution was unjustifiable?" Caught in such calamity, she said, one could cry "woe is me" and die or one could try to understand and learn from it. She said for her it was like having a front row seat on history. We talked about how the different characters in the book reacted, particularly Madame Defarge, Dickens's character whose well-justified revenge against the aristocracy went too far and included innocent people. Defarge was always knitting as the accused were executed. We began to give the people we knew names of characters from the book. Grace had often commented to me that whenever T. spoke to her or about her he would demonstrate to others his class hatred of her by twisting his face into a sneer. From that time on we referred to him as "Madame Defarge."

One day, while reading another book, mother burst out laughing and said to me, "Listen to this: 'There's more evidence to come yet, please your Majesty,' said the White Rabbit, jumping up in a great hurry . . . 'it seems to be a letter, written by the prisoner to—to somebody.'

" 'It must have been that,' said the King, 'unless it was written to nobody, which isn't usual, you know.'

". . . 'Are they in the prisoner's handwriting?' asked one of the jury men.

" 'No, they're not,' said the White Rabbit, 'and that's the queerest thing about it.' (The jury all looked puzzled.)

"'He must have imitated someone else's hand,' said the King. (The jury all brightened up again.)

" 'Please your majesty,' said the Knave, 'I didn't write it, and they can't prove I did: there's no name signed at the end.'

" 'If you didn't sign it,' said the King, 'that only makes the matter worse. You must have meant some mischief, or else you'd have signed your name like an honest man.' There was a general clapping of hands at this: it was the first really clever thing the King had said that day. 'That proves his guilt!' said the Queen."

Mother read on and we laughed until our sides ached. I had always thought *Alice in Wonderland* satirized Victorian England and had never thought it would have relevance to China, particularly to the Cultural Revolution.

But as Grace said, "Whenever fanatics rule, logic is turned on its head and language loses its meaning."

"With the 'Red Queen' around, it is a wonder that any heads are still around to be beheaded!" I replied.

We both laughed. Just at that moment I looked out of the window, "Oh, oh," I said. "Here comes Madame Defarge, I wonder which of our crimes will be knitted into his accusations this time."

Autumn came, and life became more difficult. Although the interrogations gradually dwindled and the Red Guards in the university found new targets to tear into, William noticed that the incessant interrogations and the settling in of the cold weather began to take a heavier toll on Grace:

Her cough and asthma became worse and we had nowhere to turn. We did not have enough money for food and medicine both. By then I had started to visit Nini again. She and Enhua had both been arrested, interrogated, and returned home, so I was not worried that my visits would harm them. Since my bicycle had been confiscated by the Red Guards, I went to town by bus. Nini gave me some money from the little that she had to buy medicine or food for Grace.

By the time the wind came howling down from Siberia, Mother's pleurisy worsened. She moaned in pain with each breath she took. I couldn't take her to a hospital as class enemies were not accepted at hospitals. I just sat there in our one small room and listened to her suffering. Grace would assure me, "Nothing will happen, Willy," she said calmly. "Nothing will happen; otherwise we will never be cleared."

Suddenly I heard her gasping. It seemed like her last breath.

"Willy, the pain-killer plaster, do you remember?"

She had used the pain-killing Chinese plasters a few years ago when she sprained her wrist. But I had never thought about using them for pleurisy. I had no other choice. I jumped up and said I would be right back. Fortunately, there was a drug store not far from campus; I came back with a package of these plasters and plastered her back with them. Miraculously they eased the pain and she fell asleep. She slept for a whole day and I think that saved her life. We both knew that she must live through these times. If she died, it would become more difficult to clear all these accusations. She was determined not to lose her front row seat on history no matter how hard she suffered.

Throughout this time, William was cut off from his school friend, Kelin, who years later described his feelings during this time and how he heard about Grace's arrest:

> Imagine what it was like, one day, when I was walking down a street and spotted a huge poster on a wall proclaiming some "great victory of the Red Guards" at Nankai University where a heinous American spy had been rooted out. People gathered around the poster and gasped at the shocking accusations of the class enemy and counter-revolutionary who had wished the Great Leader Chairman Mao to be buried in a tomb.
>
> And then I suddenly recognized the picture on the poster—it was my best friend's mother staring down at me, amidst all those lurid accusations!
>
> William's mother had always treated me like a son. I never thought of her as a foreigner. I came and went to their home like a member of the family. I mourned the death of my father at the same time that William mourned for his father. We had been close friends since our school days. I remember when William first came to our school, it was raining, and he wore a raincoat and rain boots. At that time most of our families were poor—we didn't have rain gear. Everybody laughed at him and called him "Big Nose." I was the only person that didn't do it. Our teacher asked us to sit together. Then we became good friends. We went to watch movies after class and we read many books when other kids were interested in other things.
>
> Before the arrest, I saw William every week. Then Enhua told me not to contact the family. When I saw the poster, I knew how much they must be suffering and I wished I could help. Yet, more than two years went by before I saw William again. And that was only when I ran into him accidentally in the summer of 1970, on the street not far from where Nini

lived. I still feel guilty to this day, guilty that I could not give a helping hand to my best friend during those years. The helplessness and hopelessness was like confronting a deadly disease; you knew it would not do anyone any good to go close to the contaminated, yet you would forever condemn yourself for not going to their aid. No matter how many books are written about the Cultural Revolution, they cannot add up to more than a snapshot of the terrible feelings we had at that time. Even after so many years, we don't want to talk about what happened. It is a deep hurt in everyone's heart.

Grace's students and colleagues were also torn by their helplessness and hopelessness. One who witnessed her public denunciation described how she felt: "We all had to go. It was required. Yet we hurt so terribly to see Grace Liu on stage, so mistreated. I felt the indignity, the fright, the humiliation, the revulsion. There was nothing we could do. Yet I knew these people attacking her were ignorant. They might have been oppressed in their lives and I understood how they felt, but I could not understand how they could hate someone who was in no way connected to their oppression."

BY 1969 THE two factions of Red Guards had taken their conflicts off the campuses and into the factories and the countryside. The nation's production was at a standstill. The nation's leaders called for the workers' organizations to quell the "leftist excesses" and bring order to the campuses. For three years there had been virtually no classes and no graduations as the students waged revolution. Grace watched with relief as the Workers' Propaganda Teams took over the Nankai campus and negotiated with the students to continue the revolution by resuming classes.

Gradually classes resumed, teachers returned to work, and those whose pay had been cut were given full salary. With her salary restored, she and William had enough money for food and medicine. Nini was pregnant again and was able to visit as before. It seemed that the most difficult years were behind but, indeed, the long ordeal was far from over. William recalls that first Nini then he came under investigation in late 1969 and 1970:

Nini was six months pregnant when they came to arrest her. It was just too much for Nini this time. She sat on the floor and cried. She

329

refused to move. Her husband Enhua yelled at the guards and told them that she had already lost one child. If she lost this one too, it would kill her. Then they would be responsible. He didn't let up, he kept yelling and threatened them with the lives of his family. Finally they went away without taking Nini.

In January 1970 her baby was born healthy. We were so glad, but before we could even celebrate things got worse. It started in the coldest part of winter when Mother's health failed. One night I found Grace spitting up blood. I rushed to the office of the workers' teams and was given permission to take her to the hospital and a school car to drive her there. While she was just beginning to recover, I became the target of attacks.

The political climate was as changeable as the weather. There was another nationwide surge to "clear the class ranks and root out 'bad' elements." This time my mother and I reversed roles. I was arrested and Grace was left alone, not knowing what was happening to me. A friend of mine and his girlfriend were caught listening to Western music in their home in the city. The girl panicked under interrogation and "confessed" to belonging to a group that opposed the government. The record player and the records were traced to me. I had loaned them out when we were forced to move from the bungalow. For the accusers the connection was electrifying. It was thought that my role was connected to Grace's case and that investigating me would lead to further evidence against her. I was arrested in April of 1970. They accused me of being a leader of a gang of bourgeois counter-revolutionaries plotting to overthrow the government.

Grace was unable to care for herself alone while William was under arrest. She moved in with Nini and had to travel back and forth daily to the campus for political meetings. Even in her weakened condition, she took that crowded bus, then walked the distance to the university, sometimes through severe wind and rain.

William recalled his arrest:

I was taken away under guard and locked in a barred cell in a dormitory on another campus that was being used for detention. My cellmates included criminals such as a rapist and thieves—the association was supposed to impress upon me the severity of my crimes. I slept in lice-infested straw on the floor, was not allowed to sleep with the lights off, and was interrogated day and night. I was told to write down all the counter-revolutionary activities I had been involved in. When I asked to be allowed to check up on my mother, I was told, "She is not your concern now. Your concern is your own crimes!"

William, 1970.

Even under these conditions, no evidence emerged. Frustrated, my jailers brought in some local high school Red Guards to intimidate me into "confession." One day when I was poking the fire in the little coal stove in the cell, a Red Guard grabbed the poker and slammed it across my face, yelling, "It is about time you confess!" A group of others came in. I was knocked to the ground and kicked around. The guards taunted me, "Look at Big Nose! See if his foreign connections can help him now!"

After two months, when no further evidence of counter-revolutionary activity turned up and Grace's case was no longer of interest to them, I was freed, but only after a thirty page confession on the evils of bourgeois literature and music was completed.

When I returned to Grace, I told her, "My crime is basically that I listen to Beethoven and read Jane Austen."

26

THE THAW

CLASSES RESUMED at Nankai University in 1971. Grace, then seventy, resumed training with the same set of young teachers as before. She had to rewrite the manuals for English language teaching because the texts that had been used before were no longer suitable. William and Grace's assistants first prepared texts for the countryside and then for factories, developing vocabulary and dialogues for activities related to farming and manufacturing.

William remembers that Ellen came to visit for the first time in years:

> Ellen brought with her two daughters. The second one had been born in 1968, at the time of Grace's denunciation. She told us that soon after the arrest, big character posters appeared at her workplace, calling on her to draw the line between herself and her reactionary mother. The worst part was not knowing what was happening to Grace. Because Ellen was pregnant at the time, she stayed low and took as much sick leave as she could. She could not contact Grace in any way, even to inform her of the birth. When she returned to work, Rei-sheng's mother came from the countryside to live with them and take care of the children. Rei-sheng was transferred to her workplace and the five of them lived in one small room in a nearby dorm. Because they worked for the government's scientific institute, the PLA took over their workplace and no Red Guard factions were allowed to fight there. Some cadres went to Tianjin to investigate Grace's case but when they returned they did not speak to Ellen. Political

meetings and infighting took place everyday but Ellen was not the target of attacks.

Two years later, Ellen had a third daughter. Since three children exceeded the central government's goal for limiting population, the third child was considered officially "not to exist." The child was given no rations, and the family was not permitted to move to a larger apartment.

In May 1971, the American Ping Pong team showed up in China. Everyone watched as China's world championship team took on the Americans. The warm reception given to the American team was the first sign that relations between America and China were beginning to thaw. The relationship with the Soviets had become more tense since the Sino-Russian border disputes began in 1969. Public meetings were held on campus to announce the change in foreign relations. The new policy excited the English teachers and students because it meant that English would again become more important.

Premier Zhou Enlai handled most of China's foreign affairs. Like many of the Chinese who sought his help during the Cultural Revolution, Grace wrote a letter to him in 1971. She explained that in order to continue her work on educational reform, she needed survivable living conditions. Grace never knew if her letter had any effect or even if it had reached its destination—her request was sent at the same time as the easing of the Cultural Revolution and the warming of relations with America—

Below left and center, Nini's daughter, Yun, 1973; Grace and Ellen's daugher Yu, 1972.

but still one day she was told that she could have another room in the same building and that William's position as English-language instructor would be restored.

Although the force of the Cultural Revolution was lessening, the political tide continued its ebb and flow. Just before Mao opened China's doors to the American president, an assassination on Mao's life was attempted. The alleged leader of the coup, Lin Biao, China's main military strategist, former head of the PLA and designated successor to Mao, was reported to have died in a plane crash with his wife and son trying to escape to Russia in September 1971.

President Richard Nixon arrived in February 1972, when China was six years into the Cultural Revolution. At the height of his revolutionary fervor, Mao welcomed the leader of capitalist world. From the American side, the ironies were just as great. The man who had built his career on opposing Communism and who had himself been confronting angry student anti-war protesters and an increasingly hostile press after the release of the Pentagon Papers, and who had released his own "enemies list" reminiscent of the McCarthy era, was now being given the red carpet treatment by the leader of the largest Communist revolution in history. Both leaders needed the other as leverage with the Soviet Union.

For the first time in nearly twenty-five years, great numbers of reporters were allowed in China. The Western media was caught unprepared. Their view into China for a whole generation had been no closer than Hong Kong or Tokyo, given to scrutinizing Chinese newspapers for nuances of words or absences of names to indicate a purge. There had been little understanding of the nation's turmoil since the Japanese occupation and almost no contact since 1949—years which were full of twists and turns.

Since television was the preferred medium of politicians in 1972, Nixon paid special attention to setting up satellite capability to transmit images worldwide. The simplistic images associated with television, combined with the fact that the Chinese government did not allow the correspondents contact with ordinary Chinese or free movement inside China, created a superficial and one-dimensional exposure to China. Each reporter interpreted his experience along the lines of his own political persuasions which were received and believed by audiences of similar persuasion. Because the opening with the West came in the middle of the Cultural Revolution, the impression of a country with a "harsh and dour reality" underneath its surface is the image of China that was indelibly printed on the Western mind.

A U.S. LIAISON office was opened in Beijing in 1973. The tie between the two nations became "normalized" for the first time in over twenty years. Grace was seventy-two years old and a generation had passed. It had been twenty years since she had heard any word from her family. The normalization of relations increased her desire to know what had happened to her family. In the fall of 1973, Grace's health was failing. She was barely able to breathe and had to stop teaching. If she was ever to contact her family, William knew it had to be soon. However, the idea was as unthinkable to William as flying to the moon.

"Who will you write to?" he asked her. "You don't know if your brothers are alive or where they live."

She had told him her experience after the war of writing to her brother Tom in Chattanooga only to find that he had moved to another city. That had been after only four years. Imagine how many changes had occurred in twenty years, he reminded her. And this time she did not have the U.S. Marine Corps to deliver the letter personally.

27

GRACE MAKES CONTACT

S ITTING AT his desk one day in late February 1974, Dr. Spencer J. McCallie, Jr., headmaster of the McCallie School, was handed a letter by his secretary.

"Dr. Spence, look at this. What beautiful stamps!" the secretary exclaimed, adding, "It's from China!"

He took the letter. It was addressed simply to "The McCallie School, Chattanooga, Tennessee, U.S.A." The letter was short, handwritten on plain rice paper.

February 12, 1974

To the Management of the McCallie School,

Since I have been completely out of contact with anyone in or concerned with Chattanooga for nearly twenty years, I do not know which elder members of my family are now living. I shall be very grateful if someone will send me some information about the elder living members of my family—both Divine and McCallie—who would remember me. When I last heard from Chattanooga, my uncle Park McCallie was living and a headmaster of McCallie School. But that was twenty years ago! I would particularly like to hear about my brother, Thomas McCallie Divine, who used to live near Kingsport.

We are all well here and I am working with English language teachers at Nankai University.

I will appreciate very much whatever you can do to help me get in touch with my family in Tennessee or wherever else they are.

Very sincerely,

Grace Divine Liu

336

"I am amazed!" Dr. Spence exclaimed. Then he called to his secretary, "Get Tom Divine on the phone. His sister is alive!"

Grace was not certain if her brothers were still alive or where they lived, but she had told William there was one thing of which she was absolutely sure—the McCallie School would still be there. She sent the letter to the school, not knowing its address beyond the city it was in. She hoped that the management of the school would know the whereabouts of her relatives. She had no idea that her cousin Spence McCallie would be the headmaster (Grace's letter arrived the year before he handed the headmaster's office over to his son, Spencer III). Dr. Spence, as he was called at the school, immediately contacted Grace's brother, who was living on a farm outside Kingsport, Tennessee. Tom had retired from Eastman Kodak, where he had been employed since leaving Oak Ridge a few years after the war.

Tom's wife, Mary Hills Divine, later wrote the following account of the day she and her husband received the news of Grace's survival:

Tom and I were going out the door when the phone rang. "I'll answer

it," Tom said and went back in. After a short greeting, he was silent. Then I heard him exclaim, "I can't believe it!"

I went in. A look of utter astonishment covered his face. He was slumped down in a nearby chair as he held the phone to his ear. Then in a voice filled with emotion, he said, "Of course, we thought she was dead."

He paused before he continued, "Please, Spence, give me her address. I want to write her at once "

He motioned to me to hand him a pencil and paper. While writing, he spoke aloud, "Building #10, North Village, Nankai University, Tientsin, People's Republic of China." Then barely audibly he choked, "Thank you, Spence," and hung up.

For what seemed a long time, Tom said nothing to me, but put his face in his hands. Then looking up with tears glistening in his eyes, he said slowly, "That was Spence. He read me a letter from my sister Grace. She's alive in Tientsin. She wrote to the school, asking about the family. She asked especially about me."

In speaking of her, he had always said, "my sister Grace," in a tone that showed his affection for her. "I must write her at once," he said as he stood up. "Grace wants to know about the whole family. It will take me awhile to bring her up to date."

Tom wrote immediately catching his sister up on what had happened to the family, including the last few years of her mother's life. Their mother, Julia McCallie Divine, had lived off and on with her sons, usually with Tom or Sam, moving from one place to the other. She had become increasingly unstable and died in the county nursing home near Chattanooga in 1954. He wrote that her brother John, the oldest of the family, had died after their mother. Sam was still alive and living in Chattanooga. And Edward, well, no one had heard from him in years. He had gone to Alaska to make his fortune and disappeared. Then there were children and grandchildren . . .

Three weeks later Tom and Mary Hills received a letter from William, opening with: "We were so happy and excited to get your long and newsy letter. Mother was going to write immediately but unfortunately she's having a severe bout of bronchial asthma; so I'm writing to give a brief sketch about ourselves, and she'll write as soon as she can get her breath." William quickly outlined the happenings in their lives since the time of Grace's last letter in 1953—F. C.'s death in September 1955, Nini and Ellen's marriages, teaching English at Nankai University, and Grace's four grandchildren: Nini's daughter, age three, and Ellen's girls, ages nine, six, and ten months. He concluded with, "Too bad none of us inherited Mother's voice; but we all have her love of music." He did not describe the price he had paid for that love.

A short time later Grace was able to write her first letter to her brother in over twenty years:

> *March 20, 1974*
>
> *Dear old Tom,*
>
> *Yes, you wrote on my birthday—February 23rd.*
>
> *I am a little better now so I'm going to try to write you at least a short letter myself. How much I appreciate your wonderful letter! But I must read it over and over again many times yet before I can properly digest all the facts. Believe me I truly never intended to let so much time pass by before I wrote and I was in a panic when I realized I did not know who was living and who wasn't or where anyone was.*
>
> *I will write what I can now and as I get better I'll write more and more. Right now you'll have to excuse my handwriting. My hand has become quite shaky since my illness. I had very bad bronchial asthma this year. I had to stop all work in September ('73) and fight for my breath— always worse during the cold, windy changeable winter months.*
>
> *Willy's letter gave you a general survey of our family's doings. I will try to gradually fill up the gaps myself—you will understand I'm sure how F. C.'s death seemed to put an end to my own life and to any desire to go on living. But I was responsible for the children who were still in school I could not allow myself to become bogged down in grief and despair. Only activity—purposeful, necessary activity—could save me. I moved with the children*

McCallie Family Gets Letter From Relative After 20 Years

RELATED TO CHATTANOOGANS — This photograph is of Ellen Liu and two of her daughters. She is the daughter of Grace McCallie Divine Liu who left Chattanooga in 1931 to live in China.

By JOHN WILSON
Staff Writer

"Since I have been completely out of contact with anyone in or concerned with Chattanooga for nearly 20 years, I do not know which other members of my family are now living.

"I shall be very grateful if someone will send me so information about the elder living members of my family — both Divine and McCallie."

So read the letter received recently at McCallie School from a descendant of two prominent Chattanooga families who went to China as a young woman and had not been heard from in 18 years.

"We had about given up hope of ever hearing from her (Grace McCallie Divine Liu) again and were wondering if she were still alive," said Miss Anne McCallie, alumni secretary at McCallie School and a first cousin of Mrs. Liu.

"We last saw Grace when she passed through Chattanooga in the early 1930s on her way to China," said Miss McCallie.

Grace McCallie Divine, who was the daughter of S.W. Divine and Julia McCallie, met her Chinese husband in New York City, where she was studying her dying voice. Her grandfathers were the Rev. Thomas Hooke McCallie and Sam Divine.

WENT TO TIENTSIN

She went to Tientsin, China, with her husband, F.C. Liu, a hydraulic engineer, to make her home about 1931.

The last Chattanoogan to see Mrs. Liu was James W. Laif, a McCallie School alumnus, who was among the First Marines, in 1945.

The family here felt that there would be word from their relative in Red China soon after the visits of President Nixon and Henry Kissinger to the Communist country. But it was only recently that the long-awaited letter came.

The family here has begun a correspondence with Mrs. Liu and learned that her husband died of lung cancer in 1955 and she began teaching English at Nankai University the following year.

She has two girls named Julian and Ellen and a son, Willy, who also teaches at Nankai University. Julian is employed at the Tientsin Water Works, where her father formerly worked, and Ellen is employed in the Academy of Science in Peking.

Julian has a girl, aged three, and Ellen has three girls, aged nine, six and ten months.

Mrs. Liu has three other first cousins in Chattanooga in addition to Miss McCallie. They are Drs. Spencer McCallie, Thomas Hooke McCallie and Dr. David McCallie.

Mrs. Liu's aunt, Margaret Ellen McCallie, for whom she named one of her children, now lives at the St. Barnabas Nursing Home.

Again, Grace's amazing life made news in Chattanooga. The article used a photo Grace sent Tom of Ellen and her daughters.

to a different part of the city where there was nothing to remind me of my old way of life. I let the servants go and we went to live in two rooms in a big house with seventeen other families, most of whom had only one room. I tried to do my own cooking and my own housework to make myself too tired to think. This is a long story I can't go into now. How I failed and what rescued me, how good these people were to me and how good for me to live in the midst of them. For the first time since I'd come to China I did not feel like a strange creature and a foreigner. The common people recognized me as another human being. They were very friendly and kind and treated me as one of themselves.

A year later we four went on a wonderful trip to the eight-hundred-year-old West Liu Village—F. C.'s old home—in Shensi Province. This is another long story that must wait to be told. When we got back to Tientsin I heard that Nankai University wanted an English teacher. I had an old friend here and it was quickly arranged that I should start immediately. I've been here ever since.

I think I've made quite a satisfactory readjustment to life. I've worked very hard and studied harder, because I knew nothing about language and language teaching when I began and had no confidence in my ability. But knowledge gives confidence and I have studied this subject diligently for the last twelve years so I have acquired enough confidence to make the most difficult work exhilarating and enjoyable.

Your family, Tom, simply bewilders me. I can't imagine Mary Hills the grandmother of ten big grandchildren. The last time I saw her she still seemed just a tiny little girl. I have already read your letter many times. but it's still bewildering. I'm not at all surprised at the many things you have done. I've always believed that you could do anything in the world and do it well, better than anybody else. You and F. C. are the only two people in the world that I've had complete faith and confidence in. I'll write about F. C.'s work later. His death was a great loss to the country—

I must stop now. I'm getting breathless. Don't you all have some pictures? Do send us some and write when ever you have time.

My very best love to dear Mary Hills and all the children and grandchildren I haven't yet succeeded in unscrambling—

Take care of yourself, Tom, and listen to Mary Hills' good advice.

Grace

When Tom read this letter he was very distressed. There was so much of his sister's life that he had missed. He had no idea that her husband had died or that she supported herself by teaching. He was most concerned about her health. He remembered how Grace had suffered from asthma as a child. He used to stay up with her and prop her head up in the big chair so that she could get her breath. But he thought she had outgrown that long ago. He did not know what kind of medical attention she was able to get now. With Mary Hills's encouragement, he wrote her back and invited her to come to the U.S. for treatment and then stay for the winter with them in Florida. For fear that she could not make the trip alone, he invited her son to come with her.

Tom's proposal that she come to the U.S. at first seemed preposterous to Grace. She had no intention of going. How could she possibly survive such a trip? But on the other hand, it was unlikely that she would survive another winter in China. Florida sounded like the perfect place—at least for one winter. And if William were ever to know his American relatives, it would have to be with her. She wrote to Tom: *"I was very intrigued by your invitation to Willy and me to visit you. I think a winter in a mild and wind-free climate would put me on my feet again (respiratorally speaking). I would like to really recover before I face another North China winter. I have already written to our department head about the matter. But I have no idea what the outcome will be. Probably many problems will arise. As you say, things are easier said than done. Well, we will see—"*

By May Grace reported that she had received approval from the university: *"I told you in my last letter that I had spoken to the chairman of our department about our making a visit to the U.S. He says the department says O.K. and so does the school. A place or two more still remain to be asked, but it seems quite possible they will all approve the trip. The problems remaining will be to find the means to carry out the project and to gather up enough strength to make the venture. If everything is favorable I hope we can get there before cold weather starts."*

Getting there before the cold weather started meant that she had until October before she would be "knocked down" again by illness. Grace had only begun to think of what had to be done in four months. The procedures for leaving were virtually unknown to her, or to anyone at that time. William had to take on most of the responsibilities, as letters had to be written and forms filled out, first seeking permission from the university and then applying for visas and passports. As permission from the university came, other obstacles arose.

Grace was frightened at the idea of flying. She said she preferred to go by sea as she had come. But it was doubtful that she could survive a long boat trip. Air service had recently been restored to Beijing, and Mary and Bob Ware, who had visited Grace in 1937, wrote her that they would meet her at the San Francisco airport, since Bob had retired from the Navy and was living in Alameda, California. But that wasn't enough to reassure Grace, as she wrote to her brother Tom: *"I don't like flying, at least I don't like the idea of it. I don't know anything about it really. I've never even been near a plane!"*

And then there was the problem of money. With hardly any salary at all for the last few years, she had no way to pay for such a trip. The university agreed to advance her salary in order to pay for the flight from Beijing to San Francisco. That part could be paid for in Chinese currency but then there was the problem of paying for the domestic travel inside the United States.

Grace's American passport had expired in 1951 and there had been no U.S. embassy in China to apply for renewal. Not wanting to be a "stateless person" she had applied to China for citizenship, but it took years to clear. She wrote to Tom in August: *"We've gone through the preliminaries and have applied for passports and visas. I have been a Chinese citizen since 1957 so we both have to have Chinese passports and entrance visas to the U.S.A. We first understood that we'd have to go through the Canadian embassy to get visas but the American Liaison Office said they can do it. I have no idea when it will all be finished . . . "*

To complete the task, William made numerous trips to Beijing to the American Liaison Office. He met with James Lilly, officer at the Liaison Office, who told him that all applicants for visas had to apply in person. William got his visa first and left Grace's passport with the office while he went back to Tianjin to get Grace:

When Grace and I arrived at the Liaison Office for her interview, the Chinese guard at the gate refused to let her enter without her passport. I explained that her passport was inside, but the guard stood firm. She could not enter unless someone from the Liaison Office invited her in. Showing my passport and visa, I was allowed to enter. I found Mr. Lilly and told him that my mother was waiting outside the gate and was not allowed in. He immediately went with me to the gate and invited her to come in. When we sat down in his office, Mr. Lilly asked her a few questions just to verify that she was who she claimed to be and then he told her that he had been authorized to give her a visa. It was a great relief to her."

Applications for passports and visas were well underway by September. The university agreed to cover domestic travel costs as well and reservations were made. Just when it looked actually possible that they might make it, a swift cold wind ripped through northern China. Grace was re-admitted to the hospital. At the same time, William heard bad news from Mary Hills:

September 2, 1974
Dear Aunt Mary Hills,

We are so sorry to hear that Uncle Tom has had a heart attack. We hope he'll be well again by the time this letter reaches you. Seeing that it is I who's writing, you must be able to guess that Mother is ill. She's having quite a bad attack of bronchitis with inflammation of the lungs and a very irregular pulse. We sent her to stay in a hospital nearby. Nini, Ellen, and I take turns to nurse her. Our colleagues have all been very nice and everybody tries to help. They made a lot of delicious things to tempt her to eat more as all the coughing, wheezing, medicine, and injections have ruined her appetite. She's very impatient to get well to continue the preparations for our visit; but of course there's no telling when she'll be well enough to travel. Anyway we still hope to get to the States in October.

But, indeed, the prospects of a cross-continental journey did not seem likely. William was worried whether his mother could survive such a journey, even if she were able to begin it. He knew it would take four hours from Peking to Tokyo and twelve hours from Tokyo to San Francisco, but he had no idea how long it would take from San Francisco to Tennessee.

When Grace came out of the hospital, she convalesced at Nini's house where Grace had lived after F. C. died. When the neighbors heard that she was going to America, they all came to see her and bid farewell. Her former cook Sun Pao-san brought her food and wished her well on her journey. She began to rebuild her strength. Her appetite was returning when she wrote her brother Tom: *"Your letter about the corn and okra made me so hungry. Okra is the one vegetable the Chinese don't have and I used to love it fried."* Uncertain, but hopeful that her weak body would sustain her, Grace wrote her last letter from China on September 22, 1974: *"I can hardly wait to get there and hear all the family history and eat!"*

28

BACK IN THE U.S.A.

M ARY AND Bob Ware met Grace and William at the San Francisco airport on October 25, 1974. Gaunt and tired, wearing a Western-style suit several sizes too big for him, William extended his arm for his mother as she exited the plane. Grace took his arm and walked steadily and with determination. She wore silken black Chinese-style pants and a loose white shirt covering her frame, now only eighty pounds. Mary and Bob greeted them at the gate. Grace refused help until they convinced her to use a wheelchair for the long walkway to the baggage claim. Eyes were on the fragile little lady sitting straight as a queen as the chair was guided through the San Francisco airport. William and Grace retrieved their small bags, filled mostly with gifts and medicines and headed for the Wares' home in Alameda. William remembered gazing out the window as they drove along the freeway:

> I was taking in the colors of San Francisco, the contrast of blue water and yellow sunshine, the brightly colored Victorian buildings and the many shades of stucco houses covering the hillsides.
>
> "Is it like you expected?" Uncle Bob asked me, as we drove along.
>
> "I didn't know what to expect," I replied. "But it doesn't seem strange to me. Everything is the way it ought to be, I suppose, which is a strange feeling."
>
> I tried to imagine what Grace was feeling. She was probably looking

for the familiar, for what she knew as home, and she must have felt assaulted by the unfamiliar—cars, freeways, tall buildings, noise, confusion, signs and names of strange places.

Grace had doubled Rip van Winkle's twenty years, lived through a revolution instead of sleeping through one, and crossed half the globe in a matter of hours. It was no wonder that she would be dazed by the unfamilar and in need of rest. She and William stayed in Alameda for five days before flying to Knoxville, Tennessee, where Tom and Mary Hills met them and took them to their farm in nearby Kingsport. Kingsport lies in the uppermost corner of Tennessee where North Carolina and Virginia also claim a patch of the wooded hills, aflame with the red and yellow leaves of fall. Tom remembered the last time he saw his sister—in 1934, when she stopped in Chattanooga before leaving for China. He recalled now with affection how his resentment of her marriage melted away when Nini, then only a toddler, reached out and hugged him.

There were many hugs again this time and again many old resentments melted away.

In their brief stay on the farm, Grace and William got little rest before Tom and Mary Hills's children and grandchildren came to meet their "long lost" aunt and cousin. Their daughter Elinor Divine Benedict, who at age fifteen had written Nini after World War II, was now married and had three grown children. Old memories came flooding back. The last time Grace had seen Elinor she was a toddler, just a year older than Nini, when Grace came to Chattanooga before leaving for China. The two little cousins had fought as soon as they met over a little

William and Grace arrive in Chattanooga, November 1974.

handmade hickory chair. Mary Hills had given the chair to Nini to take with her to China, but as Grace said, "We should have left it with Elinor, because I forgot it when I changed boats at Kobe and left it on the *Empress of Asia*. Goodness knows what child finally got it."

A welcoming luncheon had been planned in Chattanooga as they drove down from Kingsport on their way to Florida. Grace wore black Chinese pants and black slippers with a white silk

Grace and William visit her brothers, Sam (seated) and Tom. Below, Grace on the beach, Naples, Fla., January 1975.

overblouse, the only "formal" attire she brought. Her short, grayish white hair was cut off bluntly. She wore no make-up. Her face was thin. She entered the lunch room at the Holiday Inn holding William's arm, seeming small and frail, not like a returning heroine who had accomplished great feats on distant shores.

Nearly forty people gathered that day in November in Chattanooga. How hard it was for Grace to figure out who was who! She was excited but bewildered to meet so many family members. The older relatives that she had known in her youth had passed, and the ones younger than her, whom she had known only as children, had

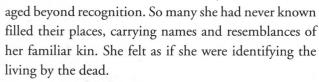

aged beyond recognition. So many she had never known filled their places, carrying names and resemblances of her familiar kin. She felt as if she were identifying the living by the dead.

The stay in Chattanooga was kept short. They had to drive on to Florida that day. When the doctors finally examined her in Naples, they said that her lungs were as black and damaged as someone who had smoked for forty years. She was hospitalized, her lungs were irrigated, and she convalesced in her brother's Florida home. As soon

346

she recovered, she wrote back to her colleagues at Nankai:

Hospital, Naples, Florida
December 28, 1974
Dear Professor Li,

I thought I would have gotten around to writing to you long before now, but I ran into difficulties soon after reaching the U.S.A. I stood the flight from Peking to San Francisco very well indeed, in fact, better than Wei-han did. He lost his appetite, but I never missed a meal. The San Francisco cold, damp weather and talking too much started me coughing again, but I still felt quite energetic when we arrived in Tennessee. Then relatives came from all over to see me in Kingsport and so much excitement and talking began to wear me out.

We started south by car after about a week. We had a terrific day in Chattanooga and I had a wonderful time seeing people I hadn't seen for forty years and more—nearly all of them had thought I must surely be dead! But thank goodness I was very lively and energetic for that one day at least, then we had two more days travel south by car. Everybody here goes either by plane or by car. The railroads have almost disappeared in the U.S. I find car travel exceedingly tiring and by the time we reached Naples in the south of Florida I was completely exhausted. I had a fever for two or three weeks and then stayed in the hospital for thirteen days. I am much better now but the doctor insists on my taking an antibiotic that makes me feel quite awful or at least it did at first. I'm getting more used to it now. I walk on the beach every morning and have had a boat trip out on the bay.

I hope Nini has shown you our letters and pictures. What we write to her is really for everybody. Please give the department and school leaders my warmest and most grateful greetings for the New Year. And remember us to all our colleagues.

All the best to you and wife.

As ever,

Grace

Picking tomatoes in Naples, 1975.

NAPLES WAS A dramatic change to this hardy survivor of hardship and scarcity. The bright and abundant flowers, long avenues of palm trees, fountains, golf courses, and beautifully painted rows of dwellings exuded the wealth of the retirees from all over the United States who settled there for half the year. Grace stayed here almost a year, regaining her strength, walking on the beach in the warm sunshine, fishing from the dock, and eating Tom's homegrown tomatoes.

In the fall of 1975, with Uncle Tom's assistance, William entered the College Scholar Program at University of Tennessee in Knoxville with a focus on linguistics. When Grace was strong enough, she joined him in Knoxville.

With Tom and Mary Hills in Naples, Spring 1975.

They had been in the country for two years before she was able to return to Chattanooga. Grace longed to see the places that had been important to her as a child. She asked her cousin's daughter, Eleanor McCallie (Cooper, the co-author of this book), who was home from San Francisco, to take her on a "search for the past." Grace wrote the following account of her return home as part of her memoirs.

SEARCH FOR THE PAST

Visiting Chattanooga after forty years in China was like seeing a well-known picture that had become warped almost beyond recognition. Both familiar and strange. The children I'd known were now middle-aged, the young were old, and the old were gone. The natural surroundings were all the same but familiar landmarks had disappeared, strange ones had taken their places. The house in the city where I'd once lived and even the street it was on couldn't be found. My grandfather's old home on Missionary Ridge had vanished and new school buildings gave it an entirely new look. It seemed as if a giant hand had jostled things around all out of place.

One morning my niece Eleanor was helping me find a few reminders of my

348

early life and was driving me around on a "search for my past." It was very frustrating. The disappearance of electric street cars which my father had worked so hard to install bewildered me. I couldn't find my way around by car. Street names had changed and some were one-way, and highways surrounded the city and there were so many cars parked everywhere. I felt I was in a maze as I told Eleanor, "Turn here, no, here, no . . ."

Suddenly I leaned forward staring, "Stop, Eleanor, I know this place."

A low stone wall and three stone steps going up into what appeared to be a park with big trees—I knew I'd been here, but when and why I didn't remember.

Eleanor stopped the car and then I saw a scattering of headstones and monuments—"Oh, it's the old citizens' cemetery I used to play in when I wasn't more than six years old." There I found the tombstone of my great-grandfather, Captain Tom McCallie, and I knew I had returned to my beginnings.

Our journey ended in the cemetery that day, but the next morning Eleanor and I set out to find my old childhood home near Fort Oglethorpe a few miles over the Tennessee-Georgia line. My father had built the house at the end of the streetcar line to demonstrate that one could live even across the state line and still commute to work on the streetcar. He eventually had to sell most of the land around the house.

Located on a hill overlooking the Chickamauga battlefield, my childhood home held such a store of early memories for me that I was choked with excitement and nostalgic emotion at the thought of seeing it again after more than fifty years. As we approached Fort Oglethorpe, I thought—we are nearly there! The familiar sight of the army post houses facing each other politely across the parade ground was exactly as I remembered. The only difference was that these formerly elegant officers' houses looked run down and disorderly. The paint was peeling, trash was left outside, and they were all different colors instead of the once uniform white. Eleanor

Top, at her cousin Spencer McCallie's in Chattanooga, 1976. Bottom, William with Civil War cannon atop Lookout Mountain, 1976.

told me that after the Second World War, the government closed the fort and sold the old army post houses to veterans for private use. Over the years, they had been sold many times and subdivided into duplexes and apartments.

"It's just beyond this rise," I said as we topped the hill and started down the steeper side.

"Here we are," I said. But where were we? When I looked to the right with my heart beating fast in anticipation and already seeing in my mind what I thought I was going to see, I was shocked to find myself looking at a totally unfamiliar scene. I expected fifty years to make changes within reason, but when I looked for the hill with the white house, beautiful trees, and big barn—I saw nothing—no house, no trees, no barn, no hill.

I was completely mystified. A house and farm can burn or be torn down, trees can be cut down, but how can a hill disappear? That was outside my experience so far.

"It's all gone," I gasped, "even the hill."

I was puzzled and disappointed. I felt I must find out something about the mystery of the hill that wasn't there.

"We'll go to Dewberrytown. They will surely know there what happened."

"Dewberrytown! What is that?" asked Eleanor.

"It was—and I'm sure it's still there—a settlement or small town at the back of our land."

Years ago my father went nearly bankrupt and sold a large section of his property to a colored woman named Emma Dewberry—we said "colored" then—and she sold off parcels to other people who wanted to build and own their own homes. During my childhood there was beginning to grow up a small black community that was called Dewberrytown. I remember going with Mama to the Dewberrytown Baptist church—I enjoyed the enthusiastic "amens" and "hallelujahs" and I loved the singing. I remember going there with Papa and the whole family to marvelous barbecues and baseball games.

My thoughts flew back to another scene on the hill—one of my very earliest remembrances. It was a December morning in 1904 when I was not quite four years old. My little two-year-old brother and I had been waked very early by "Aunt" Carrie—she was not really my aunt but rather nurse, cook, and general assistant to my mother. She was then a handsome, stout, middle-aged woman who was just the color, my Mother always said, of "coffee with cream."

Now, she gave me a little shake and said severely, "You, Miss Toe, you stop that fidgeting, stand still and let me button you up. Now then, you be real good while I git Thomas dressed."

She told us that a new little brother had come in the night and she was going to take us to see him.

The scene in Mama's bedroom that morning has become blurred in my mind—only the huge bed with the carved headboard towering, it seemed, nearly to the ceiling, is clear. Lying in the bed Mama is holding my new little brother. And in the room is another presence—I can only remember a dark wizened face. Not long before that December morning my mother had become a staunch believer in "faith healing" and from thenceforth had given up all aid from doctors and medicines; therefore she would have no doctor and no anesthetic during the birth of her last child, but was determined to rely only on prayer and faith in God to see her though the ordeal. With Aunt Carrie's advice, she sent for the midwife who delivered the Dewberrytown babies.

As our search for the past continued, we found the road to Dewberrytown and stopped in front of a big store. A few cars were parked in front and a group of men were talking beside one. Two of them came forward as Eleanor and I got out of our car. I asked them if they had ever known anyone living there named "Tom Little."

"Tom Little was my Grandfather," said one. "I'm Ed Little."

I said I'd known his grandfather when I was a little girl. I told him who I was and how long I'd been away.

"I'm looking for my old home," I said. "But I can't find it. Everything has disappeared.

"Yes, Ma'am," he said. "It's all gone.

We talked a little about his grandfather and some of the old people I'd known so long ago and then he said, "If you and Miss El'na will follow me, I'll guide you 'round."

He took us all through Dewberrytown, very much bigger than the place I'd known. I noticed that the main street was called "Divine Street." It was a dirt road that extended through the community. Out to the side of one of the small frame houses that made up the community, someone was tending a garden that reminded me of the garden Papa used to keep, full of okra, potatoes, pole beans, and tomatoes.

Leaving the cars behind, we walked in the direction of where the hill should have been. "There," said Ed Little, pointing, "right there, ma'am, is where your old home was."

"But the hill," I exclaimed. "The house was on a hill with beautiful big trees."

"Sure, the hill was right there. But they dozed it."

"Dozed it? What do you mean?" I'd never heard of such a thing.

"The bulldozers, ma'am, they dozed that hill right down."

"But . . . why?" I asked.

"They said they wuz gonna build a highway through here. They tore up the streetcar line, but that highway ain't come yet."

I stared at that low, flat piece of ground with nothing on it but wild grass and weeds and thought how unwise it was to go hunting up one's past. Time can do shocking things. The world of my youth was gone.

As we drove back into town, pictures of my childhood on that vanished hill filled my mind. I saw the white house under the big oaks and the huge mulberry tree at the left of the house. A gravel walk bordered with white narcissus curved up the left slope from the small gate at the foot of the hill to the porch steps. To the right was the big gate the cows came through on the road to the barn as the sun started down.

In the peace and quiet of the late afternoon, a little girl about eleven years old was sitting in the swing on the porch, swinging back and forth. I knew what she was feeling. I knew what she was going to do—she was going to sing. I could feel the songs filling her throat.

I remembered so clearly that long ago me. How I loved to sing from the top of that hill—to launch my voice out into the air and listen as it floated and soared through the trees and over the road and the car line and the buildings below, and in the pauses came echoing back to me from the top of the opposite hill.

I hear Mama calling from the doorway: "Sister, sing my favorite song." Then I hear the wistful words go sailing over the trees in my eleven-year-old voice:

"Believe me if all those endearing young charms, / were to change by tomorrow / and fleet in my arms, / like fairy gifts fading away, / thou woulds't still be ador'd / as the moment thou art, / let thy loveliness fade as it will, / and around the dear ruin, / each wish of my heart / would entwine itself verdantly still."

Quite an audience has gathered. There was no one in sight when I began singing. But when I look down the hill, I see some of the farmhands and a few soldiers from the fort coming in twos and threes to sit on the cross ties stacked beside the rail line. Inspired by the audience, I sing contentedly through my store of old songs until it grows darker and darker all around.

29

THE FAMILY, EAST AND WEST

B Y 1974, THE year that Grace left, it was already clear that changes in China's leadership were ahead, but no one predicted that the changes would take place so dramatically in one year. Premier Zhou Enlai died January 8, 1976. Before the year was over, the nation would be reeling from political as well as natural shocks. Zhu De, the builder of the Communist army, died in July at age ninety. Then on September 9, 1976, the Great Helmsman himself, Mao Zedong, died. While thousands passed before his casket at the Great Hall of the People, the nation watched in stunned silence as his wife Jiang Qing and three others, known as the "Gang of Four," were rounded up on October 6, and the Cultural Revolution came to its dramatic end.

Earlier that year, during the Qingming Festival in April when the Chinese traditionally paid homage to deceased ancestors, a spontaneous demonstration occurred in Tiananmen Square. Personal expressions of mourning, wreaths, poems, messages, and gifts, intended as memorials for Zhou Enlai, were laid in the square. Many people, like Grace, although she never knew if he actually intervened on her behalf, felt a great loss at his death. Vice Premier Deng Xiaoping had praised him at his funeral as one who "maintained broad and close ties with the masses and showed boundless warm-heartedness toward all." He was noted for living in a plain, hard-working way. On the morning of April 5, 1976, when the people discovered that their tokens of grief had been removed during the night, a spontaneous protest erupted into violence, resulting in the arrest of thousands.

Deng Xiaoping was held accountable for the outbursts and he was removed from office on April 7, the beginning of a campaign against him as a "capitalist roader."

There was a belief in Chinese culture that profound natural disasters accompany the end of dynasties or other major political transitions. Although this old way of thinking had been "thrown out" during the Cultural Revolution, few in China missed the significance of the event that occurred on July 28, 1976. All of northern China was ripped by the worst earthquake in China's known history. Its epicenter was only sixty miles from Tianjin. When Grace heard the news, she wrote immediately. It was a very long two weeks before she received the following letter from Nini (the notes in brackets were inserted by Grace later). Nini was living with her husband Enhua and daughter Yun in the same two rooms of the old mansion where they had moved after F. C. died.

August 9, 1976

Dear old Ma and Willy,

I got your letter of July 28th, asking me about the earthquake. What a day! I shall never forget. That night [July 27th] I couldn't go to sleep because of asthma: so I stayed up and wrote you two a letter till 1:30 a.m. [28th]. It was raining cats and dogs. Then I read a while, and about 3:45 a.m. I turned out the lights and suddenly saw a flash of reddish purple light which I thought was lighting. Then came a roar and the whole house began jumping up and down for about four times. By this time I had turned the lights on again. When the jumping stopped for a few seconds, I heard what I thought was hail and rock raining. I later found out it was house tops falling down. Then we started to rock back and forth.

Enhua was sleeping in the outer room and for the first time we had the door between the rooms shut as I did not want to disturb him with my reading with the lights on. By this time Yun had wakened. I was still sitting in the bed holding her and telling her not to be afraid and we'd go down to the basement when the rocking stopped. But the rocking seemed to get worse, and then I heard the wood frames of the windows began to crack as I said to Yun I think we better start going and I got off the bed and tried to open the door. It wouldn't open. I pulled and pulled; then I put Yun down on the floor and pulled with all my might. It was stuck tight. Then the lights went out. I heard Enhua shouting on the other side of the door and I called out that I can't open the door, and I heard him kicking the door and he finally kicked it open. When we went into the corridor, all the neighbors were in the corridor.

You can't imagine what happened to Enhua. I didn't know whether to laugh or to cry. He had been very busy and had had little sleep for quite a few days, and he had the door shut so he was sleeping very soundly like the dead. Well, he said afterwards, he didn't know what hit him: he jumped up, opened the outside door and dashed out. When he got to the stairs he said he didn't know what happened: he seemed to have stepped in a hole and went rolling down the stairs, hurting his arm. Then he jumped up and dashed outside, the most dangerous thing he could do. So many people were killed by going out too soon and were crushed by the falling debris. Outside, the cold rain on his bare skin woke him up, and he thought what am I doing here and he dashed up into the house and ran up the stairs meeting Mrs. Mopsy [her neighbor who mops all the time] dashing down the stairs. She said later on she wondered where he had been. Instead of going into the basement through the hallway, Mrs. Mopsy also dashed into the yard and then couldn't find the gate. That was just when the lights went out and the loose wire of toppled poles came coiling around her. People in the basement yelled at her to come into the house, and if she had been a few seconds later she would have been electrocuted.

We then went into the basement in Fat Mrs. Liu's room; she is the chairman of our courtyard. There were about six or seven children and I don't know how many grownups. Although frightened herself, Mrs. Liu started her stove and made what seemed to be pots and pots of mong bean soup. She kept saying: "Oh, I am so scared! Drink! Let the children drink the soup." I will never forget the kindness people showed each other. People were giving each other their last bit of things.

Our part of Tientsin was one of the hardest hit. When dawn came and everyone came out into the streets, I could barely believe my eyes. Enhua left soon afterwards for his office, returning around three in the afternoon. Then we went to Shengli Road [the widest street in Tientsin]. The rain was still pouring down. There we met one of his colleagues who welcomed us into this little tent in which were his family of five or six. I don't know if I would have had the kindness in me to have welcomed other families in so graciously. While we stayed there Enhua went to the Water Works. He came back around five, saying the Water Works said for us to go there, but we must hurry as there was going to be another quake around six. So to the Water Works we went and have been staying there off and on ever since. The forecast was really accurate, and the big aftershock came at 6:50. Food and water are easy to get, and the shops began to sell necessities the very next day. The Water Works workmen worked like mad fixing up the pipes in three days time, while the earth was still quaking. It is not over yet. Yesterday there were six medium-size ones.

I've been home the past three to four days living in front of the house; it's not so safe here so we are going back to the Water Works. We might be able to live in the outer room in the winter if no more big quakes. We are thinking of sending Yun to her grandmother's for the next six months. Her kindergarten's building is badly damaged.

Willy, all your friends are safe: Kelin and his family are well. Old Dr. Ko and his family, Professor Li and his wife all came through with flying colors; remember how the little quake last year nearly killed Mrs. Li! People with heart trouble seemed to come through all right. I have seen Mousy often [A friend of Willy's, nicknamed after the way he knocks on the door]. His uncle and aunt were killed and their three children are living with the Mousies now.

Things are so well-organized. These old ladies of the neighborhood are really something! They work night and day patrolling with the militia, seeing that everybody has food and care, looking after the old people—those who have no family. They know exactly in what condition everyone in their neighborhood is in. Many people have gone off leaving all their things in the care of the neighborhood committees. To the bad elements who want to plunder and steal, the punishment is both fast and drastic; so I haven't seen a single incident around here. You can leave things on the street for days and no one will touch it.

I must stop now as I'm very busy. I still have asthma and I have chest pain. I will have to ask for some medicine to be sent. I'll tell you in my next letter.

Love, Nini

Throughout the fall of 1976 William continued working on a degree in linguistics at the University of Tennessee where Grace joined him when her health improved. He and his mother lived on the eleventh floor of the married students' dorm. Grace loved the view she had from such a height. But, despite the open vista, Grace was often alone while William was in class. She stayed in touch with her friends in China and often sent boxes of supplies or books.

While William was at the University of Tennessee, a sea change began in U.S.-China relations. Students and professors began the

In June 1976, William and Grace attended the Golden Wedding Anniversary of Tom and Mary Hills in Memphis.

357

first wave of exchanges that were to gain momentum in the next few years. One of Grace's nephews was among the very first student groups to enter China in November 1976. Grace and William gave him Ellen's address and later heard from Ellen that, one day at work, her boss informed her that an American cousin had come to China and had asked to meet her. Ellen's letter, written in Chinese as her English was not as good as Nini's, was very lively as she told how she and Rei-sheng and her three girls went to the hotel in Beijing to meet an American cousin for the first time. This simple, yet remarkable, family reunion marked the beginning of many family reunions and academic exchanges that William was soon to become a part of.

In February 1977, William was invited to Philadelphia to meet with Dr. Labov, head of the Department of Linguistics at the University of Pennsylvania. Grace later wrote to Tom and Mary Hills:

Willy spent two weeks at U Penn, interacting with those who taught English as a second language, those who taught Chinese to English-speaking students, and those engaged in sociolinguistic research—as he was doing at UT. He was asked to give a talk at the Linguistics Club about the social significance of English teaching in China which he illustrated with examples of our work at Nankai University.

Grace enclosed a copy of the report Dr. Labov had made to the dean of University of Tennessee after the visit:

It is evident to everyone here that Mr. Liu is a talented teacher and scholar, with a great gift for observation and expression. His unique bicultural and bilingual experience makes him the ideal person to convey the experience of modern China to members of our society, and we believe that he will eventually take back to the People's Republic of China a greatly enriched view of our own goals and our approaches to scholarly and scientific work.

Dr. Labov soon put William in touch with Dr. Wang, the editor of the *Journal of Chinese Linguistics*, a publication of the University of California at Berkeley. By the time William graduated in the spring of 1977, with Phi Beta Kappa honors, he had been offered a job at Berkeley's Center for Asian Studies.

AFTER SPENDING the summer with Tom and Mary Hills in Naples, Florida, Grace and William were headed for California. Grace later described the ten-day cross-country car trip as "never to be forgotten." When they arrived, Tom and Mary Hills gave William the green 1968 Oldsmobile they had traveled in and flew back to Naples.

The college campus that spawned the sixties' "Free Speech Movement" was in the city that was tagged by some commentators as the only community in America that would have elected Mao mayor in the 1970s. William thought his mother would appreciate Berkeley's natural beauty and moderate coastal climate as well as the many "interesting people." Berkeley's liberal atmosphere expressed itself in the 1970s in various self-absorbed forms of personal growth and exaggerated styles that Grace captured in her first letter from there:

September 6, 1977

Dear Mary Hills and Tom,

Anybody who wants Berkeley can have it. Certainly Berkeley is a beautiful place and I like the climate—but, oh, the inhabitants! I couldn't feel any stranger than if I'd stumbled into a foreign country.

And so many cars! Willy got the car insurance on Friday and since has driven a couple of short distances without mishap. But it takes him about fifteen to twenty minutes to get parked in the pocket handkerchief space allotted to him behind the house and when he once gets in, he doesn't want to come out soon.

Sunday afternoon we went for a walk on the campus. It's uphill and rather strenuous walking, but so beautiful, such lovely grass and flowers, and marvelous huge trees, some so tall I almost fell backward trying to see the top.

We walked slowly along watching the cute little squirrels, waving their tails and scampering thru the leaves and up the trees, some of them fighting with the big bluejays. Suddenly off to the side some distance under the trees I saw a statue. It seemed to be a life-sized figure of the Virgin in the usual draperies and head covering.

"What an odd place to put a statue," I said to Willy. "There must be some devout Catholics here."

We walked slowly along the road. I kept my eyes on the figure and thought I saw a movement but so slight I couldn't be at all sure I actually saw it. I watched and again I felt that the thing moved.

I said "Willy, did that thing move?"

Yes," he said, "it did."

We kept on going. Suddenly, it floated off whatever it was on and moved toward the road. I grabbed Willy's arm and stifled a scream. It passed within ten feet of us and we saw it was a young woman draped in what looked like rags with a trance-like look on her face. She paid us no mind and went off down the road. Evidently it was a devotee of a yogi or meditation guru. I certainly had a real scare. I'm sure Willy was startled too, though he won't acknowledge it.

We went on a piece and came upon a sinister-looking bearded creature going in and out among the trees looking anxiously around as if he were looking for something. And a skinny old woman was walking back and forth watching him. Interspersed among the trees in the gloomy shade were what appeared to be loving couples. We didn't investigate.

And the first thing we saw coming toward us was a bare, semi-bare anyway, couple with their arms around each other stopping every now and then for a kiss or two—

On the coldest day we've had yet we came across another bare couple (more skin bare than covered) sitting on the steps of a Fried Chicken shop in a breeze that made me shiver even with a sweater under my corduroy jacket.

Yesterday was Labor Day and the Co-op [grocery store cooperative] was closed and a huge Flea Market held outside. All the sidewalk and street in front and the big vacant space at the side were running over with people selling things—everything on earth—and even more buyers and sightseers. Willy and I went around ten o'clock. When we got to the end of our street and looked down the hill at the Co-op two blocks away, Willy exclaimed, "Just look at the fleas!" The whole area was just black with "seller fleas" and "buyer fleas." It was terribly interesting and lots of fun. We bought two books, a coat for three dollars and some pots and pans. The sun gets ferocious after midmorning and I was wilted without even half a breath by the time I'd climbed back up the hill to our street.

Our apartment is convenient, but I am pursued at times by claustrophobia. The view from our window is the pink wall of the building just across the driveway.

We have finally got our phone in and now we won't feel so isolated. Willy tried to call you this morning . . .

William wrote to his aunt and uncle in October that settling into Berkeley and doing a new job at the same time was quite "nerve-wracking" and took some getting used to:

We went to a Chinese restaurant in Chinatown not far from the place where some Chinese gang killed seven people and wounded eleven a few weeks ago. We were all a bit nervous, keeping an eye on the entrance to see if any suspicious persons should come in and being prepared to duck down under the table!

Nini, center, and Ellen, left, with their daughters. The photo was made when Nini and Yun came to Beijing after the earthquake of 1976.

William and Grace also heard from Nini and Ellen. The aftershocks of the earthquake and the arrest of those associated with the Gang of Four had taken a great toll on Tianjin. They wrote to Tom and Mary Hills:

We got a letter from Nini saying that the situation in Tianjin has gotten worse even though it is getting better in the rest of the country. The mayor of Tianjin was in the clique of the Gang of Four and struggling for power and many things weren't getting done. For example, they didn't have any electricity for a long time after the earthquake. Nini put up a big fight for it. She wrote to the newspaper. At that time the newspapers were beginning to investigate what was happening and to print letters and stories. The leadership was beginning to be afraid of the newspapers. She wrote letters to the electric company and to the building company as well. Nini said that everyone has worked very hard to recover from the earthquake. They have moved back to the house now though the construction is still not complete and everything is covered in dust. She also said that there was heavy rain all summer and that our Nankai campus was flooded. Our poor university!

It was not until February, in time for Chinese New Year's, Nini wrote, that the electricity was finally restored. By then her building had been repaired and the residents had begun to clean the floors and repaint. Grace and William heard from Ellen that Beijing had not been hit as hard by the earthquake and they were beginning to teach English on television. Her daughters wanted them to bring a television back.

William's transition to life in Berkeley was aided by his work of analyzing Chinese dialects, writing articles on linguistics, and later taking courses in psycholinguistics. He was soon given an assistant to do field research in San Francisco, and he was often sent to Los Angeles to do research at UCLA. Some of his articles were published in the *Journal of Chinese Linguistics*. But what became more demanding of his time was the increasing number of academic exchanges between China and the U.S.: *"So many people are going to China now. The professor I work with led the American Linguistics delegation to Beijing and he met Ellen there . . . A higher education group from Beijing came here and I was assigned to take them around. At the luncheon at the Center for Chinese Studies I was astonished when one of the delegation said to me, 'I met your mother in New York. Your father had gone back to China. I saw your sister too—just a baby.'"* The person mentioned was head of Wuhan University and a professor of microbiology. Another member of the delegation was a top man at Ellen's place of work and was head of Qinghua University, F. C.'s alma mater.

Grace described her son as *"well and busy."* She reported that William was getting much more experienced in driving, but the problem of parking *"almost takes the pleasure out of it."* According to Grace: *"Willy's driving improves all the time. He feels quite confident going to and from San Francisco even at night in a driving rain. But I must admit the car is quite banged up now."*

Grace never quite adjusted to Berkeley's coastal climate, which she described as *"neither hot nor cold. But within the limits of about twenty degrees, the climate here is the most changeable I ever saw. It constantly rings the changes on warm, chilly, rainy, sunny, cloudy, windy, foggy, and 'whatever,' as Willy has begun to say."*

Her adjustment to Berkeley continued to show the humor with which she took the eccentric styles of the 1970s:

While I'm getting more used to it, that doesn't mean I like the place. It seems it makes no difference at all what one wears anywhere. On the street or shopping in the Co-op, I see nightgowns, evening dresses, Indian ponchos, and a great deal of messy drapery, bare legs, hairy chests, and in footwear anything from bare feet to knee-high boots. Once Willy said to me, "That woman is staring at you."

"Well," I said, "It must be because I don't look outlandish!" If I wore a Roman toga, I'm sure nobody would even glance at me.

I'm sending some fashion tips as Mary Hills is liable to get behind the times down there in old-fashioned Naples. She should get herself a "double bubble" blouson and wear it over striped wool stockings with platform shoes. Or if she prefers layers—a black turtleneck under a large bulky cable-knit sweater under a long man's overcoat with baggy pants and knee-high boots. Mao jackets, red stars and even the fur hats, like the ones the PLA wore, are the latest rage in Berkeley!

For her own clothing Grace chose "some peasant homespun" from the Chinese Cultural Center. A friend of hers made for her a Chinese-style jacket in blue and white batik that *"covers a multitude of sins,"* meaning it was loose and did not show her skin-and-bones figure (though she was beginning to fill out as she gradually gained weight with her renewed health).

The news of Grace's survival and return had spread by this time to many of her former acquaintances. She was an active correspondent again and had many visitors. Grace wrote in January 1978:

Grace in Berkeley, wearing her "peasant homespun jacket," 1978.

We had dinner last week with Dr. Starr and John Service. John Service was born in China and was on the American Embassy staff during the war and was a political advisor to General Stillwell in Chungking and Burma. He is now in the Center for Chinese Studies here at U.C. Berkeley. Dr. Starr is going on a China tour next week as advisor to the governor's group.

Bill and Sylvia Powell, who had published many of Grace's articles in the *China Monthly Review*, now lived in San Francisco and invited her to dinner for a visit with Bill Hinton, the author of *Fan Shen*, when he was in town to speak. Grace had not seen the Powells or Hinton in more than twenty-five years.

Julianne, her niece who had lived in New York with her when Grace met F. C. in 1928, invited her to Thanksgiving in 1977 at her son's house in San Carlos, California. Julianne now lived in Taos, New Mexico, and brought a wild turkey, shot by her husband, which they ate with the traditional candied yams and pumpkin pie. We don't know what Julianne thought of Grace's appearance after nearly fifty years, but Grace said of her: *"Julianne said she has lost about twenty pounds and looks better, but of course she could lose twenty or thirty more with considerable benefit."*

Eleanor, Grace's niece, lived near the Powells' antique store on Church Sreet and accompanied William and Grace on many of these visits. During her Bay Area years, Eleanor dressed the part of the alternative culture—layers of drab-colored cottons or ethnic-patterned vests over long pants—and made do with little money, living alone or with other people in various of San Francisco's many large Victorian houses with brightly painted fronts. She had just turned thirty and worked at a non-profit organization that was part of the food movement catering to the demand for low-cost, high-quality, unprocessed, unpackaged, and non-chemicalized foods, that grew from a concern for health, the environment, and social change. Eleanor recalled, "It was the politically correct eating habit of the time. It mattered whether you ate bananas, which were 'cash crops' grown on land that could be used to feed indigenous people, used vast amounts of pesticides and distributed by multinational corporations and sold by corporate food chains—or, say, strawberries, which could be grown by local farmers or farmer-worker cooperatives, distributed by a small fresh-produce group, and sold in neighborhood, cooperative stores."

This community-based network grew into an alternative food system, including warehouses, trucking, bakeries, vegetable stands, and cooperative food stores, which were run by the consumers who volunteered two or three hours a week. The alternative food movement extended to other cities across the country, but in the Bay Area alone there were about a thousand people involved as workers in this food movement and several thousand more as consumers. Among that subset of the mainstream was a smaller subset who saw themselves as "an island of socialism in a sea of capitalism." The movement spawned a number of "worker-controlled, anti-profit" units which called themselves collectives or cooperatives or communes.

Eleanor worked in a small educational collective which provided research and educational materials for the food movement. She had sent one of their publications called *Land and the Human Community* to Grace when she still lived in Knoxville. She wanted to learn all she could about China from Grace and she wanted Grace to see beyond the headlines and magazine covers in America. Grace had written back:

I was delighted to get your letter and the publication Land and the Human Community. I have read every word except the Spanish, of course, and I think it's simply wonderful. I am intensely interested in such things. Of course, you know you're fighting against terrific odds, because what you're doing is really revolutionary. You're striking at a vital point of the 'system.' I read an article in the TV Guide and a column on the editorial page of the Knoxville paper simply foaming at the mouth over the 'Dangers of the New Food Politics' which they say is 'a massive assault on reason, science, technology, industry, mass production, economic growth and freedom,' and implies that it's worked up by the 'New Socialists and Maoists.' When I got your material I understood what was making the 'powers that be' so nervous. The big agribusiness corporations are very powerful—money is power. But still more powerful are politically educated and enlightened people who work together—eventually by the millions. That is invincible. The [big corporations think] people must be kept ignorant, uninformed, misinformed, individualized, each one looking out for himself. Such people are easy to control and manipulate.

With the help of Eleanor and Paul Kivel (one of Eleanor's coworkers who had become a friend of Grace and William), they moved to a bigger place across campus. Grace liked it better because she could see a hill from the front window instead of the pink wall of the house next door. From her new location Grace could get out and walk everyday. It was a beautiful neighborhood with gorgeous flowers and wonderful flowering trees.

During this time in Berkeley, Grace began in earnest to write her life story. She filled her long days, while William worked or traveled, writing her memoir, which she mentioned in letters to Mary Hills: *"I can say I am quite busy now. I am trying to get down as much of my story as possible, but it's not fast work . . . Willy and Eleanor are really keeping my nose to the grindstone writing my 'history.' Every time Eleanor sees me, she says, 'How much more have you written?' and I feel very guilty whenever I can't report some progress. And Willy's the same. I feel very reprehensible if I sit down with a Agatha Christie or some such escapist literature."*

Pieces from her past began to resurface. Sometimes a friend or family member, hearing that she was writing her memoir, would give her an old letter or remind her of an old story. Grace was startled to receive from Sylvia Powell a copy of a letter that she could not even remember having written—it was her letter to Harriet Eddy just after F. C.'s death. Harriet had sent it to Sylvia, who had saved it. (Harriet died sev-

eral years before Grace returned to the U.S.)

Paul offered to help Grace type her memoirs. She always liked to talk to Paul because, as she wrote, he asked *"very intelligent questions and was a most interested and willing listener. This I've found rather rare as so many people can't bear to hear anything that goes against their preconceived notions."* Meanwhile, an editor at the Regional Oral History Office of the Bancroft Library contacted Grace about sitting for a series of interviews, but this would have entailed more talk for longer periods of time than Grace felt she could do.

Mary Ware's daughter, also named Mary Ware, transcribed tapes of Eleanor's earlier interviews with Grace and William, and came to see Grace in Berkeley. Soon after Mary left, Willy flew to L.A. to do some linguistics research at UCLA. While William was gone, Eleanor spent the night with Grace. The following conversation, based on Eleanor's journal entry of that time, recorded Grace's insight into her own life in China as well as Eleanor's life in Berkeley.

Grace with Mary Ware Jr. (left) and Eleanor McCallie (the co-author). Below, Ellen and Nini with cousins Helen McCallie, and Eleanor McCallie, Berkeley, August 1979.

BREAKFAST WITH GRACE

Grace was getting the strawberries out of the refrigerator when I came in for breakfast. I told her I'd have to be going right after we ate. I filled the kettle with water and put it on the stove.

"Americans always have to go somewhere—they don't just drop by and visit, do they?" she said, putting the strawberries on the table.

I was sorry . . . I knew it was Saturday morning but it was the best time to go to the office. It was quiet and I could catch up on the work I hadn't been able to do all week because of meetings. I would come again later . . . maybe after Willy got back . . .

"He's gone so much now,"

she said. "Even when he's in town, he's not here. I never really know what he is doing unless I ask questions. It makes me feel like I'm nosy. It wasn't like that in China. We were always busy together . . . we knew everything about each other, about our work, about our friends . . . I knew his friends well. They were part of the family. It's not that way here. His friends are scattered all over the place—San Carlos, San Raphael, Oakland, San Francisco—you are the closest and you live thirty minutes away by car. I don't know what the difference is, maybe it's the distance—it's so far across the bay and I never know what may happen to him in that car."

I was wiping the counter while she talked. She watched me.

"I putter around doing these things all day. I feel useless—like I have to be doing something." She paused. "In China—even when I was in the hospital—I was a part of things—I felt I was making a contribution . . . In China *lau tai tai* is a term of respect. But here being called 'old lady' is an insult."

"But, Grace," I interrupted. "You know that Willy's work, the recognition he is getting—reflects on you—it is your achievement too!"

Grace had pulled out some instant Quaker Oats and I offered to cook while she talked. We sat down to eat. She added some honey to her oatmeal with wheat germ, then sliced a few strawberries on top. I commented on how well she ate. Had she always eaten this well? I asked.

"As well as I could," she replied.

Grace and I had had many talks before about her life in China. She had recently shown me the letter to Harriet. Now that we were alone, it seemed a good time to talk about it.

"Grace, I can understand why you stayed in China with your husband when the Communists came. But when he died, didn't you think about coming home?"

"People tried to talk me into returning then, but I wouldn't think of it. I thought it would be too hard on the children. China was their home. People thought I couldn't stand it, that I couldn't survive."

"Why did they think that?"

"Because I wasn't used to it. I had always had a rather high standard of living, three servants and so forth. How could I survive if I lived like an ordinary Chinese? The place we moved—it was very primitive and . . . well, it was harsh for me, very harsh—no kitchen, no bathroom, no running water, no heating—but I welcomed harshness then. My husband's death knocked the foundations of the world right out from under me. So I didn't care how hard it was or what I had to do. I wanted to get away from everything that was familiar, to live in an entirely different place and with entirely different people. The people were just ordinary workers and they were so kind to me. And I was a foreigner—I thought they would resent me. When our neighbor saw that I didn't know how to handle the stove, she said she would help—and she did everything for me. It was *the* nicest place I have ever lived in my life. Nini still lives there and you can see from her letter after the earthquake what an organized society can be—not the 'regimented' society that scares the 'free' West, but one with a sense of security and connection with people. It creates a confident spirit. You can see that spirit in Nini's letter."

"But, Grace," I had to pursue this further. "You felt claustrophobic in your apartment in Berkeley, how could you endure such a small place there?"

"It is different in China. You can't use the same standard that you do here. In China there isn't such a great store in privacy. Our doors were always open and children of other families would just come in, running in and out, asking for this or that—a drink of water, something to eat, what time is it? If we had guests and we didn't have places to sit, we'd just go next door and get a chair and haul it over. They did the same. I think you can see that for me then—when you have had a terrible loss, when you are stricken—that kind of atmosphere is marvelous. It's healing, you know. It saved my life."

I poured some tea for both of us. She liked hers with a little milk. I got some out of the refrigerator, then she continued. "People are closer in China. There is nothing you can't talk about. Everyone listens to each other. That way each person lives several lives. That way your own problems don't seem so overwhelming. I didn't know about any of this until after my husband died. Everything was new then. It gives you a kind of security—to be connected. Here I feel alone and isolated."

Then quite unexpectedly she turned to me, "Living so long in China has made me realize the value of being old. Eleanor, there is nothing for you here in Berkeley. Why do you stay? You should go back home."

I didn't want to answer that, at least not then. I would talk about it later, when I had more time. But then, I had to go.

IN JUNE 1978, Grace made a twelve-day trip to Los Angeles to visit her cousin Katie, the daughter of "Ahnt" Lillian and Uncle Ed McCallie. Katie was also present at her grandparents' Golden Wedding Anniversary in 1912 and is in the family photo from that day. Grace's reunion with Katie was significant. Katie was the family archivist-genealogist and Grace wrote about the visit, *You can imagine all the family stories that came out!"*

Cousin Katie gave Grace two things that were crucial to her memoir-writing. The first was a copy of Grandfather's journals that Katie had typed from his handwritten manuscript. Grace had heard these stories as a child, but had never seen his journals. The second item was the letter from F. C. to Uncle Tom in 1931. Katie said she had seen it in Chattanooga when she was going through family records and when she read it, fell instantly in love with F. C. It astonished Grace to discover this letter in 1978 in Laguna Beach, California, and it touched her deeply—it was the only surviving letter from her husband, and such a good one, she felt.

On her return to Berkeley, Grace received a long letter from Nini, who was in the hospital and had nearly died. The terrible dust from the earthquake and the stress and strain of recovery and repairs had reactivated Nini's asthma and made it almost impossible for her to breathe. But, she said, things in Tianjin had improved since they had a new mayor who got things done quickly and efficiently. The building was repaired and looked better than it ever had. Nini's little girl was staying with Ellen and her cousins while Nini was hospitalized.

30

GRACE'S LAST DAYS

I N August 1978, almost a year after they came to California, William noticed a change in Grace. She didn't talk as much and her neck was misshapened. Then he discovered a large, hard growth covering most of the left side of her neck. Grace said she had been aware of it for a couple months, but no one else had noticed.

She hadn't said anything because she didn't know how her medical care would be paid for. She had no employer, no insurance, and no social security. She would just wait, she thought, until she returned to China. But William had signed a contract for another year and she needed care immediately. Eleanor offered to take her to the social security office and sign her up for Medi-Cal, coverage provided by the state of California. Eleanor recorded the expedition in her journal:

> Our trip to the Social Security Office on University Avenue in Berkeley was unforgettable. Grace wore her batik blue and white Chinese jacket and loose pants and carried a small purse over her shoulder. Just like Grace's descriptions of her grandmother, her back was straight and her posture as graceful as someone much younger. We were met by a receptionist who didn't seem to realize the import of the moment. Here is how it went:
>
> I walk up to the receptionist's window and say, I'd like to apply for Medi-Cal.
>
> The receptionist, a pale-looking young man, stares at me with no expression: Do you want Social Security Insurance or Gold Stamps?
>
> I don't know. Maybe we should apply for both.

He looks at me blankly.

I respond, It's for her—and I move aside so he can see Grace behind me.

He looks at her and says, How old are you?

Seventy-seven, she answers.

Now writing on a pad. What's your last name?

Liu.

Are you married or single?

She pauses. A widow, she says, as if she had outwitted him.

Is your income less than $370 a month?

She responds, I don't have any. I live with my son.

That's unusual, he says. Savings? Bonds?

No. None.

That's all right, he says. Please have a seat. Someone will call you.

Grace and I sit in the back of the room behind several elderly couples. We look at each other and try to suppress our giggles.

After a short wait, we are called. The eligibility worker is a young woman with a warm face and a voice so soft that Grace can't hear her. When Grace asks her to speak a little louder, the woman begins to enunciate slowly and loudly as if she is talking to a foreigner. Her questions run in the same line as the receptionist's. Then she asks, When you turned sixty-five did you apply for Social Security?

No.

Why not?

I wasn't here.

Where were you?

In China.

Puzzled look.

Were you born in the U.S.?

Yes.

Are you an American citizen?

No.

Puzzled look again. I thought if you are born in the U.S. that you are a U.S. citizen.

371

I intervene and say, Grace, show her your passport.

Grace pulls out an old, spotted, yellowed passport issued in 1946. There is a picture of Grace at forty-five with her three children, Nini, Ellen and Willy. Willy was five years old. Grace looks strong and confident.

The woman exclaims over the passport. Says the picture looks just like her. She leaves to check some records. While she is gone, I ask Grace who would pay for it if she needed care in China. She replies that she would go to the doctor and the university, where she worked, would pay for it.

That's what happened when I had cancer before.

You had cancer before!

Breast cancer. Haven't you noticed, my chest is just one big scar.

You've had a mastectomy! When was that?

Oh, about fifteen or sixteen years ago.

The doctors in China knew how to do that?

Of course they did. They were trained at the best schools all over the world and in China as well. But it wasn't just the doctors that cured me.

Who did?

It was the patients. The other women in the cancer ward . . . hearing their stories, seeing their courage . . . healing is not just the body . . .

The eligibility worker interrupts. She says she is checking to see if Grace is eligible for Medicare (federal). For Medicare you have to be a resident in the U.S. for five years, but that doesn't apply to citizens, she says.

After looking at some more records, she concludes: It looks like you have to be here for five years and you've only been here for three. Before we can do anything we have to give you a Social Security number, so I have to ask a few more questions.

The worker says that to get Grace approved for Medicare, she needs three documents verifying Grace's birth. Grace has only the passport. The eligibility worker takes the passport and leaves again. Grace and I discuss how she can get three documents. Her birth certificate of 1901 was burned in a county courthouse fire in Tennessee. Her uncle had to swear for her when she got her first passport. Her marriage license was mistakenly burned with other papers when the Japanese took over the concession in 1941. Willy's birth certificate disappeared during the Cultural Revolution. Is the passport the only surviving document proving her existence? Maybe there's a record of Nini's birth in New York . . . Then I remember Grandfather's journals that Cousin Katie gave her—there is a family genealogy in it. Grace's birth will be on that.

She returns and hands Grace the passport: "Sorry I was gone so long. The passport will count as one document. You will need two more. Since you live with your son and do not contribute to the expenses, you will get $240 a month and Medi-Cal. If you apply for SSI you have to apply for Medicare also. You have to pay for Medicare, but if you're eligible for SSI, the State of California will pay for it. When we get your Social Security number, we can proceed."

The woman hands her several booklets on Social Security Insurance and asks, Can you come back? We can't do anything until there is a Social Security number. I don't know how long it will take, but I will record it from today so you can receive Social Security back due. Possibly it will take three or four weeks for a Social Security number, two to three weeks after that for Medi-Cal and longer for Medicare. Do you have emergency medical needs?

We look blankly at her.

If you have emergency medical needs, then you will have to apply to the county. I will get you a referral form.

The next day, I took Grandfather's genealogy records to the eligibility worker and was told they would not count because the wrong year was written by Grace's name. Afterwards I wrote to the state of New York for Nini's birth records and to G.P.S. for Grace's high school records as proof of her birth.

The next day Grace was too tired to go with me to the county office in Oakland for emergency medical assistance. The county office was much more chaotic than the Social Security office. It was full of people of all ages and colors sitting in a crowded room and waiting in long lines. Names were called out from the front desk. I had to go back four times before I got everything they wanted. The emergency coverage, I was told, would take two to three weeks . . .

I handled it all quite well, except for one burst of tears after the third time to the county office and I still didn't have the right documents. But all in all I made Grace and Willy feel taken care of and Grace said that I was a bulwark of strength. Then I went home—and fell apart.

I spent the next weekend with Grace, while Willy was out of town. We had a quiet, restoring weekend together. We took a walk on Saturday and went up on top of Strawberry Canyon overlooking the whole expanse of the bay. The lights of the cars crossing the bridge shone in the evening glow of the setting sun like shimmering jewels. The fog was coming in, drifting through the Golden Gate Bridge, spilling over the hills of San Francisco and feathering its way over Alcatraz Island in the middle of the bay to Berkeley. The low-setting sun broke through under the fog and reflected across the water in brilliant streaks.

William and Eleanor immediately sought medical advice for Grace. Several diagnoses concurred that it was a tumor from the tonsil. She ended up under the care of the Tumor Board at U.C. Medical Hospital, a group of experts and interns who met weekly and reviewed cases. No one seemed quite sure what to do. The large size of the tumor was threatening to close off her throat but surgery did not look advisable, as Grace said, "it would cut off my head." The experts recommended radiation accompanied by a drug still under research for increasing the susceptibility of the cells to the radiation. Because this drug was experimental, William was asked to sign papers giving permission.

Treatment began before Labor Day. William and Eleanor alternated taking Grace every day for two weeks to U.C. Hospital in San Francisco. She did amazingly well and was a curiosity to the hospital staff, many of whom were interested in her experiences in China, especially in the fact that she had been cured of breast cancer fifteen years before using a combination of surgery, radiation, and chemotherapy. One doctor asked her about acupuncture, and Grace replied, "Well, it seems to work all right, but I'm scared to death of needles."

Grace's tumor was very responsive. It virtually disappeared in ten days. She was considered a "case to be discussed at the next convention." During that time she was doing quite well and maintaining her routine as usual with more rest.

William wrote to Nini and Ellen about Grace's condition and suggested they ask for leave of absence to visit their mother in Berkeley for a few months. Grace needed their help as he was still working. He told them that Grace had Medi-Cal, and "without it we would most probably be on our way back to China by now." In anticipation of Ellen and Nini's arrival, William and Eleanor began looking for a bigger place and Eleanor moved in to help with Grace's care.

Grace wrote to Tom and Mary Hills on September 9, 1978:

We have moved again and Eleanor has moved in with us. I feel I have three daughters now. We were so lucky to get this sunny spacious house just one block from the University. It is a quiet, lovely neighborhood, where Willy can walk to work, and Eleanor can get transportation to San Francisco very easily. It is completely furnished, even silverware, has a fireplace in the living room and a fig tree by the deck in the back yard.

The treatments are indeed causing improvement. I didn't expect anything so fast, but there is quite a definite progress for the better. Of course you know radiation therapy is very drastic—weakening and exhausting—and loss of appetite. I'm also taking a special drug that makes the tumor cells less resistant to radiation and together they seem to be working very fast. The drug is likely to cause nausea—but I'm given something to combat nausea and haven't so far suffered any. But it is not a very pleasant treatment and sometimes I feel very miserable.

I've had eight radiation treatments plus, I think, five drug doses and the doctors and all the radiation staff are astonished and pleased with my progress. I don't know if Willy told you that I'm being treated at the University of San Francisco Medical Center. People out here think it's the last word in medicine. The buildings and equipment are very very impressive. So far I've dealt with about three doctors, and I was "inspected" by about a dozen young doctors one morning! One of my doctors is the No. 1 big chief of the oncology department—that means radiation therapy.

Then by the last day of treatment, she became very weak and could scarcely swallow because her saliva glands were so burned from the radiation. Food intake became difficult and other complications began to emerge. Without eating for three weeks, her weight went down to seventy-five pounds. She was admitted to the hospital for intravenous feeding.

When she returned home, her voice was low but her spirits were high. A home-care nurse visited every day to attend her personal needs and another came once a week for technical work. Because Grace had difficulty swallowing, William got her a blender and Eleanor got her a juicer to make food that was easier for her to eat. William continued to be busy at work hosting exchange scholars from China, once being called on to make a speech in both languages. In China, Ellen and Nini applied for passports and visas.

Although the tumor had disappeared, Grace's condition deteriorated. She wrote to Tom and Mary Hills on December 5, 1978:

I'm sorry I can't write a long newsy letter. My hands are still numb and annoyingly useless—it's difficult to write, to button anything, to pick up things, or to manipulate safety pins. It's terribly frustrating. They (the doctors) say it will go away but it's not leaving fast. I am fairly active—I've been out to dinner and walk around the neighborhood. Ellen and Nini think they are leaving around the 19th—but not positive. I'm quite "writ out" now. My hand hurts. Hope we can manage to get to see you before too long. I remember so much about our time spent together.

Much love, Grace

Christmas 1978 was quiet; the weather was clear and warm in Berkeley. Eleanor had gone home to Chattanooga. Grace and William were still waiting for Nini and Ellen who were having delays getting their visas. The advisor for foreign scholars at Berkeley called the State Department and the State Department cabled the Liaison Office in Beijing to speed up the process.

In late 1978, Deng Xiaoping, twice purged and twice rehabilitated, became China's leader. Already, even before Nixon's visit in 1972, the economic and technological pressures to move China towards a more open policy were being felt. Deng supported and immediately set in place a national movement toward "The Four Modernizations" of industry, science, technology, and national defense.

The United States and China resumed full diplomatic relations on January 1, 1979. The U.S. increased its liaison office to a full embassy staff, and requests for visas moved faster. Nini and Ellen's requests were among the first to be approved.

When Deng Xiaoping arrived in Washington, D.C., on January 28, 1979, he was greeted by ecstatic crowds and press. He toured Houston, Atlanta, and Seattle, forming new corporate and political ties. Nini and Ellen had arrived in the United States in time to hear President Carter's speech welcoming Deng, at the same time that the so-called Maoist Red Guards in Berkeley demonstrated against him with sticks and banners protesting his "capitalist roader" policies. Soon after their arrival, Nini wrote to her uncle and aunt (whom she called "Juma," an affectionate term for aunt in Chinese).

January 29, 1979
Dear Uncle Tom and Juma,

We have now been six days in America. Our first impressions of America are very funny: Ellen thinks there's so few people in the streets, and I was surprised that there's no dust. The weather is much warmer here than Beijing or Tianjin. So we never quite know whether we're hot or cold.

What with the preparation of coming, the long air trip, and finally getting here and seeing our mother, we really felt all beat out and I am only now beginning to feel normal again. Mother will begin some more treatment tomorrow. She still can't swallow well and still is on liquids. I'm afraid she's gotten rather tired from too much excitement. But she's better than what we had expected. If she gets a little stronger we hope to take her back to China.

It was just when I got out of the hospital in August that Ellen came to see me with Willy's letter. We thought we better immediately get ready to go. I was real worried about Grace. I didn't know what kind of cancer she had. First we had trouble over the fare. If we didn't have the money was there any use in applying? Then Nankai University agreed to release funds from Grace and Willy's back pay. I applied to the Water Works and they were very cooperative. The municipal government was very helpful getting all the forms done and getting the money ready. The passports came fairly quickly. Then we sent them to get American visas. There it got hung up because there was just one person working on the American visas and that person only worked some days each week. It was very hard to wait knowing that Grace was so sick.

Please excuse us for this short note. We will write again soon after we get over the sleepiness.

Much love from both of us,
Nini and Ellen

Ellen making
jiaozi,
Berkeley,
1979.
Below, Ellen's
family sent this
picture while
she was with
Grace in the
States.

Their arrival coinciding with Chinese New Year's made it an occasion to celebrate. William and Eleanor invited all their and Grace's friends. William took his sister Ellen to market in Chinatown and bought Chinese food for the party. Ellen and Nini made jiaozi, Chinese dumplings, for everybody. They rolled out the dough into thin pancakes and then cut it into small round pillows and stuffed each pocket with pork, green onions, garlic, and fresh seasonings. A big pan of boiling water was kept going as plate after plate of the delicious steaming dumplings were brought forward for the happy guests.

At first after Nini and Ellen's arrival, William was triply busy, but soon, after they got used to everything, his sisters took over the care of their mother, the cooking, cleaning, and nursing, and trying to make Grace eat more. Grace's weight was now only sixty-eight pounds.

As William said in a letter to his Uncle Tom and Aunt Mary Hills, "You can positively see through her. Though chemotherapy has deterred the tumor, other complications are quite distressing; her heart and breathing are not very good. But as all her children are here, she is still in good spirits." He reported that Grace was unable to take her third session of chemotherapy because the doctors found her too thin. She spent her days resting and trying to swallow, and even that was a lot of work, as Grace said, "Something every minute." Her hands and feet were also numb making it hard for her to write, but her blood count and spirits were quite fine and "there were no bumps anywhere."

Given Grace's condition, it may seem strange to describe this as a happy time. Yet there was much joy and often laughter as the three children interacted with their mother. Ellen was studying English and they all enjoyed watching *Gone With The Wind* and *The Sound of Music* and several Shakespeare plays on television. Tours of Chinese cultural events were coming now to the States, often with stops in Berkeley. A professor at the university invited them to dinner. Again, Eleanor's journal captured the feel of the last days:

378

HER CHILDREN AT HER SIDE

One day two letters had arrived from China, both with good news. Ellen heard from Rei-sheng that they had been assigned a larger apartment—two rooms with a kitchen and bath. They had been waiting a long time for this and Ellen was excited. The second letter was from Nankai University informing Grace that she had been promoted to Associate Professor.

Grace was pleased with the news and feeling pretty good. She was sitting up in her makeshift bed in the dining room, leaning against a pile of pillows. She always wanted to be in the middle of things, not relegated to a back bedroom.

The rest of us were all sitting around the dining room table—Nini reading some papers that Grace had given her, Ellen writing a letter to Rei-sheng and the girls, and Willy catching up on some notes for work. He had just returned from giving a talk at a conference in Wisconsin preparing universities in the States to receive a great number of students from China.

I said to Willy, "I wonder how many 'F. C.s' will be coming to the States again." He replied, looking over at his mother, "I wonder how many 'Graces' there will be, too?"

"What does it mean that Grace has been promoted when she is not there?" I asked.

"It means that she has been 'rehabilitated.' Those who were accused during the Cultural Revolution are being cleared. It is just the beginning." said Willy.

Suddenly Nini chortled and said to me, "Eleanor, have you ever seen this letter my father wrote to Grace's uncle, Dr. McCallie?"

"You mean the one where he says, 'I am heathen'? Yes, Grace showed it to me. Imagine writing that to a Southern Presbyterian minister!"

Willy asked, "Didn't he also say, 'Bad people are bad and good ones are good'?"

"I haven't seen it," said Ellen, coming back from the kitchen with a glass of water for Grace.

"Both of you only remember the parts you want to remember. I'll read it to you. It is so F. C.," and Nini proceeded to read F. C.'s letter written in 1931.

When she finished reading the letter, Grace spoke from her bed in a very raspy voice, barely above a whisper, "Things haven't changed." Then she coughed and grabbed the glass of water.

"Our parents always had a great respect for each other. I never saw them fight," said Nini to me.

"They were always a 'united front' to us," Willy said with a chuckle.

"Sometimes when Ma would say something very set and determined, Dad would just mumble to himself," Ellen said and they all laughed.

"Even though your backgrounds were very different, you and F. C. saw eye to eye on most everything. This is very unusual," I remarked to Grace.

She rasped back at me, "What's so unusual about that?"

I turned to Nini, "How would F. C. have fared if he had lived longer?"

Nini looked at Grace and said, "He would have done as Grace did, given his all to his work. He might have suffered as she did, but still, I can't imagine him preferring to live in a society ruled by people like Homer Lu."

"Changing human beings is the most difficult. That will take generations," Ellen added. "But just like F. C. says in his letter, 'Good things and bad things happen.' You can't change that."

"But, so, Eleanor, do you judge other people by your own yardstick?" Willy joined in.

"And do you grumble against heaven for what happened to you?" Nini added, using F. C.'s words.

WITHIN a few days, Grace was completely unable to eat. The doctor advised that the only way to get food into her would be to put a tube directly into her stomach. Grace went back to the hospital for the operation to insert the feeding tube, but she was too weak. She went into a coma and was rushed to the emergency room. She stayed on a respirator for a couple of days until she was able to breathe again on her own. She was moved back and forth on the respirator for awhile. One night when she was on her own, her breathing stopped. A nurse found her and began pressing on her chest to resuscitate her breathing. Her bones were so weak, her ribs broke and one punctured her lung. They called the family to come immediately.

Her three children stood by her. Tubes had been inserted through her mouth, breathing for her, tubes in her veins, wires in her chest. The yellow lights beeping up and down irregularly on the machines behind her, recorded her fragile life until the last heartbeat and the last beep of the machine stopped.

Ellen stood at her head, gently stroking her forehead.

Nini at the foot of the bed, her eyes red, tears held back, touched her feet to see how warm.

William was on one side, holding her hand, no doubt wondering what she would do without him.

April 26, 1979

Dear Uncle and Juma,

It was very difficult for me to talk to you about the sad event over the phone this morning. I know how much both of you felt for her and her children. My mother has always meant so much to me, not only as a mother, but, as I had to take care of her, she was also like my child, therefore I feel a double loss. Although she did not live an easy life, it was a courageous and interesting one. She not only worked hard for her family, she also worked hard in doing her job, and she was loved and respected by many.

My mother always maintained a deep love for her family and especially for her favorite brother, and she had transmitted this feeling to her children by telling them many, many stories, and that is why I felt so much at home with all of you.

Dear Uncle Tom and Juma, I am only writing a short note, at this sad time, to say how we, her children, appreciate the love and kindness you both showed her and her children. I am enclosing one of the last pictures my mother took, and one picture of your nephew and two nieces. We love you. Take care.

Love,

Willy

31

GRACE GOES HOME

THE bone-chilling wind was again gusting over the Great Wall, sweeping down from Siberia across the mountain barriers on its way to the sea. No invaders from the North now swept along with the piercing gale. No red-cheeked army marched triumphantly down Tianjin's empty streets. The image of a lone foreign woman standing at the street by her courtyard gate watching them was now only a phantom memory. Nor was the same frail foreigner leaning into the wind as she struggled along her way to teach a class on the Nankai University campus.

On the university grounds, no large character posters announced the event. Only a small note in black and white on the official bulletin board read:

> Associate Professor Grace Divine Liu of the Foreign Language Department of Nankai University, died of illness on the 25th of April, 1979. Professor Grace Liu's memorial will be held on January 12th, 1980, 4:00 p.m. at the Tianjin Hall of Revolutionary Martyrs.

Rolling past the frozen lotus ponds and gray dusty grounds, the van with its silent passengers stopped in front of a large gray building whose red Chinese lettering proclaimed, "Hall of Revolutionary Martyrs." At the steps, the arriving passengers were handed white paper carnations. Nini escorted her American cousin Elinor Divine Benedict and Elinor's grown daughter Kathleen up the steps. William and Ellen followed them into a large cold room. A massive table with knobby, carved legs, a reminder of an ancient era, stood in the center of the room. Standing, they were

382

served tea. The cups warmed their cold hands. Other people joined them, greeting each other quietly yet kindly. Professor Li, solemn and sad, and the group of young teachers that Grace had trained, not so young any more, spoke to William. He then introduced them to his American cousins. Nini and Enhua greeted their colleagues from the Tianjin Water Works. A childhood friend of Ellen's spoke to her. And long-time friends of the family gathered.

At the proper time, an official ushered the crowd, numbering about eighty, into a large hall where dusty paper flowers on the walls commemorated the dead. On one wall hung a picture of Grace Liu, framed by a wreath of paper flowers and draped in black crepe. The crowd stood before her picture. Her soft gray eyes and her thin face looked down upon them. Crashing sounds of Chinese funeral music came over a loudspeaker. An officiating person read from a list of names of people and organizations that had sent wreaths and condolences.

Then a man rose and stood before the solemn audience. The music stopped. It was Lou Ping, Vice President of Nankai University, the same man who had stood on the stage with Grace Liu twelve years before, who had been forced with her to trudge through dirt and manure, who had been shamed and condemned before jeering crowds. Now in this silence he gazed at those gathered, both young and old. The room was heavy with the moment. He read from a prepared statement. The assembled crowd listened to the carefully chosen words:

> With profound grief, we deeply mourn Associate Professor Grace Divine Liu of our Foreign Languages Department.
>
> Grace Divine Liu was an American with Chinese nationality who was born in February 1901 in Chattanooga, Tennessee, the United States. She was educated in Chattanooga, where she also taught high school, and in New York City, where she studied music. In 1930, she married Mr. Liu Fu-chi who was a graduate of Qinghua University and an overseas student studying in the United States, and then came to China to live. Mr. Liu Fu-chi became the chief engineer at the Tianjin Water Works in 1937 and died of lung cancer in 1955. Grace Liu came to teach in the Foreign Languages Department as an English teacher and received her Chinese citizenship the same year. She became a Lecturer in 1960 and was promoted to Associate Professor in 1979. In the fall of 1974 she went to visit

William with Professor Li Jiye (Chairman of the Nankai University foreign language department who hired Grace in 1957), January 1980. The photo was taken by Grace's niece Elinor Divine Benedict, who attended the Memorial in Tianjin.

her family and to seek medical treatment in the United States. She died on April 25th, 1979, in a hospital in San Francisco. She was seventy-eight.

Grace Liu loved China. She resolutely supported her husband for devoting his knowledge and talents to the service of the motherland and its people. She broke through many barriers to come to China and willingly united her life with the fate of the Chinese nation. When the American Consulate suggested sending her whole family back to the United States in 1948, she decided to remain in China to welcome the liberation of the whole nation. From the fifties to the sixties, she endured tremendous setbacks in her life: first her husband died and she had difficulty in living, and then she herself suffered a serious illness, but she still consistently did her job well. She wrote many times to both Premier Zhou En-lai and Deputy Premier Chen Yi to report the problems in the teaching of foreign languages and to give her opinions on the subject. At the same time, she was active in writing and published many articles about New China in the progressive publications in the United States, introducing our country's great achievements under socialism. During the Cultural Revolution, she suffered serious political persecution, but she did not give up. She kept in touch with Anna Louise Strong and other international friends, and persisted in the fight for truth.

William stood silently between his two sisters. He could feel Nini's heaviness beside him. Tears welled in her swollen eyes. Her puffy hands were clasped in front of her. She had not been well in the six months since her return. He knew that she felt a great loss, not only of her mother but of a vital part of herself. The world she had known was gone. With William in the United States and Ellen in Beijing, there was no one who could share the other side of her. And what of her daughter . . . and Ellen's children, William wondered. They had never really known their grandmother. The world in which Grace lived had changed so much from their own that his sisters could never really explain to their own children this remarkable woman and what she had lived through.

Lou Ping continued listing Grace's achievements at the university:

> Grace Liu was conscientious, active, and enthusiastic in her work and made achievements in the studies of modern English and American linguistics and literature. She taught courses in advanced spoken English and English writing and continuously guided and supervised the training of English teachers in the Foreign Languages Department. She worked together with the other teachers to translate and rewrite in English the Chinese novels *Zhao Yiman, The Song of Youth, Great Changes In A Mountain Village*, and others. She also participated in editing and polishing translation works that had been done by others in the Department. For two decades, she put great effort into the study of the teaching of English and wrote many articles to introduce more advanced theories and methods from abroad, while putting forward many valuable opinions and suggestions. She led the compilation and the editing of textbooks for the teaching of basic English and rigorously trained a group of English teachers. Thus, she made very valuable contributions to the Foreign Language Department of our University. She never ceased to be concerned for the work of the Department; even after she went abroad in '74, she still wrote and mailed books and other materials back to the Department.

> While Grace Liu was in the United States, she started to write her memoir, using her personal experience to tell about the great cultural tradition of China and its achievements in the socialist revolution. Unfortunately, she could not complete this work before she died. While living in the United States, Grace Liu was always thinking about what was happening in China; even when she became seriously ill, she still instructed her children to strive for and make contribution to the Four Modernizations of China. We are all deeply impressed by her spirit.

The death of Grace Liu is a great loss to the Foreign Languages Department of Nankai University. We lost a loyal and active teacher and friend. Today, while we are striving to realize our nation's Four Modernizations, to mourn the passing of Grace Liu we must learn from her love of China, her pursuance of truth, and her tenacious revolutionary spirit; we must learn from her scientific attitude of serious pursuit in academic studies and research and the seeking of truth from facts, her diligent and conscientious style of work. We will always remember Grace Liu's profound feelings for China and the active contribution she made to the teaching of English at our university.

Grace Liu, rest in peace!

At the conclusion of the eulogy, the wreath bearing Grace's image was handed to Nini. William carried the rectangular container bearing her ashes. Together they led the crowd to an upper room in the mausoleum where he placed the container into a slot next to F. C.'s. William glanced at his father's name and then at Grace's picture. What would she be thinking now? Could she or F. C. ever have imagined that Grace would be eulogized here at this Hall of Revolutionary Martyrs? That this would be their final resting place?

As the crowd moved back through the great hall and down the steps to the outside, each one spoke condolences to the family before departing. Just as he reached the van, William was caught by an older man with a bold shock of white hair. He shook hands warmly with William. Although the man was Chinese, he spoke to William in fluent English: "I knew your mother during the Japanese Occupation. I was then about twenty years old and I remember you as just a little boy." He chuckled slightly with the memory. "I came to your house to learn English, but your mother taught me to sing. It was my dream to be a tenor in the great operas. I never did that but I sang with her. She gave me a book. It was from her teacher Proschowsky, called *The Art of Singing*. I wish I could give it back to you now but it was burned in the Cultural Revolution."

The van began to move. "Your mother was a great lady, . . . always . . . always, she was a lady . . ." His words trailed off as the van moved away and the white-haired man merged with the bundled crowd in the cold.

FOR FURTHER READING

For further reading about the times and places in which Grace lived—

Benedict, Elinor Divine, *The Green Heart,* Illinois Writers, Inc. 1994 (Elinor's version of Grace's story told in poetry, available from 8627 S. Lakeside Drive, Rapid River, MI 49878. The poem in the front of the book is used with permission from this chapbook).

Chang, Jung, *Wild Swans,* Simon and Schuster, 1991.

*Chang, Pang-mei Natasha, *Bound Feet and Western Dress,* Doubleday, 1996.

Feng Jicai, *Voices From the Whirlwind,* Pantheon Books, 1991.

Han Suyin, *The Crippled Tree,* G.P. Putnam's Sons, 1965 (volume one of a trilogy).

*Hersey, John, *The Call: An American Missionary in China,* Alfred A, Knopf, 1985.

Hinton, William, *Fanshen: Documentary of Revolution in a Chinese Village,* Random House, 1966.

*Liu, Bea Exner, *Remembering China, 1935-45, a memoir,* Minnesota Voices Project #76, New Rivers Press, 1996.

Power, Desmond, *Little Foreign Devil,* Pangli Imprint, Vancouver, BC Canada, 1996.

Seagrave, Sterling, *The Soong Dynasty,* Harper and Rowe, 1985.

Spence, Jonathan, *The Search for Modern China,* W.W. Norton and Company, Inc, 1990.

Spence, Jonathan, *The Gate of Heavenly Peace,* Viking Press, 1981.

Topping, Seymour, *Journey Between Two Chinas,* Harper and Rowe, 1972.

Weisbrot, Robert, *Father Divine,* Chelsea House Publishers, 1992.

Divine, Thomas McCallie, McDonald, Roy, and Wilson, John, eds., *The The Wit and Wisdom of Sam Divine: A Lively Look at Chattanooga from the Earliest Days to 1915,* Chattanooga News Free Press, Chattanooga.

Appendix

TEXT OF NEWS ARTICLES
ABOUT GRACE DIVINE LIU

1. CHATTANOOGA NEWS, JUNE 22, 1934.

Chattanooga Girl Who Broke Racial Ties and Married Chinese Engineer Paying Visit Here.

East and West Become One for Grace Divine, Now Mrs. Liu Fuchi.

China's Far Away, But Now It's Home

[The article appeared with a photo above this caption] "East is East and West is West and never the twain shall meet." But for Grace Divine, a Chattanooga musician, the twain have met. She is now Mrs. Liu Fuchi, the wife of a young Chinese engineer. With her 15-months-old daughter, she is finding her new home—far away China. She will sail soon to join him and make her home there.

By Nellie Kenyon

All of her life Grace Divine, talented Chattanooga girl, has wanted to travel to foreign lands, live in strange places, fall " frightfully" in love,

marry and have a nice baby. Somehow she has always felt that the fairy prince of whom she read in her childhood story books would some day come along and make possible this fantastic dream.

Today Grace Divine, as Mrs. Liu Fuchi, wife of a native Chinese, who is a brilliant scholar, feels that this dream has come true. She is deeply in love, has a beautiful baby and is in Chattanooga to tell her relatives good-by before sailing for the Orient to join her husband.

"I had to pinch myself several times coming down on the train from New York to see if it was really me, and then I wouldn't believe it," said Mrs. Liu Fuchi, as she sat holding in her arms her 15-months-old daughter, Ju Lann (Little Orchid in Chinese).

Little did Grace Divine realize several years ago when she had her first date with Liu Fuchi and went to see "Good News," a musical comedy then playing in New York, that it would mean good news to her and that she was sitting beside her future husband. Little did this Southern girl realize then that she was destined to give up a musical future and go with this man from the Land of the Rising Sun back to his native country as his wife.

WAS SENSITIVE AT FIRST

The Tennessee girl was somewhat skeptical and sensitive over her first date with a native Chinese, and he too detected this sensitiveness and remained away for some time. But gradually she grew to know him better and to admire his outstanding intellect, and then suddenly one day, as she describes it, she found herself "desperately" in love with her Chinese beau.

"I married him because I loved and admired him and wanted to more than anything I ever wanted to do," said Mrs. Liu Fuchi, when asked why she had chosen for her husband one of the Chinese race. But Grace Divine didn't marry Liu Fuchi simply because there was a deep infatuation for this man of the East. She married him because he was the man of her dreams, because as she expresses it, he seemed to possess all of the good qualities of every man whom she had ever known. She married him after cool deliberation and has never regretted her action "for one single moment."

And so it is that Mrs. Liu Fuchi will sail July 14 for China to make here future home with her husband taking with her their little daughter who will meet her father for the first time, as he returned to the Orient to accept a governmental position before Ju Lann was born.

Liu Fuchi is a member of the new school of China. Casting aside his old family traditions, he accepted the life of the modern Western world. In so doing, he himself broke an engagement negotiated by his uncle, when he was a lad of 12, with a Chinese girl, writing her from America after his uncle had refused to break the engagement in the customary fashion, that he had never seen her and that he didn't believe in the old traditional customs of his country: that she was educated in the old school and he in the new, and that they would never be congenial. The girl wrote him back that she would try to adapt herself to his modern training, but he decided otherwise.

HUSBAND ATTENDED CORNELL

When Liu Fuchi finished school at the Tsing Hua University in Peking, he was graduated with honors and because of this was given a scholarship in any American college of his own selection. He chose Cornell, and received his degree in engineering on the completion of his course at this institution. He then went to Karlruhe, Germany, for post-graduate work, later returning to the United States, where he worked for three years under the late Allan Hazen, a world authority in hydraulics. Hazen predicted that Liu Fuchi would become one of the great engineers of the world.

Liu Fuchi did not particularly want to get married. he wanted to return to his native land and give his life in trying to harness the terrible Yellow River. But he soon found himself in love with an American girl and the marriage soon followed.

About a year ago, Liu Fuchi decided to accept a position with the National Government of China and returned home as head engineer of the national health administration with headquarters in Nanking. There he conducted classes for the health inspectors, teaching them many of the modern ideas on sanitation he had learned in the United States.

When stationed in Nanking he lived next door to Pearl Buck, famous writer. He told her much about the his young American bride and promised to bring her to call when she joined him in China.

Later Liu Fuchi accepted a position as chief engineer of the Tientsin Waterworks Company , an international concern, and is now stationed at Tientsin.

When a boy, Liu Fuchi lived at Sain Fu, the capital of the Shensi province, and he went with his family during the summer months to Liu village, so named because it was usually occupied by the "Lius." Liu Fuchi's mother was a Buddhist and Fuchi was brought up under Confucian teachings. He has no scruples about the Christian religion and will not oppose his child being so trained.

Mrs. Liu Fuchi has already mastered the art of eating with chopsticks and knows a few Chinese words and expects Ju Lann to speak her father's language before she has been long in the Orient.

Mrs. Julia Divine, mother of Mrs. Liu Fuchi, who is here with her daughter, is greatly pleased with her new son-in-law, and she herself expects to join them later in China. Mrs. Liu Fuchi and her daughter will leave Chattanooga July 10 for Vancouver from which port they will sail to their new home.

2, CHATTANOOGA NEWS-FREE PRESS, FEB. 12, 1946

Mrs. F. C. Liu,
Former Grace Divine,
Found Safe In Tientsin,
Pfc. Brooks Tells Relatives Here

[This article appeared with a photograph and the following caption:] GOOD NEWS AFTER FOUR YEARS—Pvt. G. R. Brooks (center) last week brought news of Mrs. F. C. Liu, Tien-Tsin, China, to her family direct from that city, after four years of silence from Mrs. Liu due to her being at the mercy of the Japanese. Left, above, Sam Divine, Chattanooga, and right, Edward Divine, formerly of Chattanooga, who served in the Pacific war and witnessed the death of Ernie Pyle, which he was able to avenge on the spot. Divine entered the army at the age of 40, and his bald head entitled him to known by the regiment as "Pappy," a coveted honor.

MARINE FINDS EX-LOCAL WOMAN, GIVEN-UP AS DEAD BY FAMILY
by W. G. Foster

Four years of anxiety over the fate of Mrs. F. C. Liu, the former Grace Divine, ended for the Divine family last week with the information that Mrs. Liu is alive and well in Tientsin, China.

The first and last word from Mrs. Liu had

been received a few weeks before Pearl Harbor when she wrote that the Chinese coolie pushing her rickshaw had been knocked down by a Japanese bully and she had fled. She wrote that she feared serious trouble was ahead. Then there was silence until last week when G. R. Brooks, private first class in the Third Amphibious Corps of the marines, returned to Chattanooga and brought definite news from Mrs. Liu. Civilian mail is not yet coming out of Tientsin and efforts by the family of Dr. J. P. McCallie to send a Christmas box to his niece, Mrs. Liu, had been unsuccessful. Only through the soldier was she able to communicate with her relatives.

The young Chattanooga soldier, who left Central High School in February, 1943, to enlist in the marines, met Mrs. Liu by a series of circumstances which some members of the family would say indicate the hand of God. Young Brooks had been in school with Mrs. Liu's niece, daughter of Sam Divine, in Chattanooga but had no knowledge of Mrs. Liu.

ASSIGNED TO TIENTSIN

The Third Corps soon after V-J Day was assigned to the Tientsin area. The corps also steamed 40 miles up Hia Ho River to the great Chinese city of 1,000,000 souls. Last September as young Brooks stepped from a LST a large crowd was waiting, among them several American women. One approached him to welcome him and said she was from Oregon. He told her his name and that he was from Chattanooga. She answered, "I know a woman from Chattanooga and I want to tell you how to find her."

He took the address of Mrs. Liu and then went into camp. A week later he came to the city and went to the city water works where Mr. Liu is a manager. Mr. Liu had been told he was coming and welcomed him with open arms.

A most interesting experience for young Brooks ensued. He was taken into the Liu home in the English settlement where business and professional leaders were accustomed to meet. All of them, including the entire family of Mr. Liu, speak English only. With some other GIs he was entertained in the Liu home almost nightly for two months. Many of their hosts were former American college graduates.

The Chinese gave the GIs some remarkable souvenirs. Brooks has in his possession a coin dated 140 years before Christ and five coins turned out by the dies the year Christ was born. In return for the Chinese hospitality the GIs constantly brought to the "party" good American food, beer, and cigars, which the Chinese had not seen since Pearl harbor.

EVENTFUL EXPERIENCE

As the story developed yesterday in an interview with young Brooks, Sam Divine, an uncle of Mrs. Liu, and Edward Divine, his brother, Mrs. Liu has had an eventful experience since she married in New York in 1934. Mr. Liu is a graduate of Cornell and Heidelberg. He was a water works engineer in New York at the time of his marriage. Tientsin, at that time, was under Chinese puppet government dominated by Japan. He was made manager of the entire water works system and remained in charge until the time of Pearl Harbor when he refused to collaborate with the Japs. He and his wife and three children were interned in the English settlement. According to Brooks they were not mistreated and Liu retained a subordinate job with the water works. The family suffered only the hardships of war with the rest of the people.

Brooks and Edward Divine held a "fanning bee" over the Pacific war though Brooks would not talk about his own experiences. Divine was a member of the 77th Division, 305 Regiment The marine group to which Brooks belonged started out at Bougainville, then fought alongside the 77th in the storming of Guam. The two units come together again at Okinawa. In the meantime the 77th had been on Leyte, at Keramanratto, the battle of the coconut groves of Ie Jima. It was on this island that Ernie Pyle ways killed, and Divine avenged his death which he witnessed.

According to the Bealiner, army publication, "Divine" crawled stealthily around behind the shack housing the sniper and in spite of some trouble with wet matches set fire to the small building, jumping into a Jap foxhole, and covered the building, hoping to pick off the Jap when he was forced out. He was destined not to see the murderer, however, for as the flames devoured the house a and grenade explosion inside indicated that the Jap had taken his own life."

Divine is officially credited with killing 27 Japanese alone by stalking about as a scout and getting them one by one.

Thus, he said, he had fought in adjoining commands to Brooks in two campaigns without ever meeting him. Divine said he had hoped his service would enable him to go to Tientsin and look his sister up but it fell to Brooks to do this great favor for the family. "His experiences with her makes us look on him like a brother," said Divine, "and it was wonderful that the GIs and my sister's acquaintances were able to be of mutual benefit and inspiration. He was wonderful to her and wonderful to us since he came back."

Brooks trained in Camp Elliot, Calf., and was overseas within four moths after he enlisted Feb. 5, 1943. He was mustered out on Jan. 30 of this year, seven days before he would have been in three years. He was able to "double quick" home by the end of last week. He has re-entered Central High School. He expects to graduate this year and to take the four-year college course open to GIs. He lives with his parents, Mr. and Mrs. T. R. Brooks, at 909 South Watkins Street.

3. CHATTANOOGA NEWS-FREE PRESS, MARCH 24, 1975

McCallie Family Gets
Letter From Relative
After 20 Years

[This articlee appeared with a photo and the following caption:]

RELATED TO CHATTANOOGANS— This photograph is of Ellen Li and two of her daughters. She is the daughter of Grace McCallie Divine Liu who left Chattanooga in 1931 to live in China.

By John Wilson
Staff Writer

"Since I have been completely out of contact with anyone in or concerned with Chattanoga for nearly 20 years, I do not know which other members of my family are now living.

"I shall be very grateful if someone will send me some information about the elder living members of my family –- both Divine and McCallie."

So read the letter received recently at McCallie School from a descendant of two prominent Chattanooga families who went to China as a young woman and had not been heard from in 18 years.

"We had about given up hope of ever hearing from her (Grace McCallie Divine Liu) again and were wondering if she were still alive," said Miss Anne McCallie, alumni secretary at McCallie School and a first cousin to Mrs. Liu.

"We last saw Grace when she passed through Chattanooga in the early 1930s on her way to China," said Miss McCallie.

Grace McCallie Divine, who was the daughter of S.W. Divine and Julia McCallie, met her Chinese husband in New York City, where she was studying voice. Her grandfathers were the Rev. Thomas Hooke McCallie and Sam Divine.

WENT TO TIENTSIN

She went to Tientsin, China, with her husband, F. C. Liu, a hydraulic engineer, to make her home about 1931.

The last Chattanoogan to see Mrs. Liu was James W. Lail, a McCallie School alumnus, who was among the first Marines, who liberated North China in 1945.

The family here felt that there would be word from their relative in Red China soon after the visits of President Nixon and Henry Kissinger to the Communist country. But it was only recently that the long-awaited letter came.

The family here has begun a correspondence with Mrs. Liu and learned that her husband died of lung cancer in 1955 and she began teaching English at Nankai University the following year.

She has two girls named Julian and Ellen and a son, Willy, who also teaches at Nankai University. Julian is employed at the Tientsin Water Works, where her father formerly worked, and Ellen is employed in the Academy of Science in Peking.

Julian has a girl, aged three, and Ellen has three girls, aged nine, six and ten months.

Mrs. Liu has three other first cousins in Chattanooga in addition to Miss McCallie. They are Dr. Spencer McCallie, Thomas Hooke McCallie and Dr. David McCallie.

Mrs. Liu's aunt, Margaret Ellen McCallie, for whom she named one of her children now lives at the St. Barnabas Nursing Home.

The Golden Wedding Anniversary, January 28, 1912 [see page 88]

The Fiftieth Wedding Anniversary celebration of the Reverend and Mrs. Thomas Hooke McCallie was held at Founder's Home on Missionary Ridge in 1912. The people in this picture shaped Grace's childhood world. Her grandparents (seated center), were married during the Civil War and lived in Chattanooga throughout their marriage. Her grandfather died in the spring following this celebration.

After his death, her grandmother, Ellen Jarnagin McCallie, took a journey with her son Park to visit Christian missions in Japan, Korea, and China, taking the Trans-Siberian railroad into Moscow, just as the First World War broke out. They escaped through Finland and back home, but she never recovered from the trip and died in 1915.

Grace's father, Samuel Williams Divine (seated on the floor, left), once the promoter of electric street cars, authored a popular newspaper column of "wit and wisdom" in his last years and died suddenly of pneumonia in 1915.

Her mother, Julia McCallie Divine, is seated on the floor, three over to the right from Sam. Her sister Grace McCallie is directly behind her. Aunt Grace, the co-founder of Girls' Preparatory School, died in 1918, the year that Grace finished G.P.S.

Her Aunt (Margaret) Ellen is on the back row, far left. She accompanied Grace to New York and corresponded with her in China. She was the only member of her parents' generation still alive when Grace returned in 1974.

Grace's five brothers are: John and Sam, standing in the back on the left, next to their aunt Margaret Ellen, the same age as John. Sam is the one with whom Grace corresponded until he told her to write only of family matters. Robert and his wife Ruth (the young couple sitting on the floor between Sam and Julia) are the parents of Julianne, who was born in 1913 and came with Julia to New York. Grace's two younger brothers are on the floor, Edward (in Papa's lap) and Tom (in front of Julia). It was Tom, her closest brother, and his wife Mary Hills, who corresponded frequently with Grace and preserved her letters.

Grace's uncles are pictured in the back: Uncle Spence (back row, center, with black tie), read the engagement letters at this celebration. He is standing next to his wife, Alice Fletcher, who died in the influenza epidemic of 1918, leaving him with five young children. One of their children, named Thomas Hooke McCallie II, was born October 1912 and is the co-author's (Eleanor) father.

Uncle Ed (back row), next to Alice, is pictured at a great distance from his wife, "Ahnt" Lillian, who is seated on the floor in the right corner, with her baby son and daughter, Katie. The distance between them seems appropriate since they were divorced a year later and Lillian kidnapped her own daughter. After the divorce, Uncle Ed departed for China, where he joined the expedition of Roy Chapman Andrews in the Gobi Desert. Grace was reunited with "Cousin Katie" in California in 1978. Katie gave Grace a copy of this picture which led to Grace's account of this memorable event.

On the far right of the back row are Uncle Doug, a missionary to Korea, and Uncle Park, co-founder with his brother Spence of the McCallie School. Park's wife Hattie (not pictured) hosted a party for Grace when she came home in 1934 with Ju-lan. Uncle Park and Aunt Hattie were at the train station when Grace left for China in 1934.

There are a few others in the picture who appear in the story. Eula Jarnagin is in the back, almost hidden in profile behind Uncle Doug's wife. In the mid-1920s, her last years in Chattanooga, Grace lived with "Cousin Eula" at G.P.S.

Mary McCallie (third child from the left on floor) was in China with Grace in 1937 when the Japanese attacked. She and her husband, Bob Ware, met Grace at the San Francisco airport when she returned in 1974.

Spencer McCallie, Jr. was the headmaster of McCallie School when Grace first made contact in 1974. He's the baby boy in Grace McCallie's lap.

As with most family photos, there is one person we can't identify. It's the bearded guy in the back. We suppose he is a preacher friend of Grandfather's. The man taking up so much space next to Grandfather is Jonathan Waverly Bachman, the pastor of the First Presbyterian Church after Grandfather retired that position. There are a few others not mentioned because they are not a part of the story.

And Grace? Surely you have guessed by now. She is the only eleven year old girl in the picture. Of course, she's sitting at the lower far left next to her dear Papa.

INDEX